EXCERPTS FROM THE ROMAN MISSAL

ANDREAS
PETRVS

THE ROMAN MISSAL
RENEWED BY DECREE OF THE
MOST HOLY SECOND ECUMENICAL COUNCIL OF THE VATICAN,
PROMULGATED BY AUTHORITY OF POPE PAUL VI
AND REVISED AT THE DIRECTION OF POPE JOHN PAUL II

EXCERPTS FROM THE ROMAN MISSAL

For Use in the Dioceses of the United States of America

Approved by the
United States Conference of Catholic Bishops
and Confirmed by the Apostolic See

C.B. P.C.

CATHOLIC BOOK PUBLISHING CORP.
NEW JERSEY
2018

Concordat cum originali:

✠ Wilton D. Gregory
Chairman, USCCB Committee on Divine Worship
after review by Rev. Andrew Menke
Executive Director, USCCB Secretariat of Divine Worship

Published by authority of the Committee on Divine Worship,
United States Conference of Catholic Bishops

First printing, 2018.

T-37

ISBN 978-1-947070-19-6

Printed in Korea

www.catholicbookpublishing.com

GENERAL INDEX

COMMONS

RITUAL MASSES

MASSES AND PRAYERS FOR VARIOUS NEEDS AND OCCASIONS

APPENDICES

INDEX

CONGREGATION FOR DIVINE WORSHIP AND THE DISCIPLINE OF THE SACRAMENTS

Prot. n. 103/16

UNITED STATES OF AMERICA

At the request of His Excellency the Most Reverend Joseph Edward Kurtz, Archbishop of Louisville, then-President of the Conference of Bishops of the United States of America, in a letter dated February 10, 2016, and by virtue of the faculty granted to this Congregation by the Supreme Pontiff FRANCIS, we gladly confirm the edition of excerpted texts from the English-language *Roman Missal*, as found in the attached copy.

In printed editions, this decree, by which the Apostolic See has granted the requested *recognitio*, must be inserted in its entirety. Moreover, three copies of the printed text should be forwarded to this Congregation.

All things to the contrary notwithstanding.

From the offices of the Congregation for Divine Worship and the Discipline of the Sacraments, March 1, 2017, Ash Wednesday.

ROBERT Card. SARAH
Prefect

✠ Arthur Roche
Archbishop Secretary

UNITED STATES CONFERENCE OF CATHOLIC BISHOPS

DECREE OF PUBLICATION

In accord with the norms established by the Holy See, this edition of *Excerpts from the Roman Missal* is declared to be a part of the *Roman Missal* for use in the dioceses of the United States of America, and is published by authority of the United States Conference of Catholic Bishops.

Excerpts from the Roman Missal, an optional supplement of the *Roman Missal, Third Edition*, was canonically approved for use by the United States Conference of Catholic Bishops on November 17, 2015, and was subsequently confirmed by the Apostolic See by decree of the Congregation for Divine Worship and the Discipline of the Sacraments on March 1, 2017 (Prot. n. 103/16).

This ritual edition may be used in the Liturgy in the dioceses of the United States of America upon publication.

Given at the General Secretariat of the United States Conference of Catholic Bishops, Washington, DC, on September 14, 2017, the Feast of the Exaltation of the Holy Cross.

Daniel N. Cardinal DiNardo
Archbishop of Galveston-Houston
President,
United States Conference of Catholic Bishops

Rev. Msgr. J. Brian Bransfield
General Secretary

GENERAL ROMAN CALENDAR

[including the Proper Calendar for the Dioceses of the United States of America]

JANUARY

Cal.	1	The Octave Day of the Nativity of the Lord: SOLEMNITY OF MARY, THE HOLY MOTHER OF GOD	Solemnity
IV	2	Sts. Basil the Great and Gregory Nazianzen, Bishops and Doctors of the Church	Memorial
III	3	*The Most Holy Name of Jesus**	
Eve	4	[USA] St. Elizabeth Ann Seton, Religious	Memorial
Nones	5	[USA] St. John Neumann, Bishop	Memorial
VIII	6	[USA] *St. André Bessette, Religious*	
VII	7	*St. Raymond of Penyafort, Priest*	
VI	8		
V	9		
IV	10		
III	11		
Eve	12		
Ides	13	*St. Hilary, Bishop and Doctor of the Church*	
XIX	14		
XVIII	15		
XVII	16		
XVI	17	St. Anthony, Abbot	Memorial
XV	18		
XIV	19		
XIII	20	*St. Fabian, Pope and Martyr* *St. Sebastian, Martyr*	
XII	21	St. Agnes, Virgin and Martyr	Memorial
XI	22	[USA] Day of Prayer for the Legal Protection of Unborn Children**	
X	23	[USA] *St. Vincent, Deacon and Martyr* [USA] *St. Marianne Cope, Virgin*	
IX	24	St. Francis de Sales, Bishop and Doctor of the Church	Memorial
VIII	25	THE CONVERSION OF ST. PAUL THE APOSTLE	Feast
VII	26	Sts. Timothy and Titus, Bishops	Memorial
VI	27	*St. Angela Merici, Virgin*	
V	28	St. Thomas Aquinas, Priest and Doctor of the Church	Memorial
IV	29		
III	30		
Eve	31	St. John Bosco, Priest	Memorial

[USA] Sunday between January 2 and January 8:

THE EPIPHANY OF THE LORD — Solemnity

Sunday after January 6: THE BAPTISM OF THE LORD — Feast

When the Solemnity of the Epiphany is transferred to the Sunday that occurs on January 7 or 8, the Feast of the Baptism of the Lord is celebrated on the following Monday.

* When the rank of the celebration is not indicated, it is an Optional Memorial.

** January 23, when January 22 falls on a Sunday

FEBRUARY

Cal.	1		
IV	2	THE PRESENTATION OF THE LORD	Feast
III	3	*St. Blaise, Bishop and Martyr*	
		St. Ansgar, Bishop	
Eve	4		
Nones	5	St. Agatha, Virgin and Martyr	Memorial
VIII	6	St. Paul Miki and Companions, Martyrs	Memorial
VII	7		
VI	8	*St. Jerome Emiliani*	
		St. Josephine Bakhita, Virgin	
V	9		
IV	10	St. Scholastica, Virgin	Memorial
III	11	*Our Lady of Lourdes*	
Eve	12		
Ides	13		
XVI	14	Sts. Cyril, Monk, and Methodius, Bishop	Memorial
XV	15		
XIV	16		
XIII	17	*The Seven Holy Founders of the Servite Order*	
XII	18		
XI	19		
X	20		
IX	21	*St. Peter Damian, Bishop and Doctor of the Church*	
VIII	22	THE CHAIR OF ST. PETER THE APOSTLE	Feast
VII	23	St. Polycarp, Bishop and Martyr	Memorial
VI	24		
V	25		
IV	26		
III	27		
Eve	28		

MARCH

Cal.	1		
VI	2		
V	3	[USA] *St. Katharine Drexel, Virgin*	
IV	4	*St. Casimir*	
III	5		
Eve	6		
Nones	7	Sts. Perpetua and Felicity, Martyrs	Memorial
VIII	8	*St. John of God, Religious*	
VII	9	*St. Frances of Rome, Religious*	
VI	10		
V	11		
IV	12		
III	13		
Eve	14		
Ides	15		
XVII	16		
XVI	17	*St. Patrick, Bishop*	
XV	18	*St. Cyril of Jerusalem, Bishop and Doctor of the Church*	
XIV	19	ST. JOSEPH, SPOUSE OF THE BLESSED VIRGIN MARY	Solemnity
XIII	20		
XII	21		
XI	22		
X	23	*St. Turibius of Mogrovejo, Bishop*	
IX	24		
VIII	25	THE ANNUNCIATION OF THE LORD	Solemnity
VII	26		
VI	27		
V	28		
IV	29		
III	30		
Eve	31		

APRIL

Cal.	1		
IV	2	*St. Francis of Paola, Hermit*	
III	3		
Eve	4	*St. Isidore, Bishop and Doctor of the Church*	
Nones	5	*St. Vincent Ferrer, Priest*	
VIII	6		
VII	7	St. John Baptist de la Salle, Priest	Memorial
VI	8		
V	9		
IV	10		
III	11	St. Stanislaus, Bishop and Martyr	Memorial
Eve	12		
Ides	13	*St. Martin I, Pope and Martyr*	
XVIII	14		
XVII	15		
XVI	16		
XV	17		
XIV	18		
XIII	19		
XII	20		
XI	21	*St. Anselm, Bishop and Doctor of the Church*	
X	22		
IX	23	*St. George, Martyr* *St. Adalbert, Bishop and Martyr*	
VIII	24	*St. Fidelis of Sigmaringen, Priest and Martyr*	
VII	25	ST. MARK, EVANGELIST	Feast
VI	26		
V	27		
IV	28	*St. Peter Chanel, Priest and Martyr* *St. Louis Grignion de Montfort, Priest*	
III	29	St. Catherine of Siena, Virgin and Doctor of the Church	Memorial
Eve	30	*St. Pius V, Pope*	

MAY

Cal.	1	*St. Joseph the Worker*	
VI	2	St. Athanasius, Bishop and Doctor of the Church	Memorial
V	3	STS. PHILIP AND JAMES, APOSTLES	Feast
IV	4		
III	5		
Eve	6		
Nones	7		
VIII	8		
VII	9		
VI	10	[USA] *St. Damien de Veuster, Priest*	
V	11		
IV	12	*Sts. Nereus and Achilleus, Martyrs* *St. Pancras, Martyr*	
III	13	*Our Lady of Fatima*	
Eve	14	ST. MATTHIAS, APOSTLE	Feast
Ides	15	[USA] *St. Isidore*	
XVII	16		
XVI	17		
XV	18	*St. John I, Pope and Martyr*	
XIV	19		
XIII	20	*St. Bernardine of Siena, Priest*	
XII	21	*St. Christopher Magallanes, Priest, and Companions, Martyrs*	
XI	22	*St. Rita of Cascia, Religious*	
X	23		
IX	24		
VIII	25	*St. Bede the Venerable, Priest and Doctor of the Church* *St. Gregory VII, Pope* *St. Mary Magdalene de' Pazzi, Virgin*	
VII	26	St. Philip Neri, Priest	Memorial
VI	27	*St. Augustine of Canterbury, Bishop*	
V	28		
IV	29		
III	30		
Eve	31	THE VISITATION OF THE BLESSED VIRGIN MARY	Feast

First Sunday after Pentecost

THE MOST HOLY TRINITY — Solemnity

[USA] Sunday after the Most Holy Trinity

THE MOST HOLY BODY AND BLOOD OF CHRIST — Solemnity

JUNE

Cal.	1	St. Justin, Martyr	Memorial
IV	2	*Sts. Marcellinus and Peter, Martyrs*	
III	3	St. Charles Lwanga and Companions, Martyrs	Memorial
Eve	4		
Nones	5	St. Boniface, Bishop and Martyr	Memorial
VIII	6	*St. Norbert, Bishop*	
VII	7		
VI	8		
V	9	*St. Ephrem, Deacon and Doctor of the Church*	
IV	10		
III	11	St. Barnabas, Apostle	Memorial
Eve	12		
Ides	13	St. Anthony of Padua, Priest and Doctor of the Church	Memorial
XVIII	14		
XVII	15		
XVI	16		
XV	17		
XIV	18		
XIII	19	*St. Romuald, Abbot*	
XII	20		
XI	21	St. Aloysius Gonzaga, Religious	Memorial
X	22	*St. Paulinus of Nola, Bishop*	
		Sts. John Fisher, Bishop, and Thomas More, Martyrs	
IX	23		
VIII	24	THE NATIVITY OF ST. JOHN THE BAPTIST	Solemnity
VII	25		
VI	26		
V	27	*St. Cyril of Alexandria, Bishop and Doctor of the Church*	
IV	28	St. Irenaeus, Bishop and Martyr	Memorial
III	29	STS. PETER AND PAUL, APOSTLES	Solemnity
Eve	30	*The First Martyrs of the Holy Roman Church*	

Friday after the Second Sunday after Pentecost

THE MOST SACRED HEART OF JESUS — Solemnity

Saturday after the Second Sunday after Pentecost

The Immaculate Heart of the Blessed Virgin Mary — Memorial

JULY

Cal.	1	[USA] *St. Junípero Serra, Priest*	
VI	2		
V	3	ST. THOMAS, APOSTLE	Feast
IV	4	[USA] *Independence Day*	
III	5	*St. Anthony Zaccaria, Priest*	
		[USA] *St. Elizabeth of Portugal*	
Eve	6	*St. Maria Goretti, Virgin and Martyr*	
Nones	7		
VIII	8		
VII	9	*St. Augustine Zhao Rong, Priest, and Companions, Martyrs*	
VI	10		
V	11	St. Benedict, Abbot	Memorial
IV	12		
III	13	*St. Henry*	
Eve	14	[USA] St. Kateri Tekakwitha, Virgin	Memorial
Ides	15	St. Bonaventure, Bishop and Doctor of the Church	Memorial
XVII	16	*Our Lady of Mount Carmel*	
XVI	17		
XV	18	[USA] *St. Camillus de Lellis, Priest*	
XIV	19		
XIII	20	*St. Apollinaris, Bishop and Martyr*	
XII	21	*St. Lawrence of Brindisi, Priest and Doctor of the Church*	
XI	22	ST. MARY MAGDALENE	Feast
X	23	*St. Bridget, Religious*	
IX	24	*St. Sharbel Makhlūf, Priest*	
VIII	25	ST. JAMES, APOSTLE	Feast
VII	26	Sts. Joachim and Anne, Parents of the Blessed Virgin Mary	Memorial
VI	27		
V	28		
IV	29	St. Martha	Memorial
III	30	*St. Peter Chrysologus, Bishop and Doctor of the Church*	
Eve	31	St. Ignatius of Loyola, Priest	Memorial

AUGUST

Cal.	1	St. Alphonsus Liguori, Bishop and Doctor of the Church	Memorial
IV	2	*St. Eusebius of Vercelli, Bishop*	
		St. Peter Julian Eymard, Priest	
III	3		
Eve	4	St. John Vianney, Priest	Memorial
Nones	5	*The Dedication of the Basilica of St. Mary Major*	
VIII	6	THE TRANSFIGURATION OF THE LORD	Feast
VII	7	*St. Sixtus II, Pope, and Companions, Martyrs*	
		St. Cajetan, Priest	
VI	8	St. Dominic, Priest	Memorial
V	9	*St. Teresa Benedicta of the Cross, Virgin and Martyr*	
IV	10	ST. LAWRENCE, DEACON AND MARTYR	Feast
III	11	St. Clare, Virgin	Memorial
Eve	12	*St. Jane Frances de Chantal, Religious*	
Ides	13	*Sts. Pontian, Pope, and Hippolytus, Priest, Martyrs*	
XIX	14	St. Maximilian Kolbe, Priest and Martyr	Memorial
XVIII	15	THE ASSUMPTION OF THE BLESSED VIRGIN MARY	Solemnity
XVII	16	*St. Stephen of Hungary*	
XVI	17		
XV	18		
XIV	19	*St. John Eudes, Priest*	
XIII	20	St. Bernard, Abbot and Doctor of the Church	Memorial
XII	21	St. Pius X, Pope	Memorial
XI	22	The Queenship of the Blessed Virgin Mary	Memorial
X	23	*St. Rose of Lima, Virgin*	
IX	24	ST. BARTHOLOMEW, APOSTLE	Feast
VIII	25	*St. Louis*	
		St. Joseph Calasanz, Priest	
VII	26		
VI	27	St. Monica	Memorial
V	28	St. Augustine, Bishop and Doctor of the Church	Memorial
IV	29	The Passion of St. John the Baptist	Memorial
III	30		
Eve	31		

SEPTEMBER

Cal.	1		
IV	2		
III	3	St. Gregory the Great, Pope and Doctor of the Church	Memorial
Eve	4		
Nones	5		
VIII	6		
VII	7		
VI	8	THE NATIVITY OF THE BLESSED VIRGIN MARY	Feast
V	9	[USA] St. Peter Claver, Priest	Memorial
IV	10		
III	11		
Eve	12	*The Most Holy Name of Mary*	
Ides	13	St. John Chrysostom, Bishop and Doctor of the Church	Memorial
XVIII	14	THE EXALTATION OF THE HOLY CROSS	Feast
XVII	15	Our Lady of Sorrows	Memorial
XVI	16	Sts. Cornelius, Pope, and Cyprian, Bishop, Martyrs	Memorial
XV	17	*St. Robert Bellarmine, Bishop and Doctor of the Church*	
XIV	18		
XIII	19	*St. Januarius, Bishop and Martyr*	
XII	20	Sts. Andrew Kim Tae-gŏn, Priest, Paul Chŏng Ha-sang, and Companions, Martyrs	Memorial
XI	21	ST. MATTHEW, APOSTLE AND EVANGELIST	Feast
X	22		
IX	23	St. Pius of Pietrelcina, Priest	Memorial
VIII	24		
VII	25		
VI	26	*Sts. Cosmas and Damian, Martyrs*	
V	27	St. Vincent de Paul, Priest	Memorial
IV	28	*St. Wenceslaus, Martyr*	
		St. Lawrence Ruiz and Companions, Martyrs	
III	29	STS. MICHAEL, GABRIEL AND RAPHAEL, ARCHANGELS	Feast
Eve	30	St. Jerome, Priest and Doctor of the Church	Memorial

OCTOBER

Cal.	1	St. Thérèse of the Child Jesus, Virgin and Doctor of the Church	Memorial
VI	2	The Holy Guardian Angels	Memorial
V	3		
IV	4	St. Francis of Assisi	Memorial
III	5	[USA] *Bl. Francis Xavier Seelos, Priest*	
Eve	6	*St. Bruno, Priest* [USA] *Bl. Marie Rose Durocher, Virgin*	
Nones	7	Our Lady of the Rosary	Memorial
VIII	8		
VII	9	*St. Denis, Bishop, and Companions, Martyrs* *St. John Leonardi, Priest*	
VI	10		
V	11	*St. John XXIII, Pope*	
IV	12		
III	13		
Eve	14	*St. Callistus I, Pope and Martyr*	
Ides	15	St. Teresa of Jesus, Virgin and Doctor of the Church	Memorial
XVII	16	*St. Hedwig, Religious* *St. Margaret Mary Alacoque, Virgin*	
XVI	17	St. Ignatius of Antioch, Bishop and Martyr	Memorial
XV	18	ST. LUKE, EVANGELIST	Feast
XIV	19	[USA] Sts. John de Brébeuf and Isaac Jogues, Priests, and Companions, Martyrs	Memorial
XIII	20	[USA] *St. Paul of the Cross, Priest*	
XII	21		
XI	22	*St. John Paul II, Pope*	
X	23	*St. John of Capistrano, Priest*	
IX	24	*St. Anthony Mary Claret, Bishop*	
VIII	25		
VII	26		
VI	27		
V	28	STS. SIMON AND JUDE, APOSTLES	Feast
IV	29		
III	30		
Eve	31		

NOVEMBER

Cal.	1	ALL SAINTS	Solemnity
IV	2	THE COMMEMORATION OF ALL THE FAITHFUL DEPARTED (ALL SOULS' DAY)	
III	3	*St. Martin de Porres, Religious*	
Eve	4	St. Charles Borromeo, Bishop	Memorial
Nones	5		
VIII	6		
VII	7		
VI	8		
V	9	THE DEDICATION OF THE LATERAN BASILICA	Feast
IV	10	St. Leo the Great, Pope and Doctor of the Church	Memorial
III	11	St. Martin of Tours, Bishop	Memorial
Eve	12	St. Josaphat, Bishop and Martyr	Memorial
Ides	13	[USA] St. Frances Xavier Cabrini, Virgin	Memorial
XVIII	14		
XVII	15	*St. Albert the Great, Bishop and Doctor of the Church*	
XVI	16	*St. Margaret of Scotland* *St. Gertrude, Virgin*	
XV	17	St. Elizabeth of Hungary, Religious	Memorial
XIV	18	*The Dedication of the Basilicas of Sts. Peter and Paul, Apostles* [USA] *St. Rose Philippine Duchesne, Virgin*	
XIII	19		
XII	20		
XI	21	The Presentation of the Blessed Virgin Mary	Memorial
X	22	St. Cecilia, Virgin and Martyr	Memorial
IX	23	*St. Clement I, Pope and Martyr* *St. Columban, Abbot* [USA] *Bl. Miguel Agustín Pro, Priest and Martyr*	
VIII	24	St. Andrew Dũng-Lạc, Priest, and Companions, Martyrs	Memorial
VII	25	*St. Catherine of Alexandria, Virgin and Martyr*	
VI	26		
V	27		
IV	28		
III	29		
Eve	30	ST. ANDREW, APOSTLE	Feast

Last Sunday in Ordinary Time:
OUR LORD JESUS CHRIST, KING OF THE UNIVERSE Solemnity

[USA] Fourth Thursday: *Thanksgiving Day*

DECEMBER

Cal.	1		
IV	2		
III	3	St. Francis Xavier, Priest	Memorial
Eve	4	*St. John Damascene, Priest and Doctor of the Church*	
Nones	5		
VIII	6	*St. Nicholas, Bishop*	
VII	7	St. Ambrose, Bishop and Doctor of the Church	Memorial
VI	8	[USA] THE IMMACULATE CONCEPTION OF THE BLESSED VIRGIN MARY (Patronal Feastday of the United States of America)	Solemnity
V	9	*St. Juan Diego Cuauhtlatoatzin*	
IV	10		
III	11	*St. Damasus I, Pope*	
Eve	12	[USA] OUR LADY OF GUADALUPE	Feast
Ides	13	St. Lucy, Virgin and Martyr	Memorial
XIX	14	St. John of the Cross, Priest and Doctor of the Church	Memorial
XVIII	15		
XVII	16		
XVI	17		
XV	18		
XIV	19		
XIII	20		
XII	21	*St. Peter Canisius, Priest and Doctor of the Church*	
XI	22		
X	23	*St. John of Kanty, Priest*	
IX	24		
VIII	25	THE NATIVITY OF THE LORD (CHRISTMAS)	Solemnity
VII	26	ST. STEPHEN, THE FIRST MARTYR	Feast
VI	27	ST. JOHN, APOSTLE AND EVANGELIST	Feast
V	28	THE HOLY INNOCENTS, MARTYRS	Feast
IV	29	*St. Thomas Becket, Bishop and Martyr*	
III	30		
Eve	31	*St. Sylvester I, Pope*	

Sunday within the Octave of the Nativity, or, if there is no Sunday, December 30:

THE HOLY FAMILY OF JESUS, MARY AND JOSEPH — Feast

SPECIAL DAYS OF PRAYER FOR THE DIOCESES OF THE UNITED STATES OF AMERICA

In all the Dioceses of the United States of America, January 22 (or January 23, when January 22 falls on a Sunday) shall be observed as a particular day of prayer for the full restoration of the legal guarantee of the right to life and of penance for violations to the dignity of the human person committed through acts of abortion. The liturgical celebrations for this day may be the Mass "For Giving Thanks to God for the Gift of Human Life" (no. 48/1 of the Masses and Prayers for Various Needs and Occasions), celebrated with white vestments, or the Mass "For the Preservation of Peace and Justice" (no. 30 of the Masses and Prayers for Various Needs and Occasions), celebrated with violet vestments.

TABLE OF DATES
of the Principal Celebrations of the Liturgical Year

A.D.	Lectionary Cycles		Ash Wednesday	Easter	Ascension	Pentecost
	Dominical Letter	Sunday Cycle				
2016*	c b	C - A	February 10	March 27	May 5	May 15
2017	A	A - B	March 1	April 16	May 25	June 4
2018	g	B - C	February 14	April 1	May 10	May 20
2019	f	C - A	March 6	April 21	May 30	June 9
2020*	e d	A - B	February 26	April 12	May 21	May 31
2021	c	B - C	February 17	April 4	May 13	May 23
2022	b	C - A	March 2	April 17	May 26	June 5
2023	A	A - B	February 22	April 9	May 18	May 28
2024*	g f	B - C	February 14	March 31	May 9	May 19
2025	e	C - A	March 5	April 20	May 29	June 8
2026	d	A - B	February 18	April 5	May 14	May 24
2027	c	B - C	February 10	March 28	May 6	May 16
2028*	b A	C - A	March 1	April 16	May 25	June 4
2029	g	A - B	February 14	April 1	May 10	May 20
2030	f	B - C	March 6	April 21	May 30	June 9
2031	e	C - A	February 26	April 13	May 22	June 1
2032*	d c	A - B	February 11	March 28	May 6	May 16
2033	b	B - C	March 2	April 17	May 26	June 5
2034	A	C - A	February 22	April 9	May 18	May 28
2035	g	A - B	February 7	March 25	May 3	May 13
2036*	f e	B - C	February 27	April 13	May 22	June 1
2037	d	C - A	February 18	April 5	May 14	May 24
2038	c	A - B	March 10	April 25	June 3	June 13
2039	b	B - C	February 23	April 10	May 19	May 29

* Leap Years

TABLE OF DATES

of the Principal Celebrations of the Liturgical Year

A.D.	Lectionary Cycles		Ordinary Time				First Sunday of Advent
	Dominical Letter	Sunday Cycle	Before Lent		After Easter Time		
			Up Until	Weeks	From	From Week	
2016*	c b	C - A	February 9	5	May 16	7	November 27
2017	A	A - B	February 28	8	June 5	9	December 3
2018	g	B - C	February 13	6	May 21	7	December 2
2019	f	C - A	March 5	8	June 10	10	December 1
2020*	e d	A - B	February 25	7	June 1	9	November 29
2021	c	B - C	February 16	6	May 24	8	November 28
2022	b	C - A	March 1	8	June 6	10	November 27
2023	A	A - B	February 21	7	May 29	8	December 3
2024*	g f	B - C	February 13	6	May 20	7	December 1
2025	e	C - A	March 4	8	June 9	10	November 30
2026	d	A - B	February 17	6	May 25	8	November 29
2027	c	B - C	February 9	5	May 17	7	November 28
2028*	b A	C - A	February 29	8	June 5	9	December 3
2029	g	A - B	February 13	6	May 21	7	December 2
2030	f	B - C	March 5	8	June 10	10	December 1
2031	e	C - A	February 25	7	June 2	9	November 30
2032*	d c	A - B	February 10	5	May 17	7	November 28
2033	b	B - C	March 1	8	June 6	10	November 27
2034	A	C - A	February 21	7	May 29	8	December 3
2035	g	A - B	February 6	5	May 14	6	December 2
2036*	f e	B - C	February 26	7	June 2	9	November 30
2037	d	C - A	February 17	6	May 25	8	November 29
2038	c	A - B	March 9	9	June 14	11	November 28
2039	b	B - C	February 22	7	May 30	9	November 27

* Leap Years

PROPER OF TIME

ADVENT

FIRST SUNDAY OF ADVENT

Entrance Antiphon

To you, I lift up my soul, O my God.
In you, I have trusted; let me not be put to shame.
Nor let my enemies exult over me;
and let none who hope in you be put to shame.

Cf. Ps 25 (24): 1-3

The Gloria in excelsis (Glory to God in the highest) is not said.

COLLECT

Grant your faithful, we pray, almighty God,
the resolve to run forth to meet your Christ
with righteous deeds at his coming,
so that, gathered at his right hand,
they may be worthy to possess the heavenly Kingdom.
Through our Lord Jesus Christ, your Son,
who lives and reigns with you
in the unity of the Holy Spirit,
one God, for ever and ever.

The Creed is said.

PRAYER AFTER COMMUNION

May these mysteries, O Lord,
in which we have participated,
profit us, we pray,
for even now, as we walk amid passing things,
you teach us by them
to love the things of heaven
and hold fast to what endures.
Through Christ our Lord.

A formula of Solemn Blessing, p. 310, may be used.

MONDAY

Entrance Antiphon

Hear the word of the Lord, O nations;
declare it to the distant lands:
Behold, our Savior will come; you need no longer fear.
Cf. Jer 31: 10; Is 35: 4

COLLECT

Keep us alert, we pray, O Lord our God,
as we await the advent of Christ your Son,
so that, when he comes and knocks,
he may find us watchful in prayer
and exultant in his praise.
Who lives and reigns with you
in the unity of the Holy Spirit,
one God, for ever and ever.

PRAYER AFTER COMMUNION

May these mysteries, O Lord,
in which we have participated,
profit us, we pray,
for even now, as we walk amid passing things,
you teach us by them
to love the things of heaven
and hold fast to what endures.
Through Christ our Lord.

TUESDAY

Entrance Antiphon

Behold, the Lord will come, and all his holy ones with him;
and on that day there will be a great light. Cf. Zec 14: 5, 7

COLLECT

Look with favor, Lord God, on our petitions,
and in our trials grant us your compassionate help,
that, consoled by the presence of your Son,
whose coming we now await,
we may be tainted no longer
by the corruption of former ways.
Through our Lord Jesus Christ, your Son,
who lives and reigns with you
in the unity of the Holy Spirit,
one God, for ever and ever.

PRAYER AFTER COMMUNION

Replenished by the food of spiritual nourishment,
we humbly beseech you, O Lord,
that, through our partaking in this mystery,
you may teach us to judge wisely the things of earth
and hold firm to the things of heaven.
Through Christ our Lord.

WEDNESDAY

Entrance Antiphon

The Lord will come and he will not delay.
He will illumine what is hidden in darkness
and reveal himself to all the nations. Cf. Hb 2: 3; 1 Cor 4: 5

COLLECT

Prepare our hearts, we pray, O Lord our God,
by your divine power,
so that at the coming of Christ your Son
we may be found worthy of the banquet of eternal life
and merit to receive heavenly nourishment
from his hands.
Who lives and reigns with you
in the unity of the Holy Spirit,
one God, for ever and ever.

PRAYER AFTER COMMUNION

We implore your mercy, Lord,
that this divine sustenance
may cleanse us of our faults
and prepare us for the coming feasts.
Through Christ our Lord.

THURSDAY

Entrance Antiphon

You, O Lord, are close, and all your ways are truth.
From of old I have known of your decrees, for you are eternal.
Cf. Ps 119 (118): 151-152

COLLECT

Stir up your power, O Lord,
and come to our help with mighty strength,
that what our sins impede
the grace of your mercy may hasten.
Through our Lord Jesus Christ, your Son,
who lives and reigns with you
in the unity of the Holy Spirit,
one God, for ever and ever.

PRAYER AFTER COMMUNION

May these mysteries, O Lord,
in which we have participated,
profit us, we pray,
for even now, as we walk amid passing things,
you teach us by them
to love the things of heaven
and hold fast to what endures.
Through Christ our Lord.

FRIDAY

Entrance Antiphon

Behold, the Lord will come
descending with splendor to visit his people with peace,
and he will bestow on them eternal life.

COLLECT

Stir up your power, we pray, O Lord, and come,
that with you to protect us,
we may find rescue
from the pressing dangers of our sins,
and with you to set us free,
we may be found worthy of salvation.
Who live and reign with God the Father
in the unity of the Holy Spirit,
one God, for ever and ever.

PRAYER AFTER COMMUNION

Replenished by the food of spiritual nourishment,
we humbly beseech you, O Lord,
that, through our partaking in this mystery,
you may teach us to judge wisely the things of earth
and hold firm to the things of heaven.
Through Christ our Lord.

SATURDAY

Entrance Antiphon

Come and show us your face, O Lord,
who are seated upon the Cherubim, and we will be saved.
Cf. Ps 80 (79): 4, 2

COLLECT

O God, who sent your Only Begotten Son into this world
to free the human race from its ancient enslavement,
bestow on those who devoutly await him
the grace of your compassion from on high,
that we may attain the prize of true freedom.
Through our Lord Jesus Christ, your Son,
who lives and reigns with you
in the unity of the Holy Spirit,
one God, for ever and ever.

PRAYER AFTER COMMUNION

We implore your mercy, Lord,
that this divine sustenance
may cleanse us of our faults
and prepare us for the coming feasts.
Through Christ our Lord.

SECOND SUNDAY OF ADVENT

Entrance Antiphon

O people of Sion, behold,
the Lord will come to save the nations,
and the Lord will make the glory of his voice heard
in the joy of your heart. Cf. Is 30: 19, 30

The Gloria in excelsis (Glory to God in the highest) is not said.

COLLECT

Almighty and merciful God,
may no earthly undertaking hinder those
who set out in haste to meet your Son,
but may our learning of heavenly wisdom
gain us admittance to his company.
Who lives and reigns with you
in the unity of the Holy Spirit,
one God, for ever and ever.

The Creed is said.

PRAYER AFTER COMMUNION

Replenished by the food of spiritual nourishment,
we humbly beseech you, O Lord,
that, through our partaking in this mystery,
you may teach us to judge wisely the things of earth
and hold firm to the things of heaven.
Through Christ our Lord.

A formula of Solemn Blessing, p. 310, may be used.

MONDAY

Entrance Antiphon

Hear the word of the Lord, O nations;
declare it to the distant lands:
Behold, our Savior will come; you need no longer fear.
Cf. Jer 31: 10; Is 35: 4

COLLECT

May our prayer of petition
rise before you, we pray, O Lord,
that, with purity unblemished,
we, your servants, may come, as we desire,
to celebrate the great mystery
of the Incarnation of your Only Begotten Son.
Who lives and reigns with you
in the unity of the Holy Spirit,
one God, for ever and ever.

PRAYER AFTER COMMUNION

May these mysteries, O Lord,
in which we have participated,
profit us, we pray,
for even now, as we walk amid passing things,
you teach us by them
to love the things of heaven
and hold fast to what endures.
Through Christ our Lord.

TUESDAY

Entrance Antiphon

Behold, the Lord will come, and all his holy ones with him;
and on that day there will be a great light. Cf. Zec 14: 5, 7

COLLECT

O God, who have shown forth your salvation
to all the ends of the earth,
grant, we pray,
that we may look forward in joy
to the glorious Nativity of Christ.
Who lives and reigns with you
in the unity of the Holy Spirit,
one God, for ever and ever.

PRAYER AFTER COMMUNION

Replenished by the food of spiritual nourishment,
we humbly beseech you, O Lord,
that, through our partaking in this mystery,
you may teach us to judge wisely the things of earth
and hold firm to the things of heaven.
Through Christ our Lord.

WEDNESDAY

Entrance Antiphon

The Lord will come and he will not delay.
He will illumine what is hidden in darkness
and reveal himself to all the nations. Cf. Hb 2: 3; 1 Cor 4: 5

COLLECT

Almighty God, who command us
to prepare the way for Christ the Lord,
grant in your kindness, we pray,
that no infirmity may weary us
as we long for the comforting presence
of our heavenly physician.
Who lives and reigns with you
in the unity of the Holy Spirit,
one God, for ever and ever.

PRAYER AFTER COMMUNION

We implore your mercy, Lord,
that this divine sustenance
may cleanse us of our faults
and prepare us for the coming feasts.
Through Christ our Lord.

THURSDAY

Entrance Antiphon

You, O Lord, are close, and all your ways are truth.
From of old I have known of your decrees, for you are eternal.
Cf. Ps 119 (118): 151-152

COLLECT

Stir up our hearts, O Lord,
to make ready the paths
of your Only Begotten Son,
that through his coming,
we may be found worthy to serve you
with minds made pure.
Through our Lord Jesus Christ, your Son,
who lives and reigns with you
in the unity of the Holy Spirit,
one God, for ever and ever.

PRAYER AFTER COMMUNION

May these mysteries, O Lord,
in which we have participated,
profit us, we pray,
for even now, as we walk amid passing things,
you teach us by them
to love the things of heaven
and hold fast to what endures.
Through Christ our Lord.

FRIDAY

Entrance Antiphon

Behold, the Lord will come
descending with splendor to visit his people with peace,
and he will bestow on them eternal life.

COLLECT

Grant that your people, we pray, almighty God,
may be ever watchful
for the coming of your Only Begotten Son,
that, as the author of our salvation himself has taught us,
we may hasten, alert and with lighted lamps,
to meet him when he comes.
Who lives and reigns with you
in the unity of the Holy Spirit,
one God, for ever and ever.

PRAYER AFTER COMMUNION

Replenished by the food of spiritual nourishment,
we humbly beseech you, O Lord,
that, through our partaking in this mystery,
you may teach us to judge wisely the things of earth
and hold firm to the things of heaven.
Through Christ our Lord.

SATURDAY

Entrance Antiphon

**Come and show us your face, O Lord,
who are seated upon the Cherubim, and we will be saved.**
Cf. Ps 80 (79): 4, 2

COLLECT

**May the splendor of your glory dawn in our hearts,
we pray, almighty God,
that all shadows of the night may be scattered
and we may be shown to be children of light
by the advent of your Only Begotten Son.
Who lives and reigns with you
in the unity of the Holy Spirit,
one God, for ever and ever.**

PRAYER AFTER COMMUNION

**We implore your mercy, Lord,
that this divine sustenance
may cleanse us of our faults
and prepare us for the coming feasts.
Through Christ our Lord.**

THIRD SUNDAY OF ADVENT

In this Mass the color violet or rose is used.

Entrance Antiphon

**Rejoice in the Lord always; again I say, rejoice.
Indeed, the Lord is near.** Phil 4: 4-5

The Gloria in excelsis (Glory to God in the highest) is not said.

COLLECT

**O God, who see how your people
faithfully await the feast of the Lord's Nativity,
enable us, we pray,
to attain the joys of so great a salvation
and to celebrate them always
with solemn worship and glad rejoicing.
Through our Lord Jesus Christ, your Son,
who lives and reigns with you
in the unity of the Holy Spirit,
one God, for ever and ever.**

The Creed is said.

PRAYER AFTER COMMUNION

**We implore your mercy, Lord,
that this divine sustenance
may cleanse us of our faults
and prepare us for the coming feasts.
Through Christ our Lord.**

A formula of Solemn Blessing, p. 310, may be used.

When during the week a Mass of the weekday is to be said, the texts given below are used, unless the day is one of the Advent weekdays that occur from December 17 to 24.

MONDAY

Entrance Antiphon

Hear the word of the Lord, O nations;
declare it to the distant lands:
Behold, our Savior will come; you need no longer fear.
Cf. Jer 31: 10; Is 35: 4

COLLECT

Incline a merciful ear to our cry, we pray, O Lord,
and, casting light on the darkness of our hearts,
visit us with the grace of your Son.
Who lives and reigns with you
in the unity of the Holy Spirit,
one God, for ever and ever.

PRAYER AFTER COMMUNION

May these mysteries, O Lord,
in which we have participated,
profit us, we pray,
for even now, as we walk amid passing things,
you teach us by them
to love the things of heaven
and hold fast to what endures.
Through Christ our Lord.

TUESDAY

Entrance Antiphon

Behold, the Lord will come, and all his holy ones with him;
and on that day there will be a great light. Cf. Zec 14: 5, 7

COLLECT

O God, who through your Only Begotten Son
have made us a new creation,
look kindly, we pray,
on the handiwork of your mercy,
and at your Son's coming
cleanse us from every stain of the old way of life.
Through our Lord Jesus Christ, your Son,
who lives and reigns with you
in the unity of the Holy Spirit,
one God, for ever and ever.

PRAYER AFTER COMMUNION

Replenished by the food of spiritual nourishment,
we humbly beseech you, O Lord,
that, through our partaking in this mystery,
you may teach us to judge wisely the things of earth
and hold firm to the things of heaven.
Through Christ our Lord.

WEDNESDAY

Entrance Antiphon

The Lord will come and he will not delay.
He will illumine what is hidden in darkness
and reveal himself to all the nations. Cf. Hb 2: 3; 1 Cor 4: 5

COLLECT

Grant, we pray, almighty God,
that the coming solemnity of your Son
may bestow healing upon us in this present life
and bring us the rewards of life eternal.
Through our Lord Jesus Christ, your Son,
who lives and reigns with you
in the unity of the Holy Spirit,
one God, for ever and ever.

PRAYER AFTER COMMUNION

We implore your mercy, Lord,
that this divine sustenance
may cleanse us of our faults
and prepare us for the coming feasts.
Through Christ our Lord.

THURSDAY

Entrance Antiphon

You, O Lord, are close, and all your ways are truth.
From of old I have known of your decrees, for you are eternal.
Cf. Ps 119 (118): 151-152

COLLECT

Unworthy servants that we are, O Lord,
grieved by the guilt of our deeds,
we pray that you may gladden us
by the saving advent of your Only Begotten Son.
Who lives and reigns with you
in the unity of the Holy Spirit,
one God, for ever and ever.

PRAYER AFTER COMMUNION

May these mysteries, O Lord,
in which we have participated,
profit us, we pray,
for even now, as we walk amid passing things,
you teach us by them
to love the things of heaven
and hold fast to what endures.
Through Christ our Lord.

FRIDAY

Entrance Antiphon

Behold, the Lord will come
descending with splendor to visit his people with peace,
and he will bestow on them eternal life.

COLLECT

May your grace, almighty God,
always go before us and follow after,
so that we, who await with heartfelt desire
the coming of your Only Begotten Son,
may receive your help both now and in the life to come.
Through our Lord Jesus Christ, your Son,
who lives and reigns with you
in the unity of the Holy Spirit,
one God, for ever and ever.

PRAYER AFTER COMMUNION

Replenished by the food of spiritual nourishment,
we humbly beseech you, O Lord,
that, through our partaking in this mystery,
you may teach us to judge wisely the things of earth
and hold firm to the things of heaven.
Through Christ our Lord.

FOURTH SUNDAY OF ADVENT

Entrance Antiphon

Drop down dew from above, you heavens,
and let the clouds rain down the Just One;
let the earth be opened and bring forth a Savior. Cf. Is 45: 8

The Gloria in excelsis (Glory to God in the highest) is not said.

COLLECT

Pour forth, we beseech you, O Lord,
your grace into our hearts,
that we, to whom the Incarnation of Christ your Son
was made known by the message of an Angel,
may by his Passion and Cross
be brought to the glory of his Resurrection.
Who lives and reigns with you
in the unity of the Holy Spirit,
one God, for ever and ever.

The Creed is said.

PRAYER AFTER COMMUNION

Having received this pledge of eternal redemption,
we pray, almighty God,
that, as the feast day of our salvation draws ever nearer,
so we may press forward all the more eagerly
to the worthy celebration of the mystery
of your Son's Nativity.
Who lives and reigns for ever and ever.

A formula of Solemn Blessing, p. 310, may be used.

THE WEEKDAYS OF ADVENT

from December 17 to 24

The following Masses are used on the days to which they are assigned, with the exception of Sunday, which retains its own Mass.

December 17

Entrance Antiphon

Rejoice, O heavens, and exult, O earth,
for our Lord will come to show mercy to his poor. Cf. Is 49: 13

COLLECT

O God, Creator and Redeemer of human nature,
who willed that your Word should take flesh
in an ever-virgin womb,
look with favor on our prayers,
that your Only Begotten Son,
having taken to himself our humanity,
may be pleased to grant us a share in his divinity.
Who lives and reigns with you
in the unity of the Holy Spirit,
one God, for ever and ever.

PRAYER AFTER COMMUNION

Nourished by these divine gifts, almighty God.
we ask you to grant our desire:
that, aflame with your Spirit,
we may shine like bright torches
before your Christ when he comes.
Who lives and reigns for ever and ever.

December 18

Entrance Antiphon

Christ our King is coming,
he is the Lamb foretold by John.

COLLECT

Grant, we pray, almighty God,
that we, who are weighed down from of old
by slavery beneath the yoke of sin,
may be set free by the newness
of the long-awaited Nativity
of your Only Begotten Son.
Who lives and reigns with you
in the unity of the Holy Spirit,
one God, for ever and ever.

PRAYER AFTER COMMUNION

May we receive your mercy
in the midst of your temple, O Lord,
and show fitting honor
to the coming solemnities of our redemption.
Through Christ our Lord.

December 19

Entrance Antiphon

He who is to come will come and will not delay,
and now there will be no fear within our land,
for he is our Savior. Cf. Heb 10: 37

COLLECT

O God, who through the child-bearing of the holy Virgin
graciously revealed the radiance of your glory
to the world,
grant, we pray,
that we may venerate with integrity of faith
the mystery of so wondrous an Incarnation
and always celebrate it with due reverence.
Through our Lord Jesus Christ, your Son,
who lives and reigns with you
in the unity of the Holy Spirit,
one God, for ever and ever.

PRAYER AFTER COMMUNION

As we give thanks, almighty God,
for these gifts you have bestowed,
graciously arouse in us, we pray,
the desire for those yet to come,
that we may welcome the Nativity of our Savior
and honor it with minds made pure.
Through Christ our Lord.

December 20

Entrance Antiphon

A branch shall sprout from the root of Jesse,
and the glory of the Lord will fill the whole earth,
and all flesh will see the salvation of God.
Cf. Is 11: 1; 40: 5; Lk 3: 6

COLLECT

O God, eternal majesty, whose ineffable Word
the immaculate Virgin received through
the message of an Angel
and so became the dwelling-place of divinity,
filled with the light of the Holy Spirit,
grant, we pray, that by her example
we may in humility hold fast to your will.
Through our Lord Jesus Christ, your Son,
who lives and reigns with you
in the unity of the Holy Spirit,
one God, for ever and ever.

PRAYER AFTER COMMUNION

Grant divine protection, O Lord,
to those you renew with this heavenly gift,
that to those who delight in your mysteries
you may give the joy of true peace.
Through Christ our Lord.

December 21

Entrance Antiphon

The Lord and Ruler will be coming soon,
and his name will be called Emmanuel,
because he will be God-with-us. Cf. Is 7: 14; 8: 10

COLLECT

Hear in kindness, O Lord,
the prayers of your people,
that those who rejoice
at the coming of your Only Begotten Son in our flesh
may, when at last he comes in glory,
gain the reward of eternal life.
Through our Lord Jesus Christ, your Son,
who lives and reigns with you
in the unity of the Holy Spirit,
one God, for ever and ever.

PRAYER AFTER COMMUNION

Lord, may participation in this divine mystery
provide enduring protection for your people,
so that, being subject to your glorious majesty
in dedicated service,
they may know abundant health in mind and body.
Through Christ our Lord.

December 22

Entrance Antiphon

O gates, lift high your heads; grow higher, ancient doors.
Let him enter, the king of glory! Ps 24 (23): 7

COLLECT

O God, who, seeing the human race fallen into death,
willed to redeem it by the coming
of your Only Begotten Son,
grant, we pray,
that those who confess his Incarnation with humble fervor
may merit his company as their Redeemer.
Who lives and reigns with you
in the unity of the Holy Spirit,
one God, for ever and ever.

PRAYER AFTER COMMUNION

May reception of your Sacrament strengthen us, O Lord,
so that we may go out to meet our Savior
with worthy deeds when he comes
and merit the rewards of the blessed.
Through Christ our Lord.

December 23

Entrance Antiphon

A child shall be born for us,
and he will be called God, the Almighty;
every tribe of the earth shall be blest in him.
Cf. Is 9: 5; Ps 72 (71): 17

COLLECT

Almighty ever-living God,
as we see how the Nativity of your Son
according to the flesh draws near,
we pray that to us, your unworthy servants,
mercy may flow from your Word,
who chose to become flesh of the Virgin Mary
and establish among us his dwelling,
Jesus Christ our Lord.
Who lives and reigns with you
in the unity of the Holy Spirit,
one God, for ever and ever.

PRAYER AFTER COMMUNION

Grant your peace, O Lord,
to those you have nourished with these heavenly gifts,
that we may be ready, with lighted lamps,
to meet your dearly beloved Son at his coming.
Who lives and reigns for ever and ever.

December 24

At the Morning Mass

Entrance Antiphon

Behold, when the fullness of time had come,
God sent his Son into the world. Cf. Gal 4: 4

COLLECT

Come quickly, we pray, Lord Jesus,
and do not delay,
that those who trust in your compassion
may find solace and relief in your coming.
Who live and reign with God the Father
in the unity of the Holy Spirit,
one God, for ever and ever.

PRAYER AFTER COMMUNION

Grant to us who find new vigor, O Lord,
in these your wondrous gifts,
that, as we prepare to celebrate in adoration
the festivities of your Son's Nativity,
so we may possess in gladness
his everlasting rewards.
Who lives and reigns for ever and ever.

CHRISTMAS TIME

December 25

THE NATIVITY OF THE LORD [CHRISTMAS]

Solemnity

MCCCC
LXXXV
ENSE CADENS SOLYMO POMPEI FVLVI
AVGVR
NVMEN AIT QVAE ME
VRNA DABIT

At the Vigil Mass

This Mass is used on the evening of December 24, either before or after First Vespers (Evening Prayer I) of the Nativity.

Entrance Antiphon **Today you will know that the Lord will come, and he will save us, and in the morning you will see his glory.** Cf. Ex 16: 6-7

The Gloria in excelsis (Glory to God in the highest) is said.

COLLECT

O God, who gladden us year by year
as we wait in hope for our redemption,
grant that, just as we joyfully welcome
your Only Begotten Son as our Redeemer,
we may also merit to face him confidently
when he comes again as our Judge.
Who lives and reigns with you
in the unity of the Holy Spirit,
one God, for ever and ever.

The Creed is said. All kneel at the words and by the Holy Spirit was incarnate.

PRAYER AFTER COMMUNION

Grant, O Lord, we pray,
that we may draw new vigor
from celebrating the Nativity of your Only Begotten Son,
by whose heavenly mystery we receive
both food and drink.
Who lives and reigns for ever and ever.

A formula of Solemn Blessing, p. 310, may be used.

At the Mass during the Night

On the Nativity of the Lord all Priests may celebrate or concelebrate three Masses, provided the Masses are celebrated at their proper times.

Entrance Antiphon

The Lord said to me: You are my Son.
It is I who have begotten you this day. Ps 2: 7

Or:

Let us all rejoice in the Lord,
for our Savior has been born in the world.
Today true peace has come down to us from heaven.

The Gloria in excelsis (Glory to God in the highest) is said.

COLLECT

O God, who have made this most sacred night
radiant with the splendor of the true light,
grant, we pray, that we, who have known the mysteries
of his light on earth,
may also delight in his gladness in heaven.
Who lives and reigns with you
in the unity of the Holy Spirit,
one God, for ever and ever.

The Creed is said. All kneel at the words and by the Holy Spirit was incarnate.

PRAYER AFTER COMMUNION

Grant us, we pray, O Lord our God,
that we, who are gladdened by participation
in the feast of our Redeemer's Nativity,
may through an honorable way of life
become worthy of union with him.
Who lives and reigns for ever and ever.

A formula of Solemn Blessing, p. 310, may be used.

At the Mass at Dawn

Entrance Antiphon

Today a light will shine upon us, for the Lord is born for us;
and he will be called Wondrous God,
Prince of peace, Father of future ages:
and his reign will be without end. Cf. Is 9: 1, 5; Lk 1: 33

The Gloria in excelsis (Glory to God in the highest) is said.

COLLECT

Grant, we pray, almighty God,
that, as we are bathed in the new radiance
of your incarnate Word,
the light of faith, which illumines our minds,
may also shine through in our deeds.
Through our Lord Jesus Christ, your Son,
who lives and reigns with you
in the unity of the Holy Spirit,
one God, for ever and ever.

The Creed is said. All kneel at the words and by the Holy Spirit was incarnate.

PRAYER AFTER COMMUNION

Grant us, Lord, as we honor with joyful devotion
the Nativity of your Son,
that we may come to know with fullness of faith
the hidden depths of this mystery
and to love them ever more and more.
Through Christ our Lord.

A formula of Solemn Blessing, p. 310, may be used.

At the Mass during the Day

Entrance Antiphon

A child is born for us, and a son is given to us;
his scepter of power rests upon his shoulder,
and his name will be called Messenger of great counsel.

Cf. Is 9: 5

The Gloria in excelsis (Glory to God in the highest) is said.

COLLECT

O God, who wonderfully created the dignity
of human nature
and still more wonderfully restored it,
grant, we pray,
that we may share in the divinity of Christ,
who humbled himself to share in our humanity.
Who lives and reigns with you
in the unity of the Holy Spirit,
one God, for ever and ever.

The Creed is said. All kneel at the words and by the Holy Spirit was incarnate.

PRAYER AFTER COMMUNION

Grant, O merciful God,
that just as the Savior of the world, born this day,
is the author of divine generation for us,
so he may be the giver even of immortality.
Who lives and reigns for ever and ever.

A formula of Solemn Blessing, p. 310, may be used.

The Sunday within the Octave of the Nativity of the Lord [Christmas], or, if there is no Sunday, December 30

THE HOLY FAMILY OF JESUS, MARY AND JOSEPH

Feast

Entrance Antiphon

The shepherds went in haste,
and found Mary and Joseph and the Infant lying in a manger.
Lk 2: 16

The Gloria in excelsis (Glory to God in the highest) is said.

COLLECT

O God, who were pleased to give us
the shining example of the Holy Family,
graciously grant that we may imitate them
in practicing the virtues of family life and
in the bonds of charity,
and so, in the joy of your house,
delight one day in eternal rewards.
Through our Lord Jesus Christ, your Son,
who lives and reigns with you
in the unity of the Holy Spirit,
one God, for ever and ever.

When this Feast is celebrated on Sunday, the Creed is said.

PRAYER AFTER COMMUNION

Bring those you refresh with this heavenly Sacrament,
most merciful Father,
to imitate constantly the example of the Holy Family,
so that, after the trials of this world,
we may share their company for ever.
Through Christ our Lord.

December 29

FIFTH DAY WITHIN THE OCTAVE OF THE NATIVITY OF THE LORD [CHRISTMAS]

Entrance Antiphon

**God so loved the world that he gave his Only Begotten Son,
so that all who believe in him may not perish,
but may have eternal life.** Jn 3: 16

The Gloria in excelsis (Glory to God in the highest) is said.

COLLECT

**Almighty and invisible God,
who dispersed the darkness of this world
by the coming of your light,
look, we pray, with serene countenance upon us,
that we may acclaim with fitting praise
the greatness of the Nativity of your Only Begotten Son.
Who lives and reigns with you
in the unity of the Holy Spirit,
one God, for ever and ever.**

PRAYER AFTER COMMUNION

**Grant, we pray, almighty God,
that, by the power of these holy mysteries,
our life may be constantly sustained.
Through Christ our Lord.**

December 30

SIXTH DAY WITHIN THE OCTAVE OF THE NATIVITY OF THE LORD [CHRISTMAS]

When there is no Sunday within the Octave of the Nativity [Christmas], the Feast of the Holy Family of Jesus, Mary and Joseph is celebrated on this day (cf. p. 35).

Entrance Antiphon

When a profound silence covered all things
and night was in the middle of its course,
your all-powerful Word, O Lord,
bounded from heaven's royal throne. Wis 18: 14-15

The Gloria in excelsis (Glory to God in the highest) is said.

COLLECT

Grant, we pray, almighty God,
that the newness of the Nativity in the flesh
of your Only Begotten Son may set us free,
for ancient servitude holds us bound
beneath the yoke of sin.
Through our Lord Jesus Christ, your Son,
who lives and reigns with you
in the unity of the Holy Spirit,
one God, for ever and ever.

PRAYER AFTER COMMUNION

O God, who touch us through our partaking
of your Sacrament,
work, we pray, the effects of its power in our hearts,
that we may be made fit to receive your gift
through this very gift itself.
Through Christ our Lord.

December 31

SEVENTH DAY WITHIN THE OCTAVE OF THE NATIVITY OF THE LORD [CHRISTMAS]

Entrance Antiphon

A child is born for us, and a son is given to us;
his scepter of power rests upon his shoulder,
and his name will be called Messenger of great counsel. Is 9: 5

The Gloria in excelsis (Glory to God in the highest) is said.

COLLECT

Almighty ever-living God,
who in the Nativity of your Son
established the beginning and fulfillment of all religion,
grant, we pray, that we may be numbered
among those who belong to him,
in whom is the fullness of human salvation.
Who lives and reigns with you
in the unity of the Holy Spirit,
one God, for ever and ever.

PRAYER AFTER COMMUNION

May your people, O Lord,
whom you guide and sustain in many ways,
experience, both now and in the future,
the remedies which you bestow,
that, with the needed solace of things that pass away,
they may strive with ever deepened trust
for things eternal.
Through Christ our Lord.

January 1

The Octave Day of the Nativity of the Lord [Christmas]

SOLEMNITY OF MARY, THE HOLY MOTHER OF GOD

Entrance Antiphon

Hail, Holy Mother, who gave birth to the King
who rules heaven and earth for ever.

Or:

Today a light will shine upon us, for the Lord is born for us;
and he will be called Wondrous God,
Prince of peace, Father of future ages:
and his reign will be without end. Cf. Is 9: 1, 5; Lk 1: 33

The Gloria in excelsis (Glory to God in the highest) is said.

COLLECT

O God, who through the fruitful virginity of Blessed Mary
bestowed on the human race
the grace of eternal salvation,
grant, we pray,
that we may experience the intercession of her,
through whom we were found worthy
to receive the author of life,
our Lord Jesus Christ, your Son.
Who lives and reigns with you
in the unity of the Holy Spirit,
one God, for ever and ever.

The Creed is said.

PRAYER AFTER COMMUNION

We have received this heavenly Sacrament with joy,
O Lord:
grant, we pray,
that it may lead us to eternal life,
for we rejoice to proclaim the blessed ever-Virgin Mary
Mother of your Son and Mother of the Church.
Through Christ our Lord.

A formula of Solemn Blessing, p. 311, may be used.

On the days following, when the Mass of the weekday is to be said, the texts given below are used, p. 45.

SECOND SUNDAY AFTER THE NATIVITY [CHRISTMAS]

Entrance Antiphon

When a profound silence covered all things
and night was in the middle of its course,
your all-powerful Word, O Lord,
bounded from heaven's royal throne. Wis 18: 14-15

The Gloria in excelsis (Glory to God in the highest) is said.

COLLECT

Almighty ever-living God,
splendor of faithful souls,
graciously be pleased to fill the world with your glory,
and show yourself to all peoples by the radiance of your light.
Through our Lord Jesus Christ, your Son,
who lives and reigns with you in the unity of the Holy Spirit,
one God, for ever and ever.

The Creed is said.

PRAYER AFTER COMMUNION

Lord our God, we humbly ask you,
that, through the working of this mystery,
our offenses may be cleansed
and our just desires fulfilled.
Through Christ our Lord.

A formula of Solemn Blessing, p. 310, may be used.

[In the Dioceses of the United States]

Sunday between January 2 and January 8

THE EPIPHANY OF THE LORD

Solemnity

At the Vigil Mass

This Mass is used on the evening of the day before the Solemnity, either before or after First Vespers (Evening Prayer I) of the Epiphany.

Entrance Antiphon

Arise, Jerusalem, and look to the East
and see your children gathered from the rising to the setting
of the sun. Cf. Bar 5: 5

The Gloria in excelsis (Glory to God in the highest) is said.

COLLECT

May the splendor of your majesty, O Lord, we pray,
shed its light upon our hearts,
that we may pass through the shadows of this world
and reach the brightness of our eternal home.
Through our Lord Jesus Christ, your Son,
who lives and reigns with you
in the unity of the Holy Spirit,
one God, for ever and ever.

The Creed is said.

PRAYER AFTER COMMUNION

Renewed by sacred nourishment,
we implore your mercy, O Lord,
that the star of your justice
may shine always bright in our minds
and that our true treasure may ever consist
in our confession of you.
Through Christ our Lord.

A formula of Solemn Blessing, p. 312, may be used.

At the Mass during the Day

Entrance Antiphon

Behold, the Lord, the Mighty One, has come;
and kingship is in his grasp, and power and dominion.

Cf. Mal 3: 1; 1 Chr 29: 12

The Gloria in excelsis (Glory to God in the highest) is said.

COLLECT

O God, who on this day
revealed your Only Begotten Son to the nations
by the guidance of a star,
grant in your mercy
that we, who know you already by faith,
may be brought to behold the beauty
of your sublime glory.
Through our Lord Jesus Christ, your Son,
who lives and reigns with you
in the unity of the Holy Spirit,
one God, for ever and ever.

Where it is the practice, if appropriate, the moveable Feasts of the current year may be proclaimed after the Gospel, according to the formula given below, pp. 724-725.

The Creed is said.

PRAYER AFTER COMMUNION

Go before us with heavenly light, O Lord,
always and everywhere,
that we may perceive with clear sight
and revere with true affection
the mystery in which you have willed us to participate.
Through Christ our Lord.

A formula of Solemn Blessing, p. 312, may be used.

WEEKDAYS OF CHRISTMAS TIME

from January 2
to the Saturday before the Feast of the Baptism of the Lord

These Masses are used on the weekdays to which they are assigned, with the Collect selected as indicated.

Monday

Entrance Antiphon

A holy day has dawned upon us:
Come, you nations, and adore the Lord,
for a great light has come down upon the earth.

COLLECT

Before the Solemnity of the Epiphany

Grant your people, O Lord, we pray,
unshakable strength of faith,
so that all who profess that your Only Begotten Son
is with you for ever in your glory
and was born of the Virgin Mary
in a body truly like our own
may be freed from present trials
and given a place in abiding gladness.
Through our Lord Jesus Christ, your Son,
who lives and reigns with you
in the unity of the Holy Spirit,
one God, for ever and ever.

After the Solemnity of the Epiphany

O God, whose eternal Word adorns the face of the heavens
yet accepted from the Virgin Mary the frailty of our flesh,
grant, we pray,
that he who appeared among us as the splendor of truth
may go forth in the fullness of power
for the redemption of the world.
Who lives and reigns with you
in the unity of the Holy Spirit,
one God, for ever and ever.

PRAYER AFTER COMMUNION

Grant, we pray, almighty God,
that, by the power of these holy mysteries,
our life may be constantly sustained.
Through Christ our Lord.

TUESDAY

Entrance Antiphon

Blessed is he who comes in the name of the Lord:
The Lord is God and has given us light. Ps 118 (117): 26-27

COLLECT

Before the Solemnity of the Epiphany

O God, who in the blessed childbearing
of the holy Virgin Mary
kept the flesh of your Son
free from the sentence incurred by the human race,
grant, we pray,
that we, who have been taken up into this new creation,
may be freed from the ancient taint of sin.
Through our Lord Jesus Christ, your Son,
who lives and reigns with you
in the unity of the Holy Spirit,
one God, for ever and ever.

After the Solemnity of the Epiphany

O God, whose Only Begotten Son
has appeared in our very flesh,
grant, we pray, that we may be inwardly transformed
through him whom we recognize
as outwardly like ourselves.
Who lives and reigns with you
in the unity of the Holy Spirit,
one God, for ever and ever.

PRAYER AFTER COMMUNION

O God, who touch us through our partaking
of your Sacrament,
work, we pray, the effects of its power in our hearts,
that we may be made fit to receive your gift
through this very gift itself.
Through Christ our Lord.

WEDNESDAY

Entrance Antiphon

A people who walked in darkness has seen a great light;
for those dwelling in a land of deep gloom, a light has shone.
Is 9: 1

COLLECT

Before the Solemnity of the Epiphany

Grant us, almighty God, that the bringer of your salvation,
who for the world's redemption came forth
with newness of heavenly light,
may dawn afresh in our hearts
and bring us constant renewal.
Who lives and reigns with you
in the unity of the Holy Spirit,
one God, for ever and ever.

After the Solemnity of the Epiphany

O God, who bestow light on all the nations,
grant your peoples the gladness of lasting peace
and pour into our hearts that brilliant light
by which you purified the minds of our fathers in faith.
Through our Lord Jesus Christ, your Son,
who lives and reigns with you
in the unity of the Holy Spirit,
one God, for ever and ever.

PRAYER AFTER COMMUNION

May your people, O Lord,
whom you guide and sustain in many ways,
experience, both now and in the future,
the remedies which you bestow,
that, with the needed solace of things that pass away,
they may strive with ever deepened trust
for things eternal.
Through Christ our Lord.

THURSDAY

Entrance Antiphon

**In the beginning and before all ages, the Word was God
and he humbled himself to be born the Savior of the world.**

Cf. Jn 1: 1

COLLECT

Before the Solemnity of the Epiphany

**O God, who by the Nativity of your Only Begotten Son
wondrously began for your people
the work of redemption,
grant, we pray, to your servants such firmness of faith,
that by his guidance they may attain the glorious prize
you have promised.
Through our Lord Jesus Christ, your Son,
who lives and reigns with you
in the unity of the Holy Spirit,
one God, for ever and ever.**

After the Solemnity of the Epiphany

**O God, who through your Son raised up
your eternal light for all nations,
grant that your people may come to acknowledge
the full splendor of their Redeemer,
that, bathed ever more in his radiance,
they may reach everlasting glory.
Through our Lord Jesus Christ, your Son,
who lives and reigns with you
in the unity of the Holy Spirit,
one God, for ever and ever.**

PRAYER AFTER COMMUNION

**Grant, we pray, almighty God,
that, by the power of these holy mysteries,
our life may be constantly sustained.
Through Christ our Lord.**

FRIDAY

Entrance Antiphon

A light has risen in the darkness for the upright of heart;
the Lord is generous, merciful and just. Ps 112 (111): 4

COLLECT

Before the Solemnity of the Epiphany

Cast your kindly light upon your faithful, Lord, we pray,
and with the splendor of your glory
set their hearts ever aflame,
that they may never cease to acknowledge their Savior
and may truly hold fast to him.
Who lives and reigns with you
in the unity of the Holy Spirit,
one God, for ever and ever.

After the Solemnity of the Epiphany

Grant, we ask, almighty God,
that the Nativity of the Savior of the world,
made known by the guidance of a star,
may be revealed ever more fully to our minds.
Through our Lord Jesus Christ, your Son,
who lives and reigns with you
in the unity of the Holy Spirit,
one God, for ever and ever.

PRAYER AFTER COMMUNION

O God, who touch us through our partaking
of your Sacrament,
work, we pray, the effects of its power in our hearts,
that we may be made fit to receive your gift
through this very gift itself.
Through Christ our Lord.

SATURDAY

Entrance Antiphon

**God sent his Son, born of a woman,
so that we might receive adoption as children.** Gal 4: 4-5

COLLECT

Before the Solemnity of the Epiphany

**Almighty ever-living God,
who were pleased to shine forth with new light
through the coming of your Only Begotten Son,
grant, we pray,
that, just as he was pleased to share our bodily form
through the childbearing of the Virgin Mary,
so we, too, may one day merit
to become companions in his kingdom of grace.
Who lives and reigns with you
in the unity of the Holy Spirit,
one God, for ever and ever.**

After the Solemnity of the Epiphany

**Almighty ever-living God,
who through your Only Begotten Son
have made us a new creation for yourself,
grant, we pray,
that by your grace we may be found in the likeness of him,
in whom our nature is united to you.
Who lives and reigns with you
in the unity of the Holy Spirit,
one God, for ever and ever.**

PRAYER AFTER COMMUNION

**May your people, O Lord,
whom you guide and sustain in many ways,
experience, both now and in the future,
the remedies which you bestow,
that, with the needed solace of things that pass away,
they may strive with ever deepened trust
for things eternal.
Through Christ our Lord.**

Sunday after the Epiphany of the Lord

THE BAPTISM OF THE LORD

Feast

Where the Solemnity of the Epiphany is transferred to Sunday, if this Sunday occurs on January 7 or 8, the Feast of the Baptism of the Lord is celebrated on the following Monday.

Entrance Antiphon

After the Lord was baptized, the heavens were opened,
and the Spirit descended upon him like a dove,
and the voice of the Father thundered:
This is my beloved Son, with whom I am well pleased.

Cf. Mt 3: 16-17

The Gloria in excelsis (Glory to God in the highest) is said.

COLLECT

Almighty ever-living God,
who, when Christ had been baptized in the River Jordan
and as the Holy Spirit descended upon him,
solemnly declared him your beloved Son,
grant that your children by adoption,
reborn of water and the Holy Spirit,
may always be well pleasing to you.
Through our Lord Jesus Christ, your Son,
who lives and reigns with you
in the unity of the Holy Spirit,
one God, for ever and ever.

Or:

O God, whose Only Begotten Son
has appeared in our very flesh,
grant, we pray, that we may be inwardly transformed
through him whom we recognize
as outwardly like ourselves.
Who lives and reigns with you
in the unity of the Holy Spirit,
one God, for ever and ever.

The Creed is said.

PRAYER AFTER COMMUNION

**Nourished with these sacred gifts,
we humbly entreat your mercy, O Lord,
that, faithfully listening to your Only Begotten Son,
we may be your children in name and in truth.
Through Christ our Lord.**

Ordinary Time lasts from the Monday after this Sunday to the Tuesday before Lent. For Masses both on Sundays and on weekdays, the texts given below, pp. 257ff., are used.

INRI

LENT

1. It is strongly recommended that the tradition of gathering the local Church after the fashion of the Roman "stations" be kept and promoted, especially during Lent and at least in larger towns and cities, in a way best suited to individual places.

Such gatherings of the faithful can take place, especially with the chief Pastor of the diocese presiding, on Sundays or on other more convenient days during the week, either at the tombs of the Saints, or in the principal churches or shrines of a city, or even in the more frequently visited places of pilgrimage in the diocese.

If a procession precedes a Mass celebrated for such a gathering, according to circumstances and local conditions, the faithful gather at a smaller church or some other suitable place other than in the church to which the procession will head.

After greeting the people, the Priest says a Collect of The Mystery of the Holy Cross (cf. below, p. 669), For the Forgiveness of Sins (cf. below, p. 649), or For the Church, especially For the Particular Church (cf. below, p. 603), or one of the Prayers over the People. Then the procession makes its way to the church in which Mass will be celebrated and meanwhile the Litany of the Saints is sung. Invocations to the Patron Saint or the Founder Saint and to the Saints of the local Church may be inserted at the appropriate point in the Litany.

When the procession reaches the church, the Priest venerates the altar and, if appropriate, incenses it. Afterwards, omitting the Introductory Rites and, if appropriate, the Kyrie, he says the Collect of the Mass, and then continues the Mass in the usual way.

2. At these gatherings, instead of Mass, some celebration of the Word of God may also take place, especially in the form of the penitential celebrations given in the Roman Ritual for Lent.

3. On weekdays of Lent, at the end of Mass and before the final blessing, the Prayer over the People indicated for each day may appropriately be used.

4. During Lent, it is not permitted to decorate the altar with flowers, and the use of musical instruments is allowed only so as to support the singing. Nevertheless, Laetare Sunday (the Fourth Sunday of Lent), Solemnities, and Feasts are exceptions to this rule.

ASH WEDNESDAY

In the course of today's Mass, ashes are blessed and distributed. These are made from the olive branches or branches of other trees that were blessed the previous year.

INTRODUCTORY RITES AND LITURGY OF THE WORD

Entrance Antiphon

You are merciful to all, O Lord,
and despise nothing that you have made.
You overlook people's sins, to bring them to repentance,
and you spare them, for you are the Lord our God.

Wis 11: 24, 25, 27

The Penitential Act is omitted, and the Distribution of Ashes takes its place.

COLLECT

Grant, O Lord, that we may begin with holy fasting
this campaign of Christian service,
so that, as we take up battle against spiritual evils,
we may be armed with weapons of self-restraint.
Through our Lord Jesus Christ, your Son,
who lives and reigns with you
in the unity of the Holy Spirit,
one God, for ever and ever.

BLESSING AND DISTRIBUTION OF ASHES

After the Homily, the Priest, standing with hands joined, says:

Dear brethren (brothers and sisters),
let us humbly ask God our Father
that he be pleased to bless with the abundance of his grace
these ashes, which we will put on our heads in penitence.

After a brief prayer in silence, and, with hands extended, he continues:

O God, who are moved by acts of humility
and respond with forgiveness to works of penance,
lend your merciful ear to our prayers
and in your kindness pour out the grace of your ✠ blessing
on your servants who are marked with these ashes,
that, as they follow the Lenten observances,
they may be worthy to come with minds made pure
to celebrate the Paschal Mystery of your Son.
Through Christ our Lord.

℟. Amen.

Or:

**O God, who desire not the death of sinners,
but their conversion,
mercifully hear our prayers
and in your kindness be pleased to bless ✠ these ashes,
which we intend to receive upon our heads,
that we, who acknowledge we are but ashes
and shall return to dust,
may, through a steadfast observance of Lent,
gain pardon for sins and newness of life
after the likeness of your Risen Son.
Who lives and reigns for ever and ever.**

℟. Amen.

He sprinkles the ashes with holy water, without saying anything.

Then the Priest places ashes on the head of all those present who come to him, and says to each one:

Repent, and believe in the Gospel.

Or:

Remember that you are dust, and to dust you shall return.

Meanwhile, the following are sung:

Antiphon 1 — Let us change our garments to sackcloth and ashes,
let us fast and weep before the Lord,
that our God, rich in mercy, might forgive us our sins.

Antiphon 2 — Let the priests, the ministers of the Lord,
stand between the porch and the altar and weep and cry out:
Spare, O Lord, spare your people;
do not close the mouths of those who sing your praise, O Lord.
Cf. Jl 2: 17; Est 4: 17

Antiphon 3 — Blot out my transgressions, O Lord. Ps 51 (50): 3

This may be repeated after each verse of Psalm 51 (50) (Have mercy on me, O God).

Responsory — ℟. Let us correct our faults which we have committed in ignorance, let us not be taken unawares by the day of our death, looking in vain for leisure to repent. * Hear us, O Lord, and show us your mercy, for we have sinned against you.

℣. Help us, O God our Savior; for the sake of your name, O Lord, set us free. * Hear us, O Lord . . . Cf. Bar 3: 2; Ps 79 (78): 9

Another appropriate chant may also be sung.

After the distribution of ashes, the Priest washes his hands and proceeds to the Universal Prayer, and continues the Mass in the usual way.

The Creed is not said.

THE LITURGY OF THE EUCHARIST

PRAYER AFTER COMMUNION

May the Sacrament we have received sustain us, O Lord,
that our Lenten fast may be pleasing to you
and be for us a healing remedy.
Through Christ our Lord.

PRAYER OVER THE PEOPLE

For the dismissal, the Priest stands facing the people and, extending his hands over them, says this prayer:

Pour out a spirit of compunction, O God,
on those who bow before your majesty,
and by your mercy may they merit the rewards
you promise
to those who do penance.
Through Christ our Lord.

The blessing and distribution of ashes may also take place outside Mass. In this case, the rite is preceded by a Liturgy of the Word, with the Entrance Antiphon, the Collect, and the readings with their chants as at Mass. Then there follow the Homily and the blessing and distribution of ashes. The rite is concluded with the Universal Prayer, the Blessing, and the Dismissal of the Faithful.

THURSDAY AFTER ASH WEDNESDAY

Entrance Antiphon

When I cried to the Lord, he heard my voice;
he rescued me from those who attack me.
Entrust your cares to the Lord, and he will support you.

Cf. Ps 55 (54): 17-20, 23

COLLECT

Prompt our actions with your inspiration, we pray, O Lord,
and further them with your constant help,
that all we do may always begin from you
and by you be brought to completion.
Through our Lord Jesus Christ, your Son,
who lives and reigns with you
in the unity of the Holy Spirit,
one God, for ever and ever.

PRAYER AFTER COMMUNION

Having received the blessing of your heavenly gifts,
we humbly beseech you, almighty God,
that they may always be for us
a source both of pardon and of salvation.
Through Christ our Lord.

PRAYER OVER THE PEOPLE

for optional use

Almighty God,
who have made known to your people
the ways of eternal life,
lead them by that path, we pray,
to you, the unfading light.
Through Christ our Lord.

FRIDAY AFTER ASH WEDNESDAY

Entrance Antiphon

The Lord heard and had mercy on me;
the Lord became my helper. Ps 30 (29): 11

COLLECT

Show gracious favor, O Lord, we pray,
to the works of penance we have begun,
that we may have strength to accomplish with sincerity
the bodily observances we undertake.
Through our Lord Jesus Christ, your Son,
who lives and reigns with you
in the unity of the Holy Spirit,
one God, for ever and ever.

PRAYER AFTER COMMUNION

We pray, almighty God,
that, through partaking of this mystery,
we may be cleansed of all our misdeeds,
and so be suited for the remedies of your compassion.
Through Christ our Lord.

PRAYER OVER THE PEOPLE

for optional use

For your mighty deeds, O God of mercy,
may your people offer endless thanks,
and, by observing the age-old disciplines
along their pilgrim journey,
may they merit to come and behold you for ever.
Through Christ our Lord.

SATURDAY AFTER ASH WEDNESDAY

Entrance Antiphon

Answer us, Lord, for your mercy is kind;
in the abundance of your mercies, look upon us.
Cf. Ps 69 (68): 17

COLLECT

Almighty ever-living God,
look with compassion on our weakness
and ensure us your protection
by stretching forth the right hand of your majesty.
Through our Lord Jesus Christ, your Son,
who lives and reigns with you
in the unity of the Holy Spirit,
one God, for ever and ever.

PRAYER AFTER COMMUNION

Nourished with the gift of heavenly life,
we pray, O Lord,
that what remains for us a mystery in this present life
may be for us a help to reach eternity.
Through Christ our Lord.

PRAYER OVER THE PEOPLE

for optional use

Abide graciously, O Lord, with your people,
who have touched the sacred mysteries,
that no dangers may bring affliction
to those who trust in you, their protector.
Through Christ our Lord.

FIRST SUNDAY OF LENT

On this Sunday is celebrated the rite of "election" or "enrollment of names" for the catechumens who are to be admitted to the Sacraments of Christian Initiation at the Easter Vigil, using the proper prayers and intercessions as given in the Roman Missal.

Entrance Antiphon

When he calls on me, I will answer him;
I will deliver him and give him glory,
I will grant him length of days. Cf. Ps 91 (90): 15-16

The Gloria in excelsis (Glory to God in the highest) is not said.

COLLECT

Grant, almighty God,
through the yearly observances of holy Lent,
that we may grow in understanding
of the riches hidden in Christ
and by worthy conduct pursue their effects.
Through our Lord Jesus Christ, your Son,
who lives and reigns with you
in the unity of the Holy Spirit,
one God, for ever and ever.

The Creed is said.

PRAYER AFTER COMMUNION

Renewed now with heavenly bread,
by which faith is nourished, hope increased,
and charity strengthened,
we pray, O Lord,
that we may learn to hunger for Christ,
the true and living Bread,
and strive to live by every word
which proceeds from your mouth.
Through Christ our Lord.

PRAYER OVER THE PEOPLE

May bountiful blessing, O Lord, we pray,
come down upon your people,
that hope may grow in tribulation,
virtue be strengthened in temptation,
and eternal redemption be assured.
Through Christ our Lord.

MONDAY

Entrance Antiphon

Like the eyes of slaves on the hand of their lords,
so our eyes are on the Lord our God, till he show us his mercy.
Have mercy on us, Lord, have mercy. Cf. Ps 123 (122): 2-3

COLLECT

Convert us, O God our Savior,
and instruct our minds by heavenly teaching,
that we may benefit from the works of Lent.
Through our Lord Jesus Christ, your Son,
who lives and reigns with you
in the unity of the Holy Spirit,
one God, for ever and ever.

PRAYER AFTER COMMUNION

We pray, O Lord, that, in receiving your Sacrament,
we may experience help in mind and body
so that, kept safe in both,
we may glory in the fullness of heavenly healing.
Through Christ our Lord.

PRAYER OVER THE PEOPLE

for optional use

Enlighten the minds of your people, Lord, we pray,
with the light of your glory,
that they may see what must be done
and have the strength to do what is right.
Through Christ our Lord.

TUESDAY

Entrance Antiphon

O Lord, you have been our refuge,
from generation to generation;
from age to age, you are. Cf. Ps 90 (89): 1-2

COLLECT

Look upon your family, Lord,
that, through the chastening effects of bodily discipline,
our minds may be radiant in your presence
with the strength of our yearning for you.
Through our Lord Jesus Christ, your Son,
who lives and reigns with you
in the unity of the Holy Spirit,
one God, for ever and ever.

PRAYER AFTER COMMUNION

Grant us through these mysteries, Lord,
that by moderating earthly desires
we may learn to love the things of heaven.
Through Christ our Lord.

PRAYER OVER THE PEOPLE

for optional use

May your faithful be strengthened,
O God, by your blessing:
in grief, may you be their consolation,
in tribulation, their power to endure,
and in peril, their protection.
Through Christ our Lord.

WEDNESDAY

Entrance Antiphon

Remember your compassion, O Lord,
and your merciful love, for they are from of old.
Let not our enemies exult over us.
Redeem us, O God of Israel, from all our distress.
Cf. Ps 25 (24): 6, 2, 22

COLLECT

Look kindly, Lord, we pray,
on the devotion of your people,
that those who by self-denial are restrained in body
may by the fruit of good works be renewed in mind.
Through our Lord Jesus Christ, your Son,
who lives and reigns with you
in the unity of the Holy Spirit,
one God, for ever and ever.

PRAYER AFTER COMMUNION

O God, who never cease to nourish us by your Sacrament,
grant that the refreshment you give us through it
may bring us unending life.
Through Christ our Lord.

PRAYER OVER THE PEOPLE

for optional use

Watch over your people, Lord,
and in your kindness cleanse them from all sins,
for if evil has no dominion over them,
no trial can do them harm.
Through Christ our Lord.

THURSDAY

Entrance Antiphon

To my words give ear, O Lord; give heed to my sighs.
Attend to the sound of my cry, my King and my God.
Cf. Ps 5: 2-3

COLLECT

Bestow on us, we pray, O Lord,
a spirit of always pondering on what is right
and of hastening to carry it out,
and, since without you we cannot exist,
may we be enabled to live according to your will.
Through our Lord Jesus Christ, your Son,
who lives and reigns with you
in the unity of the Holy Spirit,
one God, for ever and ever.

PRAYER AFTER COMMUNION

We pray, O Lord our God,
that, as you have given these most sacred mysteries
to be the safeguard of our salvation,
so you may make them a healing remedy for us,
both now and in time to come.
Through Christ our Lord.

PRAYER OVER THE PEOPLE

for optional use

May the mercy they have hoped for, O Lord,
come to those who make supplication to you,
and may the riches of heaven be given them,
that they may know what it is right to ask
and receive what they have sought.
Through Christ our Lord.

FRIDAY

Entrance Antiphon

Set me free from my distress, O Lord.
See my lowliness and suffering,
and take away all my sins.
Cf. Ps 25 (24): 17-18

COLLECT

Grant that your faithful, O Lord, we pray,
may be so conformed to the paschal observances,
that the bodily discipline now solemnly begun
may bear fruit in the souls of all.
Through our Lord Jesus Christ, your Son,
who lives and reigns with you
in the unity of the Holy Spirit,
one God, for ever and ever.

PRAYER AFTER COMMUNION

May the holy refreshment of your Sacrament
restore us anew, O Lord,
and, cleansing us of old ways,
take us up into the mystery of salvation.
Through Christ our Lord.

PRAYER OVER THE PEOPLE

for optional use

Look with favor on your people, O Lord,
that what their observance outwardly declares
it may inwardly bring about.
Through Christ our Lord.

SATURDAY

Entrance Antiphon

The law of the Lord is perfect; it revives the soul.
The decrees of the Lord are steadfast;
they give wisdom to the simple. Cf. Ps 19 (18): 8

COLLECT

Turn our hearts to you, eternal Father,
and grant that, seeking always the one thing necessary
and carrying out works of charity,
we may be dedicated to your worship.
Through our Lord Jesus Christ, your Son,
who lives and reigns with you
in the unity of the Holy Spirit,
one God, for ever and ever.

PRAYER AFTER COMMUNION

Show unceasing favor, O Lord,
to those you refresh with this divine mystery,
and accompany with salutary consolations
those you have imbued with heavenly teaching.
Through Christ our Lord.

PRAYER OVER THE PEOPLE

for optional use

May the blessing for which they have longed
strengthen your faithful, O God,
so that, never straying from your will,
they may always rejoice in your benefits.
Through Christ our Lord.

SECOND SUNDAY OF LENT

Entrance Antiphon

Of you my heart has spoken: Seek his face.
It is your face, O Lord, that I seek;
hide not your face from me. Cf. Ps 27 (26): 8-9

Or:

Remember your compassion, O Lord,
and your merciful love, for they are from of old.
Let not our enemies exult over us.
Redeem us, O God of Israel, from all our distress.
Cf. Ps 25 (24): 6, 2, 22

The Gloria in excelsis (Glory to God in the highest) is not said.

COLLECT

O God, who have commanded us
to listen to your beloved Son,
be pleased, we pray,
to nourish us inwardly by your word,
that, with spiritual sight made pure,
we may rejoice to behold your glory.
Through our Lord Jesus Christ, your Son,
who lives and reigns with you
in the unity of the Holy Spirit,
one God, for ever and ever.

The Creed is said.

PRAYER AFTER COMMUNION

As we receive these glorious mysteries,
we make thanksgiving to you, O Lord,
for allowing us while still on earth
to be partakers even now of the things of heaven.
Through Christ our Lord.

PRAYER OVER THE PEOPLE

Bless your faithful, we pray, O Lord,
with a blessing that endures for ever,
and keep them faithful
to the Gospel of your Only Begotten Son,
so that they may always desire and at last attain
that glory whose beauty he showed in his own Body,
to the amazement of his Apostles.
Through Christ our Lord.

MONDAY

Entrance Antiphon

Redeem me, O Lord, and have mercy on me.
My foot stands on level ground;
I will bless the Lord in the assembly. Cf. Ps 26 (25): 11-12

COLLECT

O God, who have taught us
to chasten our bodies
for the healing of our souls,
enable us, we pray,
to abstain from all sins,
and strengthen our hearts
to carry out your loving commands.
Through our Lord Jesus Christ, your Son,
who lives and reigns with you
in the unity of the Holy Spirit,
one God, for ever and ever.

PRAYER AFTER COMMUNION

May this Communion, O Lord,
cleanse us of wrongdoing
and make us heirs to the joy of heaven.
Through Christ our Lord.

PRAYER OVER THE PEOPLE

for optional use

Confirm the hearts of your faithful, O Lord, we pray,
and strengthen them by the power of your grace,
that they may be constant in making supplication to you
and sincere in love for one another.
Through Christ our Lord.

TUESDAY

Entrance Antiphon

Give light to my eyes lest I fall asleep in death,
lest my enemy say: I have overcome him. Cf. Ps 13 (12): 4-5

COLLECT

Guard your Church, we pray, O Lord,
in your unceasing mercy,
and, since without you mortal humanity is sure to fall,
may we be kept by your constant helps from all harm
and directed to all that brings salvation.
Through our Lord Jesus Christ, your Son,
who lives and reigns with you
in the unity of the Holy Spirit,
one God, for ever and ever.

PRAYER AFTER COMMUNION

May the refreshment of this sacred table,
O Lord, we pray,
bring us an increase in devoutness of life
and the constant help of your work of conciliation.
Through Christ our Lord.

PRAYER OVER THE PEOPLE

for optional use

Graciously hear the cries of your faithful, O Lord,
and relieve the weariness of their souls,
that, having received your forgiveness,
they may ever rejoice in your blessing.
Through Christ our Lord.

WEDNESDAY

Entrance Antiphon

Forsake me not, O Lord! My God, be not far from me!
Make haste and come to my help, O Lord, my strong salvation!
Cf. Ps 38 (37): 22-23

COLLECT

Keep your family, O Lord,
schooled always in good works,
and so comfort them with your protection here
as to lead them graciously to gifts on high.
Through our Lord Jesus Christ, your Son,
who lives and reigns with you
in the unity of the Holy Spirit,
one God, for ever and ever.

PRAYER AFTER COMMUNION

Grant, we pray, O Lord our God,
that what you have given us as the pledge of immortality
may work for our eternal salvation.
Through Christ our Lord.

PRAYER OVER THE PEOPLE

for optional use

Bestow upon your servants, Lord,
abundance of grace and protection;
grant health of mind and body;
grant fullness of fraternal charity,
and make them always devoted to you.
Through Christ our Lord.

THURSDAY

Entrance Antiphon

Test me, O God, and know my thoughts.
See that my path is not wicked,
and lead me in the way everlasting. Cf. Ps 139 (138): 23-24

COLLECT

O God, who delight in innocence and restore it,
direct the hearts of your servants to yourself,
that, caught up in the fire of your Spirit,
we may be found steadfast in faith
and effective in works.
Through our Lord Jesus Christ, your Son,
who lives and reigns with you
in the unity of the Holy Spirit,
one God, for ever and ever.

PRAYER AFTER COMMUNION

May this sacrifice, O God,
remain active in its effects
and work ever more strongly within us.
Through Christ our Lord.

PRAYER OVER THE PEOPLE

for optional use

Abide with your servants, O Lord,
who implore the help of your grace,
that they may receive from you
the support and guidance of your protection.
Through Christ our Lord.

FRIDAY

Entrance Antiphon

In you, O Lord, I put my trust, let me never be put to shame;
release me from the snare they have hidden for me,
for you indeed are my refuge. Cf. Ps 31 (30): 2, 5

COLLECT

Grant, we pray, almighty God,
that, purifying us by the sacred practice of penance,
you may lead us in sincerity of heart
to attain the holy things to come.
Through our Lord Jesus Christ, your Son,
who lives and reigns with you
in the unity of the Holy Spirit,
one God, for ever and ever.

PRAYER AFTER COMMUNION

Having received this pledge of eternal salvation,
we pray, O Lord,
that we may set our course so well
as to attain the redemption you promise.
Through Christ our Lord.

PRAYER OVER THE PEOPLE

for optional use

Grant your people, O Lord, we pray,
health of mind and body,
that by constancy in good deeds
they may always merit the defense of your protection.
Through Christ our Lord.

SATURDAY

Entrance Antiphon

The Lord is kind and full of compassion,
slow to anger, abounding in mercy.
How good is the Lord to all,
compassionate to all his creatures. Ps 145 (144): 8-9

COLLECT

O God, who grant us by glorious healing remedies while still on earth
to be partakers of the things of heaven,
guide us, we pray, through this present life
and bring us to that light in which you dwell.
Through our Lord Jesus Christ, your Son,
who lives and reigns with you
in the unity of the Holy Spirit,
one God, for ever and ever.

PRAYER AFTER COMMUNION

May your divine Sacrament, O Lord,
which we have received,
fill the inner depths of our heart
and, by its working mightily within us,
make us partakers of its grace.
Through Christ our Lord.

PRAYER OVER THE PEOPLE

for optional use

May the ears of your mercy be open, O Lord,
to the prayers of those who call upon you;
and that you may grant what they desire,
have them ask what is pleasing to you.
Through Christ our Lord.

THIRD SUNDAY OF LENT

On this Sunday is celebrated the first scrutiny in preparation for the Baptism of the catechumens who are to be admitted to the Sacraments of Christian Initiation at the Easter Vigil, using the proper prayers and intercessions as given below, p. 572.

Entrance Antiphon

My eyes are always on the Lord,
for he rescues my feet from the snare.
Turn to me and have mercy on me,
for I am alone and poor. Cf. Ps 25 (24): 15-16

Or:

When I prove my holiness among you,
I will gather you from all the foreign lands;
and I will pour clean water upon you
and cleanse you from all your impurities,
and I will give you a new spirit, says the Lord. Ez 36: 23-26

The Gloria in excelsis (Glory to God in the highest) is not said.

COLLECT

O God, author of every mercy and of all goodness,
who in fasting, prayer and almsgiving
have shown us a remedy for sin,
look graciously on this confession of our lowliness,
that we, who are bowed down by our conscience,
may always be lifted up by your mercy.
Through our Lord Jesus Christ, your Son,
who lives and reigns with you
in the unity of the Holy Spirit,
one God, for ever and ever.

The Creed is said.

PRAYER AFTER COMMUNION

As we receive the pledge
of things yet hidden in heaven
and are nourished while still on earth
with the Bread that comes from on high,
we humbly entreat you, O Lord,
that what is being brought about in us in mystery
may come to true completion.
Through Christ our Lord.

PRAYER OVER THE PEOPLE

Direct, O Lord, we pray, the hearts of your faithful,
and in your kindness grant your servants this grace:
that, abiding in the love of you and their neighbor,
they may fulfill the whole of your commands.
Through Christ our Lord.

MONDAY

Entrance Antiphon

My soul is longing and yearning for the courts of the Lord.
My heart and my flesh cry out to the living God. Ps 84 (83): 3

COLLECT

May your unfailing compassion, O Lord,
cleanse and protect your Church,
and, since without you she cannot stand secure,
may she be always governed by your grace.
Through our Lord Jesus Christ, your Son,
who lives and reigns with you
in the unity of the Holy Spirit,
one God, for ever and ever.

PRAYER AFTER COMMUNION

May communion in this your Sacrament,
we pray, O Lord,
bring with it purification and the unity that is your gift.
Through Christ our Lord.

PRAYER OVER THE PEOPLE

for optional use

May your right hand, we ask, O Lord,
protect this people that makes entreaty to you:
graciously purify them and give them instruction,
that, finding solace in this life,
they may reach the good things to come.
Through Christ our Lord.

TUESDAY

Entrance Antiphon

To you I call, for you will surely heed me, O God;
turn your ear to me; hear my words.
Guard me as the apple of your eye;
in the shadow of your wings protect me. Cf. Ps 17 (16): 6, 8

COLLECT

May your grace not forsake us, O Lord, we pray,
but make us dedicated to your holy service
and at all times obtain for us your help.
Through our Lord Jesus Christ, your Son,
who lives and reigns with you
in the unity of the Holy Spirit,
one God, for ever and ever.

PRAYER AFTER COMMUNION

May the holy partaking of this mystery
give us life, O Lord, we pray,
and grant us both pardon and protection.
Through Christ our Lord.

PRAYER OVER THE PEOPLE

for optional use

O God, founder and ruler of your people,
drive away the sins that assail them,
that they may always be pleasing to you
and ever safe under your protection.
Through Christ our Lord.

WEDNESDAY

Entrance Antiphon Let my steps be guided by your promise; may evil never rule me.
Cf. Ps 119 (118): 133

COLLECT

Grant, we pray, O Lord,
that, schooled through Lenten observance
and nourished by your word,
through holy restraint
we may be devoted to you with all our heart
and be ever united in prayer.
Through our Lord Jesus Christ, your Son,
who lives and reigns with you
in the unity of the Holy Spirit,
one God, for ever and ever.

PRAYER AFTER COMMUNION

May the heavenly banquet, at which we have been fed,
sanctify us, O Lord,
and, cleansing us of all errors,
make us worthy of your promises from on high.
Through Christ our Lord.

PRAYER OVER THE PEOPLE

for optional use

Give to your people, our God,
a resolve that is pleasing to you,
for, by conforming them to your teachings,
you bestow on them every favor.
Through Christ our Lord.

THURSDAY

Entrance Antiphon

I am the salvation of the people, says the Lord.
Should they cry to me in any distress,
I will hear them, and I will be their Lord for ever.

COLLECT

We implore your majesty most humbly, O Lord,
that, as the feast of our salvation draws ever closer,
so we may press forward all the more eagerly
towards the worthy celebration of the Paschal Mystery.
Through our Lord Jesus Christ, your Son,
who lives and reigns with you
in the unity of the Holy Spirit,
one God, for ever and ever.

PRAYER AFTER COMMUNION

Graciously raise up, O Lord,
those you renew with this Sacrament,
that we may come to possess your salvation
both in mystery and in the manner of our life.
Through Christ our Lord.

PRAYER OVER THE PEOPLE

for optional use

We call on your loving kindness
and trust in your mercy, O Lord,
that, since we have from you all that we are,
through your grace we may seek what is right
and have strength to do the good we desire.
Through Christ our Lord.

FRIDAY

Entrance Antiphon

Among the gods there is none like you, O Lord,
for you are great and do marvelous deeds; you alone are God.
Ps 86 (85): 8, 10

COLLECT

Pour your grace into our hearts, we pray, O Lord,
that we may be constantly drawn away
from unruly desires
and obey by your own gift the heavenly teaching
you give us.
Through our Lord Jesus Christ, your Son,
who lives and reigns with you
in the unity of the Holy Spirit,
one God, for ever and ever.

PRAYER AFTER COMMUNION

May your strength be at work in us, O Lord,
pervading our minds and bodies,
that what we have received
by participating in this Sacrament
may bring us the fullness of redemption.
Through Christ our Lord.

PRAYER OVER THE PEOPLE

for optional use

Look graciously, O Lord,
upon the faithful who implore your mercy,
that, trusting in your kindness,
they may spread far and wide
the gifts your charity has bestowed.
Through Christ our Lord.

SATURDAY

Entrance Antiphon

Bless the Lord, O my soul, and never forget all his benefits;
it is he who forgives all your sins. Ps 103 (102): 2-3

COLLECT

Rejoicing in this annual celebration
of our Lenten observance,
we pray, O Lord,
that, with our hearts set on the paschal mysteries,
we may be gladdened by their full effects.
Through our Lord Jesus Christ, your Son,
who lives and reigns with you
in the unity of the Holy Spirit,
one God, for ever and ever.

PRAYER AFTER COMMUNION

May we truly revere, O merciful God,
these holy gifts, by which you ceaselessly nourish us,
and may we always partake of them
with abundant faith in our heart.
Through Christ our Lord.

PRAYER OVER THE PEOPLE

for optional use

Hold out to your faithful people, Lord,
the right hand of heavenly assistance,
that they may seek you with all their heart
and merit the granting of what they ask.
Through Christ our Lord.

FOURTH SUNDAY OF LENT

In this Mass, the color violet or rose is used. Instrumental music is permitted, and the altar may be decorated with flowers.

On this Sunday is celebrated the second scrutiny in preparation for the Baptism of the catechumens who are to be admitted to the Sacraments of Christian Initiation at the Easter Vigil, using the proper prayers and intercessions as given below, p. 573.

Entrance Antiphon

Rejoice, Jerusalem, and all who love her.
Be joyful, all who were in mourning;
exult and be satisfied at her consoling breast. Cf. Is 66: 10-11

The Gloria in excelsis (Glory to God in the highest) is not said.

COLLECT

O God, who through your Word
reconcile the human race to yourself in a wonderful way,
grant, we pray,
that with prompt devotion and eager faith
the Christian people may hasten
toward the solemn celebrations to come.
Through our Lord Jesus Christ, your Son,
who lives and reigns with you
in the unity of the Holy Spirit,
one God, for ever and ever.

The Creed is said.

PRAYER AFTER COMMUNION

O God, who enlighten everyone who comes into this world,
illuminate our hearts, we pray,
with the splendor of your grace,
that we may always ponder
what is worthy and pleasing to your majesty
and love you in all sincerity.
Through Christ our Lord.

PRAYER OVER THE PEOPLE

Look upon those who call to you, O Lord,
and sustain the weak;
give life by your unfailing light
to those who walk in the shadow of death,
and bring those rescued by your mercy from every evil
to reach the highest good.
Through Christ our Lord.

MONDAY

Entrance Antiphon

As for me, I trust in the Lord.
Let me be glad and rejoice in your mercy,
for you have seen my affliction. Cf. Ps 31 (30): 7-8

COLLECT

O God, who renew the world
through mysteries beyond all telling,
grant, we pray,
that your Church may be guided by your eternal design
and not be deprived of your help in this present age.
Through our Lord Jesus Christ, your Son,
who lives and reigns with you
in the unity of the Holy Spirit,
one God, for ever and ever.

PRAYER AFTER COMMUNION

May your holy gifts, O Lord, we pray,
give us life by making us new,
and, by sanctifying us, lead us to things eternal.
Through Christ our Lord.

PRAYER OVER THE PEOPLE

for optional use

Renew your people within and without, O Lord,
and, since it is your will
that they be unhindered by bodily delights,
give them, we pray,
perseverance in their spiritual intent.
Through Christ our Lord.

TUESDAY

Entrance Antiphon

All who are thirsty, come to the waters, says the Lord.
Though you have no money, come and drink with joy. Cf. Is 55: 1

COLLECT

May the venerable exercises of holy devotion
shape the hearts of your faithful, O Lord,
to welcome worthily the Paschal Mystery
and proclaim the praises of your salvation.
Through our Lord Jesus Christ, your Son,
who lives and reigns with you
in the unity of the Holy Spirit,
one God, for ever and ever.

PRAYER AFTER COMMUNION

Purify our minds, O Lord, we pray,
and renew them with this heavenly Sacrament,
that we may find help for our bodies
now and likewise in times to come.
Through Christ our Lord.

PRAYER OVER THE PEOPLE

for optional use

Grant, O merciful God,
that your people may remain always devoted to you
and may constantly receive from your kindness
whatever is for their good.
Through Christ our Lord.

WEDNESDAY

Entrance Antiphon

I pray to you, O Lord, for a time of your favor.
In your great mercy, answer me, O God,
with your salvation that never fails. Ps 69 (68): 14

COLLECT

O God, who reward the merits of the just
and offer pardon to sinners who do penance,
have mercy, we pray, on those who call upon you,
that the admission of our guilt
may serve to obtain your pardon for our sins.
Through our Lord Jesus Christ, your Son,
who lives and reigns with you
in the unity of the Holy Spirit,
one God, for ever and ever.

PRAYER AFTER COMMUNION

May your heavenly gifts, O Lord, we pray,
which you bestow as a heavenly remedy on your people,
not bring judgment to those who receive them.
Through Christ our Lord.

PRAYER OVER THE PEOPLE

for optional use

May your servants be shielded, O Lord,
by the protection of your loving-kindness,
that, doing what is good in this world,
they may reach you, their highest good.
Through Christ our Lord.

THURSDAY

Entrance Antiphon

Let the hearts that seek the Lord rejoice;
turn to the Lord and his strength;
constantly seek his face. Cf. Ps 105 (104): 3-4

COLLECT

We invoke your mercy in humble prayer, O Lord,
that you may cause us, your servants,
corrected by penance and schooled by good works,
to persevere sincerely in your commands
and come safely to the paschal festivities.
Through our Lord Jesus Christ, your Son,
who lives and reigns with you
in the unity of the Holy Spirit,
one God, for ever and ever.

PRAYER AFTER COMMUNION

May this Sacrament we have received purify us,
we pray, O Lord,
and grant your servants freedom from all blame,
that those bound by a guilty conscience
may glory in the fullness of heavenly remedy.
Through Christ our Lord.

PRAYER OVER THE PEOPLE

for optional use

O God, protector of all who hope in you,
bless your people, keep them safe,
defend them, prepare them,
that, free from sin and safe from the enemy,
they may persevere always in your love.
Through Christ our Lord.

FRIDAY

Entrance Antiphon

O God, save me by your name;
by your power, defend my cause.
O God, hear my prayer;
give ear to the words of my mouth. Cf. Ps 54 (53): 3-4

COLLECT

O God, who have prepared
fitting helps for us in our weakness,
grant, we pray, that we may receive
their healing effects with joy
and reflect them in a holy way of life.
Through our Lord Jesus Christ, your Son,
who lives and reigns with you
in the unity of the Holy Spirit,
one God, for ever and ever.

PRAYER AFTER COMMUNION

Grant, we pray, O Lord,
that as we pass from old to new,
so, with former ways left behind,
we may be renewed in holiness of mind.
Through Christ our Lord.

PRAYER OVER THE PEOPLE

for optional use

Look upon your servants, O Lord,
and in your goodness protect with heavenly assistance
those who trust in your mercy.
Through Christ our Lord.

SATURDAY

Entrance Antiphon

The waves of death rose about me;
the pains of the netherworld surrounded me.
In my anguish I called to the Lord,
and from his holy temple he heard my voice. Cf. Ps 18 (17): 5, 7

COLLECT

May the working of your mercy, O Lord, we pray,
direct our hearts aright,
for without your grace
we cannot find favor in your sight.
Through our Lord Jesus Christ, your Son,
who lives and reigns with you
in the unity of the Holy Spirit,
one God, for ever and ever.

PRAYER AFTER COMMUNION

May your holy gifts purify us, O Lord, we pray,
and by their working render us fully pleasing to you.
Through Christ our Lord.

PRAYER OVER THE PEOPLE

for optional use

Look upon your people, O Lord,
and, as they draw near to the coming festivities,
bestow upon them abundance of heavenly grace,
that, helped by the consolations of this world,
they may be impelled more readily
towards higher goods that cannot be seen.
Through Christ our Lord.

FIFTH SUNDAY OF LENT

In the Dioceses of the United States, the practice of covering crosses and images throughout the church from this Sunday may be observed. Crosses remain covered until the end of the celebration of the Lord's Passion on Good Friday, but images remain covered until the beginning of the Easter Vigil.

On this Sunday is celebrated the third scrutiny in preparation for the Baptism of the catechumens who are to be admitted to the Sacraments of Christian Initiation at the Easter Vigil, using the proper prayers and intercessions as given below, p. 574.

Entrance Antiphon

Give me justice, O God,
and plead my cause against a nation that is faithless.
From the deceitful and cunning rescue me,
for you, O God, are my strength. Cf. Ps 43 (42): 1-2

The Gloria in excelsis (Glory to God in the highest) is not said.

COLLECT

By your help, we beseech you, Lord our God,
may we walk eagerly in that same charity
with which, out of love for the world,
your Son handed himself over to death.
Through our Lord Jesus Christ, your Son,
who lives and reigns with you
in the unity of the Holy Spirit,
one God, for ever and ever.

The Creed is said.

PRAYER AFTER COMMUNION

We pray, almighty God,
that we may always be counted
among the members of Christ,
in whose Body and Blood we have communion.
Who lives and reigns for ever and ever.

PRAYER OVER THE PEOPLE

Bless, O Lord, your people,
who long for the gift of your mercy,
and grant that what, at your prompting, they desire
they may receive by your generous gift.
Through Christ our Lord.

MONDAY

Entrance Antiphon

**Have mercy on me, O God, for people assail me;
they fight me all day long and oppress me.** Cf. Ps 56 (55): 2

COLLECT

**O God, by whose wondrous grace
we are enriched with every blessing,
grant us so to pass from former ways to newness of life,
that we may be made ready for the glory
of the heavenly Kingdom.
Through our Lord Jesus Christ, your Son,
who lives and reigns with you
in the unity of the Holy Spirit,
one God, for ever and ever.**

PRAYER AFTER COMMUNION

**Strengthened by the blessing of your Sacraments,
we pray, O Lord,
that through them we may constantly be cleansed
of our faults
and, by following Christ,
hasten our steps upward toward you.
Through Christ our Lord.**

PRAYER OVER THE PEOPLE

for optional use

**Set free from their sins, O Lord, we pray,
the people who call upon you,
that, living a holy way of life,
they may be kept safe from every trial.
Through Christ our Lord.**

TUESDAY

Entrance Antiphon

Wait for the Lord; be strong;
be stouthearted, and wait for the Lord! Ps 27 (26): 14

COLLECT

Grant us, we pray, O Lord,
perseverance in obeying your will,
that in our days the people dedicated to your service
may grow in both merit and number.
Through our Lord Jesus Christ, your Son,
who lives and reigns with you
in the unity of the Holy Spirit,
one God, for ever and ever.

PRAYER AFTER COMMUNION

Grant, we pray, almighty God,
that, ever seeking what is divine,
we may always be worthy
to approach these heavenly gifts.
Through Christ our Lord.

PRAYER OVER THE PEOPLE

for optional use

O God, who choose to show mercy not anger
to those who hope in you,
grant that your faithful may weep, as they should,
for the evil they have done,
and so merit the grace of your consolation.
Through Christ our Lord.

WEDNESDAY

Entrance Antiphon

My deliverer from angry nations, you set me above my assailants;
you saved me from the violent man, O Lord.

Cf. Ps 18 (17): 48-49

COLLECT

Enlighten, O God of compassion,
the hearts of your children, sanctified by penance,
and in your kindness
grant those you stir to a sense of devotion
a gracious hearing when they cry out to you.
Through our Lord Jesus Christ, your Son,
who lives and reigns with you
in the unity of the Holy Spirit,
one God, for ever and ever.

PRAYER AFTER COMMUNION

May the mysteries we have received, O Lord,
bring us heavenly medicine,
that they may purge all evil from our heart
and strengthen us with eternal protection.
Through Christ our Lord.

PRAYER OVER THE PEOPLE

for optional use

Attend, almighty God,
to the prayers of your people,
and, as you endow them
with confident hope in your compassion,
let them feel as ever the effects of your mercy.
Through Christ our Lord.

THURSDAY

Entrance Antiphon

Christ is mediator of a New Covenant,
so that by means of his death, those who are called
may receive the promise of an eternal inheritance. Heb 9: 15

COLLECT

Be near, O Lord, to those who plead before you,
and look kindly on those who place their hope
in your mercy,
that, cleansed from the stain of their sins,
they may persevere in holy living
and be made full heirs of your promise.
Through our Lord Jesus Christ, your Son,
who lives and reigns with you
in the unity of the Holy Spirit,
one God, for ever and ever.

PRAYER AFTER COMMUNION

Nourished by your saving gifts,
we beseech your mercy, Lord,
that by this same Sacrament,
with which you feed us in the present age,
you may make us partakers of life eternal.
Through Christ our Lord.

PRAYER OVER THE PEOPLE

for optional use

Be gracious to your people, Lord, we pray,
that, as from day to day they reject
what does not please you,
they may be filled instead with delight at your commands.
Through Christ our Lord.

FRIDAY

Entrance Antiphon

Have mercy on me, O Lord, for I am in distress.
Deliver me from the hands of my enemies
and those who pursue me.
O Lord, let me never be put to shame, for I call on you.

Ps 31 (30): 10, 16, 18

COLLECT

Pardon the offenses of your peoples, we pray, O Lord,
and in your goodness set us free
from the bonds of the sins
we have committed in our weakness.
Through our Lord Jesus Christ, your Son,
who lives and reigns with you
in the unity of the Holy Spirit,
one God, for ever and ever.

Or:

O God, who in this season
give your Church the grace
to imitate devoutly the Blessed Virgin Mary
in contemplating the Passion of Christ,
grant, we pray, through her intercession,
that we may cling more firmly each day
to your Only Begotten Son
and come at last to the fullness of his grace.
Who lives and reigns with you
in the unity of the Holy Spirit,
one God, for ever and ever.

PRAYER AFTER COMMUNION

May the unfailing protection
of the sacrifice we have received
never leave us, O Lord,
and may it always drive far from us
all that would do us harm.
Through Christ our Lord.

PRAYER OVER THE PEOPLE

for optional use

Grant, we pray, almighty God,
that your servants, who seek the grace of your protection,
may be free from every evil
and serve you in peace of mind.
Through Christ our Lord.

SATURDAY

Entrance Antiphon

O Lord, do not stay afar off;
my strength, make haste to help me!
For I am a worm and no man,
scorned by everyone, despised by the people. Cf. Ps 22 (21): 20, 7

COLLECT

O God, who have made all those reborn in Christ
a chosen race and a royal priesthood,
grant us, we pray, the grace to will and to do
what you command,
that the people called to eternal life
may be one in the faith of their hearts
and the homage of their deeds.
Through our Lord Jesus Christ, your Son,
who lives and reigns with you
in the unity of the Holy Spirit,
one God, for ever and ever.

PRAYER AFTER COMMUNION

We entreat your majesty most humbly, O Lord,
that, as you feed us with the nourishment
which comes from the most holy Body and Blood
of your Son,
so you may make us sharers of his divine nature.
Who lives and reigns for ever and ever.

PRAYER OVER THE PEOPLE

for optional use

Have mercy, Lord, on your Church,
as she brings you her supplications,
and be attentive to those who incline their hearts
before you:
do not allow, we pray, those you have redeemed
by the Death of your Only Begotten Son,
to be harmed by their sins or weighed down by their trials.
Through Christ our Lord.

HOLY WEEK

PALM SUNDAY OF THE PASSION OF THE LORD

1. On this day the Church recalls the entrance of Christ the Lord into Jerusalem to accomplish his Paschal Mystery. Accordingly, the memorial of this entrance of the Lord takes place at all Masses, by means of the Procession or the Solemn Entrance before the principal Mass or the Simple Entrance before other Masses. The Solemn Entrance, but not the Procession, may be repeated before other Masses that are usually celebrated with a large gathering of people.

It is desirable that, where neither the Procession nor the Solemn Entrance can take place, there be a sacred celebration of the Word of God on the messianic entrance and on the Passion of the Lord, either on Saturday evening or on Sunday at a convenient time.

The Commemoration of the Lord's Entrance into Jerusalem

First Form: The Procession

2. At an appropriate hour, a gathering takes place at a smaller church or other suitable place other than inside the church to which the procession will go. The faithful hold branches in their hands.

3. Wearing the red sacred vestments as for Mass, the Priest and the Deacon, accompanied by other ministers, approach the place where the people are gathered. Instead of the chasuble, the Priest may wear a cope, which he leaves aside when the procession is over, and puts on a chasuble.

4. Meanwhile, the following antiphon or another appropriate chant is sung.

Ant.

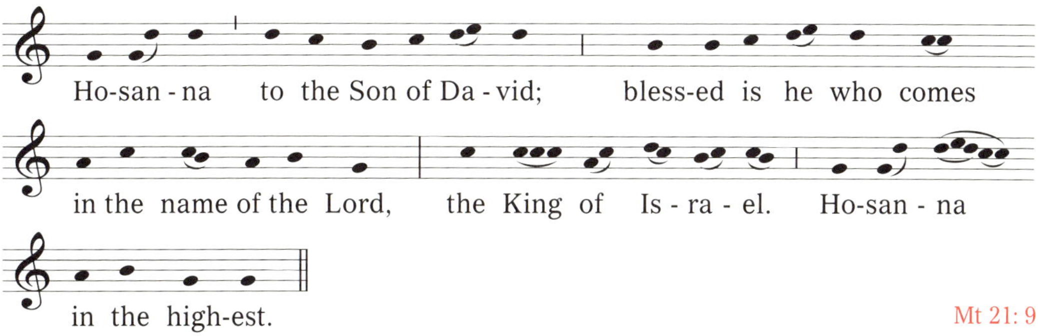

Mt 21: 9

Or:

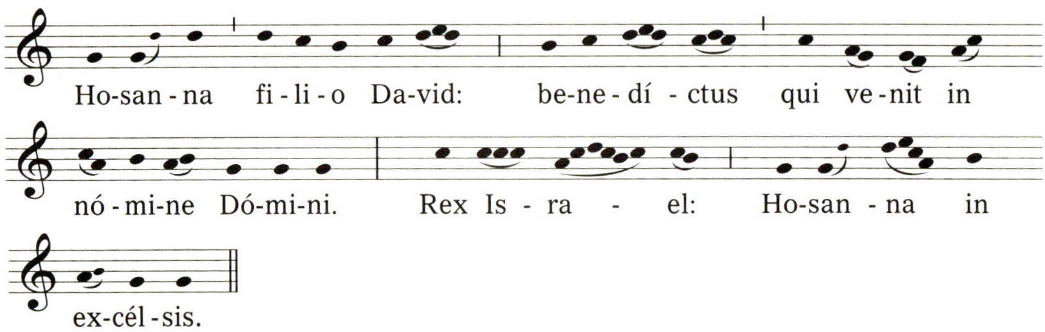

5. After this, the Priest and people sign themselves, while the Priest says: In the name of the Father, and of the Son, and of the Holy Spirit. Then he greets the people in the usual way. A brief address is given, in which the faithful are invited to participate actively and consciously in the celebration of this day, in these or similar words:

Dear brethren (brothers and sisters),
since the beginning of Lent until now
we have prepared our hearts
by penance and charitable works.
Today we gather together to herald with the whole Church
the beginning of the celebration
of our Lord's Paschal Mystery,
that is to say, of his Passion and Resurrection.
For it was to accomplish this mystery
that he entered his own city of Jerusalem.
Therefore, with all faith and devotion,
let us commemorate
the Lord's entry into the city for our salvation,
following in his footsteps,
so that, being made by his grace partakers of the Cross,
we may have a share also
in his Resurrection and in his life.

6. After the address, the Priest says one of the following prayers with hands extended.

Let us pray.

Almighty ever-living God,
sanctify ✠ these branches with your blessing,
that we, who follow Christ the King in exultation,
may reach the eternal Jerusalem through him.
Who lives and reigns for ever and ever.
℟. Amen.

Or:

**Increase the faith of those who place their hope in you,
O God,
and graciously hear the prayers of those who call on you,
that we, who today hold high these branches
to hail Christ in his triumph,
may bear fruit for you by good works accomplished in him.
Who lives and reigns for ever and ever.**

℟. Amen.

He sprinkles the branches with holy water without saying anything.

7. Then a Deacon or, if there is no Deacon, a Priest, proclaims in the usual way the Gospel concerning the Lord's entrance according to one of the four Gospels. If appropriate, incense may be used.

"Blessed is he who comes in the name of the Lord"

Year A

✠ **A reading from the holy Gospel according to Matthew.**

21: 1-11

**1 When Jesus and the disciples drew near Jerusalem
and came to Bethphage on the Mount of Olives,
Jesus sent two disciples, 2 saying to them,
"Go into the village opposite you,
and immediately you will find an ass tethered,
and a colt with her.
Untie them and bring them here to me.
3 And if anyone should say anything to you, reply,
'The master has need of them.'
Then he will send them at once."
4 This happened so that what had been spoken through the prophet might be fulfilled:
5 *Say to daughter Zion,
"Behold, your king comes to you,
meek and riding on an ass,
and on a colt, the foal of a beast of burden."*
6 The disciples went and did as Jesus had ordered them.
7 They brought the ass and the colt and laid their cloaks over them,
and he sat upon them.**

8 The very large crowd spread their cloaks on the road,
while others cut branches from the trees
and strewed them on the road.
9 The crowds preceding him and those following
kept crying out and saying:
"Hosanna to the Son of David;
blessed is he who comes in the name of the Lord;
hosanna in the highest."
10 And when he entered Jerusalem
the whole city was shaken and asked, "Who is this?"
11 And the crowds replied,
"This is Jesus the prophet, from Nazareth in Galilee."

The Gospel of the Lord.

Year B

✠ A reading from the holy Gospel according to Mark.

11: 1-10

1 When Jesus and his disciples drew near to Jerusalem,
to Bethphage and Bethany at the Mount of Olives,
he sent two of his disciples 2 and said to them,
"Go into the village opposite you,
and immediately on entering it,
you will find a colt tethered on which no one has ever sat.
Untie it and bring it here.
3 If anyone should say to you,
'Why are you doing this?' reply,
'The Master has need of it
and will send it back here at once.' "
4 So they went off
and found a colt tethered at a gate outside on the street,
and they untied it.
5 Some of the bystanders said to them,
"What are you doing, untying the colt?"
6 They answered them just as Jesus had told them to,
and they permitted them to do it.
7 So they brought the colt to Jesus
and put their cloaks over it.
And he sat on it.
8 Many people spread their cloaks on the road,
and others spread leafy branches
that they had cut from the fields.

9 Those preceding him as well as those following kept
crying out:
"Hosanna!
Blessed is he who comes in the name of the Lord!
10 Blessed is the kingdom of our father David that is
to come!
Hosanna in the highest!"

The Gospel of the Lord.

Or:

✠ A reading from the holy Gospel according to John.

12: 12-16

12 When the great crowd that had come to the feast heard
that Jesus was coming to Jerusalem,
13 they took palm branches and went out to meet him,
and cried out:
"Hosanna!
Blessed is he who comes in the name of the Lord,
the king of Israel."
14 Jesus found an ass and sat upon it, as is written:
15 *Fear no more, O daughter Zion;*
see, your king comes, seated upon an ass's colt.
16 His disciples did not understand this at first,
but when Jesus had been glorified
they remembered that these things were written about
him
and that they had done this for him.
The Gospel of the Lord.

Year C

✠ A reading from the holy Gospel according to Luke.

19: 28-40

28 Jesus proceeded on his journey up to Jerusalem.
29 As he drew near to Bethphage and Bethany
at the place called the Mount of Olives,
he sent two of his disciples.
30 He said, "Go into the village opposite you,
and as you enter it you will find a colt tethered
on which no one has ever sat.
Untie it and bring it here.

31 And if anyone should ask you,
'Why are you untying it?'
you will answer,
'The Master has need of it.' "
32 So those who had been sent went off
and found everything just as he had told them.
33 And as they were untying the colt, its owners said to them,
"Why are you untying this colt?"
34 They answered,
"The Master has need of it."
35 So they brought it to Jesus,
threw their cloaks over the colt,
and helped Jesus to mount.
36 As he rode along,
the people were spreading their cloaks on the road;
37 and now as he was approaching the slope of the Mount of Olives,
the whole multitude of his disciples
began to praise God aloud with joy
for all the mighty deeds they had seen.
38 They proclaimed:
"Blessed is the king who comes
in the name of the Lord.
39 Peace in heaven
and glory in the highest."
Some of the Pharisees in the crowd said to him,
"Teacher, rebuke your disciples."
40 He said in reply,
"I tell you, if they keep silent,
the stones will cry out!"

The Gospel of the Lord.

8. After the Gospel, a brief homily may be given. Then, to begin the Procession, an invitation may be given by a Priest or a Deacon or a lay minister, in these or similar words:

Dear brethren (brothers and sisters),
like the crowds who acclaimed Jesus in Jerusalem,
let us go forth in peace.

Or:

In this latter case, all respond:

9. The Procession to the church where Mass will be celebrated then sets off in the usual way. If incense is used, the thurifer goes first, carrying a thurible with burning incense, then an acolyte or another minister, carrying a cross decorated with palm branches according to local custom, between two ministers with lighted candles. Then follow the Deacon carrying the Book of the Gospels, the Priest with the ministers, and, after them, all the faithful carrying branches.

As the Procession moves forward, the following or other suitable chants in honor of Christ the King are sung by the choir and people.

Antiphon 1 The children of the Hebrews, carrying olive branches,
went to meet the Lord, crying out and saying:
Hosanna in the highest.

If appropriate, this antiphon is repeated between the strophes of the following Psalm.

Psalm 24 (23)

The LORD's is the earth and its fullness,*
the world, and those who dwell in it.
It is he who set it on the seas;*
on the rivers he made it firm.

(The antiphon is repeated)

Who shall climb the mountain of the LORD?*
Who shall stand in his holy place?
The clean of hands and pure of heart,†
whose soul is not set on vain things,*
who has not sworn deceitful words.

(The antiphon is repeated)

Blessings from the LORD shall he receive,*
and right reward from the God who saves him.
Such are the people who seek him,*
who seek the face of the God of Jacob.

(The antiphon is repeated)

O gates, lift high your heads; †
grow higher, ancient doors.*
Let him enter, the king of glory!
(The antiphon is repeated)

Who is this king of glory?*
The LORD, the mighty, the valiant; †
the LORD, the valiant in war.
(The antiphon is repeated)

O gates, lift high your heads; †
grow higher, ancient doors.*
Let him enter, the king of glory!
(The antiphon is repeated)

Who is this king of glory?*
He, the LORD of hosts, †
he is the king of glory.
(The antiphon is repeated)

Antiphon 2 The children of the Hebrews spread their garments on the road,
crying out and saying: Hosanna to the Son of David;
blessed is he who comes in the name of the Lord.

If appropriate, this antiphon is repeated between the strophes of the following Psalm.

Psalm 47 (46)

All peoples, clap your hands.*
Cry to God with shouts of joy!
For the LORD, the Most High, is awesome,*
the great king over all the earth.
(The antiphon is repeated)

He humbles peoples under us*
and nations under our feet.
Our heritage he chose for us,*
the pride of Jacob whom he loves.
(The antiphon is repeated)

God goes up with shouts of joy.*
The LORD goes up with trumpet blast.
Sing praise for God; sing praise!*
Sing praise to our king; sing praise!
(The antiphon is repeated)

God is king of all the earth.*
Sing praise with all your skill.
God reigns over the nations.*
God sits upon his holy throne.
(The antiphon is repeated)

The princes of the peoples are assembled *
with the people of the God of Abraham.
The rulers of the earth belong to God,*
who is greatly exalted.
(The antiphon is repeated)

Hymn to Christ the King

Chorus:
Glory and honor and praise be to you, Christ, King and Redeemer,
to whom young children cried out loving Hosannas with joy.

All repeat: Glory and honor . . .

Chorus:
Israel's King are you, King David's magnificent offspring;
you are the ruler who come blest in the name of the Lord.

All repeat: Glory and honor . . .

Chorus:
Heavenly hosts on high unite in singing your praises;
men and women on earth and all creation join in.

All repeat: Glory and honor . . .

Chorus:
Bearing branches of palm, Hebrews came crowding to greet you;
see how with prayers and hymns we come to pay you our vows.

All repeat: Glory and honor . . .

Chorus:
They offered gifts of praise to you, so near to your Passion;
see how we sing this song now to you reigning on high.

All repeat: Glory and honor . . .

Chorus:
Those you were pleased to accept; now accept our gifts of devotion,
good and merciful King, lover of all that is good.

All repeat: Glory and honor . . .

10. As the procession enters the church, there is sung the following responsory or another chant, which should speak of the Lord's entrance.

℟. As the Lord entered the holy city, the children of the Hebrews proclaimed the resurrection of life. * Waving their branches of palm, they cried: Hosanna in the Highest.
℣. When the people had heard that Jesus was coming to Jerusalem, they went out to meet him. * Waving their branches.

11. When the Priest arrives at the altar, he venerates it and, if appropriate, incenses it. Then he goes to the chair, where he puts aside the cope, if he has worn one, and puts on the chasuble. Omitting the other Introductory Rites of the Mass and, if appropriate, the Kyrie (Lord, have mercy), he says the Collect of the Mass, and then continues the Mass in the usual way.

Second Form: The Solemn Entrance

12. When a procession outside the church cannot take place, the entrance of the Lord is celebrated inside the church by means of a Solemn Entrance before the principal Mass.

13. Holding branches in their hands, the faithful gather either outside, in front of the church door, or inside the church itself. The Priest and ministers and a representative group of the faithful go to a suitable place in the church outside the sanctuary, where at least the greater part of the faithful can see the rite.

14. While the Priest approaches the appointed place, the antiphon Hosanna or another appropriate chant is sung. Then the blessing of branches and the proclamation of the Gospel of the Lord's entrance into Jerusalem take place as above (nos. 5-7). After the Gospel, the Priest processes solemnly with the ministers and the representative group of the faithful through the church to the sanctuary, while the responsory As the Lord entered (no. 10) or another appropriate chant is sung.

15. Arriving at the altar, the Priest venerates it. He then goes to the chair and, omitting the Introductory Rites of the Mass and, if appropriate, the Kyrie (Lord, have mercy), he says the Collect of the Mass, and then continues the Mass in the usual way.

Third Form: The Simple Entrance

16. At all other Masses of this Sunday at which the Solemn Entrance is not held, the memorial of the Lord's entrance into Jerusalem takes place by means of a Simple Entrance.

17. While the Priest proceeds to the altar, the Entrance Antiphon with its Psalm (no. 18) or another chant on the same theme is sung. Arriving at the altar, the Priest venerates it and goes to the chair. After the Sign of the Cross, he greets the people and continues the Mass in the usual way.

At other Masses, in which singing at the entrance cannot take place, the Priest, as soon as he has arrived at the altar and venerated it, greets the people, reads the Entrance Antiphon, and continues the Mass in the usual way.

18. **Entrance Antiphon**

Six days before the Passover,
when the Lord came into the city of Jerusalem,
the children ran to meet him;
in their hands they carried palm branches
and with a loud voice cried out:
***Hosanna in the highest!**
Blessed are you, who have come in your abundant mercy!

O gates, lift high your heads;
grow higher, ancient doors.
Let him enter, the king of glory!
Who is this king of glory?
He, the Lord of hosts, he is the king of glory.
***Hosanna in the highest!**
Blessed are you, who have come in your abundant mercy!

Cf. Jn 12: 1, 12-13; Ps 24 (23): 9-10

At the Mass

19. After the Procession or Solemn Entrance the Priest begins the Mass with the Collect.

20. **COLLECT**

**Almighty ever-living God,
who as an example of humility
for the human race to follow
caused our Savior to take flesh and submit to the Cross,
graciously grant that we may heed his lesson
of patient suffering
and so merit a share in his Resurrection.
Who lives and reigns with you
in the unity of the Holy Spirit,
one God, for ever and ever.**

21. The narrative of the Lord's Passion is read without candles and without incense, with no greeting or signing of the book. It is read by a Deacon or, if there is no Deacon, by a Priest. It may also be read by readers, with the part of Christ, if possible, reserved to a Priest.

Deacons, but not others, ask for the blessing of the Priest before singing the Passion, as at other times before the Gospel.

22. After the narrative of the Passion, a brief homily should take place, if appropriate. A period of silence may also be observed.

The Creed is said, and the Universal Prayer takes place.

[For nos. 23–25, see the Roman Missal.]

26. **PRAYER AFTER COMMUNION**

**Nourished with these sacred gifts,
we humbly beseech you, O Lord,
that, just as through the death of your Son
you have brought us to hope for what we believe,
so by his Resurrection
you may lead us to where you call.
Through Christ our Lord.**

27. **PRAYER OVER THE PEOPLE**

**Look, we pray, O Lord, on this your family,
for whom our Lord Jesus Christ
did not hesitate to be delivered
into the hands of the wicked
and submit to the agony of the Cross.
Who lives and reigns for ever and ever.**

MONDAY OF HOLY WEEK

Entrance Antiphon

Contend, O Lord, with my contenders;
fight those who fight me.
Take up your buckler and shield;
arise in my defense, Lord, my mighty help.
Cf. Ps 35 (34): 1-2; 140 (139): 8

COLLECT

Grant, we pray, almighty God,
that, though in our weakness we fail,
we may be revived through
the Passion of your Only Begotten Son.
Who lives and reigns with you
in the unity of the Holy Spirit,
one God, for ever and ever.

PRAYER AFTER COMMUNION

Visit your people, O Lord, we pray,
and with ever-watchful love
look upon the hearts dedicated to you by means
of these sacred mysteries,
so that under your protection
we may keep safe this remedy of eternal salvation,
which by your mercy we have received.
Through Christ our Lord.

PRAYER OVER THE PEOPLE

for optional use

May your protection, O Lord, we pray,
defend the humble
and keep ever safe those who trust in your mercy,
that they may celebrate the paschal festivities
not only with bodily observance
but above all with purity of mind.
Through Christ our Lord.

TUESDAY OF HOLY WEEK

Entrance Antiphon

Do not leave me to the will of my foes, O Lord,
for false witnesses rise up against me
and they breathe out violence. Cf. Ps 27 (26): 12

COLLECT

Almighty ever-living God,
grant us so to celebrate
the mysteries of the Lord's Passion
that we may merit to receive your pardon.
Through our Lord Jesus Christ, your Son,
who lives and reigns with you
in the unity of the Holy Spirit,
one God, for ever and ever.

PRAYER AFTER COMMUNION

Nourished by your saving gifts,
we beseech your mercy, Lord,
that by this same Sacrament,
with which you have fed us in the present age
you may make us partakers of life eternal.
Through Christ our Lord.

PRAYER OVER THE PEOPLE

for optional use

May your mercy, O God,
cleanse the people that are subject to you
from all seduction of former ways
and make them capable of new holiness.
Through Christ our Lord.

WEDNESDAY OF HOLY WEEK

Entrance Antiphon

At the name of Jesus, every knee should bend,
of those in heaven and on the earth and under the earth,
for the Lord became obedient to death, death on a cross:
therefore Jesus Christ is Lord, to the glory of God the Father.
Cf. Phil 2: 10, 8, 11

COLLECT

O God, who willed your Son to submit for our sake
to the yoke of the Cross,
so that you might drive from us the power of the enemy,
grant us, your servants,
to attain the grace of the resurrection.
Through our Lord Jesus Christ, your Son,
who lives and reigns with you
in the unity of the Holy Spirit,
one God, for ever and ever.

PRAYER AFTER COMMUNION

Endow us, almighty God, with the firm conviction
that through your Son's Death in time,
to which the revered mysteries bear witness,
we may be assured of perpetual life.
Through Christ our Lord.

PRAYER OVER THE PEOPLE

for optional use

Grant your faithful, O Lord, we pray,
to partake unceasingly of the paschal mysteries
and to await with longing the gifts to come,
that, persevering in the Sacraments of their rebirth,
they may be led by Lenten works to newness of life.
Through Christ our Lord.

THURSDAY OF HOLY WEEK [HOLY THURSDAY]

1. In accordance with a most ancient tradition of the Church, on this day all Masses without the people are forbidden.

The Chrism Mass

2. The blessing of the Oil of the Sick and of the Oil of Catechumens and the consecration of the Chrism are carried out by the Bishop, according to the Rite described in the Roman Pontifical, usually on this day, at a proper Mass to be celebrated during the morning.

3. If, however, it is very difficult for the clergy and the people to gather with the Bishop on this day, the Chrism Mass may be anticipated on another day, but near to Easter.

4. This Mass, which the Bishop concelebrates with his presbyterate, should be, as it were, a manifestation of the Priests' communion with their Bishop. Accordingly it is desirable that all the Priests participate in it, insofar as is possible, and during it receive Communion even under both kinds. To signify the unity of the presbyterate of the diocese, the Priests who concelebrate with the Bishop should be from different regions of the diocese.

5. In accord with traditional practice, the blessing of the Oil of the Sick takes place before the end of the Eucharistic Prayer, but the blessing of the Oil of Catechumens and the consecration of the Chrism take place after Communion. Nevertheless, for pastoral reasons, it is permitted for the entire rite of blessing to take place after the Liturgy of the Word.

6. **Entrance Antiphon**

Jesus Christ has made us into a kingdom,
priests for his God and Father.
To him be glory and power for ever and ever. Amen. Rev 1: 6

The Gloria in excelsis (Glory to God in the highest) is said.

7. **COLLECT**

O God, who anointed your Only Begotten Son
with the Holy Spirit
and made him Christ and Lord,
graciously grant
that, being made sharers in his consecration,
we may bear witness to your Redemption in the world.
Through our Lord Jesus Christ, your Son,
who lives and reigns with you
in the unity of the Holy Spirit,
one God, for ever and ever.

8. After the reading of the Gospel, the Bishop preaches the Homily in which, taking his starting point from the text of the readings proclaimed in the Liturgy of the Word, he speaks to the people and to his Priests about priestly anointing, urging the Priests to be faithful in their office and calling on them to renew publicly their priestly promises.

Renewal of Priestly Promises

9. After the Homily, the Bishop speaks with the Priests in these or similar words.

Beloved sons,
on the anniversary of that day
when Christ our Lord conferred his priesthood
on his Apostles and on us,
are you resolved to renew,
in the presence of your Bishop and God's holy people,
the promises you once made?

The Priests, all together, respond: **I am.**

Are you resolved to be more united with the Lord Jesus
and more closely conformed to him,
denying yourselves and confirming those promises
about sacred duties towards Christ's Church
which, prompted by love of him,
you willingly and joyfully pledged
on the day of your priestly ordination?

Priests: **I am.**

Are you resolved to be faithful stewards
of the mysteries of God
in the Holy Eucharist and the other liturgical rites
and to discharge faithfully the sacred office of teaching,
following Christ the Head and Shepherd,
not seeking any gain,
but moved only by zeal for souls?

Priests: **I am.**

Then, turned towards the people, the Bishop continues:

As for you, dearest sons and daughters,
pray for your Priests,
that the Lord may pour out his gifts
abundantly upon them,
and keep them faithful as ministers of Christ,
the High Priest,
so that they may lead you to him,
who is the source of salvation.

People: Christ, hear us. Christ, graciously hear us.

And pray also for me,
that I may be faithful to the apostolic office
entrusted to me in my lowliness
and that in your midst I may be made day by day
a living and more perfect image of Christ,
the Priest, the Good Shepherd,
the Teacher and the Servant of all.

People: Christ, hear us. Christ, graciously hear us.

May the Lord keep us all in his charity
and lead all of us,
shepherds and flock,
to eternal life.

All: Amen.

10. The Creed is not said.

[For nos. 11–13, see the Roman Missal.]

14. **PRAYER AFTER COMMUNION**

We beseech you, almighty God,
that those you renew by your Sacraments
may merit to become the pleasing fragrance of Christ.
Who lives and reigns for ever and ever.

15. The reception of the Holy Oils may take place in individual parishes either before the celebration of the Evening Mass of the Lord's Supper or at another time that seems more appropriate.

THE SACRED PASCHAL TRIDUUM

1. In the Sacred Triduum, the Church solemnly celebrates the greatest mysteries of our redemption, keeping by means of special celebrations the memorial of her Lord, crucified, buried, and risen.

   The Paschal Fast should also be kept sacred. It is to be celebrated everywhere on the Friday of the Lord's Passion and, where appropriate, prolonged also through Holy Saturday as a way of coming, with spirit uplifted, to the joys of the Lord's Resurrection.

2. For a fitting celebration of the Sacred Triduum, a sufficient number of lay ministers is required, who must be carefully instructed as to what they are to do.

   The singing of the people, the ministers, and the Priest Celebrant has a special importance in the celebrations of these days, for when texts are sung, they have their proper impact.

   Pastors should, therefore, not fail to explain to the Christian faithful, as best they can, the meaning and order of the celebrations and to prepare them for active and fruitful participation.

3. The celebrations of the Sacred Triduum are to be carried out in cathedral and parochial churches and only in those churches in which they can be performed with dignity, that is, with a good attendance of the faithful, an appropriate number of ministers, and the means to sing at least some of the parts.

   Consequently, it is desirable that small communities, associations, and special groups of various kinds join together in these churches to carry out the sacred celebrations in a more noble manner.

THURSDAY OF THE LORD'S SUPPER

At the Evening Mass

1. The Mass of the Lord's Supper is celebrated in the evening, at a convenient time, with the full participation of the whole local community and with all the Priests and ministers exercising their office.

2. All Priests may concelebrate even if they have already concelebrated the Chrism Mass on this day, or if they have to celebrate another Mass for the good of the Christian faithful.

3. Where a pastoral reason requires it, the local Ordinary may permit another Mass to be celebrated in churches and oratories in the evening and, in case of genuine necessity, even in the morning, but only for the faithful who are in no way able to participate in the evening Mass. Care should, nevertheless, be taken that celebrations of this sort do not take place for the advantage of private persons or special small groups, and do not prejudice the evening Mass.

4. Holy Communion may only be distributed to the faithful during Mass; but it may be brought to the sick at any hour of the day.

5. The altar may be decorated with flowers with a moderation that accords with the character of this day. The tabernacle should be entirely empty; but a sufficient amount of bread should be consecrated in this Mass for the Communion of the clergy and the people on this and the following day.

6. **Entrance Antiphon**

We should glory in the Cross of our Lord Jesus Christ,
in whom is our salvation, life and resurrection,
through whom we are saved and delivered. Cf. Gal 6: 14

7. The Gloria in excelsis (Glory to God in the highest) is said. While the hymn is being sung, bells are rung, and when it is finished, they remain silent until the Gloria in excelsis of the Easter Vigil, unless, if appropriate, the Diocesan Bishop has decided otherwise. Likewise, during this same period, the organ and other musical instruments may be used only so as to support the singing.

8. **COLLECT**

O God, who have called us to participate
in this most sacred Supper,
in which your Only Begotten Son,
when about to hand himself over to death,
entrusted to the Church a sacrifice new for all eternity,
the banquet of his love,
grant, we pray,
that we may draw from so great a mystery,
the fullness of charity and of life.
Through our Lord Jesus Christ, your Son,
who lives and reigns with you
in the unity of the Holy Spirit,
one God, for ever and ever.

9. After the proclamation of the Gospel, the Priest gives a homily in which light is shed on the principal mysteries that are commemorated in this Mass, namely, the institution of the Holy Eucharist and of the priestly Order, and the commandment of the Lord concerning fraternal charity.

The Washing of Feet

10. After the Homily, where a pastoral reason suggests it, the Washing of Feet follows.

11. Those who are chosen from among the people of God are led by the ministers to seats prepared in a suitable place. Then the Priest (removing his chasuble if necessary) goes to each one, and, with the help of the ministers, pours water over each one's feet and then dries them.

12. Meanwhile some of the following antiphons or other appropriate chants are sung.

Antiphon 1

After the Lord had risen from supper,
he poured water into a basin
and began to wash the feet of his disciples:
he left them this example. Cf. Jn 13: 4, 5, 15

Antiphon 2

The Lord Jesus, after eating supper with his disciples,
washed their feet and said to them:
Do you know what I, your Lord and Master, have done for you?
I have given you an example, that you should do likewise.
Cf. Jn 13: 12, 13, 15

Antiphon 3

Lord, are you to wash my feet? Jesus said to him in answer:
If I do not wash your feet, you will have no share with me.

℣. So he came to Simon Peter and Peter said to him:
—Lord.

℣. What I am doing, you do not know for now,
but later you will come to know.
—Lord. Jn 13: 6, 7, 8

Antiphon 4 If I, your Lord and Master, have washed your feet,
how much more should you wash each other's feet? Cf. Jn 13: 14

Antiphon 5 This is how all will know that you are my disciples:
if you have love for one another.

℣. Jesus said to his disciples:
—This is how. Jn 13: 35

Antiphon 6 I give you a new commandment,
that you love one another
as I have loved you, says the Lord. Jn 13: 34

Antiphon 7 Let faith, hope and charity, these three, remain among you,
but the greatest of these is charity.

℣. Now faith, hope and charity, these three, remain;
but the greatest of these is charity.
—Let. 1 Cor 13: 13

13. After the Washing of Feet, the Priest washes and dries his hands, puts the chasuble back on, and returns to the chair, and from there he directs the Universal Prayer.

The Creed is not said.

[For nos. 14–34, see the Roman Missal.]

35. After the distribution of Communion, a ciborium with hosts for Communion on the following day is left on the altar. The Priest, standing at the chair, says the Prayer after Communion.

36. PRAYER AFTER COMMUNION

Grant, almighty God,
that, just as we are renewed
by the Supper of your Son in this present age,
so we may enjoy his banquet for all eternity.
Who lives and reigns for ever and ever.

The Transfer of the Most Blessed Sacrament

37. After the Prayer after Communion, the Priest puts incense in the thurible while standing, blesses it and then, kneeling, incenses the Blessed Sacrament three times. Then, having put on a white humeral veil, he rises, takes the ciborium, and covers it with the ends of the veil.

38. A procession is formed in which the Blessed Sacrament, accompanied by torches and incense, is carried through the church to a place of repose prepared in a part of the church or in a chapel suitably decorated. A lay minister with a cross, standing between two other ministers with lighted candles leads off. Others carrying lighted candles follow. Before the Priest carrying the Blessed Sacrament comes the thurifer with a smoking thurible. Meanwhile, the hymn Pange, lingua (exclusive of the last two stanzas) or another eucharistic chant is sung.

39. When the procession reaches the place of repose, the Priest, with the help of the Deacon if necessary, places the ciborium in the tabernacle, the door of which remains open. Then he puts incense in the thurible and, kneeling, incenses the Blessed Sacrament, while Tantum ergo Sacramentum or another eucharistic chant is sung. Then the Deacon or the Priest himself places the Sacrament in the tabernacle and closes the door.

40. After a period of adoration in silence, the Priest and ministers genuflect and return to the sacristy.

41. At an appropriate time, the altar is stripped and, if possible, the crosses are removed from the church. It is expedient that any crosses which remain in the church be veiled.

42. Vespers (Evening Prayer) is not celebrated by those who have attended the Mass of the Lord's Supper.

43. The faithful are invited to continue adoration before the Blessed Sacrament for a suitable length of time during the night, according to local circumstances, but after midnight the adoration should take place without solemnity.

44. If the celebration of the Passion of the Lord on the following Friday does not take place in the same church, the Mass is concluded in the usual way and the Blessed Sacrament is placed in the tabernacle.

INRI

FRIDAY OF THE PASSION OF THE LORD
[GOOD FRIDAY]

1. On this and the following day, by a most ancient tradition, the Church does not celebrate the Sacraments at all, except for Penance and the Anointing of the Sick.

2. On this day, Holy Communion is distributed to the faithful only within the celebration of the Lord's Passion; but it may be brought at any hour of the day to the sick who cannot participate in this celebration.

3. The altar should be completely bare: without a cross, without candles and without cloths.

The Celebration of the Passion of the Lord

4. On the afternoon of this day, about three o'clock (unless a later hour is chosen for a pastoral reason), there takes place the celebration of the Lord's Passion consisting of three parts, namely, the Liturgy of the Word, the Adoration of the Cross, and Holy Communion.

   In the United States, if the size or nature of a parish or other community indicates the pastoral need for an additional liturgical service, the Diocesan Bishop may permit the service to be repeated later. This liturgy by its very nature may not, however, be celebrated in the absence of a Priest.

5. The Priest and the Deacon, if a Deacon is present, wearing red vestments as for Mass, go to the altar in silence and, after making a reverence to the altar, prostrate themselves or, if appropriate, kneel and pray in silence for a while. All others kneel.

6. Then the Priest, with the ministers, goes to the chair where, facing the people, who are standing, he says, with hands extended, one of the following prayers, omitting the invitation Let us pray.

PRAYER

Remember your mercies, O Lord,
and with your eternal protection sanctify your servants,
for whom Christ your Son,
by the shedding of his Blood,
established the Paschal Mystery.
Who lives and reigns for ever and ever.

℟. Amen.

Or:

O God, who by the Passion of Christ your Son, our Lord,
abolished the death inherited from ancient sin
by every succeeding generation,
grant that just as, being conformed to him,
we have borne by the law of nature
the image of the man of earth,
so by the sanctification of grace
we may bear the image of the Man of heaven.
Through Christ our Lord.

℟. Amen.

FIRST PART: THE LITURGY OF THE WORD

7. Then all sit and the First Reading, from the Book of the Prophet Isaiah (52: 13–53: 12), is read with its Psalm.

8. The Second Reading, from the Letter to the Hebrews (4: 14-16; 5: 7-9), follows, and then the chant before the Gospel.

9. Then the narrative of the Lord's Passion according to John (18: 1–19: 42) is read in the same way as on the preceding Sunday.

10. After the reading of the Lord's Passion, the Priest gives a brief homily and, at its end, the faithful may be invited to spend a short time in prayer.

The Solemn Intercessions

11. The Liturgy of the Word concludes with the Solemn Intercessions, which take place in this way: the Deacon, if a Deacon is present, or if he is not, a lay minister, stands at the ambo, and sings or says the invitation in which the intention is expressed. Then all pray in silence for a while, and afterwards the Priest, standing at the chair or, if appropriate, at the altar, with hands extended, sings or says the prayer.

The faithful may remain either kneeling or standing throughout the entire period of the prayers.

12. Before the Priest's prayer, in accord with tradition, it is permissible to use the Deacon's invitations Let us kneel — Let us stand, with all kneeling for silent prayer.

Text with music:

The Conferences of Bishops may provide other invitations to introduce the prayer of the Priest.

13. In a situation of grave public need, the Diocesan Bishop may permit or order the addition of a special intention.

I. For Holy Church

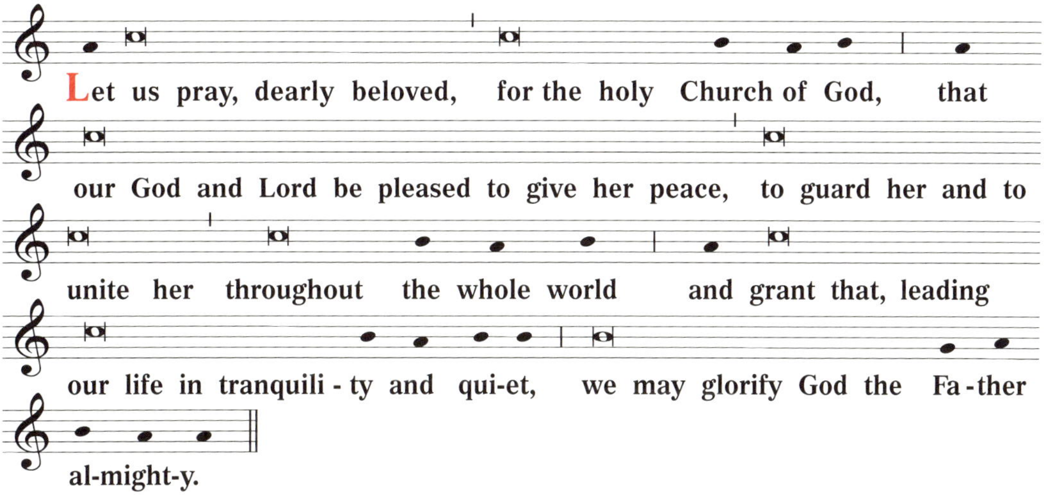

The prayer is sung in the simple tone or, if the invitations Let us kneel — Let us stand are used, in the solemn tone.

Let us pray, dearly beloved, for the holy Church of God, that our God and Lord be pleased to give her peace, to guard her and to unite her throughout the whole world and grant that, leading our life in tranquility and quiet, we may glorify God the Father almighty.

Prayer in silence. Then the Priest says:

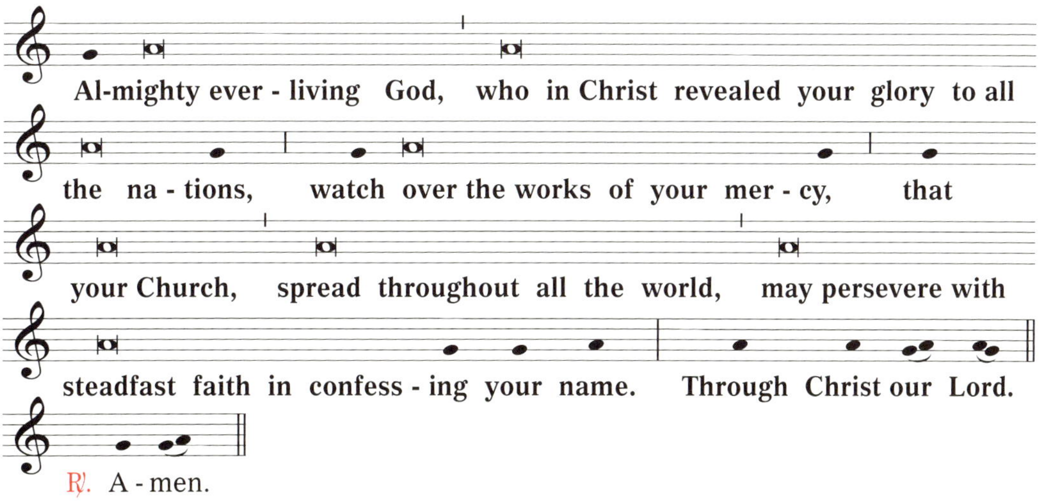

Almighty ever-living God,
who in Christ revealed your glory to all the nations,
watch over the works of your mercy,
that your Church, spread throughout all the world,
may persevere with steadfast faith
  in confessing your name.
Through Christ our Lord.

℟. Amen.

II. For the Pope

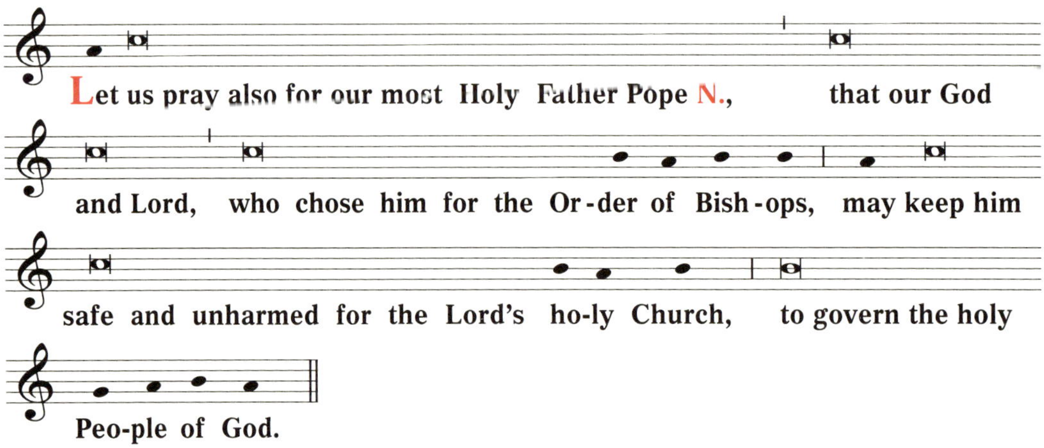

Let us pray also for our most Holy Father Pope N.,
that our God and Lord,
who chose him for the Order of Bishops,
may keep him safe and unharmed
  for the Lord's holy Church,
to govern the holy People of God.

Prayer in silence. Then the Priest says:

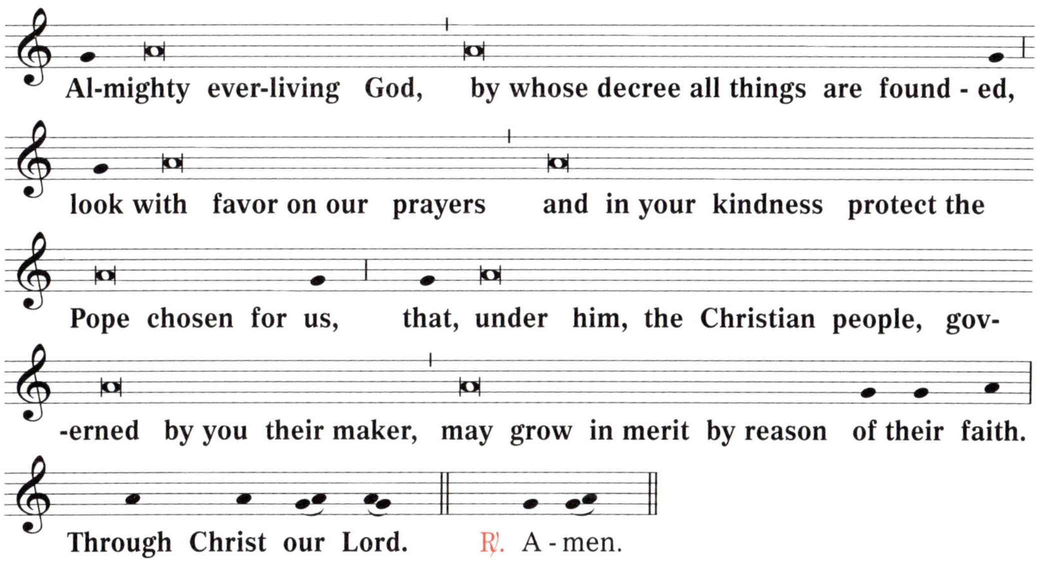

Almighty ever-living God,
by whose decree all things are founded,
look with favor on our prayers
and in your kindness protect the Pope chosen for us,
that, under him, the Christian people,
governed by you their maker,
may grow in merit by reason of their faith.
Through Christ our Lord.

R/. Amen.

III. For all orders and degrees of the faithful

* Mention may be made here of the Coadjutor Bishop, or Auxiliary Bishops, as noted in the *General Instruction of the Roman Missal*, no. 149.

Let us pray also for our Bishop N.,*
for all Bishops, Priests, and Deacons of the Church
and for the whole of the faithful people.

Prayer in silence. Then the Priest says:

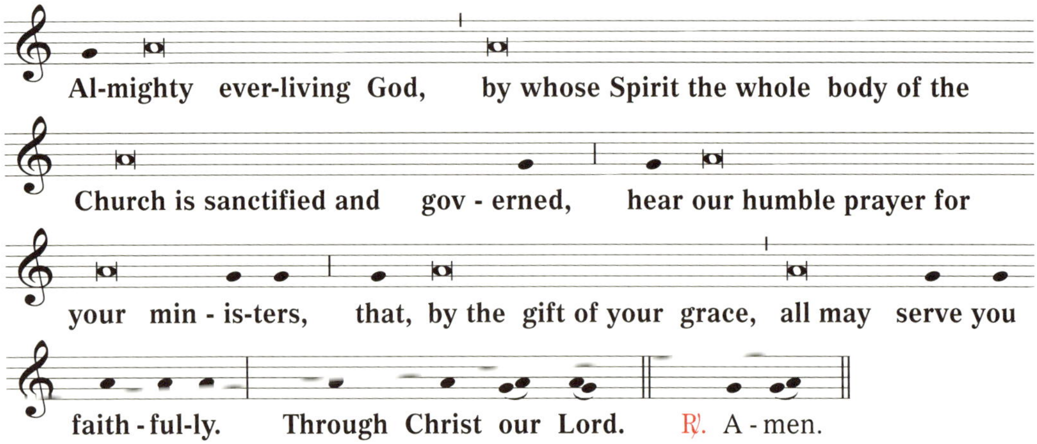

Almighty ever-living God,
by whose Spirit the whole body of the Church
is sanctified and governed,
hear our humble prayer for your ministers,
that, by the gift of your grace,
all may serve you faithfully.
Through Christ our Lord.
℟. Amen.

IV. For catechumens

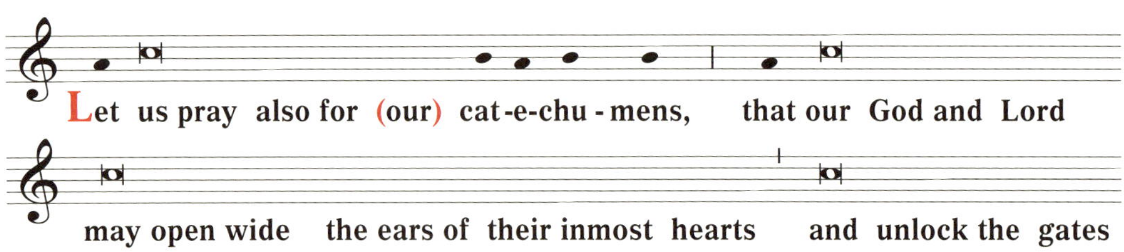

* Mention may be made here of the Coadjutor Bishop, or Auxiliary Bishops, as noted in the *General Instruction of the Roman Missal*, no. 149.

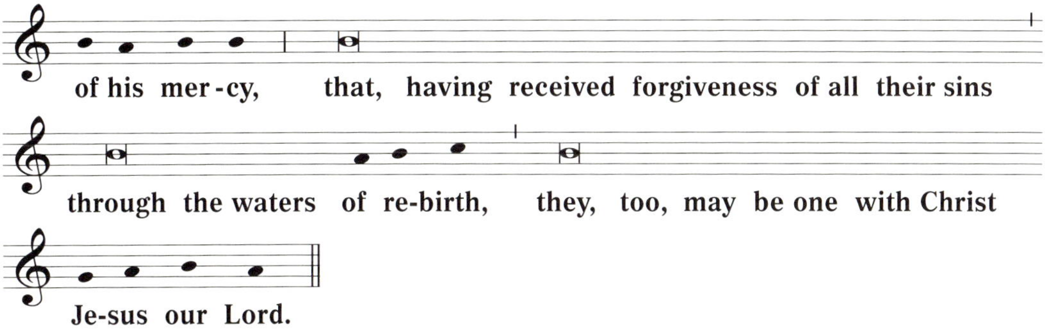

Let us pray also for (our) catechumens,
that our God and Lord
may open wide the ears of their inmost hearts
and unlock the gates of his mercy,
that, having received forgiveness of all their sins
through the waters of rebirth,
they, too, may be one with Christ Jesus our Lord.

Prayer in silence. Then the Priest says:

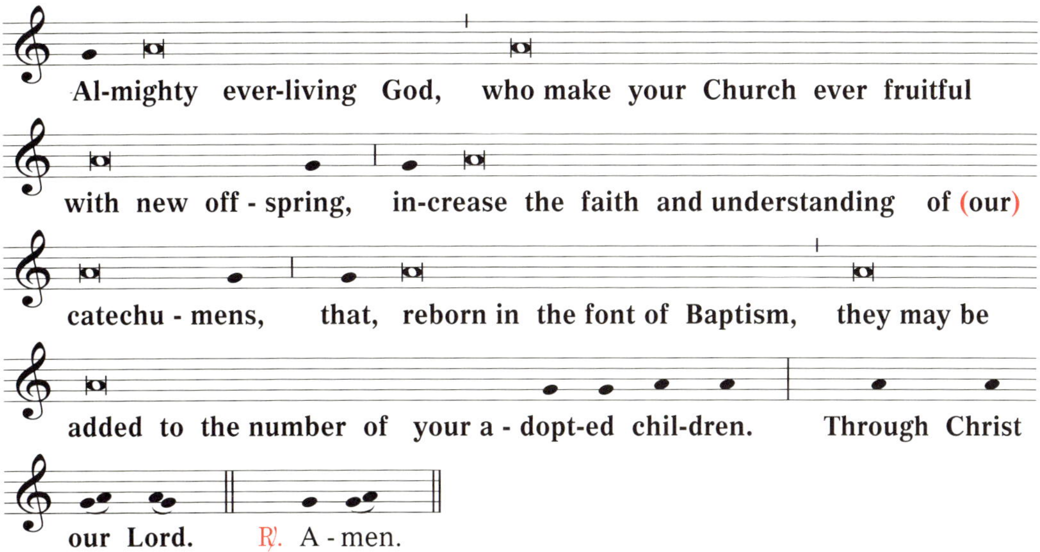

Almighty ever-living God,
who make your Church ever fruitful with new offspring,
increase the faith and understanding of (our) catechumens,
that, reborn in the font of Baptism,
they may be added
to the number of your adopted children.
Through Christ our Lord.

℟. Amen.

V. For the unity of Christians

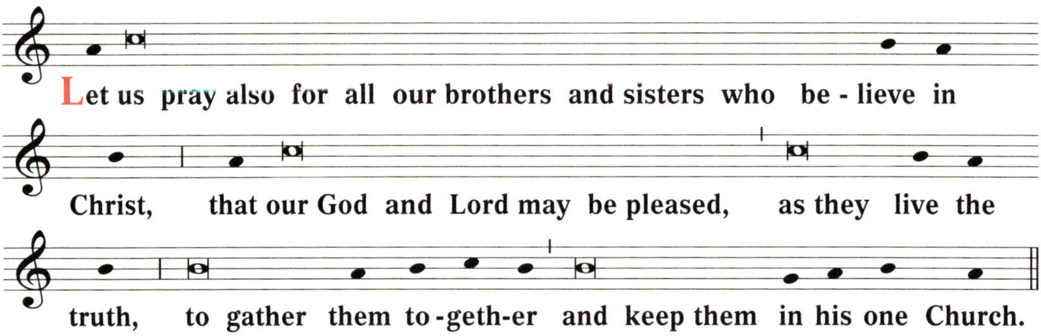

Let us pray also for all our brothers and sisters
who believe in Christ,
that our God and Lord may be pleased,
as they live the truth,
to gather them together and keep them in his one Church.

Prayer in silence. Then the Priest says:

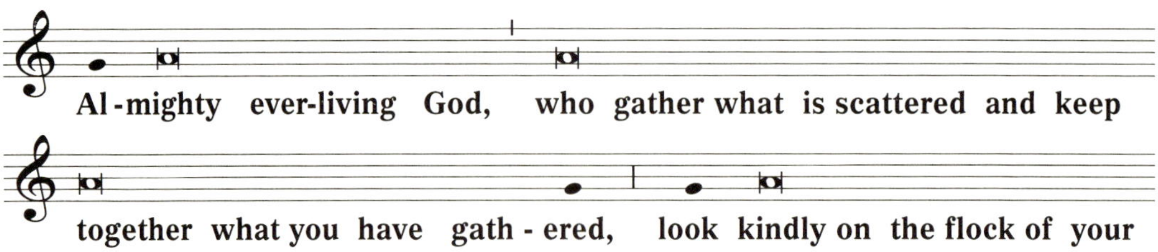

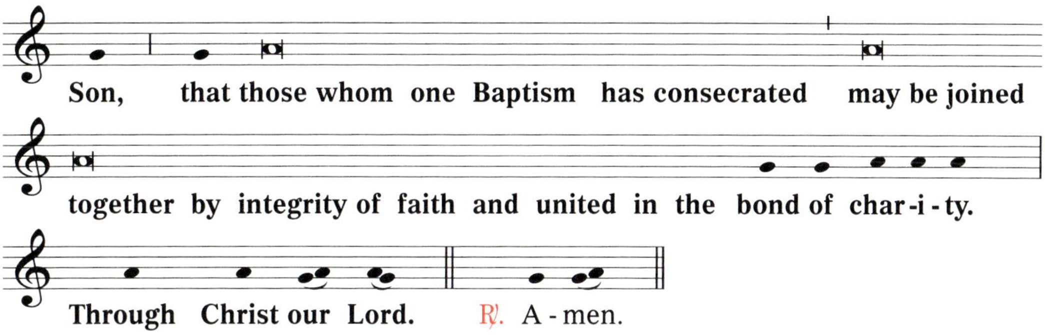

Almighty ever-living God,
who gather what is scattered
and keep together what you have gathered,
look kindly on the flock of your Son,
that those whom one Baptism has consecrated
may be joined together by integrity of faith
and united in the bond of charity.
Through Christ our Lord.

℟. Amen.

VI. For the Jewish people

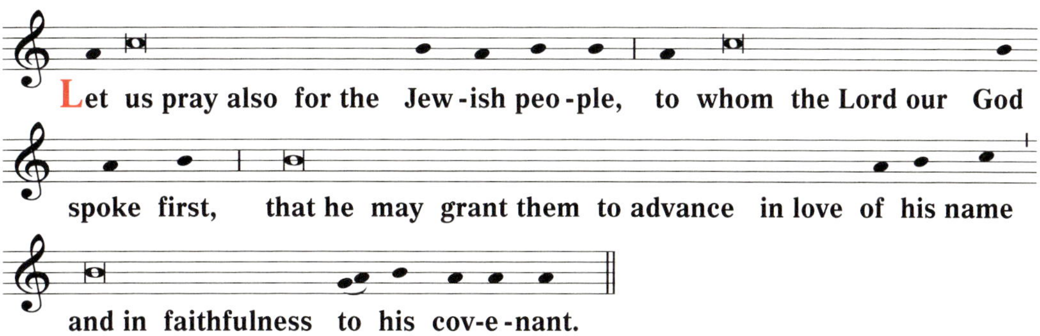

Let us pray also for the Jewish people,
to whom the Lord our God spoke first,
that he may grant them to advance in love of his name
and in faithfulness to his covenant.

Prayer in silence. Then the Priest says:

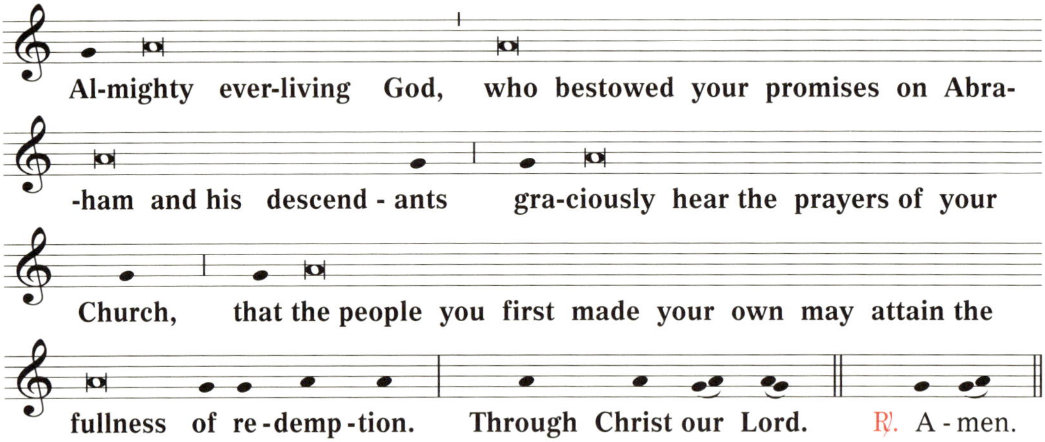

Almighty ever-living God,
who bestowed your promises on Abraham
and his descendants,
graciously hear the prayers of your Church,
that the people you first made your own
may attain the fullness of redemption.
Through Christ our Lord.

℟. Amen.

VII. For those who do not believe in Christ

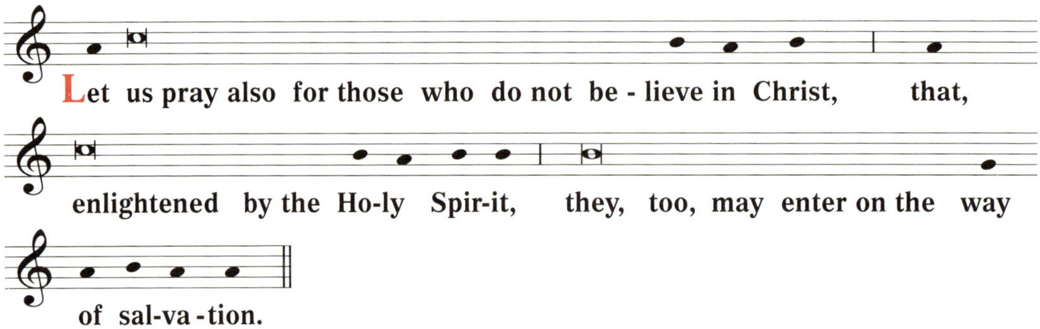

Let us pray also for those who do not believe in Christ,
that, enlightened by the Holy Spirit,
they, too, may enter on the way of salvation.

Prayer in silence. Then the Priest says:

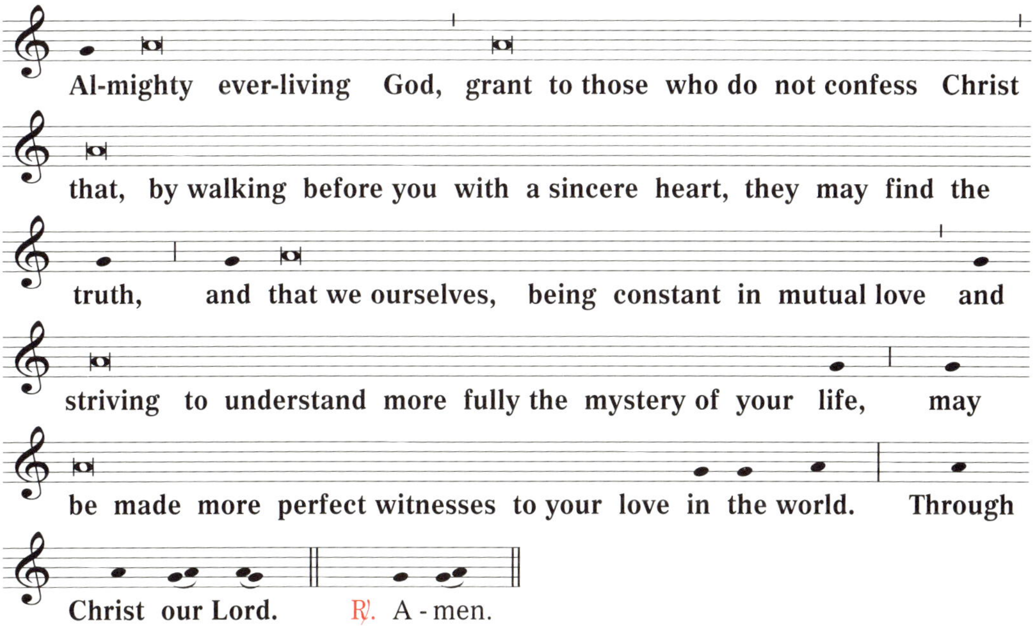

Almighty ever-living God,
grant to those who do not confess Christ
that, by walking before you with a sincere heart,
they may find the truth
and that we ourselves, being constant in mutual love
and striving to understand more fully
 the mystery of your life,
may be made more perfect witnesses
 to your love in the world.
Through Christ our Lord.

℟. Amen.

VIII. For those who do not believe in God

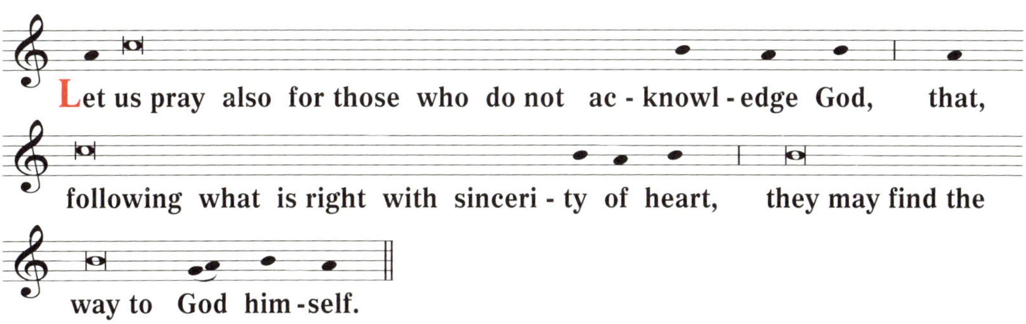

Let us pray also for those who do not acknowledge God,
that, following what is right in sincerity of heart,
they may find the way to God himself.

Prayer in silence. Then the Priest says:

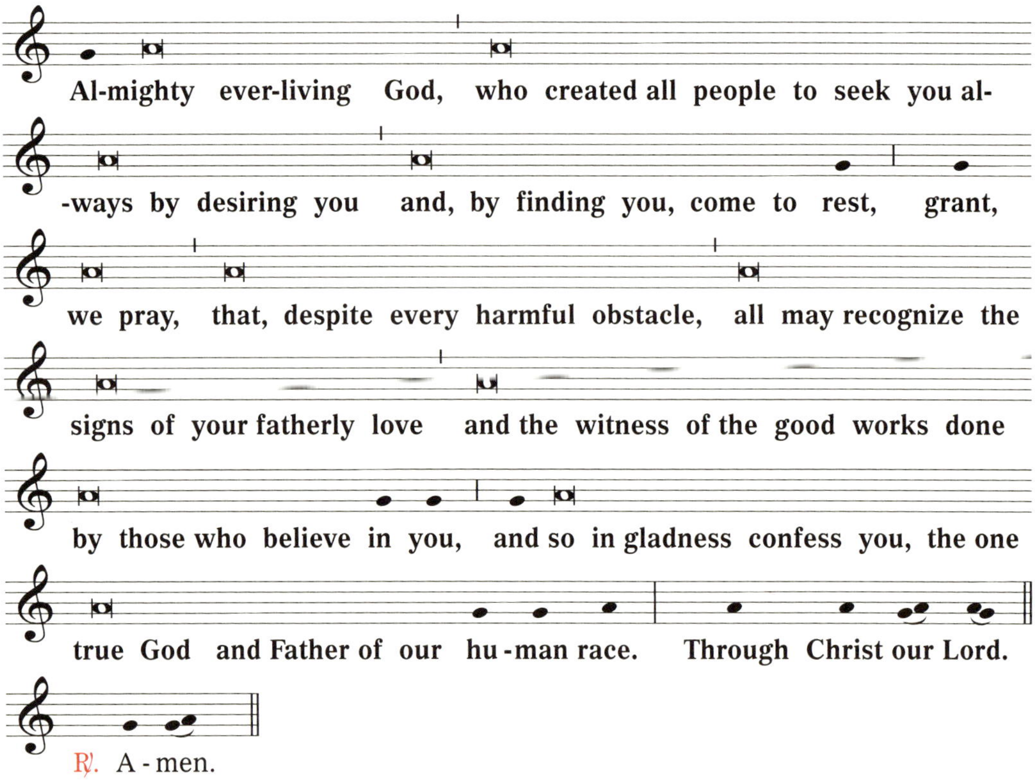

Almighty ever-living God,
who created all people
to seek you always by desiring you
and, by finding you, come to rest,
grant, we pray,
that, despite every harmful obstacle,
all may recognize the signs of your fatherly love
and the witness of the good works
done by those who believe in you,
and so in gladness confess you,
the one true God and Father of our human race.
Through Christ our Lord.

℟. Amen.

IX. For those in public office

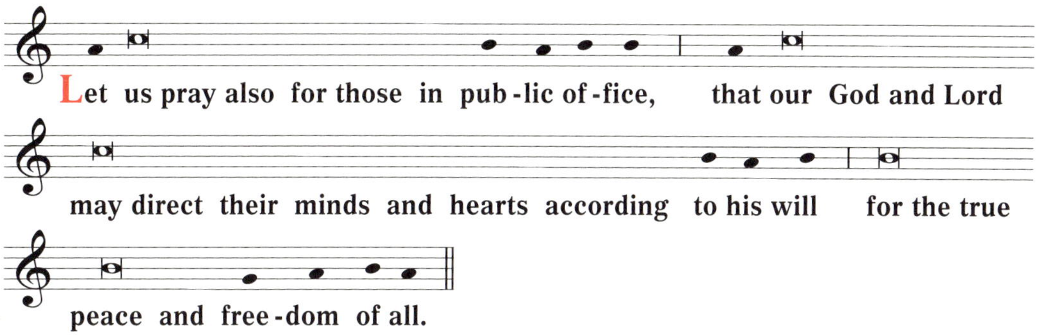

Let us pray also for those in public office,
that our God and Lord
may direct their minds and hearts according to his will
for the true peace and freedom of all.

Prayer in silence. Then the Priest says:

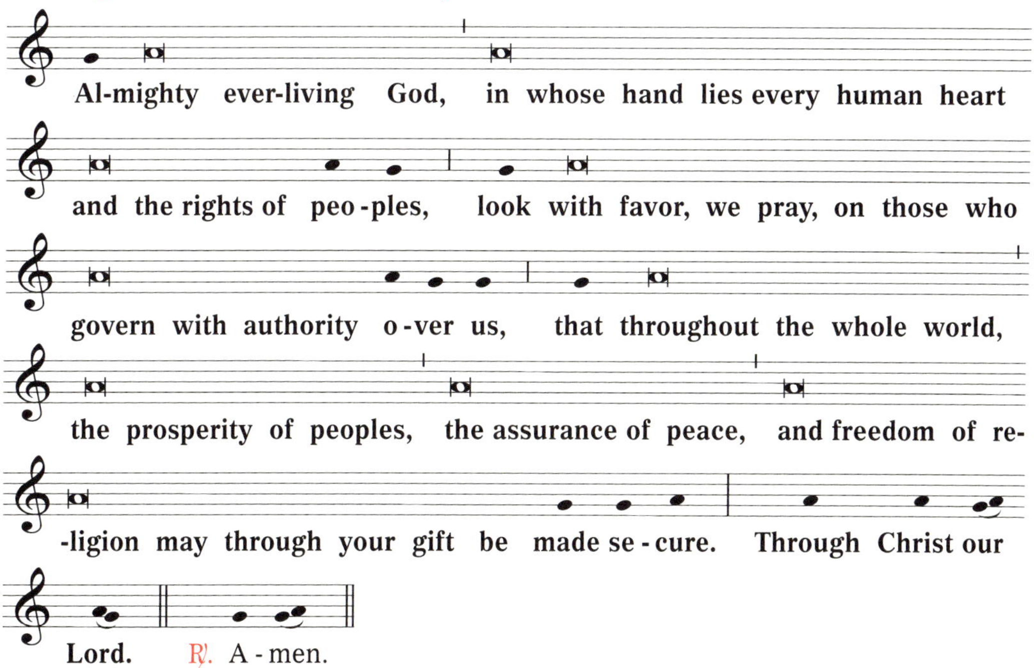

Almighty ever-living God,
in whose hand lies every human heart
and the rights of peoples,
look with favor, we pray,
on those who govern with authority over us,
that throughout the whole world,
the prosperity of peoples,
the assurance of peace,
and freedom of religion
may through your gift be made secure.
Through Christ our Lord.

℟. Amen.

X. For those in tribulation

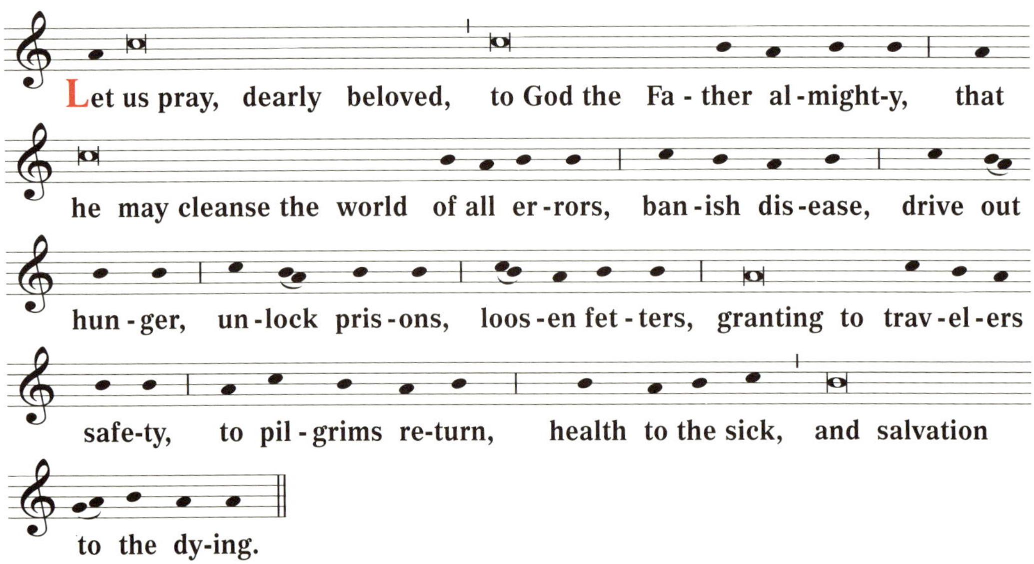

Let us pray, dearly beloved,
to God the Father almighty,
that he may cleanse the world of all errors,
banish disease, drive out hunger,
unlock prisons, loosen fetters,
granting to travelers safety, to pilgrims return,
health to the sick, and salvation to the dying.

Prayer in silence. Then the Priest says:

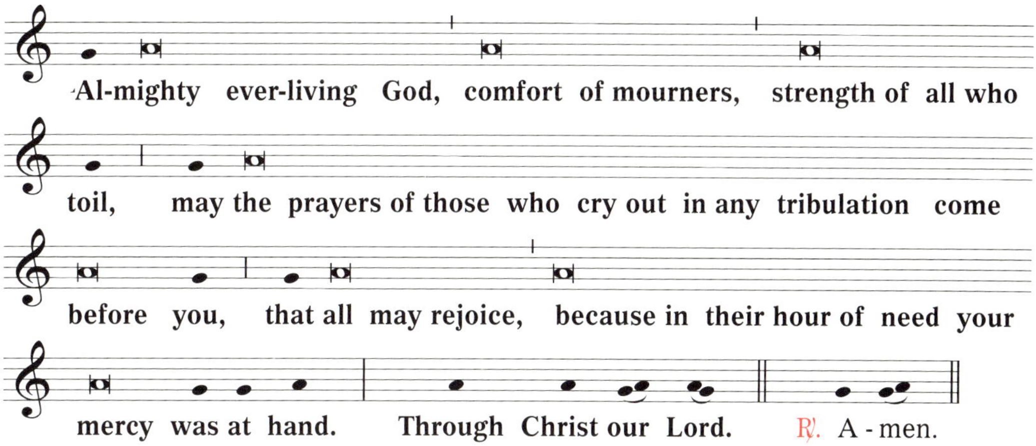

Almighty ever-living God,
comfort of mourners, strength of all who toil,
may the prayers of those who cry out in any tribulation
come before you,
that all may rejoice,
because in their hour of need
your mercy was at hand.
Through Christ our Lord.

℟. Amen.

SECOND PART:
THE ADORATION OF THE HOLY CROSS

14. After the Solemn Intercessions, the solemn Adoration of the Holy Cross takes place. Of the two forms of the showing of the Cross presented here, the more appropriate one, according to pastoral needs, should be chosen.

The Showing of the Holy Cross

First Form

15. The Deacon accompanied by ministers, or another suitable minister, goes to the sacristy, from which, in procession, accompanied by two ministers with lighted candles, he carries the Cross, covered with a violet veil, through the church to the middle of the sanctuary.

The Priest, standing before the altar and facing the people, receives the Cross, uncovers a little of its upper part and elevates it while beginning the Ecce lignum Crucis (Behold the wood of the Cross). He is assisted in singing by the Deacon or, if need be, by the choir. All respond, Come, let us adore. At the end of the singing, all kneel and for a brief moment adore in silence, while the Priest stands and holds the Cross raised.

Or:

Or:

Behold the wood of the Cross,
on which hung the salvation of the world.

℟. Come, let us adore.

Then the Priest uncovers the right arm of the Cross and again, raising up the Cross, begins, Behold the wood of the Cross and everything takes place as above.

Finally, he uncovers the Cross entirely and, raising it up, he begins the invitation Behold the wood of the Cross a third time and everything takes place like the first time.

Second Form

16. The Priest or the Deacon accompanied by ministers, or another suitable minister, goes to the door of the church, where he receives the unveiled Cross, and the ministers take lighted candles; then the procession sets off through the church to the sanctuary. Near the door, in the middle of the church and before the entrance of the sanctuary, the one who carries the Cross elevates it, singing, Behold the wood of the Cross, to which all respond, Come, let us adore. After each response all kneel and for a brief moment adore in silence, as above.

The Adoration of the Holy Cross

17. Then, accompanied by two ministers with lighted candles, the Priest or the Deacon carries the Cross to the entrance of the sanctuary or to another suitable place and there puts it down or hands it over to the ministers to hold. Candles are placed on the right and left sides of the Cross.

18. For the Adoration of the Cross, first the Priest Celebrant alone approaches, with the chasuble and his shoes removed, if appropriate. Then the clergy, the lay ministers, and the faithful approach, moving as if in procession, and showing reverence to the Cross by a simple genuflection or by some other sign appropriate to the usage of the region, for example, by kissing the Cross.

19. Only one Cross should be offered for adoration. If, because of the large number of people, it is not possible for all to approach individually, the Priest, after some of the clergy and faithful have adored, takes the Cross and, standing in the middle before the altar, invites the people in a few words to adore the Holy Cross and afterwards holds the Cross elevated higher for a brief time, for the faithful to adore it in silence.

20. While the adoration of the Holy Cross is taking place, the antiphon Crucem tuam adoramus (We adore your Cross, O Lord), the Reproaches, the hymn Crux fidelis (Faithful Cross) or other suitable chants are sung, during which all who have already adored the Cross remain seated.

Chants to Be Sung during the Adoration of the Holy Cross

Antiphon

We adore your Cross, O Lord,
we praise and glorify your holy Resurrection,
for behold, because of the wood of a tree
joy has come to the whole world.

May God have mercy on us and bless us;
may he let his face shed its light upon us
and have mercy on us. Cf. Ps 67 (66): 2

And the antiphon is repeated: We adore . . .

The Reproaches

Parts assigned to one of the two choirs separately are indicated by the numbers 1 (first choir) and 2 (second choir); parts sung by both choirs together are marked: 1 and 2. Some of the verses may also be sung by two cantors.

I

1 and 2 My people, what have I done to you?
Or how have I grieved you? Answer me!
1 Because I led you out of the land of Egypt,
you have prepared a Cross for your Savior.
1 Hagios o Theos,
2 Holy is God,
1 Hagios Ischyros,
2 Holy and Mighty,
1 Hagios Athanatos, eleison himas.
2 Holy and Immortal One, have mercy on us.

1 and 2 Because I led you out through the desert forty years
and fed you with manna and brought you into a land of plenty,
you have prepared a Cross for your Savior.
1 Hagios o Theos,
2 Holy is God,
1 Hagios Ischyros,
2 Holy and Mighty,
1 Hagios Athanatos, eleison himas.
2 Holy and Immortal One, have mercy on us.

1 and 2 What more should I have done for you and have not done?
Indeed, I planted you as my most beautiful chosen vine
and you have turned very bitter for me,
for in my thirst you gave me vinegar to drink
and with a lance you pierced your Savior's side.
1 Hagios o Theos,
2 Holy is God,
1 Hagios Ischyros,
2 Holy and Mighty,
1 Hagios Athanatos, eleison himas.
2 Holy and Immortal One, have mercy on us.

II

Cantors: I scourged Egypt for your sake with its firstborn sons,
and you scourged me and handed me over.

1 and 2 repeat: My people, what have I done to you?
Or how have I grieved you? Answer me!

Cantors: I led you out from Egypt as Pharaoh lay sunk in the Red Sea,
and you handed me over to the chief priests.

1 and 2 repeat: My people . . .

Cantors: I opened up the sea before you,
and you opened my side with a lance.

1 and 2 repeat: My people . . .

Cantors: I went before you in a pillar of cloud,
and you led me into Pilate's palace.

1 and 2 repeat: My people . . .

Cantors: I fed you with manna in the desert,
and on me you rained blows and lashes.

1 and 2 repeat: My people . . .

Cantors: I gave you saving water from the rock to drink,
and for drink you gave me gall and vinegar.

1 and 2 repeat: My people . . .

Cantors: I struck down for you the kings of the Canaanites,
and you struck my head with a reed.

1 and 2 repeat: My people . . .

Cantors: I put in your hand a royal scepter,
and you put on my head a crown of thorns.

1 and 2 repeat: My people . . .

Cantors: I exalted you with great power,
and you hung me on the scaffold of the Cross.

1 and 2 repeat: My people . . .

Hymn

All: Faithful Cross the Saints rely on,
Noble tree beyond compare!
Never was there such a scion,
Never leaf or flower so rare.
Sweet the timber, sweet the iron,
Sweet the burden that they bear!

Cantors: Sing, my tongue, in exultation
Of our banner and device!
Make a solemn proclamation
Of a triumph and its price:
How the Savior of creation
Conquered by his sacrifice!

All: Faithful Cross the Saints rely on,
Noble tree beyond compare!
Never was there such a scion,
Never leaf or flower so rare.

Cantors: For, when Adam first offended,
Eating that forbidden fruit,
Not all hopes of glory ended
With the serpent at the root:
Broken nature would be mended
By a second tree and shoot.

All: Sweet the timber, sweet the iron,
Sweet the burden that they bear!

Cantors: Thus the tempter was outwitted
By a wisdom deeper still:
Remedy and ailment fitted,
Means to cure and means to kill;
That the world might be acquitted,
Christ would do his Father's will.

All: Faithful Cross the Saints rely on,
Noble tree beyond compare!
Never was there such a scion,
Never leaf or flower so rare.

Cantors: So the Father, out of pity
For our self-inflicted doom,
Sent him from the heavenly city
When the holy time had come:
He, the Son and the Almighty,
Took our flesh in Mary's womb.

All: Sweet the timber, sweet the iron,
Sweet the burden that they bear!

Cantors: Hear a tiny baby crying,
Founder of the seas and strands:
See his virgin Mother tying
Cloth around his feet and hands:
Find him in a manger lying
Tightly wrapped in swaddling-bands!

All: Faithful Cross the Saints rely on,
Noble tree beyond compare!
Never was there such a scion,
Never leaf or flower so rare.

Cantors: So he came, the long-expected,
Not in glory, not to reign;
Only born to be rejected,
Choosing hunger, toil and pain,
Till the scaffold was erected
And the Paschal Lamb was slain.

All: Sweet the timber, sweet the iron,
Sweet the burden that they bear!

Cantors: No disgrace was too abhorrent:
Nailed and mocked and parched he died;
Blood and water, double warrant,
Issue from his wounded side,
Washing in a mighty torrent
Earth and stars and oceantide.

All: Faithful Cross the Saints rely on,
Noble tree beyond compare!
Never was there such a scion,
Never leaf or flower so rare.

Cantors: Lofty timber, smooth your roughness,
Flex your boughs for blossoming:
Let your fibers lose their toughness,
Gently let your tendrils cling;
Lay aside your native gruffness,
Clasp the body of your King!

All: Sweet the timber, sweet the iron,
Sweet the burden that they bear!

Cantors: Noblest tree of all created,
Richly jeweled and embossed:
Post by Lamb's blood consecrated;
Spar that saves the tempest-tossed;
Scaffold-beam which, elevated,
Carries what the world has cost!

All: Faithful Cross the Saints rely on,
Noble tree beyond compare!
Never was there such a scion,
Never leaf or flower so rare.

The following conclusion is never to be omitted:

All: Wisdom, power, and adoration
To the blessed Trinity
For redemption and salvation
Through the Paschal Mystery,
Now, in every generation,
And for all eternity. Amen.

In accordance with local circumstances or popular traditions and if it is pastorally appropriate, the Stabat Mater may be sung, as found in the Graduale Romanum, or another suitable chant in memory of the compassion of the Blessed Virgin Mary.

21. When the adoration has been concluded, the Cross is carried by the Deacon or a minister to its place at the altar. Lighted candles are placed around or on the altar or near the Cross.

THIRD PART:
HOLY COMMUNION

[For nos. 22–28, see the Roman Missal.]

29. When the distribution of Communion has been completed, the ciborium is taken by the Deacon or another suitable minister to a place prepared outside the church or, if circumstances so require, it is placed in the tabernacle.

30. Then the Priest says: Let us pray, and, after a period of sacred silence, if circumstances so suggest, has been observed, he says the Prayer after Communion.

Almighty ever-living God,
who have restored us to life
by the blessed Death and Resurrection of your Christ,
preserve in us the work of your mercy,
that, by partaking of this mystery,
we may have a life unceasingly devoted to you.
Through Christ our Lord.

℟. Amen.

31. For the Dismissal the Deacon or, if there is no Deacon, the Priest himself, may say the invitation Bow down for the blessing.

Then the Priest, standing facing the people and extending his hands over them, says this Prayer over the People:

May abundant blessing, O Lord, we pray,
descend upon your people,
who have honored the Death of your Son
in the hope of their resurrection:
may pardon come,
comfort be given,
holy faith increase,
and everlasting redemption be made secure.
Through Christ our Lord.

℟. Amen.

32. And all, after genuflecting to the Cross, depart in silence.

33. After the celebration, the altar is stripped, but the Cross remains on the altar with two or four candlesticks.

34. Vespers (Evening Prayer) is not celebrated by those who have been present at the solemn afternoon liturgical celebration.

HOLY SATURDAY

1. On Holy Saturday the Church waits at the Lord's tomb in prayer and fasting, meditating on his Passion and Death and on his Descent into Hell, and awaiting his Resurrection.

2. The Church abstains from the Sacrifice of the Mass, with the sacred table left bare, until after the solemn Vigil, that is, the anticipation by night of the Resurrection, when the time comes for paschal joys, the abundance of which overflows to occupy fifty days.

3. Holy Communion may only be given on this day as Viaticum.

EASTER TIME

EASTER SUNDAY OF THE RESURRECTION OF THE LORD

THE EASTER VIGIL IN THE HOLY NIGHT

1. By most ancient tradition, this is the night of keeping vigil for the Lord (Ex 12: 42), in which, following the Gospel admonition (Lk 12: 35-37), the faithful, carrying lighted lamps in their hands, should be like those looking for the Lord when he returns, so that at his coming he may find them awake and have them sit at his table.

2. Of this night's Vigil, which is the greatest and most noble of all solemnities, there is to be only one celebration in each church. It is arranged, moreover, in such a way that after the Lucernarium and Easter Proclamation (which constitutes the first part of this Vigil), Holy Church meditates on the wonders the Lord God has done for his people from the beginning, trusting in his word and promise (the second part, that is, the Liturgy of the Word) until, as day approaches, with new members reborn in Baptism (the third part), the Church is called to the table the Lord has prepared for his people, the memorial of his Death and Resurrection until he comes again (the fourth part).

3. The entire celebration of the Easter Vigil must take place during the night, so that it begins after nightfall and ends before daybreak on the Sunday.

4. The Mass of the Vigil, even if it is celebrated before midnight, is a paschal Mass of the Sunday of the Resurrection.

5. Anyone who participates in the Mass of the night may receive Communion again at Mass during the day. A Priest who celebrates or concelebrates the Mass of the night may again celebrate or concelebrate Mass during the day.

   The Easter Vigil takes the place of the Office of Readings.

6. The Priest is usually assisted by a Deacon. If, however, there is no Deacon, the duties of his Order, except those indicated below, are assumed by the Priest Celebrant or by a concelebrant.

   The Priest and Deacon vest as at Mass, in white vestments.

7. Candles should be prepared for all who participate in the Vigil. The lights of the church are extinguished.

FIRST PART:
THE SOLEMN BEGINNING OF THE VIGIL OR LUCERNARIUM

The Blessing of the Fire and Preparation of the Candle

8. A blazing fire is prepared in a suitable place outside the church. When the people are gathered there, the Priest approaches with the ministers, one of whom carries the paschal candle. The processional cross and candles are not carried.

Where, however, a fire cannot be lit outside the church, the rite is carried out as in no. 13, below.

9. The Priest and faithful sign themselves while the Priest says: In the name of the Father, and of the Son, and of the Holy Spirit, and then he greets the assembled people in the usual way and briefly instructs them about the night vigil in these or similar words:

Dear brethren (brothers and sisters),
on this most sacred night,
in which our Lord Jesus Christ
passed over from death to life,
the Church calls upon her sons and daughters,
scattered throughout the world,
to come together to watch and pray.
If we keep the memorial
of the Lord's paschal solemnity in this way,
listening to his word and celebrating his mysteries,
then we shall have the sure hope
of sharing his triumph over death
and living with him in God.

10. Then the Priest blesses the fire, saying, with hands extended:

Let us pray.

O God, who through your Son
bestowed upon the faithful the fire of your glory,
sanctify ✠ this new fire, we pray,
and grant that,
by these paschal celebrations,
we may be so inflamed with heavenly desires,
that with minds made pure
we may attain festivities of unending splendor.
Through Christ our Lord.

℟. Amen.

11. After the blessing of the new fire, one of the ministers brings the paschal candle to the Priest, who cuts a cross into the candle with a stylus. Then he makes the Greek letter Alpha above the cross, the letter Omega below, and the four numerals of the current year between the arms of the cross, saying meanwhile:

1. **Christ yesterday and today**	(he cuts a vertical line);
2. **the Beginning and the End**	(he cuts a horizontal line);
3. **the Alpha**	(he cuts the letter Alpha above the vertical line);
4. **and the Omega**	(he cuts the letter Omega below the vertical line).
5. **All time belongs to him**	(he cuts the first numeral of the current year in the upper left corner of the cross);
6. **and all the ages**	(he cuts the second numeral of the current year in the upper right corner of the cross).
7. **To him be glory and power**	(he cuts the third numeral of the current year in the lower left corner of the cross);
8. **through every age and for ever. Amen.**	(he cuts the fourth numeral of the current year in the lower right corner of the cross).

A

2	0
1	8

Ω

12. When the cutting of the cross and of the other signs has been completed, the Priest may insert five grains of incense into the candle in the form of a cross, meanwhile saying:

1. **By his holy**	1
2. **and glorious wounds,**	
3. **may Christ the Lord**	4 2 5
4. **guard us**	
5. **and protect us. Amen.**	3

13. Where, because of difficulties that may occur, a fire is not lit, the blessing of fire is adapted to the circumstances. When the people are gathered in the church as on other occasions, the Priest comes to the door of the church, along with the ministers carrying the paschal candle. The people, insofar as is possible, turn to face the Priest.

The greeting and address take place as in no. 9 above; then the fire is blessed and the candle is prepared, as above in nos. 10-12.

14. The Priest lights the paschal candle from the new fire, saying:

May the light of Christ rising in glory
dispel the darkness of our hearts and minds.

As regards the preceding elements, Conferences of Bishops may also establish other forms more adapted to the culture of the different peoples.

Procession

15. When the candle has been lit, one of the ministers takes burning coals from the fire and places them in the thurible, and the Priest puts incense into it in the usual way. The Deacon or, if there is no Deacon, another suitable minister, takes the paschal candle and a procession forms. The thurifer with the smoking thurible precedes the Deacon or other minister who carries the paschal candle. After them follows the Priest with the ministers and the people, all holding in their hands unlit candles.

At the door of the church the Deacon, standing and raising up the candle, sings:

Or:

The Light of Christ.

And all reply:

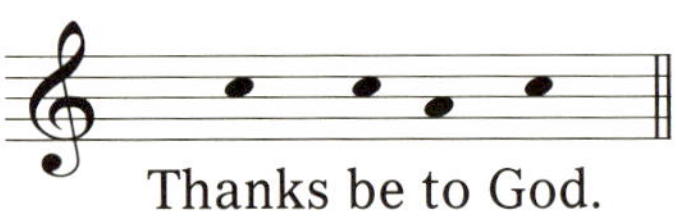

Or:

Thanks be to God.

The Priest lights his candle from the flame of the paschal candle.

16. Then the Deacon moves forward to the middle of the church and, standing and raising up the candle, sings a second time:

The Light of Christ.

And all reply:

Thanks be to God.

All light their candles from the flame of the paschal candle and continue in procession.

17. When the Deacon arrives before the altar, he stands facing the people, raises up the candle and sings a third time:

The Light of Christ.

And all reply:

Thanks be to God.

Then the Deacon places the paschal candle on a large candlestand prepared next to the ambo or in the middle of the sanctuary.

And lights are lit throughout the church, except for the altar candles.

The Easter Proclamation (Exsultet)

18. Arriving at the altar, the Priest goes to his chair, gives his candle to a minister, puts incense into the thurible and blesses the incense as at the Gospel at Mass. The Deacon goes to the Priest and saying, Your blessing, Father, asks for and receives a blessing from the Priest, who says in a low voice:

May the Lord be in your heart and on your lips,
that you may proclaim his paschal praise
worthily and well,
in the name of the Father and of the Son, ✠ and
of the Holy Spirit.

The Deacon replies: Amen.

This blessing is omitted if the Proclamation is made by someone who is not a Deacon.

19. The Deacon, after incensing the book and the candle, proclaims the Easter Proclamation (Exsultet) at the ambo or at a lectern, with all standing and holding lighted candles in their hands.

The Easter Proclamation may be made, in the absence of a Deacon, by the Priest himself or by another concelebrating Priest. If, however, because of necessity, a lay cantor sings the Proclamation, the words Therefore, dearest friends up to the end of the invitation are omitted, along with the greeting The Lord be with you.

The Proclamation may also be sung in the shorter form (pp. 166-169).

Longer Form of the Easter Proclamation

(℣. The Lord be with you. ℟. And with your spir-it.)
℣. Lift up your hearts. ℟. We lift them up to the Lord.
℣. Let us give thanks to the Lord our God. ℟. It is right and just.
It is truly right and just, with ardent love of mind and heart and
with devoted service of our voice, to acclaim our God in-vis-i-ble,
the al - might - y Fa-ther, and Jesus Christ our Lord, his Son, his
On - ly Be-got-ten. Who for our sake paid Adam's debt to the e-
-ter-nal Fa-ther, and, pouring out his own dear Blood, wiped clean
the re-cord of our an-cient sin-ful - ness. These then are the feasts
of Pass-o-ver, in which is slain the Lamb, the one true Lamb,
whose Blood anoints the door - posts of be - liev-ers. This is the
night, when once you led our fore - bears, Is-ra-el's chil - dren,
from slaver - y in E-gypt and made them pass dry - shod through

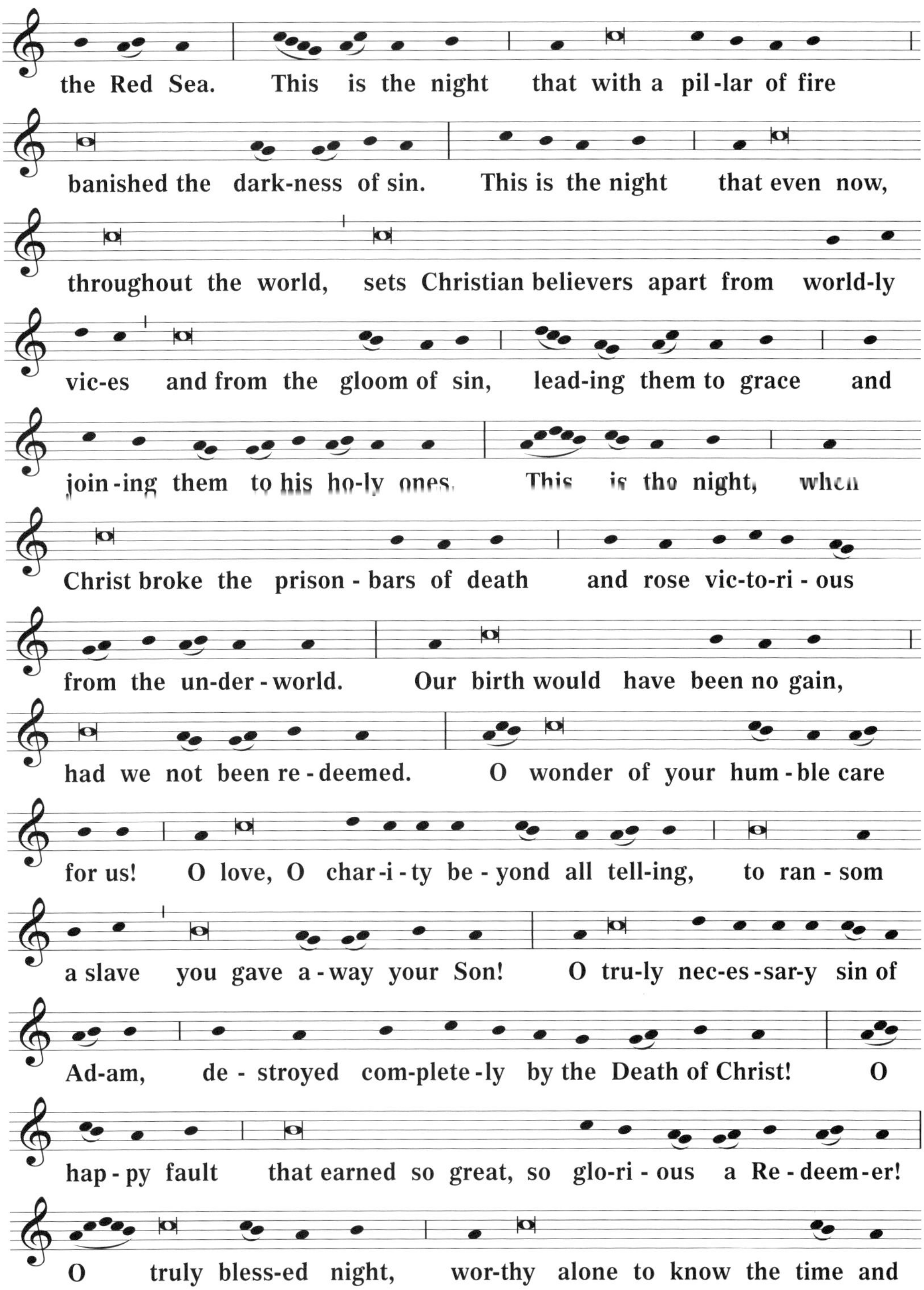
the Red Sea. This is the night that with a pil-lar of fire
banished the dark-ness of sin. This is the night that even now,
throughout the world, sets Christian believers apart from world-ly
vic-es and from the gloom of sin, lead-ing them to grace and
join-ing them to his ho-ly ones. This is the night, when
Christ broke the prison-bars of death and rose vic-to-ri-ous
from the un-der-world. Our birth would have been no gain,
had we not been re-deemed. O wonder of your hum-ble care
for us! O love, O char-i-ty be-yond all tell-ing, to ran-som
a slave you gave a-way your Son! O tru-ly nec-es-sar-y sin of
Ad-am, de-stroyed com-plete-ly by the Death of Christ! O
hap-py fault that earned so great, so glo-ri-ous a Re-deem-er!
O truly bless-ed night, wor-thy alone to know the time and

hour when Christ rose from the un-der - world! This is the night
of which it is writ - ten: The night shall be as bright as day,
dazzling is the night for me, and full of glad - ness. The sanctifying
power of this night dis - pels wick-ed - ness, washes faults a-way,
re-stores innocence to the fall-en, and joy to mourn - ers, drives
out ha - tred, fos - ters con - cord, and brings down the might - y.
On this, your night of grace, O ho - ly Fa - ther, accept this candle, a
sol - emn of - fer - ing, the work of bees and of your serv - ants' hands,
an evening sacri - fice of praise, this gift from your most ho - ly
Church. But now we know the praises of this pil - lar, which glow-
-ing fire ig - nites for God's hon - or, a fire into many flames
di - vid - ed, yet nev - er dimmed by shar - ing of its light, for it is
fed by melt - ing wax, drawn out by moth - er bees to build a torch

so pre - cious. O truly bless - ed night, when things of heaven
are wed to those of earth, and di - vine to the hu - man.
There - fore, O Lord, we pray you that this candle, hallowed to the
honor of your name, may perse - vere un - dimmed, to overcome
the dark - ness of this night. Re - ceive it as a pleas - ing fra - grance,
and let it min - gle with the lights of heav - en. May this flame
be found still burn - ing by the Morn - ing Star: the one Morning
Star who nev - er sets, Christ your Son, who, coming back from
death's do - main, has shed his peaceful light on hu - man - i - ty, and
lives and reigns for ev - er and ev - er. ℟. A - men.

Text without music:

Longer Form of the Easter Proclamation

**Exult, let them exult, the hosts of heaven,
exult, let Angel ministers of God exult,
let the trumpet of salvation
sound aloud our mighty King's triumph!
Be glad, let earth be glad, as glory floods her,
ablaze with light from her eternal King,
let all corners of the earth be glad,
knowing an end to gloom and darkness.
Rejoice, let Mother Church also rejoice,
arrayed with the lightning of his glory,
let this holy building shake with joy,
filled with the mighty voices of the peoples.
(Therefore, dearest friends,
standing in the awesome glory of this holy light,
invoke with me, I ask you,
the mercy of God almighty,
that he, who has been pleased to number me,
though unworthy, among the Levites,
may pour into me his light unshadowed,
that I may sing this candle's perfect praises).**

(℣. **The Lord be with you.**
℟. And with your spirit.)

℣. **Lift up your hearts.**
℟. We lift them up to the Lord.

℣. **Let as give thanks to the Lord our God.**
℟. It is right and just.

**It is truly right and just,
with ardent love of mind and heart
and with devoted service of our voice,
to acclaim our God invisible, the almighty Father,
and Jesus Christ, our Lord, his Son, his Only Begotten.**

**Who for our sake paid Adam's debt to the eternal Father,
and, pouring out his own dear Blood,
wiped clean the record of our ancient sinfulness.**

These then are the feasts of Passover,
in which is slain the Lamb, the one true Lamb,
whose Blood anoints the doorposts of believers.

This is the night,
when once you led our forebears, Israel's children,
from slavery in Egypt
and made them pass dry-shod through the Red Sea.

This is the night
that with a pillar of fire
banished the darkness of sin.

This is the night
that even now, throughout the world,
sets Christian believers apart from worldly vices
and from the gloom of sin,
leading them to grace
and joining them to his holy ones.

This is the night,
when Christ broke the prison-bars of death
and rose victorious from the underworld.

Our birth would have been no gain,
had we not been redeemed.
O wonder of your humble care for us!
O love, O charity beyond all telling,
to ransom a slave you gave away your Son!

O truly necessary sin of Adam,
destroyed completely by the Death of Christ!

O happy fault
that earned so great, so glorious a Redeemer!

O truly blessed night,
worthy alone to know the time and hour
when Christ rose from the underworld!

This is the night
of which it is written:
The night shall be as bright as day,
dazzling is the night for me,
and full of gladness.

The sanctifying power of this night
dispels wickedness, washes faults away,
restores innocence to the fallen, and joy to mourners,
drives out hatred, fosters concord, and brings down the mighty.

On this, your night of grace, O holy Father,
accept this candle, a solemn offering,
the work of bees and of your servants' hands,
an evening sacrifice of praise,
this gift from your most holy Church.

But now we know the praises of this pillar,
which glowing fire ignites for God's honor,
a fire into many flames divided,
yet never dimmed by sharing of its light,
for it is fed by melting wax,
drawn out by mother bees
to build a torch so precious.

O truly blessed night,
when things of heaven are wed to those of earth,
and divine to the human.

Therefore, O Lord,
we pray you that this candle,
hallowed to the honor of your name,
may persevere undimmed,
to overcome the darkness of this night.
Receive it as a pleasing fragrance,
and let it mingle with the lights of heaven.
May this flame be found still burning
by the Morning Star:
the one Morning Star who never sets,
Christ your Son,
who, coming back from death's domain,
has shed his peaceful light on humanity,
and lives and reigns for ever and ever.

℟. Amen.

Shorter Form of the Easter Proclamation

the al - might - y Fa-ther, and Jesus Christ our Lord, his Son, his
On - ly Be-got-ten. Who for our sake paid Adam's debt to the e-
-ter-nal Fa-ther, and, pouring out his own dear Blood, wiped clean
the re-cord of our an-cient sin-ful -ness. These then are the feasts
of Pass-o-ver, in which is slain the Lamb, the one true Lamb,
whose Blood anoints the door - posts of be - liev-ers. This is the
night, when once you led our fore - bears, Is-ra-el's chil - dren,
from slaver - y in E-gypt and made them pass dry - shod through
the Red Sea. This is the night that with a pil-lar of fire
banished the dark-ness of sin. This is the night that even now,
throughout the world, sets Christian believers apart from world-ly
vic-es and from the gloom of sin, lead-ing them to grace and
join - ing them to his ho-ly ones. This is the night, when

Christ broke the prison - bars of death and rose vic-to-ri - ous
from the un-der - world. O wonder of your hum - ble care for us!
O love, O char - i - ty be - yond all tell-ing, to ran - som a slave
you gave a - way your Son! O tru-ly nec-es - sar-y sin of Ad-am,
de - stroyed com-plete - ly by the Death of Christ! O hap - py fault
that earned so great, so glo-ri - ous a Re-deem - er! The sanctifying
power of this night dis - pels wick-ed - ness, washes faults a-way,
re-stores innocence to the fall-en, and joy to mourn - ers. O truly
bless - ed night, when things of heaven are wed to those of earth,
and di - vine to the hu - man.
On this, your night of grace, O ho - ly Fa - ther, accept this candle, a
sol - emn of - fer - ing, the work of bees and of your serv - ants' hands,

an evening sacri - fice of praise, this gift from your most ho - ly
Church.
There - fore, O Lord, we pray you that this candle, hallowed to the
honor of your name, may perse - vere un - dimmed, to overcome
the dark - ness of this night. Re - ceive it as a pleas - ing fra - grance,
and let it min - gle with the lights of heav - en. May this flame
be found still burn - ing by the Morn - ing Star: the one Morning
Star who nev - er sets, Christ your Son, who, coming back from
death's do - main, has shed his peaceful light on hu - man - i - ty, and
lives and reigns for ev - er and ev - er. ℟. A - men.

Text without music:

Shorter Form of the Easter Proclamation

Exult, let them exult, the hosts of heaven,
exult, let Angel ministers of God exult,
let the trumpet of salvation
sound aloud our mighty King's triumph!
Be glad, let earth be glad, as glory floods her,
ablaze with light from her eternal King,
let all corners of the earth be glad,
knowing an end to gloom and darkness.
Rejoice, let Mother Church also rejoice,
arrayed with the lightning of his glory,
let this holy building shake with joy,
filled with the mighty voices of the peoples.

(℣. **The Lord be with you.**
℟. And with your spirit.)

℣. **Lift up your hearts.**
℟. We lift them up to the Lord.

℣. **Let us give thanks to the Lord our God.**
℟. It is right and just.

It is truly right and just,
with ardent love of mind and heart
and with devoted service of our voice,
to acclaim our God invisible, the almighty Father,
and Jesus Christ, our Lord, his Son, his Only Begotten.

Who for our sake paid Adam's debt to the eternal Father,
and, pouring out his own dear Blood,
wiped clean the record of our ancient sinfulness.

These then are the feasts of Passover,
in which is slain the Lamb, the one true Lamb,
whose Blood anoints the doorposts of believers.

This is the night,
when once you led our forebears, Israel's children,
from slavery in Egypt
and made them pass dry-shod through the Red Sea.

This is the night
that with a pillar of fire
banished the darkness of sin.

This is the night
that even now, throughout the world,
sets Christian believers apart from worldly vices
and from the gloom of sin,
leading them to grace
and joining them to his holy ones.

This is the night,
when Christ broke the prison-bars of death
and rose victorious from the underworld.

O wonder of your humble care for us!
O love, O charity beyond all telling,
to ransom a slave you gave away your Son!

O truly necessary sin of Adam,
destroyed completely by the Death of Christ!

O happy fault
that earned so great, so glorious a Redeemer!
The sanctifying power of this night
dispels wickedness, washes faults away,
restores innocence to the fallen, and joy to mourners.

O truly blessed night,
when things of heaven are wed to those of earth
and divine to the human.

On this, your night of grace, O holy Father,
accept this candle, a solemn offering,
the work of bees and of your servants' hands,
an evening sacrifice of praise,
this gift from your most holy Church.

Therefore, O Lord,
we pray you that this candle,
hallowed to the honor of your name,
may persevere undimmed,
to overcome the darkness of this night.

**Receive it as a pleasing fragrance,
and let it mingle with the lights of heaven.
May this flame be found still burning
by the Morning Star:
the one Morning Star who never sets,
Christ your Son,
who, coming back from death's domain,
has shed his peaceful light on humanity,
and lives and reigns for ever and ever.**

℟. Amen.

SECOND PART:
THE LITURGY OF THE WORD

20. In this Vigil, the mother of all Vigils, nine readings are provided, namely seven from the Old Testament and two from the New (the Epistle and Gospel), all of which should be read whenever this can be done, so that the character of the Vigil, which demands an extended period of time, may be preserved.

21. Nevertheless, where more serious pastoral circumstances demand it, the number of readings from the Old Testament may be reduced, always bearing in mind that the reading of the Word of God is a fundamental part of this Easter Vigil. At least three readings should be read from the Old Testament, both from the Law and from the Prophets, and their respective Responsorial Psalms should be sung. Never, moreover, should the reading of chapter 14 of Exodus with its canticle be omitted.

22. After setting aside their candles, all sit. Before the readings begin, the Priest instructs the people in these or similar words:

**Dear brethren (brothers and sisters),
now that we have begun our solemn Vigil,
let us listen with quiet hearts to the Word of God.
Let us meditate on how God in times past saved his people
and in these, the last days,
has sent us his Son as our Redeemer.
Let us pray that our God may complete
this paschal work of salvation
by the fullness of redemption.**

23. Then the readings follow. A reader goes to the ambo and proclaims the reading. Afterwards a psalmist or a cantor sings or says the Psalm with the people making the response. Then all rise, the Priest says, Let us pray and, after all have prayed for a while in silence, he says the prayer corresponding to the reading. In place of the Responsorial Psalm a period of sacred silence may be observed, in which case the pause after Let us pray is omitted.

Prayers after the Readings

24. After the first reading (On creation: Gn 1: 1–2: 2 or 1: 1, 26-31a) and the Psalm (104 [103] or 33 [32]).

Let us pray.

**Almighty ever-living God,
who are wonderful in the ordering of all your works,
may those you have redeemed understand
that there exists nothing more marvelous
than the world's creation in the beginning
except that, at the end of the ages,
Christ our Passover has been sacrificed.
Who lives and reigns for ever and ever.**

℟. Amen.

Or, On the creation of man:

O God, who wonderfully created human nature
and still more wonderfully redeemed it,
grant us, we pray,
to set our minds against the enticements of sin,
that we may merit to attain eternal joys.
Through Christ our Lord.

℟. Amen.

25. After the second reading (On Abraham's sacrifice: Gn 22: 1-18 or 1-2, 9a, 10-13, 15-18) and the Psalm (16 [15]).

Let us pray.

O God, supreme Father of the faithful,
who increase the children of your promise
by pouring out the grace of adoption
throughout the whole world
and who through the Paschal Mystery
make your servant Abraham father of nations,
as once you swore,
grant, we pray,
that your peoples may enter worthily
into the grace to which you call them.
Through Christ our Lord.

℟. Amen.

26. After the third reading (On the passage through the Red Sea: Ex 14: 15–15: 1) and its canticle (Ex 15).

Let us pray.

O God, whose ancient wonders
remain undimmed in splendor even in our day,
for what you once bestowed on a single people,
freeing them from Pharaoh's persecution
by the power of your right hand,
now you bring about as the salvation of the nations
through the waters of rebirth,
grant, we pray, that the whole world
may become children of Abraham
and inherit the dignity of Israel's birthright.
Through Christ our Lord.

℟. Amen.

Or:

O God, who by the light of the New Testament
have unlocked the meaning
of wonders worked in former times,
so that the Red Sea prefigures the sacred font
and the nation delivered from slavery
foreshadows the Christian people,
grant, we pray, that all nations,
obtaining the privilege of Israel by merit of faith,
may be reborn by partaking of your Spirit.
Through Christ our Lord.

℟. Amen.

27. After the fourth reading (On the new Jerusalem: Is 54: 5-14) and the Psalm (30 [29]).

Let us pray.

Almighty ever-living God,
surpass, for the honor of your name,
what you pledged to the Patriarchs by reason of their faith,
and through sacred adoption increase
the children of your promise,
so that what the Saints of old never doubted
would come to pass
your Church may now see in great part fulfilled.
Through Christ our Lord.

℟. Amen.

Alternatively, other prayers may be used from among those which follow the readings that have been omitted.

28. After the fifth reading (On salvation freely offered to all: Is 55: 1-11) and the canticle (Is 12).

Let us pray.

Almighty ever-living God,
sole hope of the world,
who by the preaching of your Prophets
unveiled the mysteries of this present age,
graciously increase the longing of your people,
for only at the prompting of your grace
do the faithful progress in any kind of virtue.
Through Christ our Lord.

℟. Amen.

29. After the sixth reading (On the fountain of wisdom: Bar 3: 9-15, 32–4: 4) and the Psalm (19 [18]).

Let us pray.

O God, who constantly increase your Church
by your call to the nations,
graciously grant
to those you wash clean in the waters of Baptism
the assurance of your unfailing protection.
Through Christ our Lord.

℟. Amen.

30. After the seventh reading (On a new heart and new spirit: Ez 36: 16-28) and the Psalm (42-43 [41-42]).

Let us pray.

O God of unchanging power and eternal light,
look with favor on the wondrous mystery of
the whole Church
and serenely accomplish the work of human salvation,
which you planned from all eternity;
may the whole world know and see
that what was cast down is raised up,
what had become old is made new,
and all things are restored to integrity through Christ,
just as by him they came into being.
Who lives and reigns for ever and ever.

℟. Amen.

Or:

O God, who by the pages of both Testaments
instruct and prepare us to celebrate the Paschal Mystery,
grant that we may comprehend your mercy,
so that the gifts we receive from you this night
may confirm our hope of the gifts to come.
Through Christ our Lord.

℟. Amen.

31. After the last reading from the Old Testament with its Responsorial Psalm and its prayer, the altar candles are lit, and the Priest intones the hymn Gloria in excelsis Deo (Glory to God in the highest), which is taken up by all, while bells are rung, according to local custom.

32. When the hymn is concluded, the Priest says the Collect in the usual way.

Let us pray.

O God, who make this most sacred night radiant
with the glory of the Lord's Resurrection,
stir up in your Church a spirit of adoption,
so that, renewed in body and mind,
we may render you undivided service.
Through our Lord Jesus Christ, your Son,
who lives and reigns with you
in the unity of the Holy Spirit,
one God, for ever and ever.

33. Then the reader proclaims the reading from the Apostle.

34. After the Epistle has been read, all rise, then the Priest solemnly intones the Alleluia three times, raising his voice by a step each time, with all repeating it. If necessary, the psalmist intones the Alleluia.

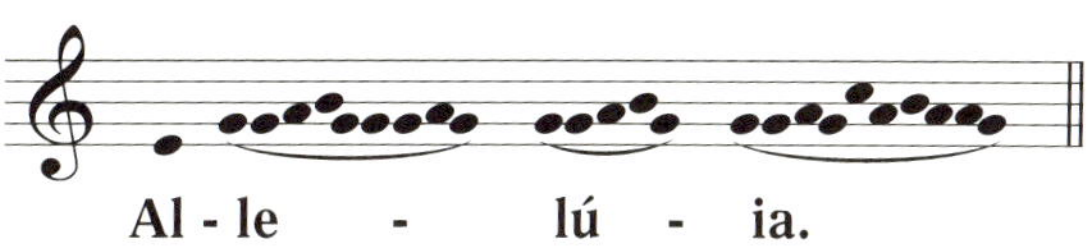

Then the psalmist or cantor proclaims Psalm 118 (117) with the people responding Alleluia.

35. The Priest, in the usual way, puts incense in the thurible and blesses the Deacon. At the Gospel lights are not carried, but only incense.

36. After the Gospel, the Homily, even if brief, is not to be omitted.

THIRD PART:
BAPTISMAL LITURGY

37. After the Homily the Baptismal Liturgy begins. The Priest goes with the ministers to the baptismal font, if this can be seen by the faithful. Otherwise a vessel with water is placed in the sanctuary.

38. Catechumens, if there are any, are called forward and presented by their godparents in front of the assembled Church or, if they are small children, are carried by their parents and godparents.

39. Then, if there is to be a procession to the baptistery or to the font, it forms immediately. A minister with the paschal candle leads off, and those to be baptized follow him with their godparents, then the ministers, the Deacon, and the Priest. During the procession, the Litany (no. 43) is sung. When the Litany is completed, the Priest gives the address (no. 40).

40. If, however, the Baptismal Liturgy takes place in the sanctuary, the Priest immediately makes an introductory statement in these or similar words.

If there are candidates to be baptized:

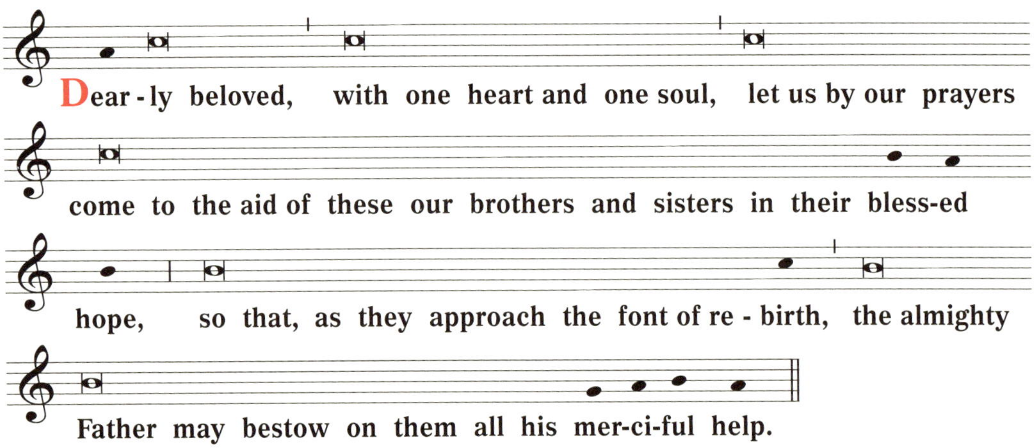

Dearly beloved,
with one heart and one soul, let us by our prayers
come to the aid of these our brothers and sisters
in their blessed hope,
so that, as they approach the font of rebirth,
the almighty Father may bestow on them
all his merciful help.

If the font is to be blessed, but no one is to be baptized:

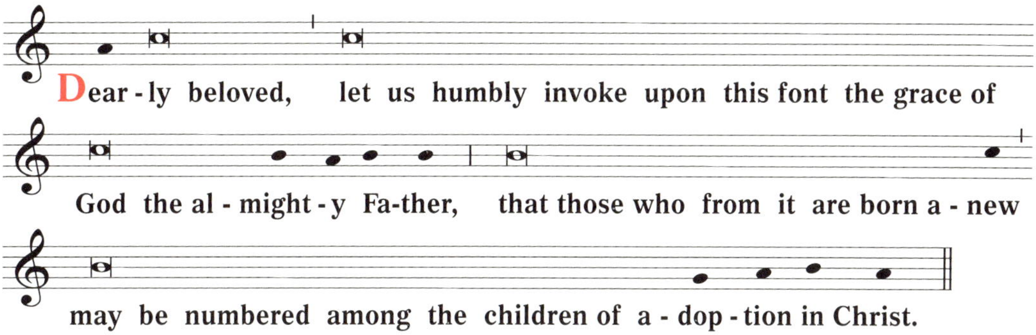

Dearly beloved,
let us humbly invoke upon this font
the grace of God the almighty Father,
that those who from it are born anew
may be numbered among the children of adoption
in Christ.

41. The Litany is sung by two cantors, with all standing (because it is Easter Time) and responding.

If, however, there is to be a procession of some length to the baptistery, the Litany is sung during the procession; in this case, those to be baptized are called forward before the procession begins, and the procession takes place led by the paschal candle, followed by the catechumens with their godparents, then the ministers, the Deacon, and the Priest. The address should occur before the Blessing of Water.

---

42. If no one is to be baptized and the font is not to be blessed, the Litany is omitted, and the Blessing of Water (no. 54) takes place at once.

---

43. In the Litany the names of some Saints may be added, especially the Titular Saint of the church and the Patron Saints of the place and of those to be baptized.

Holy Mary, Mother of God, [ ] ℟. pray for us.
Saint Mich - ael,
Holy Angels of God, [ ]
Saint John the Bap - tist,
Saint Jo - seph,
Saint Peter and Saint Paul, [ ]
Saint An - drew,
Saint John, [ ]
Saint Mary Mag - da - lene,
Saint Ste - phen,
Saint Ignatius of An - ti - och,
Saint Law - rence,
Saint Perpetua and Saint Fe - li - ci - ty,
Saint Ag - nes,
Saint Gre - go - ry,
Saint Au - gus - tine,
Saint Atha - na - sius,
Saint Bas - il,
Saint Mar - tin,
Saint Ben - e - dict,
Saint Francis and Saint Dom - i - nic,
Saint Francis Xa - vi - er,
Saint John Vi - an - ney,
Saint Catherine of Si - e - na,
Saint Teresa of Je - sus,
All holy men and women, Saints of God, [ ]

Lord, be mer-ci-ful, ℟. Lord, de-liv-er us, we pray.

From all e - vil, ℟. Lord, de-liv-er us, we pray.
From eve - ry sin,
From ever - last-ing death,
By your In - car - na - tion,
By your Death and Res - ur - rec - tion,
By the out - pouring of the Ho - ly Spir - it,

Be merciful to us sin-ners, ℟. Lord, we ask you, hear our prayer.

If there are candidates to be baptized:

Bring these chosen ones to new birth through the grace of Bap-tism,

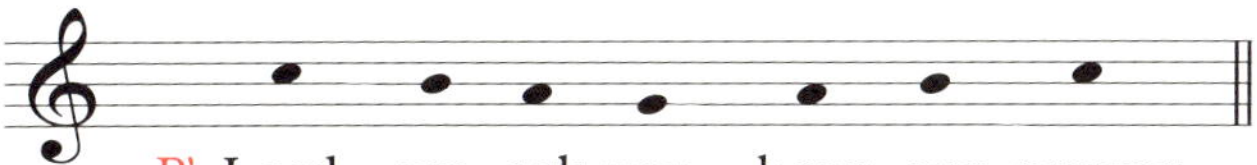

℟. Lord, we ask you, hear our prayer.

If there is no one to be baptized:

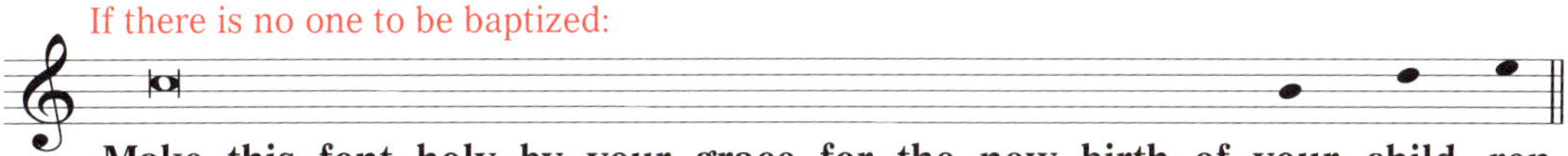

Make this font holy by your grace for the new birth of your child - ren,

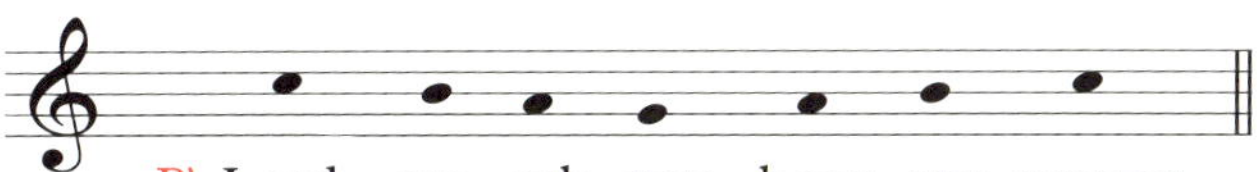

℟. Lord, we ask you, hear our prayer.

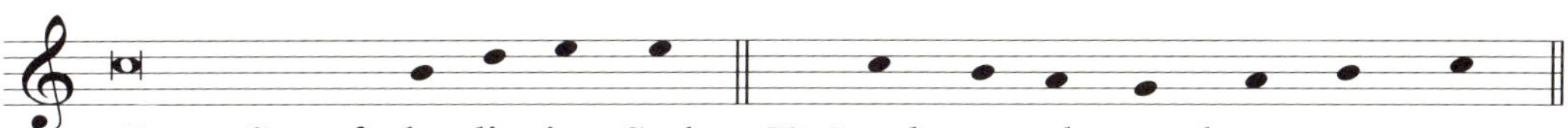

Jesus, Son of the liv - ing God, ℟. Lord, we ask you, hear our prayer.

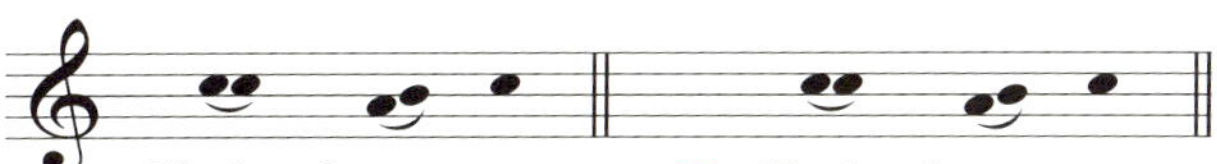

Christ, hear us. ℟. Christ, hear us.

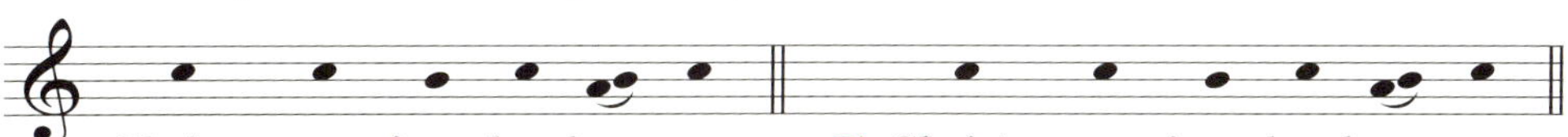

Christ, gra-cious-ly hear us. ℟. Christ, gra-cious-ly hear us.

If there are candidates to be baptized, the Priest, with hands extended, says the following prayer:

Almighty ever-living God,
be present by the mysteries of your great love
and send forth the spirit of adoption
to create the new peoples
brought to birth for you in the font of Baptism,
so that what is to be carried out by our humble service
may be brought to fulfillment by your mighty power.
Through Christ our Lord.

℟. Amen.

Blessing of Baptismal Water

44. The Priest then blesses the baptismal water, saying the following prayer with hands extended:

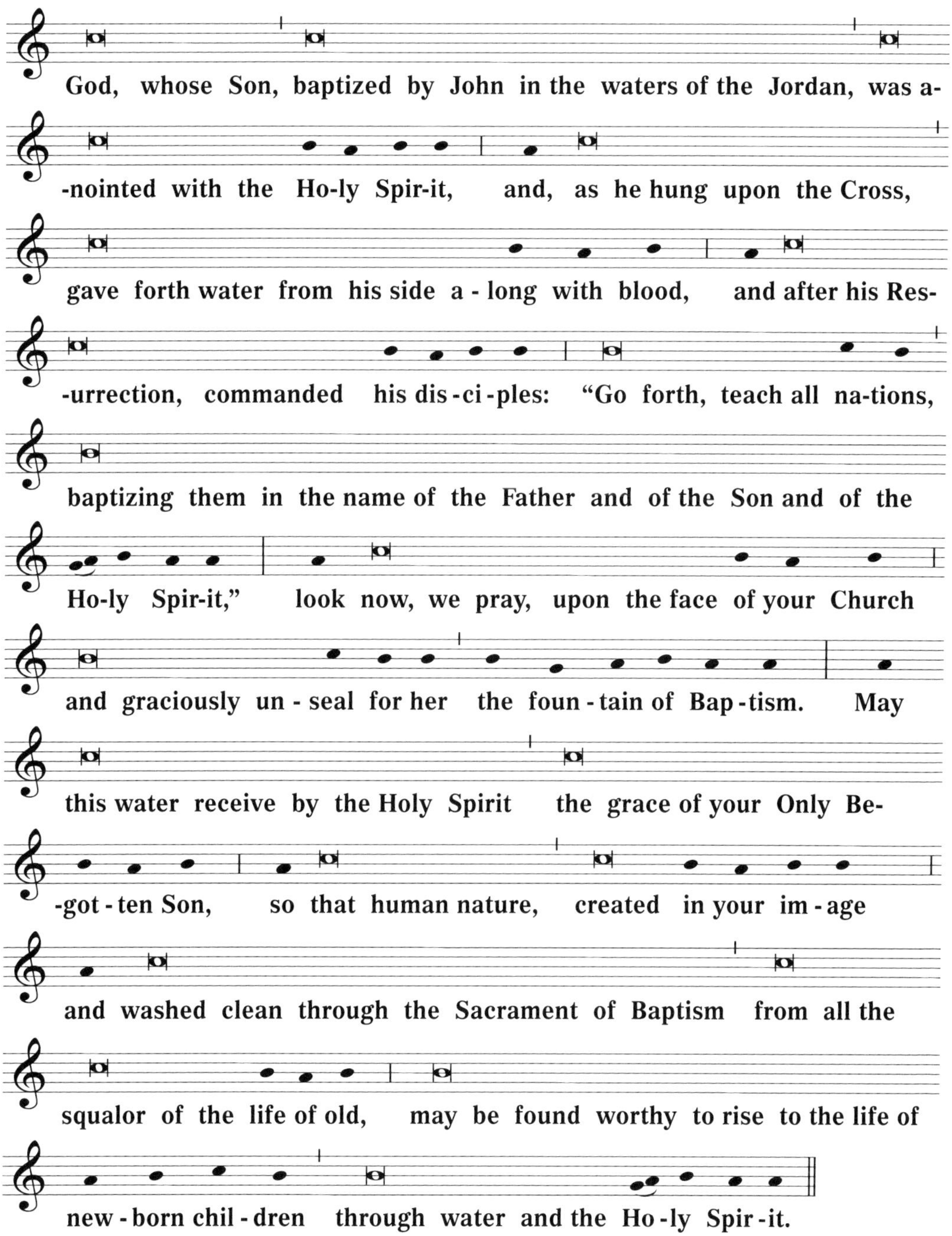
God, whose Son, baptized by John in the waters of the Jordan, was a-
-nointed with the Ho-ly Spir-it, and, as he hung upon the Cross,
gave forth water from his side a - long with blood, and after his Res-
-urrection, commanded his dis - ci - ples: "Go forth, teach all na-tions,
baptizing them in the name of the Father and of the Son and of the
Ho-ly Spir-it," look now, we pray, upon the face of your Church
and graciously un - seal for her the foun - tain of Bap - tism. May
this water receive by the Holy Spirit the grace of your Only Be-
-got - ten Son, so that human nature, created in your im - age
and washed clean through the Sacrament of Baptism from all the
squalor of the life of old, may be found worthy to rise to the life of
new - born chil - dren through water and the Ho - ly Spir - it.

And, if appropriate, lowering the paschal candle into the water either once or three times, he continues:

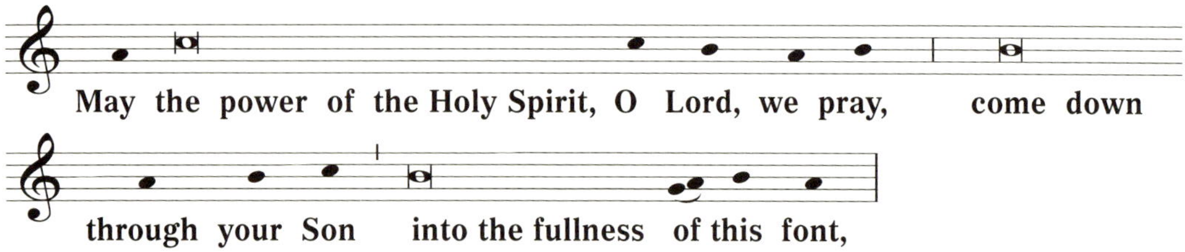

and, holding the candle in the water, he continues:

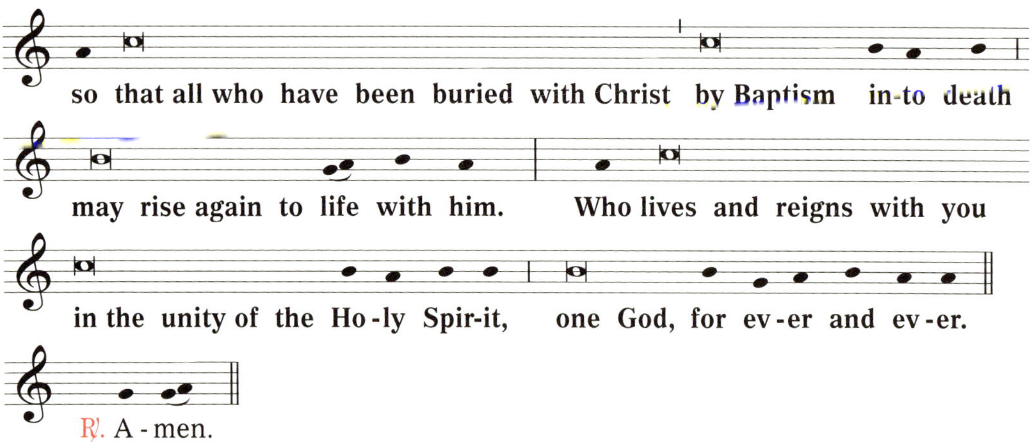

45. Then the candle is lifted out of the water, as the people acclaim:

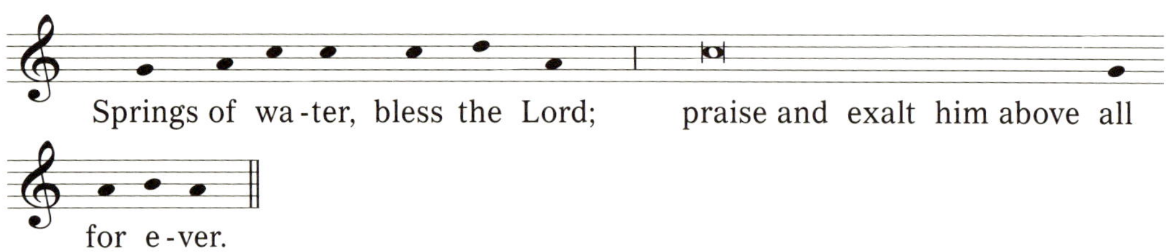

Text without music:

46. The Priest then blesses the baptismal water, saying the following prayer with hands extended:

O God, who by invisible power
accomplish a wondrous effect
through sacramental signs
and who in many ways have prepared water,
your creation,
to show forth the grace of Baptism;

O God, whose Spirit
in the first moments of the world's creation
hovered over the waters,
so that the very substance of water
would even then take to itself the power to sanctify;

O God, who by the outpouring of the flood
foreshadowed regeneration,
so that from the mystery of one and the same
element of water
would come an end to vice and a beginning of virtue;

O God, who caused the children of Abraham
to pass dry-shod through the Red Sea,
so that the chosen people,
set free from slavery to Pharaoh,
would prefigure the people of the baptized;

O God, whose Son,
baptized by John in the waters of the Jordan,
was anointed with the Holy Spirit,
and, as he hung upon the Cross,
gave forth water from his side along with blood,
and after his Resurrection, commanded his disciples:
"Go forth, teach all nations, baptizing them
in the name of the Father and of the Son and
of the Holy Spirit,"
look now, we pray, upon the face of your Church
and graciously unseal for her the fountain of Baptism.

May this water receive by the Holy Spirit
the grace of your Only Begotten Son,
so that human nature, created in your image
and washed clean through the Sacrament of Baptism
from all the squalor of the life of old,
may be found worthy to rise to the life of
newborn children
through water and the Holy Spirit.

And, if appropriate, lowering the paschal candle into the water either once or three times, he continues:

May the power of the Holy Spirit,
O Lord, we pray,
come down through your Son
into the fullness of this font,

and, holding the candle in the water, he continues:

so that all who have been buried with Christ
by Baptism into death
may rise again to life with him.
Who lives and reigns with you
in the unity of the Holy Spirit,
one God, for ever and ever.
℟. Amen.

47. Then the candle is lifted out of the water, as the people acclaim:

Springs of water, bless the Lord;
praise and exalt him above all for ever.

48. After the blessing of baptismal water and the acclamation of the people, the Priest, standing, puts the prescribed questions to the adults and the parents or godparents of the children, as is set out in the respective Rites of the Roman Ritual, in order for them to make the required renunciation.

If the anointing of the adults with the Oil of Catechumens has not taken place beforehand, as part of the immediately preparatory rites, it occurs at this moment.

49. Then the Priest questions the adults individually about the faith and, if there are children to be baptized, he requests the triple profession of faith from all the parents and godparents together, as is indicated in the respective Rites.

Where many are to be baptized on this night, it is possible to arrange the rite so that, immediately after the response of those to be baptized and of the godparents and the parents, the Celebrant asks for and receives the renewal of baptismal promises of all present.

50. When the interrogation is concluded, the Priest baptizes the adult elect and the children.

51. After the Baptism, the Priest anoints the infants with chrism. A white garment is given to each, whether adults or children. Then the Priest or Deacon receives the paschal candle from the hand of the minister, and the candles of the newly baptized are lighted. For infants the rite of Ephphetha is omitted.

52. Afterwards, unless the baptismal washing and the other explanatory rites have occurred in the sanctuary, a procession returns to the sanctuary, formed as before, with the newly baptized or the godparents or parents carrying lighted candles. During this procession, the baptismal canticle Vidi aquam (I saw water) or another appropriate chant is sung (no. 56).

53. If adults have been baptized, the Bishop or, in his absence, the Priest who has conferred Baptism, should at once administer the Sacrament of Confirmation to them in the sanctuary, as is indicated in the Roman Pontifical or Roman Ritual.

The Blessing of Water

54. If no one present is to be baptized and the font is not to be blessed, the Priest introduces the faithful to the blessing of water, saying:

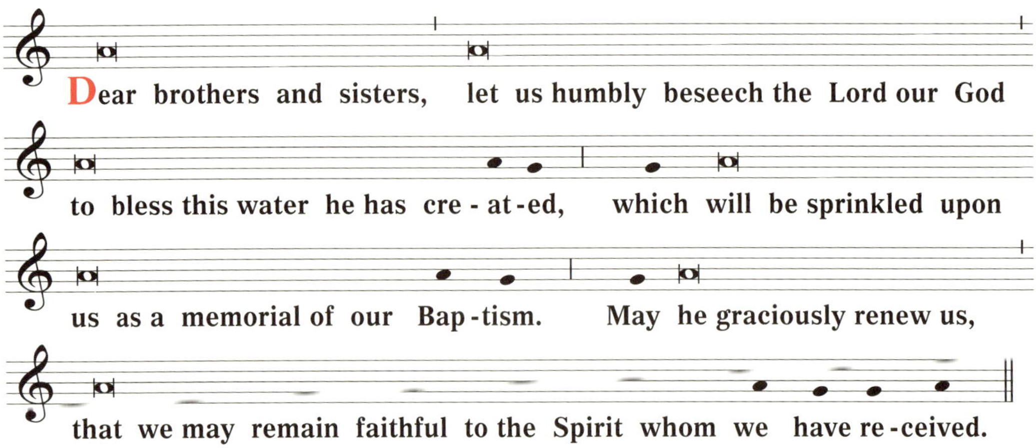

And after a brief pause in silence, he proclaims the following prayer with hands extended:

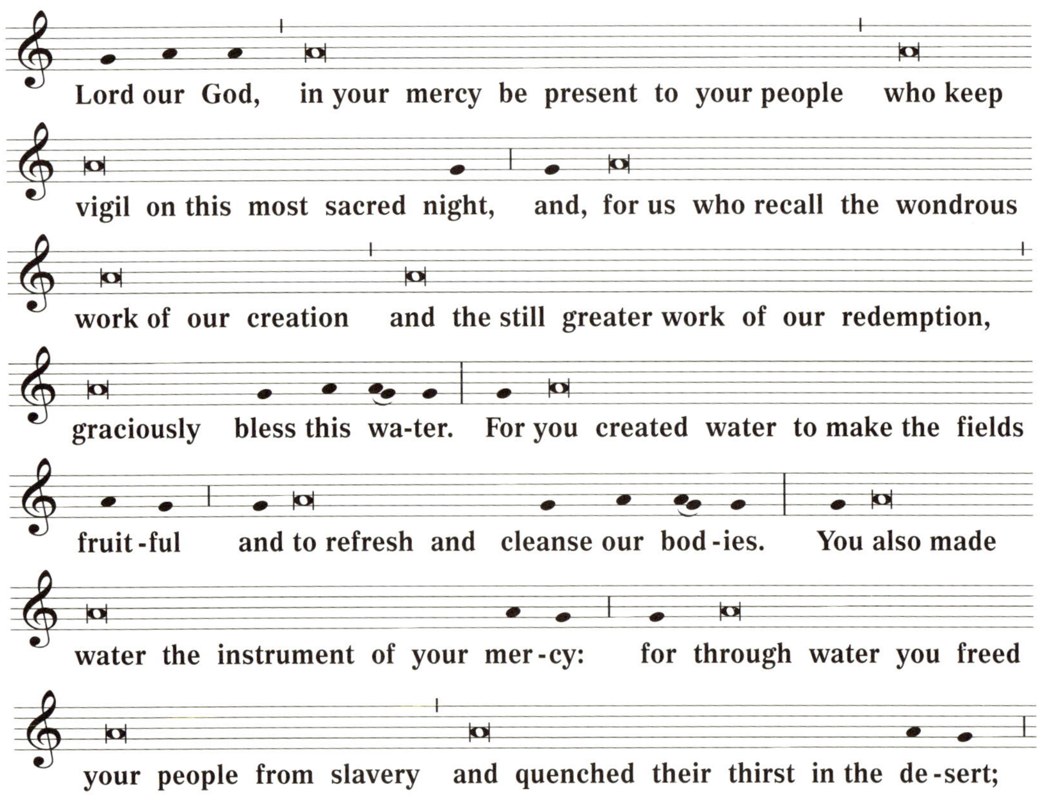

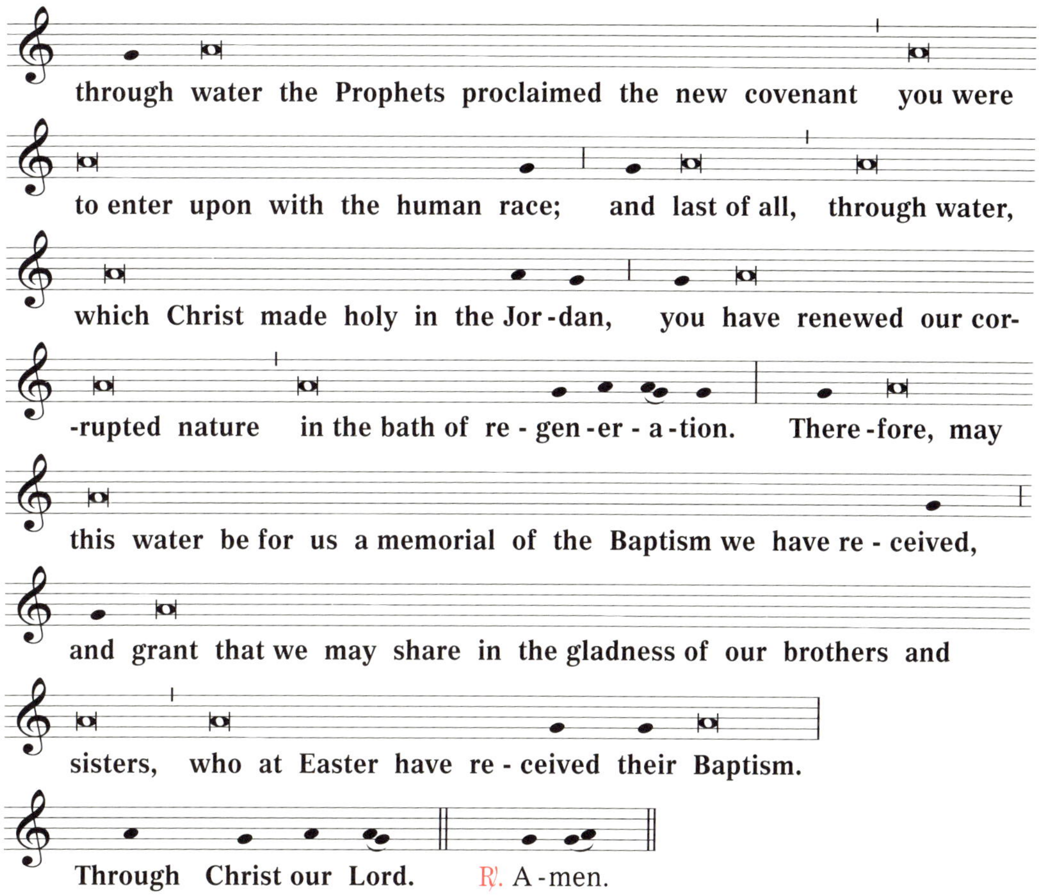
through water the Prophets proclaimed the new covenant you were
to enter upon with the human race; and last of all, through water,
which Christ made holy in the Jor-dan, you have renewed our cor-
-rupted nature in the bath of re-gen-er-a-tion. There-fore, may
this water be for us a memorial of the Baptism we have re-ceived,
and grant that we may share in the gladness of our brothers and
sisters, who at Easter have re-ceived their Baptism.
Through Christ our Lord. ℟. A-men.

Text without music:

**Dear brothers and sisters,
let us humbly beseech the Lord our God
to bless this water he has created,
which will be sprinkled upon us
as a memorial of our Baptism.
May he graciously renew us,
that we may remain faithful to the Spirit
whom we have received.**

And after a brief pause in silence, he proclaims the following prayer, with hands extended:

**Lord our God,
in your mercy be present to your people
who keep vigil on this most sacred night,
and, for us who recall the wondrous work of our creation
and the still greater work of our redemption,
graciously bless this water.
For you created water to make the fields fruitful
and to refresh and cleanse our bodies.
You also made water the instrument of your mercy:
for through water you freed your people from slavery
and quenched their thirst in the desert;
through water the Prophets proclaimed the new covenant
you were to enter upon with the human race;
and last of all,
through water, which Christ made holy in the Jordan,
you have renewed our corrupted nature
in the bath of regeneration.**

**Therefore, may this water be for us
a memorial of the Baptism we have received,
and grant that we may share
in the gladness of our brothers and sisters,
who at Easter have received their Baptism.
Through Christ our Lord.**

℟. Amen.

The Renewal of Baptismal Promises

55. When the Rite of Baptism (and Confirmation) has been completed or, if this has not taken place, after the blessing of water, all stand, holding lighted candles in their hands, and renew the promise of baptismal faith, unless this has already been done together with those to be baptized (cf. no. 49).

The Priest addresses the faithful in these or similar words:

Dear brethren (brothers and sisters),
through the Paschal Mystery
we have been buried with Christ in Baptism,
so that we may walk with him in newness of life.
And so, now that our Lenten observance is concluded,
let us renew the promises of Holy Baptism,
by which we once renounced Satan and his works
and promised to serve God in the holy catholic Church.
And so I ask you:

Priest: **Do you renounce Satan?**

All: I do.

Priest: **And all his works?**

All: I do.

Priest: **And all his empty show?**

All: I do.

Or:

Priest: **Do you renounce sin,**
so as to live in the freedom of the children of God?

All: I do.

Priest: **Do you renounce the lure of evil,**
so that sin may have no mastery over you?

All: I do.

Priest: **Do you renounce Satan,**
the author and prince of sin?

All: I do.

If the situation warrants, this second formula may be adapted by Conferences of Bishops according to local needs.

Then the Priest continues:

Priest: **Do you believe in God,**
the Father almighty,
Creator of heaven and earth?

All: I do.

Priest: **Do you believe in Jesus Christ, his only Son, our Lord,**
who was born of the Virgin Mary,
suffered death and was buried,
rose again from the dead
and is seated at the right hand of the Father?

All: I do.

Priest: **Do you believe in the Holy Spirit,**
the holy catholic Church,
the communion of saints,
the forgiveness of sins,
the resurrection of the body,
and life everlasting?

All: I do.

And the Priest concludes:

And may almighty God, the Father of our Lord Jesus Christ,
who has given us new birth by water and the Holy Spirit
and bestowed on us forgiveness of our sins,
keep us by his grace,
in Christ Jesus our Lord,
for eternal life.

All: Amen.

56. The Priest sprinkles the people with the blessed water, while all sing:

Antiphon

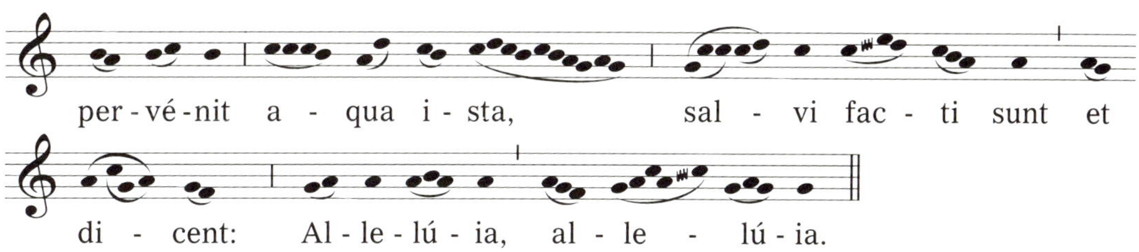

Or:

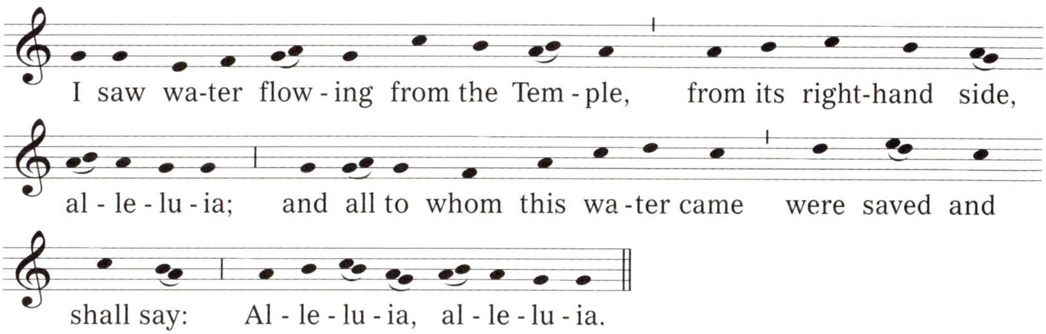

Ant. I saw water flowing from the Temple,
from its right-hand side, alleluia;
and all to whom this water came were saved
and shall say: Alleluia, alleluia.

Another chant that is baptismal in character may also be sung.

57. Meanwhile the newly baptized are led to their place among the faithful.

If the blessing of baptismal water has not taken place in the baptistery, the Deacon and the ministers reverently carry the vessel of water to the font.

If the blessing of the font has not occurred, the blessed water is put aside in an appropriate place.

58. After the sprinkling, the Priest returns to the chair where, omitting the Creed, he directs the Universal Prayer, in which the newly baptized participate for the first time.

FOURTH PART:
THE LITURGY OF THE EUCHARIST

59. The Priest goes to the altar and begins the Liturgy of the Eucharist in the usual way.

60. It is desirable that the bread and wine be brought forward by the newly baptized or, if they are children, by their parents or godparents.

[For nos. 61–66, see the Roman Missal.]

67. **PRAYER AFTER COMMUNION**

Pour out on us, O Lord, the Spirit of your love,
and in your kindness make those you have nourished
by this paschal Sacrament
one in mind and heart.
Through Christ our Lord.

68. **SOLEMN BLESSING**

May almighty God bless you
through today's Easter Solemnity
and, in his compassion,
defend you from every assault of sin.

℟. Amen.

And may he, who restores you to eternal life
in the Resurrection of his Only Begotten,
endow you with the prize of immortality.

℟. Amen.

Now that the days of the Lord's Passion have drawn
to a close,
may you who celebrate the gladness of the Paschal Feast
come with Christ's help, and exulting in spirit,
to those feasts that are celebrated in eternal joy.

℟. Amen.

And may the blessing of almighty God,
the Father, and the Son, ✠ and the Holy Spirit,
come down on you and remain with you for ever.

℟. Amen.

The final blessing formula from the Rite of Baptism of Adults or of Children may also be used, according to circumstances.

69. To dismiss the people the Deacon or, if there is no Deacon, the Priest himself sings or says:

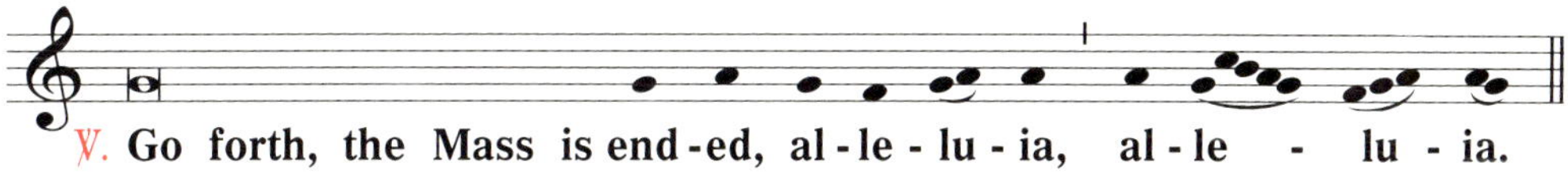

Or:

All reply:

This practice is observed throughout the Octave of Easter.

70. The paschal candle is lit in all the more solemn liturgical celebrations of this period.

At the Mass during the Day

71. Entrance Antiphon

I have risen, and I am with you still, alleluia.
You have laid your hand upon me, alleluia.
Too wonderful for me, this knowledge, alleluia, alleluia.

Cf. Ps 139 (138): 18, 5-6

Or:

The Lord is truly risen, alleluia.
To him be glory and power
for all the ages of eternity, alleluia, alleluia.

Lk 24: 34; cf. Rev 1: 6

The Gloria in excelsis (Glory to God in the highest) is said.

72. COLLECT

O God, who on this day,
through your Only Begotten Son,
have conquered death
and unlocked for us the path to eternity,
grant, we pray, that we who keep
the solemnity of the Lord's Resurrection
may, through the renewal brought by your Spirit,
rise up in the light of life.
Through our Lord Jesus Christ, your Son,
who lives and reigns with you
in the unity of the Holy Spirit,
one God, for ever and ever.

The Creed is said.

However, in Easter Sunday Masses which are celebrated with a congregation, the rite of the renewal of baptismal promises may take place after the Homily, according to the text used at the Easter Vigil (p. 191). In that case the Creed is omitted.

[For nos. 73–75, see the Roman Missal.]

76. **PRAYER AFTER COMMUNION**

Look upon your Church, O God,
with unfailing love and favor,
so that, renewed by the paschal mysteries,
she may come to the glory of the resurrection.
Through Christ our Lord.

77. To impart the blessing at the end of Mass, the Priest may appropriately use the formula of Solemn Blessing for the Mass of the Easter Vigil, p. 194.

78. For the dismissal of the people, there is sung (as above no. 69) or said:

Go forth, the Mass is ended, alleluia, alleluia.

Or:

Go in peace, alleluia, alleluia.

℟. Thanks be to God, alleluia, alleluia.

MONDAY WITHIN THE OCTAVE OF EASTER

Entrance Antiphon

The Lord has led you into a land flowing with milk and honey,
that the law of the Lord may always be on your lips, alleluia.
Ex 13: 5, 9

Or:

The Lord has risen from the dead, as he said;
let us all exult and rejoice,
for he reigns for all eternity, alleluia.

The Gloria in excelsis (Glory to God in the highest) is said.

COLLECT

O God, who give constant increase
to your Church by new offspring,
grant that your servants may hold fast in their lives
to the Sacrament they have received in faith.
Through our Lord Jesus Christ, your Son,
who lives and reigns with you
in the unity of the Holy Spirit,
one God, for ever and ever.

PRAYER AFTER COMMUNION

May the grace of this paschal Sacrament
abound in our minds, we pray, O Lord,
and make those you have set on the way
of eternal salvation
worthy of your gifts.
Through Christ our Lord.

TUESDAY WITHIN THE OCTAVE OF EASTER

Entrance Antiphon

He gave them the water of wisdom to drink;
it will be made strong in them and will not be moved;
it will raise them up for ever, alleluia. Cf. Sir 15: 3-4

The Gloria in excelsis (Glory to God in the highest) is said.

COLLECT

O God, who have bestowed on us paschal remedies,
endow your people with heavenly gifts,
so that, possessed of perfect freedom,
they may rejoice in heaven
over what gladdens them now on earth.
Through our Lord Jesus Christ, your Son,
who lives and reigns with you
in the unity of the Holy Spirit,
one God, for ever and ever.

PRAYER AFTER COMMUNION

Hear us, almighty God,
and, as you have bestowed on your family
the perfect grace of Baptism,
so prepare their hearts
for the reward of eternal happiness.
Through Christ our Lord.

WEDNESDAY WITHIN THE OCTAVE OF EASTER

Entrance Antiphon

Come, you blessed of my Father;
receive the kingdom prepared for you
from the foundation of the world, alleluia. Cf. Mt 25: 34

The Gloria in excelsis (Glory to God in the highest) is said.

COLLECT

O God, who gladden us year by year
with the solemnity of the Lord's Resurrection,
graciously grant
that, by celebrating these present festivities,
we may merit through them to reach eternal joys.
Through our Lord Jesus Christ, your Son,
who lives and reigns with you
in the unity of the Holy Spirit,
one God, for ever and ever.

PRAYER AFTER COMMUNION

We pray, O Lord,
that the reverent reception of the Sacrament of your Son
may cleanse us from our old ways
and transform us into a new creation.
Through Christ our Lord.

THURSDAY WITHIN THE OCTAVE OF EASTER

Entrance Antiphon

They praised in unison your conquering hand, O Lord,
for wisdom opened mouths that were mute
and gave eloquence to the tongues of infants, alleluia.
Wis 10: 20-21

The Gloria in excelsis (Glory to God in the highest) is said.

COLLECT

O God, who have united the many nations
in confessing your name,
grant that those reborn in the font of Baptism
may be one in the faith of their hearts
and the homage of their deeds.
Through our Lord Jesus Christ, your Son,
who lives and reigns with you
in the unity of the Holy Spirit,
one God, for ever and ever.

PRAYER AFTER COMMUNION

Hear, O Lord, our prayers,
that this most holy exchange,
by which you have redeemed us,
may bring your help in this present life
and ensure for us eternal gladness.
Through Christ our Lord.

FRIDAY WITHIN THE OCTAVE OF EASTER

Entrance Antiphon

The Lord led his people in hope,
while the sea engulfed their foes, alleluia. Cf. Ps 78 (77): 53

The Gloria in excelsis (Glory to God in the highest) is said.

COLLECT

Almighty ever-living God,
who gave us the Paschal Mystery
in the covenant you established
for reconciling the human race,
so dispose our minds, we pray,
that what we celebrate by professing the faith
we may express in deeds.
Through our Lord Jesus Christ, your Son,
who lives and reigns with you
in the unity of the Holy Spirit,
one God, for ever and ever.

PRAYER AFTER COMMUNION

Keep safe, O Lord, we pray,
those whom you have saved by your kindness
that, redeemed by the Passion of your Son,
they may rejoice in his Resurrection.
Who lives and reigns for ever and ever.

SATURDAY WITHIN THE OCTAVE OF EASTER

Entrance Antiphon

The Lord brought out his people with joy,
his chosen ones with shouts of rejoicing, alleluia.

Ps 105 (104): 43

The Gloria in excelsis (Glory to God in the highest) is said.

COLLECT

O God, who by the abundance of your grace
give increase to the peoples who believe in you,
look with favor on those you have chosen
and clothe with blessed immortality
those reborn through the Sacrament of Baptism.
Through our Lord Jesus Christ, your Son,
who lives and reigns with you
in the unity of the Holy Spirit,
one God, for ever and ever.

PRAYER AFTER COMMUNION

Look with kindness upon your people, O Lord,
and grant, we pray,
that those you were pleased to renew by eternal mysteries
may attain in their flesh
the incorruptible glory of the resurrection.
Through Christ our Lord.

SECOND SUNDAY OF EASTER
(or of Divine Mercy)

Entrance Antiphon

Like newborn infants, you must long for the pure, spiritual milk, that in him you may grow to salvation, alleluia. 1 Pt 2: 2

Or:

Receive the joy of your glory, giving thanks to God, who has called you into the heavenly kingdom, alleluia. 4 Esdr 2: 36-37

The Gloria in excelsis (Glory to God in the highest) is said.

COLLECT

God of everlasting mercy,
who in the very recurrence of the paschal feast
kindle the faith of the people you have made your own,
increase, we pray, the grace you have bestowed,
that all may grasp and rightly understand
in what font they have been washed,
by whose Spirit they have been reborn,
by whose Blood they have been redeemed.
Through our Lord Jesus Christ, your Son,
who lives and reigns with you
in the unity of the Holy Spirit,
one God, for ever and ever.

The Creed is said.

PRAYER AFTER COMMUNION

Grant, we pray, almighty God,
that our reception of this paschal Sacrament
may have a continuing effect
in our minds and hearts.
Through Christ our Lord.

A formula of Solemn Blessing, p. 194, may be used.

For the dismissal of the people, there is sung (as above, p. 195) or said: Go forth, the Mass is ended, alleluia, alleluia. Or: Go in peace, alleluia, alleluia. The people respond: Thanks be to God, alleluia, alleluia.

MONDAY

Entrance Antiphon

Christ, having risen from the dead, dies now no more;
death will no longer have dominion over him, alleluia. Rom 6: 9

COLLECT

Grant, we pray, almighty God,
that we, who have been renewed by paschal remedies,
transcending the likeness of our earthly parentage,
may be transformed in the image of our heavenly maker.
Through our Lord Jesus Christ, your Son,
who lives and reigns with you
in the unity of the Holy Spirit,
one God, for ever and ever.

PRAYER AFTER COMMUNION

Look with kindness upon your people, O Lord,
and grant, we pray,
that those you were pleased to renew by eternal mysteries
may attain in their flesh
the incorruptible glory of the resurrection.
Through Christ our Lord.

TUESDAY

Entrance Antiphon

Let us rejoice and be glad and give glory to God,
for the Lord our God the Almighty reigns, alleluia. Rev 19: 7, 6

COLLECT

Enable us, we pray, almighty God,
to proclaim the power of the risen Lord,
that we, who have received the pledge of his gift,
may come to possess all he gives
when it is fully revealed.
Through our Lord Jesus Christ, your Son,
who lives and reigns with you
in the unity of the Holy Spirit,
one God, for ever and ever.

PRAYER AFTER COMMUNION

Hear, O Lord, our prayers,
that this most holy exchange,
by which you have redeemed us,
may bring your help in this present life
and ensure for us eternal gladness.
Through Christ our Lord.

WEDNESDAY

Entrance Antiphon

I will praise you, Lord, among the nations;
I will tell of your name to my kin, alleluia.
Cf. Ps 18 (17): 50; 22 (21): 23

COLLECT

As we recall year by year the mysteries
by which, through the restoration of its original dignity,
human nature has received the hope of rising again,
we earnestly beseech your mercy, Lord,
that what we celebrate in faith
we may possess in unending love.
Through our Lord Jesus Christ, your Son,
who lives and reigns with you
in the unity of the Holy Spirit,
one God, for ever and ever.

PRAYER AFTER COMMUNION

Graciously be present to your people, we pray, O Lord,
and lead those you have imbued with heavenly mysteries
to pass from former ways to newness of life.
Through Christ our Lord.

THURSDAY

Entrance Antiphon

**O God, when you went forth before your people,
marching with them and living among them,
the earth trembled, heavens poured down rain, alleluia.**

Cf. Ps 68 (67): 8-9, 20

COLLECT

**O God, who for the salvation of the world
brought about the paschal sacrifice,
be favorable to the supplications of your people,
so that Christ our High Priest, interceding on our behalf,
may by his likeness to ourselves
bring us reconciliation,
and by his equality with you
free us from our sins.
Through our Lord Jesus Christ, your Son,
who lives and reigns with you
in the unity of the Holy Spirit,
one God, for ever and ever.**

PRAYER AFTER COMMUNION

**Almighty ever-living God,
who restore us to eternal life
in the Resurrection of Christ,
increase in us, we pray,
the fruits of this paschal Sacrament
and pour into our hearts the strength of this saving food.
Through Christ our Lord.**

FRIDAY

Entrance Antiphon

You have redeemed us, Lord, by your Blood,
from every tribe and tongue and people and nation,
and have made us into a kingdom, priests for our God, alleluia.
Rev 5: 9-10

COLLECT

O God, hope and light of the sincere,
we humbly entreat you to dispose our hearts
to offer you worthy prayer
and ever to extol you
by dutiful proclamation of your praise.
Through our Lord Jesus Christ, your Son,
who lives and reigns with you
in the unity of the Holy Spirit,
one God, for ever and ever.

PRAYER AFTER COMMUNION

Keep safe, O Lord, we pray,
those whom you have saved by your kindness,
that, redeemed by the Passion of your Son,
they may rejoice in his Resurrection.
Who lives and reigns for ever and ever.

SATURDAY

Entrance Antiphon

O chosen people, proclaim the mighty works of him
who called you out of darkness into his wonderful light, alleluia.
Cf. 1 Pt 2: 9

COLLECT

Set aside, O Lord,
the bond of sentence written for us by the law of sin,
which in the Paschal Mystery you canceled
through the Resurrection of Christ your Son.
Who lives and reigns with you
in the unity of the Holy Spirit,
one God, for ever and ever.

Or:

O God, who willed that through the paschal mysteries
the gates of mercy should stand open for your faithful,
look upon us and have mercy,
that as we follow, by your gift, the way you desire for us,
so may we never stray from the paths of life.
Through our Lord Jesus Christ, your Son,
who lives and reigns with you
in the unity of the Holy Spirit,
one God, for ever and ever.

PRAYER AFTER COMMUNION

We have partaken of the gifts of this sacred mystery,
humbly imploring, O Lord,
that what your Son commanded us to do
in memory of him
may bring us growth in charity.
Through Christ our Lord.

THIRD SUNDAY OF EASTER

Entrance Antiphon

Cry out with joy to God, all the earth;
O sing to the glory of his name.
O render him glorious praise, alleluia. Cf. Ps 66 (65): 1-2

The Gloria in excelsis (Glory to God in the highest) is said.

COLLECT

May your people exult for ever, O God,
in renewed youthfulness of spirit,
so that, rejoicing now in the restored glory of our adoption,
we may look forward in confident hope
to the rejoicing of the day of resurrection.
Through our Lord Jesus Christ, your Son,
who lives and reigns with you
in the unity of the Holy Spirit,
one God, for ever and ever.

The Creed is said.

PRAYER AFTER COMMUNION

Look with kindness upon your people, O Lord,
and grant, we pray,
that those you were pleased to renew by eternal mysteries
may attain in their flesh
the incorruptible glory of the resurrection.
Through Christ our Lord.

A formula of Solemn Blessing, p. 313, may be used.

MONDAY

Entrance Antiphon

The Good Shepherd has risen,
who laid down his life for his sheep
and willingly died for his flock, alleluia.

COLLECT

Grant, we pray, almighty God,
that, putting off our old self with all its ways,
we may live as Christ did,
for through the healing paschal remedies
you have conformed us to his nature.
Who lives and reigns with you
in the unity of the Holy Spirit,
one God, for ever and ever.

PRAYER AFTER COMMUNION

Almighty ever-living God,
who restore us to eternal life
in the Resurrection of Christ,
increase in us, we pray, the fruits of this paschal Sacrament
and pour into our hearts the strength of this saving food.
Through Christ our Lord.

TUESDAY

Entrance Antiphon

Sing praise to our God,
all you who fear God, both small and great,
for now salvation and strength have come,
and the power of his Christ, alleluia. Rev 19: 5; 12: 10

COLLECT

O God, who open wide the gates of the heavenly Kingdom
to those reborn of water and the Holy Spirit,
pour out on your servants
an increase of the grace you have bestowed,
that, having been purged of all sins,
they may lack nothing
that in your kindness you have promised.
Through our Lord Jesus Christ, your Son,
who lives and reigns with you
in the unity of the Holy Spirit,
one God, for ever and ever.

PRAYER AFTER COMMUNION

Look with kindness upon your people, O Lord,
and grant, we pray,
that those you were pleased to renew by eternal mysteries
may attain in their flesh
the incorruptible glory of the resurrection.
Through Christ our Lord.

WEDNESDAY

Entrance Antiphon Let my mouth be filled with your praise, that I may sing aloud;
my lips shall shout for joy, when I sing to you, alleluia.
Cf. Ps 71 (70): 8, 23

COLLECT Be present to your family, O Lord, we pray,
and graciously ensure
those you have endowed with the grace of faith
an eternal share in the Resurrection
of your Only Begotten Son.
Who lives and reigns with you
in the unity of the Holy Spirit,
one God, for ever and ever.

PRAYER AFTER COMMUNION Hear, O Lord, our prayers,
that this most holy exchange,
by which you have redeemed us,
may bring your help in this present life
and ensure for us eternal gladness.
Through Christ our Lord.

THURSDAY

Entrance Antiphon

Let us sing to the Lord, for he has gloriously triumphed.
The Lord is my strength and my might;
he has become my salvation, alleluia. Cf. Ex 15: 1-2

COLLECT

Almighty ever-living God,
let us feel your compassion more readily
during these days when, by your gift,
we have known it more fully,
so that those you have freed from the darkness of error
may cling more firmly to the teachings of your truth.
Through our Lord Jesus Christ, your Son,
who lives and reigns with you
in the unity of the Holy Spirit,
one God, for ever and ever.

PRAYER AFTER COMMUNION

Graciously be present to your people, we pray, O Lord,
and lead those you have imbued with heavenly mysteries
to pass from former ways to newness of life.
Through Christ our Lord.

FRIDAY

Entrance Antiphon

Worthy is the Lamb who was slain,
to receive power and divinity,
and wisdom and strength and honor, alleluia. Rev 5: 12

COLLECT

Grant, we pray, almighty God,
that we, who have come to know
the grace of the Lord's Resurrection,
may, through the love of the Spirit,
ourselves rise to newness of life.
Through our Lord Jesus Christ, your Son,
who lives and reigns with you
in the unity of the Holy Spirit,
one God, for ever and ever.

PRAYER AFTER COMMUNION

We have partaken of the gifts of this sacred mystery,
humbly imploring, O Lord,
that what your Son commanded us to do
in memory of him
may bring us growth in charity.
Through Christ our Lord.

SATURDAY

Entrance Antiphon

You have been buried with Christ in Baptism,
through which you also rose again
by faith in the working of God,
who raised him from the dead, alleluia. Col 2: 12

COLLECT

O God, who in the font of Baptism
have made new those who believe in you,
keep safe those reborn in Christ,
that, defeating every onslaught of error,
they may faithfully preserve the grace of your blessing.
Through our Lord Jesus Christ, your Son,
who lives and reigns with you
in the unity of the Holy Spirit,
one God, for ever and ever.

PRAYER AFTER COMMUNION

Keep safe, O Lord, we pray,
those whom you have saved by your kindness,
that, redeemed by the Passion of your Son,
they may rejoice in his Resurrection.
Who lives and reigns for ever and ever.

FOURTH SUNDAY OF EASTER

Entrance Antiphon

The merciful love of the Lord fills the earth;
by the word of the Lord the heavens were made, alleluia.

Cf. Ps 33 (32): 5-6

The Gloria in excelsis (Glory to God in the highest) is said.

COLLECT

Almighty ever-living God,
lead us to a share in the joys of heaven,
so that the humble flock may reach
where the brave Shepherd has gone before.
Who lives and reigns with you
in the unity of the Holy Spirit,
one God, for ever and ever.

The Creed is said.

PRAYER AFTER COMMUNION

Look upon your flock, kind Shepherd,
and be pleased to settle in eternal pastures
the sheep you have redeemed
by the Precious Blood of your Son.
Who lives and reigns for ever and ever.

A formula of Solemn Blessing, p. 313, may be used.

MONDAY

Entrance Antiphon

Christ, having risen from the dead, dies now no more;
death will no longer have dominion over him, alleluia. Rom 6: 9

COLLECT

O God, perfect light of the blessed,
by whose gift we celebrate the paschal mysteries on earth,
bring us, we pray,
to rejoice in the full measure of your grace
for ages unending.
Through our Lord Jesus Christ, your Son,
who lives and reigns with you
in the unity of the Holy Spirit,
one God, for ever and ever.

PRAYER AFTER COMMUNION

Look with kindness upon your people, O Lord,
and grant, we pray,
that those you were pleased to renew by eternal mysteries
may attain in their flesh
the incorruptible glory of the resurrection.
Through Christ our Lord.

TUESDAY

Entrance Antiphon

Let us rejoice and be glad and give glory to God,
for the Lord our God the Almighty reigns, alleluia. Rev 19: 7, 6

COLLECT

Grant, we pray, almighty God,
that, celebrating the mysteries of the Lord's Resurrection,
we may merit to receive the joy of our redemption.
Through our Lord Jesus Christ, your Son,
who lives and reigns with you
in the unity of the Holy Spirit,
one God, for ever and ever.

PRAYER AFTER COMMUNION

Hear, O Lord, our prayers,
that this most holy exchange,
by which you have redeemed us,
may bring your help in this present life
and ensure for us eternal gladness.
Through Christ our Lord.

WEDNESDAY

Entrance Antiphon

I will praise you, Lord, among the nations;
I will tell of your name to my kin, alleluia.

Cf. Ps 18 (17): 50; 22 (21): 23

COLLECT

O God, life of the faithful,
glory of the humble, blessedness of the just,
listen kindly to the prayers
of those who call on you,
that they who thirst for what you generously promise
may always have their fill of your plenty.
Through our Lord Jesus Christ, your Son,
who lives and reigns with you
in the unity of the Holy Spirit,
one God, for ever and ever.

PRAYER AFTER COMMUNION

Graciously be present to your people, we pray, O Lord,
and lead those you have imbued with heavenly mysteries
to pass from former ways to newness of life.
Through Christ our Lord.

THURSDAY

Entrance Antiphon

O God, when you went forth before your people,
marching with them and living among them,
the earth trembled, heavens poured down rain, alleluia.
Cf. Ps 68 (67): 8-9, 20

COLLECT

O God, who restore human nature
to yet greater dignity than at its beginnings,
look upon the amazing mystery of your loving kindness,
and in those you have chosen to make new
through the wonder of rebirth
may you preserve the gifts
of your enduring grace and blessing.
Through our Lord Jesus Christ, your Son,
who lives and reigns with you
in the unity of the Holy Spirit,
one God, for ever and ever.

PRAYER AFTER COMMUNION

Almighty ever-living God,
who restore us to eternal life
in the Resurrection of Christ,
increase in us, we pray,
the fruits of this paschal Sacrament
and pour into our hearts the strength of this saving food.
Through Christ our Lord.

FRIDAY

Entrance Antiphon

You have redeemed us, Lord, by your Blood,
from every tribe and tongue and people and nation,
and have made us into a kingdom, priests for our God, alleluia.
Rev 5: 9-10

COLLECT

O God, author of our freedom and of our salvation,
listen to the voice of our pleading
and grant that those you have redeemed
by the shedding of your Son's Blood
may have life through you
and, under your protection,
rejoice for ever unharmed.
Through our Lord Jesus Christ, your Son,
who lives and reigns with you
in the unity of the Holy Spirit,
one God, for ever and ever.

PRAYER AFTER COMMUNION

Keep safe, O Lord, we pray,
those whom you have saved by your kindness,
that, redeemed by the Passion of your Son,
they may rejoice in his Resurrection.
Who lives and reigns for ever and ever.

SATURDAY

Entrance Antiphon

O chosen people, proclaim the mighty works of him
who called you out of darkness into his wonderful light, alleluia.
Cf. 1 Pt 2: 9

COLLECT

O God, who in the celebration of Easter
graciously give to the world
the healing of heavenly remedies,
show benevolence to your Church,
that our present observance
may benefit us for eternal life.
Through our Lord Jesus Christ, your Son,
who lives and reigns with you
in the unity of the Holy Spirit,
one God, for ever and ever.

PRAYER AFTER COMMUNION

We have partaken of the gifts of this sacred mystery,
humbly imploring, O Lord,
that what your Son commanded us to do
in memory of him
may bring us growth in charity.
Through Christ our Lord.

FIFTH SUNDAY OF EASTER

Entrance Antiphon

O sing a new song to the Lord,
for he has worked wonders;
in the sight of the nations
he has shown his deliverance, alleluia. Cf. Ps 98 (97): 1-2

The Gloria in excelsis (Glory to God in the highest) is said.

COLLECT

Almighty ever-living God,
constantly accomplish the Paschal Mystery within us,
that those you were pleased to make new in Holy Baptism
may, under your protective care, bear much fruit
and come to the joys of life eternal.
Through our Lord Jesus Christ, your Son,
who lives and reigns with you
in the unity of the Holy Spirit,
one God, for ever and ever.

The Creed is said.

PRAYER AFTER COMMUNION

Graciously be present to your people, we pray, O Lord,
and lead those you have imbued with heavenly mysteries
to pass from former ways to newness of life.
Through Christ our Lord.

A formula of Solemn Blessing, p. 313, may be used.

MONDAY

Entrance Antiphon

The Good Shepherd has risen,
who laid down his life for his sheep
and willingly died for his flock, alleluia.

COLLECT

May your right hand, O Lord, we pray,
encompass your family with perpetual help,
so that, defended from all wickedness
by the Resurrection of your Only Begotten Son,
we may make our way by means of your heavenly gifts.
Through our Lord Jesus Christ, your Son,
who lives and reigns with you
in the unity of the Holy Spirit,
one God, for ever and ever.

PRAYER AFTER COMMUNION

Almighty ever-living God,
who restore us to eternal life
in the Resurrection of Christ,
increase in us, we pray, the fruits of this paschal Sacrament
and pour into our hearts the strength of this saving food.
Through Christ our Lord.

TUESDAY

Entrance Antiphon

Sing praise to our God,
all you who fear God, both small and great,
for now salvation and strength have come,
and the power of his Christ, alleluia. Rev 19: 5; 12: 10

COLLECT

O God, who restore us to eternal life
in the Resurrection of Christ,
grant your people constancy in faith and hope,
that we may never doubt the promises
of which we have learned from you.
Through our Lord Jesus Christ, your Son,
who lives and reigns with you
in the unity of the Holy Spirit,
one God, for ever and ever.

PRAYER AFTER COMMUNION

Look with kindness upon your people, O Lord,
and grant, we pray,
that those you were pleased to renew by eternal mysteries
may attain in their flesh
the incorruptible glory of the resurrection.
Through Christ our Lord.

WEDNESDAY

Entrance Antiphon

Let my mouth be filled with your praise, that I may sing aloud;
my lips shall shout for joy, when I sing to you, alleluia.
Cf. Ps 71 (70): 8, 23

COLLECT

O God, restorer and lover of innocence,
direct the hearts of your servants towards yourself,
that those you have set free from the darkness of unbelief
may never stray from the light of your truth.
Through our Lord Jesus Christ, your Son,
who lives and reigns with you
in the unity of the Holy Spirit,
one God, for ever and ever.

PRAYER AFTER COMMUNION

Hear, O Lord, our prayers,
that this most holy exchange,
by which you have redeemed us,
may bring your help in this present life
and ensure for us eternal gladness.
Through Christ our Lord.

THURSDAY

Entrance Antiphon

Let us sing to the Lord, for he has gloriously triumphed.
The Lord is my strength and my might;
he has become my salvation, alleluia. Cf. Ex 15: 1-2

COLLECT

O God, by whose grace,
though sinners, we are made just
and, though pitiable, made blessed,
stand, we pray, by your works,
stand by your gifts,
that those justified by faith
may not lack the courage of perseverance.
Through our Lord Jesus Christ, your Son,
who lives and reigns with you
in the unity of the Holy Spirit,
one God, for ever and ever.

PRAYER AFTER COMMUNION

Graciously be present to your people, we pray, O Lord,
and lead those you have imbued with heavenly mysteries
to pass from former ways to newness of life.
Through Christ our Lord.

FRIDAY

Entrance Antiphon

Worthy is the Lamb who was slain,
to receive power and divinity,
and wisdom and strength and honor, alleluia. Rev 5: 12

COLLECT

Grant us, Lord, we pray,
that, being rightly conformed to the paschal mysteries,
what we celebrate in joy
may protect and save us with perpetual power.
Through our Lord Jesus Christ, your Son,
who lives and reigns with you
in the unity of the Holy Spirit,
one God, for ever and ever.

PRAYER AFTER COMMUNION

We have partaken of the gifts of this sacred mystery,
humbly imploring, O Lord,
that what your Son commanded us to do
in memory of him
may bring us growth in charity.
Through Christ our Lord.

SATURDAY

Entrance Antiphon

You have been buried with Christ in Baptism,
through which you also rose again
by faith in the working of God,
who raised him from the dead, alleluia. Col 2: 12

COLLECT

Almighty and eternal God,
who through the regenerating power of Baptism
have been pleased to confer on us heavenly life,
grant, we pray,
that those you render capable of immortality
by justifying them
may by your guidance
attain the fullness of glory.
Through our Lord Jesus Christ, your Son,
who lives and reigns with you
in the unity of the Holy Spirit,
one God, for ever and ever.

PRAYER AFTER COMMUNION

Keep safe, O Lord, we pray,
those whom you have saved by your kindness,
that, redeemed by the Passion of your Son,
they may rejoice in his Resurrection.
Who lives and reigns for ever and ever.

SIXTH SUNDAY OF EASTER

Entrance Antiphon

Proclaim a joyful sound and let it be heard;
proclaim to the ends of the earth:
The Lord has freed his people, alleluia. Cf. Is 48: 20

The Gloria in excelsis (Glory to God in the highest) is said.

COLLECT

Grant, almighty God,
that we may celebrate with heartfelt devotion
these days of joy,
which we keep in honor of the risen Lord,
and that what we relive in remembrance
we may always hold to in what we do.
Through our Lord Jesus Christ, your Son,
who lives and reigns with you
in the unity of the Holy Spirit,
one God, for ever and ever.

The Creed is said.

PRAYER AFTER COMMUNION

Almighty ever-living God,
who restore us to eternal life in the Resurrection of Christ,
increase in us, we pray, the fruits of this paschal Sacrament
and pour into our hearts the strength of this saving food.
Through Christ our Lord.

A formula of Solemn Blessing, p. 313, may be used.

MONDAY

Entrance Antiphon

Christ, having risen from the dead, dies now no more;
death will no longer have dominion over him, alleluia.
Rom 6: 9

COLLECT

Grant, O merciful God,
that we may experience at all times
the fruit produced by the paschal observances.
Through our Lord Jesus Christ, your Son,
who lives and reigns with you
in the unity of the Holy Spirit,
one God, for ever and ever.

PRAYER AFTER COMMUNION

Look with kindness upon your people, O Lord,
and grant, we pray,
that those you were pleased to renew by eternal mysteries
may attain in their flesh
the incorruptible glory of the resurrection.
Through Christ our Lord.

TUESDAY

Entrance Antiphon

Let us rejoice and be glad and give glory to God,
for the Lord our God the Almighty reigns, alleluia. Rev 19: 7, 6

COLLECT

Grant, almighty and merciful God,
that we may in truth receive a share
in the Resurrection of Christ your Son.
Who lives and reigns with you
in the unity of the Holy Spirit,
one God, for ever and ever.

PRAYER AFTER COMMUNION

Hear, O Lord, our prayers,
that this most holy exchange,
by which you have redeemed us,
may bring your help in this present life
and ensure for us eternal gladness.
Through Christ our Lord.

WEDNESDAY

At the Morning Mass

In regions where the Solemnity of the Ascension occurs on the following Sunday, this Mass is also used in the evening.

Entrance Antiphon

I will praise you, Lord, among the nations;
I will tell of your name to my kin, alleluia.
Cf. Ps 18 (17): 50; 22 (21): 23

COLLECT

Grant, we pray, O Lord,
that, as we celebrate in mystery
the solemnities of your Son's Resurrection,
so, too, we may be worthy
to rejoice at his coming with all the Saints.
Through our Lord Jesus Christ, your Son,
who lives and reigns with you
in the unity of the Holy Spirit,
one God, for ever and ever.

PRAYER AFTER COMMUNION

Graciously be present to your people, we pray, O Lord,
and lead those you have imbued with heavenly mysteries
to pass from former ways to newness of life.
Through Christ our Lord.

THE ASCENSION OF THE LORD

Solemnity

Where the Solemnity of the Ascension is not to be observed as a Holyday of Obligation, it is assigned to the Seventh Sunday of Easter as its proper day.

At the Vigil Mass

This Mass is used on the evening of the day before the Solemnity, either before or after First Vespers (Evening Prayer I) of the Ascension.

Entrance Antiphon

You kingdoms of the earth, sing to God;
praise the Lord, who ascends above the highest heavens;
his majesty and might are in the skies, alleluia. Ps 68 (67): 33, 35

The Gloria in excelsis (Glory to God in the highest) is said.

COLLECT

O God, whose Son today ascended to the heavens
as the Apostles looked on,
grant, we pray, that, in accordance with his promise,
we may be worthy for him to live with us always on earth,
and we with him in heaven.
Who lives and reigns with you
in the unity of the Holy Spirit,
one God, for ever and ever.

The Creed is said.

PRAYER AFTER COMMUNION

May the gifts we have received from your altar, Lord,
kindle in our hearts a longing for the heavenly homeland
and cause us to press forward,
following in the Savior's footsteps,
to the place where for our sake he entered before us.
Who lives and reigns for ever and ever.

A formula of Solemn Blessing, p. 314, may be used.

At the Mass during the Day

Entrance Antiphon

Men of Galilee, why gaze in wonder at the heavens?
This Jesus whom you saw ascending into heaven
will return as you saw him go, alleluia. Acts 1: 11

The Gloria in excelsis (Glory to God in the highest) is said.

COLLECT

Gladden us with holy joys, almighty God,
and make us rejoice with devout thanksgiving,
for the Ascension of Christ your Son
is our exaltation,
and, where the Head has gone before in glory,
the Body is called to follow in hope.
Through our Lord Jesus Christ, your Son,
who lives and reigns with you
in the unity of the Holy Spirit,
one God, for ever and ever.

Or:

Grant, we pray, almighty God,
that we, who believe that your Only Begotten Son,
our Redeemer,
ascended this day to the heavens,
may in spirit dwell already in heavenly realms.
Who lives and reigns with you
in the unity of the Holy Spirit,
one God, for ever and ever.

The Creed is said.

PRAYER AFTER COMMUNION

Almighty ever-living God,
who allow those on earth to celebrate divine mysteries,
grant, we pray,
that Christian hope may draw us onward
to where our nature is united with you.
Through Christ our Lord.

A formula of Solemn Blessing, p. 314, may be used.

THURSDAY

In regions where the Solemnity of the Ascension occurs on the following Sunday.

Entrance Antiphon

O God, when you went forth before your people,
marching with them and living among them,
the earth trembled, heavens poured down rain, alleluia.

Cf. Ps 68 (67): 8-9, 20

COLLECT

O God, who made your people
partakers in your redemption,
grant, we pray,
that we may perpetually render thanks
for the Resurrection of the Lord.
Who lives and reigns with you
in the unity of the Holy Spirit,
one God, for ever and ever.

PRAYER AFTER COMMUNION

Almighty ever-living God,
who restore us to eternal life
in the Resurrection of Christ,
increase in us, we pray, the fruits of this paschal Sacrament
and pour into our hearts the strength of this saving food.
Through Christ our Lord.

FRIDAY

Entrance Antiphon

You have redeemed us, Lord, by your Blood
from every tribe and tongue and people and nation,
and have made us into a kingdom, priests for our God, alleluia.
Rev 5: 9-10

COLLECT

O God, who restore us to eternal life
in the Resurrection of Christ,
raise us up, we pray, to the author of our salvation,
who is seated at your right hand,
so that, when our Savior comes again in majesty,
those you have given new birth in Baptism
may be clothed with blessed immortality.
Through our Lord Jesus Christ, your Son,
who lives and reigns with you
in the unity of the Holy Spirit,
one God, for ever and ever.

In regions where the Solemnity of the Ascension is celebrated on the following Sunday:

Hear our prayers, O Lord,
so that what was promised
by the sanctifying power of your Word
may everywhere be accomplished
through the working of the Gospel
and that all your adopted children may attain
what the testimony of truth has foretold.
Through our Lord Jesus Christ, your Son,
who lives and reigns with you
in the unity of the Holy Spirit,
one God, for ever and ever.

PRAYER AFTER COMMUNION

Keep safe, O Lord, we pray,
those whom you have saved by your kindness,
that, redeemed by the Passion of your Son,
they may rejoice in his Resurrection.
Who lives and reigns for ever and ever.

SATURDAY

Entrance Antiphon

O chosen people, proclaim the mighty works of him
who called you out of darkness into his wonderful light, alleluia.
Cf. 1 Pt 2: 9

COLLECT

O God, whose Son, at his Ascension to the heavens,
was pleased to promise the Holy Spirit to the Apostles,
grant, we pray,
that, just as they received manifold gifts
of heavenly teaching,
so on us, too, you may bestow spiritual gifts.
Through our Lord Jesus Christ, your Son,
who lives and reigns with you
in the unity of the Holy Spirit,
one God, for ever and ever.

In regions where the Solemnity of the Ascension is celebrated on the following Sunday:

Constantly shape our minds, we pray, O Lord,
by the practice of good works,
that, trying always for what is better,
we may strive to hold ever fast to the Paschal Mystery.
Through our Lord Jesus Christ, your Son,
who lives and reigns with you
in the unity of the Holy Spirit,
one God, for ever and ever.

PRAYER AFTER COMMUNION

We have partaken of the gifts of this sacred mystery,
humbly imploring, O Lord,
that what your Son commanded us to do in memory of him
may bring us growth in charity.
Through Christ our Lord.

SEVENTH SUNDAY OF EASTER

Entrance Antiphon

O Lord, hear my voice, for I have called to you;
of you my heart has spoken: Seek his face;
hide not your face from me, alleluia. Cf. Ps 27 (26): 7-9

The Gloria in excelsis (Glory to God in the highest) is said.

COLLECT

Graciously hear our supplications, O Lord,
so that we, who believe that the Savior of the human race
is with you in your glory,
may experience, as he promised,
until the end of the world,
his abiding presence among us.
Who lives and reigns with you
in the unity of the Holy Spirit,
one God, for ever and ever.

The Creed is said.

PRAYER AFTER COMMUNION

Hear us, O God our Savior,
and grant us confidence,
that through these sacred mysteries
there will be accomplished in the body
of the whole Church
what has already come to pass in Christ her Head.
Who lives and reigns for ever and ever.

A formula of Solemn Blessing, pp. 313-314, may be used.

MONDAY

Entrance Antiphon

You will receive the power of the Holy Spirit coming upon you,
and you will be my witnesses,
even to the ends of the earth, alleluia. Acts 1: 8

COLLECT

May the power of the Holy Spirit
come to us, we pray, O Lord,
that we may keep your will faithfully in mind
and express it in a devout way of life.
Through our Lord Jesus Christ, your Son,
who lives and reigns with you
in the unity of the Holy Spirit,
one God, for ever and ever.

PRAYER AFTER COMMUNION

Graciously be present to your people, we pray, O Lord,
and lead those you have imbued with heavenly mysteries
to pass from former ways to newness of life.
Through Christ our Lord.

TUESDAY

Entrance Antiphon

I am the first and the last,
I was dead and am now alive.
Behold, I am alive for ever and ever, alleluia. Rev 1: 17-18

COLLECT

Grant, we pray, almighty and merciful God,
that the Holy Spirit, coming near
and dwelling graciously within us,
may make of us a perfect temple of his glory.
Through our Lord Jesus Christ, your Son,
who lives and reigns with you
in the unity of the Holy Spirit,
one God, for ever and ever.

PRAYER AFTER COMMUNION

We have partaken of the gifts of this sacred mystery,
humbly imploring, O Lord,
that what your Son commanded us to do
in memory of him
may bring us growth in charity.
Through Christ our Lord.

WEDNESDAY

Entrance Antiphon

All peoples, clap your hands.
Cry to God with shouts of joy, alleluia. Ps 47 (46): 2

COLLECT

Graciously grant to your Church, O merciful God,
that, gathered by the Holy Spirit,
she may be devoted to you with all her heart
and united in purity of intent.
Through our Lord Jesus Christ, your Son,
who lives and reigns with you
in the unity of the Holy Spirit,
one God, for ever and ever.

PRAYER AFTER COMMUNION

May our partaking of this divine Sacrament, O Lord,
constantly increase your grace within us,
and, by cleansing us with its power,
make us always ready to receive so great a gift.
Through Christ our Lord.

THURSDAY

Entrance Antiphon

With boldness let us approach the throne of grace,
that we may receive mercy
and find grace as a timely help, alleluia. Heb 4: 16

COLLECT

May your Spirit, O Lord, we pray,
imbue us powerfully with spiritual gifts,
that he may give us a mind pleasing to you
and graciously conform us to your will.
Through our Lord Jesus Christ, your Son,
who lives and reigns with you
in the unity of the Holy Spirit,
one God, for ever and ever.

PRAYER AFTER COMMUNION

May the mysteries we have received, O Lord, we pray,
enlighten us by the instruction they bring
and restore us through our participation in them,
that we may merit the gifts of the Spirit.
Through Christ our Lord.

FRIDAY

Entrance Antiphon

Christ loved us and washed us clean of our sins by his Blood,
and made us into a kingdom,
priests for his God and Father, alleluia. Rev 1: 5-6

COLLECT

O God, who by the glorification of your Christ
and the light of the Holy Spirit
have unlocked for us the gates of eternity,
grant, we pray,
that, partaking of so great a gift,
our devotion may grow deeper
and our faith be strengthened.
Through our Lord Jesus Christ, your Son,
who lives and reigns with you
in the unity of the Holy Spirit,
one God, for ever and ever.

PRAYER AFTER COMMUNION

O God, by whose mysteries
we are cleansed and nourished,
grant, we pray,
that this banquet which you give us
may bring everlasting life.
Through Christ our Lord.

SATURDAY

At the Morning Mass

Entrance Antiphon

The disciples devoted themselves with one accord to prayer
with the women, and Mary the Mother of Jesus,
and his brethren, alleluia. Acts 1: 14

COLLECT

Grant, we pray, almighty God,
that we, who have celebrated the paschal festivities,
may by your gift hold fast to them
in the way that we live our lives.
Through our Lord Jesus Christ, your Son,
who lives and reigns with you
in the unity of the Holy Spirit,
one God, for ever and ever.

PRAYER AFTER COMMUNION

Hear in your compassion our prayers, O Lord,
that, as we have been brought
from things of the past to new mysteries,
so, with former ways left behind,
we may be made new in holiness of mind.
Through Christ our Lord.

PENTECOST SUNDAY

Solemnity

At the Vigil Mass

Extended form

This Vigil Mass may be celebrated on the Saturday evening, either before or after First Vespers (Evening Prayer I) of Pentecost Sunday.

1. In churches where the Vigil Mass is celebrated in an extended form, this may be done as follows.

2. a) If First Vespers (Evening Prayer I) celebrated in choir or in common immediately precede Mass, the celebration may begin either from the introductory verse and the hymn (Veni, creator Spiritus) or else from the singing of the Entrance Antiphon with the procession and greeting of the Priest; in either case the Penitential Act is omitted (cf. *General Instruction of the Liturgy of the Hours*, nos. 94 and 96).

Then the Psalmody prescribed for Vespers follows, up to but not including the Short Reading.

After the Psalmody, omitting the Penitential Act, and if appropriate, the Kyrie (Lord, have mercy), the Priest says the prayer Grant, we pray, almighty God, that the splendor, as at the Vigil Mass.

3. b) If Mass is begun in the usual way, after the Kyrie (Lord, have mercy), the Priest says the prayer Grant, we pray, almighty God, that the splendor, as at the Vigil Mass.

Then the Priest may address the people in these or similar words:

Dear brethren (brothers and sisters),
we have now begun our Pentecost Vigil,
after the example of the Apostles and disciples,
who with Mary, the Mother of Jesus, persevered in prayer,
awaiting the Spirit promised by the Lord;
like them, let us, too, listen with quiet hearts
to the Word of God.
Let us meditate on how many great deeds
God in times past did for his people
and let us pray that the Holy Spirit,
whom the Father sent as the first fruits
for those who believe,
may bring to perfection his work in the world.

4. Then follow the readings proposed as options in the Lectionary. A reader goes to the ambo and proclaims the reading. Afterwards a psalmist or a cantor sings or says the Psalm with the people making the response. Then all rise, the Priest says, Let us pray and, after all have prayed for a while in silence, he says the prayer corresponding to the reading. In place of the Responsorial Psalm a period of sacred silence may be observed, in which case the pause after Let us pray is omitted.

Prayers after the Readings

5. After the first reading (On Babel: Gn 11: 1-9) and the Psalm (33 [32]: 10-11, 12-13, 14-15; ℟. v. 12b).

Let us pray.

Grant, we pray, almighty God,
that your Church may always remain that holy people,
formed as one by the unity of Father, Son and Holy Spirit,
which manifests to the world
the Sacrament of your holiness and unity
and leads it to the perfection of your charity.
Through Christ our Lord.
℟. Amen.

6. After the second reading (On God's Descent on Mount Sinai: Ex 19: 3-8, 16-20b) and the canticle (Dn 3: 52, 53, 54, 55, 56; ℟. v. 52b) or the Psalm (19 [18]: 8, 9, 10, 11; ℟. Jn 6: 68c).

Let us pray.

O God, who in fire and lightning
gave the ancient Law to Moses on Mount Sinai
and on this day manifested the new covenant
in the fire of the Spirit,
grant, we pray,
that we may always be aflame with that same Spirit
whom you wondrously poured out on your Apostles,
and that the new Israel,
gathered from every people,
may receive with rejoicing
the eternal commandment of your love.
Through Christ our Lord.
℟. Amen.

7. After the third reading (On the dry bones and God's spirit: Ez 37: 1-14) and the Psalm (107 [106]: 2-3, 4-5, 6-7, 8-9; ℟. v. 1 or Alleluia).

Let us pray.

Lord, God of power,
who restore what has fallen
and preserve what you have restored,
increase, we pray, the peoples
to be renewed by the sanctification of your name,

that all who are washed clean by holy Baptism
may always be directed by your prompting.
Through Christ our Lord.
℟. Amen.

Or:

O God, who have brought us to rebirth by the word of life,
pour out upon us your Holy Spirit,
that, walking in oneness of faith,
we may attain in our flesh
the incorruptible glory of the resurrection.
Through Christ our Lord.
℟. Amen.

Or:

May your people exult for ever, O God,
in renewed youthfulness of spirit,
so that, rejoicing now in the restored glory of our adoption,
we may look forward in confident hope
to the rejoicing of the day of resurrection.
Through Christ our Lord.
℟. Amen.

8. After the fourth reading (On the outpouring of the Spirit: Joel 3: 1-5) and the Psalm (104 [103]: 1-2a, 24, 35c, 27-28, 29bc-30; ℟. v. 30 or Alleluia).

Let us pray.

Fulfill for us your gracious promise,
O Lord, we pray, so that by his coming
the Holy Spirit may make us witnesses before the world
to the Gospel of our Lord Jesus Christ.
Who lives and reigns for ever and ever.
℟. Amen.

9. Then the Priest intones the hymn Gloria in excelsis Deo (Glory to God in the highest).

10. When the hymn is concluded, the Priest says the Collect in the usual way: Almighty ever-living God, who willed, as here below.

11. Then the reader proclaims the reading from the Apostle (Rom 8: 22-27), and Mass continues in the usual way.

12. If Vespers (Evening Prayer) are joined to Mass, after Communion with the Communion Antiphon (On the last day), the Magnificat is sung, with its Vespers antiphon (Veni, Sancte Spiritus); then the Prayer after Communion is said and the rest follows as usual.

13. It is appropriate that the formula of Solemn Blessing be used, p. 314.

To dismiss the people the Deacon or, if there is no Deacon, the Priest himself sings or says:

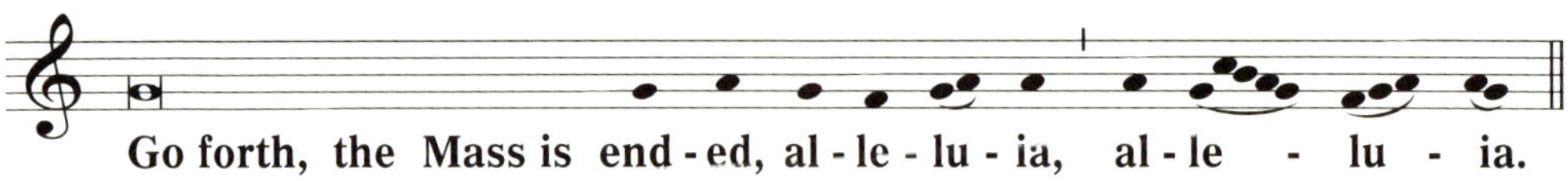

Or:

And the people reply:

At the Vigil Mass

Simple form

This Mass is used on the Saturday evening, either before or after First Vespers (Evening Prayer I) of Pentecost Sunday.

Entrance Antiphon

The love of God has been poured into our hearts
through the Spirit of God dwelling within us, alleluia.

Rom 5: 5; cf. 8: 11

The Gloria in excelsis (Glory to God in the highest) is said.

COLLECT

Almighty ever-living God,
who willed the Paschal Mystery
to be encompassed as a sign in fifty days,
grant that from out of the scattered nations
the confusion of many tongues
may be gathered by heavenly grace
into one great confession of your name.
Through our Lord Jesus Christ, your Son,
who lives and reigns with you
in the unity of the Holy Spirit,
one God, for ever and ever.

Or:

Grant, we pray, almighty God,
that the splendor of your glory
may shine forth upon us
and that, by the bright rays of the Holy Spirit,
the light of your light may confirm the hearts
of those born again by your grace.
Through our Lord Jesus Christ, your Son,
who lives and reigns with you
in the unity of the Holy Spirit,
one God, for ever and ever.

The Creed is said.

PRAYER AFTER COMMUNION

May these gifts we have consumed
benefit us, O Lord,
that we may always be aflame with the same Spirit,
whom you wondrously poured out on your Apostles.
Through Christ our Lord.

A formula of Solemn Blessing, p. 314, may be used.

To dismiss the people the Deacon or, if there is no Deacon, the Priest himself sings (as above p. 248) or says:

Go forth, the Mass is ended, alleluia, alleluia.

Or:

Go in peace, alleluia, alleluia.

And the people reply:

Thanks be to God, alleluia, alleluia.

At the Mass during the Day

Entrance Antiphon

The Spirit of the Lord has filled the whole world
and that which contains all things
understands what is said, alleluia. Wis 1: 7

Or:

The love of God has been poured into our hearts
through the Spirit of God dwelling within us, alleluia.
Rom 5: 5; cf. 8: 11

The Gloria in excelsis (Glory to God in the highest) is said.

COLLECT

O God, who by the mystery of today's great feast
sanctify your whole Church in every people and nation,
pour out, we pray, the gifts of the Holy Spirit
across the face of the earth
and, with the divine grace that was at work
when the Gospel was first proclaimed,
fill now once more the hearts of believers.
Through our Lord Jesus Christ, your Son,
who lives and reigns with you
in the unity of the Holy Spirit,
one God, for ever and ever.

The Creed is said.

PRAYER AFTER COMMUNION

O God, who bestow heavenly gifts upon your Church,
safeguard, we pray, the grace you have given,
that the gift of the Holy Spirit poured out upon her
may retain all its force
and that this spiritual food
may gain her abundance of eternal redemption.
Through Christ our Lord.

A formula of Solemn Blessing, p. 314, may be used.

To dismiss the people the Deacon or, if there is no Deacon, the Priest himself sings or says:

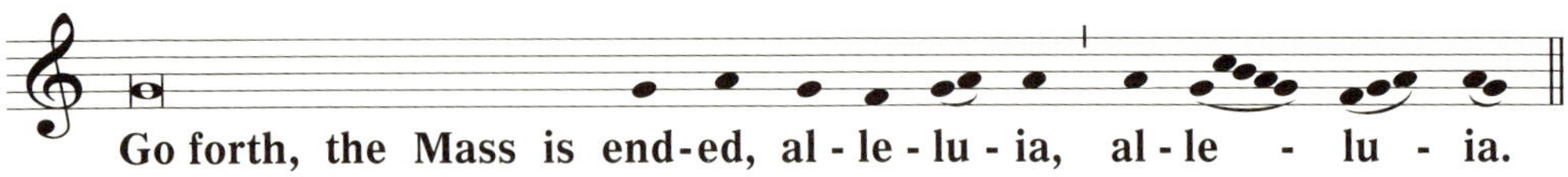

Or:

And the people reply:

Go forth, the Mass is ended, alleluia, alleluia.

Or:

Go in peace, alleluia, alleluia.

And the people reply:

Thanks be to God, alleluia, alleluia.

With Easter Time now concluded, the paschal candle is extinguished. It is desirable to keep the paschal candle in the baptistery with due honor so that it is lit at the celebration of Baptism and the candles of those baptized are lit from it.

Where the Monday or Tuesday after Pentecost are days on which the faithful are obliged or accustomed to attend Mass, the Mass of Pentecost Sunday may be repeated, or a Mass of the Holy Spirit, pp. 673-675, may be said.

ORDINARY TIME

1. Ordinary Time contains thirty-three or thirty-four weeks. It begins on the Monday following the Sunday after January 6 and continues until the beginning of Lent; it begins again on the Monday after Pentecost Sunday and ends on the Saturday before the First Sunday of Advent.

2. The numbering of Sundays and weeks in Ordinary Time is calculated as follows:

a) The Sunday on which the Feast of the Baptism of the Lord occurs takes the place of the first Sunday in Ordinary Time; the week that follows is counted as the first week in Ordinary Time. The remaining Sundays and weeks are numbered in order until the beginning of Lent.

b) If there are thirty-four weeks in Ordinary Time, after Pentecost the series is resumed with the week that follows immediately the last week celebrated before Lent; it should be noted, however, that the Masses of Pentecost Sunday and of the Solemnity of the Most Holy Trinity take the place of the Sunday Masses. If, however, there are thirty-three weeks in Ordinary Time, the first week that would otherwise follow Pentecost is omitted.

3. Thus, in the Missal, thirty-four Masses for the Sundays and weekdays in Ordinary Time are found. They are used in this way:

a) On Sundays the Mass corresponding to the number of the Sunday in Ordinary Time is ordinarily used, unless there occurs a Solemnity or a Feast of the Lord which takes the place of the Sunday.

b) On weekdays, however, any of the thirty-four Masses may be used, provided the pastoral needs of the faithful are taken into consideration.

4. The Gloria in excelsis (Glory to God in the highest) and the Creed are said on Sundays; on weekdays, however, both are omitted.

5. Unless a Eucharistic Prayer is used that has a proper Preface, on Sundays one of the Prefaces for Sundays in Ordinary Time is said; but on weekdays, a Common Preface is said.

6. Two antiphons are provided for Communion, the first from the Psalms, and the second for the most part from the Gospel. One or the other may be selected, as circumstances suggest, but preference should be given to an antiphon that is in harmony with the Gospel of the Mass.

SUNDAY AND DAILY MASSES

FIRST WEEK IN ORDINARY TIME

On the first Sunday in Ordinary Time there occurs the Feast of the Baptism of the Lord, pp. 52-53.

Entrance Antiphon

Upon a lofty throne, I saw a man seated,
whom a host of angels adore, singing in unison:
Behold him, the name of whose empire is eternal.

COLLECT

Attend to the pleas of your people with heavenly care,
O Lord, we pray,
that they may see what must be done
and gain strength to do what they have seen.
Through our Lord Jesus Christ, your Son,
who lives and reigns with you
in the unity of the Holy Spirit,
one God, for ever and ever.

PRAYER AFTER COMMUNION

Humbly we ask you, almighty God,
be graciously pleased to grant
that those you renew with your Sacraments
may also serve with lives pleasing to you.
Through Christ our Lord.

SECOND SUNDAY IN ORDINARY TIME

Entrance Antiphon

**All the earth shall bow down before you, O God,
and shall sing to you,
shall sing to your name, O Most High!** Ps 66 (65): 4

COLLECT

**Almighty ever-living God,
who govern all things,
both in heaven and on earth,
mercifully hear the pleading of your people
and bestow your peace on our times.
Through our Lord Jesus Christ, your Son,
who lives and reigns with you
in the unity of the Holy Spirit,
one God, for ever and ever.**

PRAYER AFTER COMMUNION

**Pour on us, O Lord, the Spirit of your love,
and in your kindness
make those you have nourished
by this one heavenly Bread
one in mind and heart.
Through Christ our Lord.**

THIRD SUNDAY IN ORDINARY TIME

Entrance Antiphon

O sing a new song to the Lord;
sing to the Lord, all the earth.
In his presence are majesty and splendor,
strength and honor in his holy place. Cf. Ps 96 (95): 1, 6

COLLECT

Almighty ever-living God,
direct our actions according to your good pleasure,
that in the name of your beloved Son
we may abound in good works.
Through our Lord Jesus Christ, your Son,
who lives and reigns with you
in the unity of the Holy Spirit,
one God, for ever and ever.

PRAYER AFTER COMMUNION

Grant, we pray, almighty God,
that, receiving the grace
by which you bring us to new life,
we may always glory in your gift.
Through Christ our Lord.

FOURTH SUNDAY IN ORDINARY TIME

Entrance Antiphon

Save us, O Lord our God!
And gather us from the nations,
to give thanks to your holy name,
and make it our glory to praise you. Ps 106 (105): 47

COLLECT

Grant us, Lord our God,
that we may honor you with all our mind,
and love everyone in truth of heart.
Through our Lord Jesus Christ, your Son,
who lives and reigns with you
in the unity of the Holy Spirit,
one God, for ever and ever.

PRAYER AFTER COMMUNION

Nourished by these redeeming gifts,
we pray, O Lord,
that through this help to eternal salvation
true faith may ever increase.
Through Christ our Lord.

FIFTH SUNDAY IN ORDINARY TIME

Entrance Antiphon

O come, let us worship God
and bow low before the God who made us,
for he is the Lord our God. Ps 95 (94): 6-7

COLLECT

Keep your family safe, O Lord, with unfailing care,
that, relying solely on the hope of heavenly grace,
they may be defended always by your protection.
Through our Lord Jesus Christ, your Son,
who lives and reigns with you
in the unity of the Holy Spirit,
one God, for ever and ever.

PRAYER AFTER COMMUNION

O God, who have willed that we be partakers
in the one Bread and the one Chalice,
grant us, we pray, so to live
that, made one in Christ,
we may joyfully bear fruit
for the salvation of the world.
Through Christ our Lord.

SIXTH SUNDAY IN ORDINARY TIME

Entrance Antiphon

Be my protector, O God,
a mighty stronghold to save me.
For you are my rock, my stronghold!
Lead me, guide me, for the sake of your name.

Cf. Ps 31 (30): 3-4

COLLECT

O God, who teach us that you abide
in hearts that are just and true,
grant that we may be so fashioned by your grace
as to become a dwelling pleasing to you.
Through our Lord Jesus Christ, your Son,
who lives and reigns with you
in the unity of the Holy Spirit,
one God, for ever and ever.

PRAYER AFTER COMMUNION

Having fed upon these heavenly delights,
we pray, O Lord,
that we may always long
for that food by which we truly live.
Through Christ our Lord.

SEVENTH SUNDAY IN ORDINARY TIME

Entrance Antiphon

O Lord, I trust in your merciful love.
My heart will rejoice in your salvation.
I will sing to the Lord who has been bountiful with me.

Ps 13 (12): 6

COLLECT

Grant, we pray, almighty God,
that, always pondering spiritual things,
we may carry out in both word and deed
that which is pleasing to you.
Through our Lord Jesus Christ, your Son,
who lives and reigns with you
in the unity of the Holy Spirit,
one God, for ever and ever.

PRAYER AFTER COMMUNION

Grant, we pray, almighty God,
that we may experience the effects of the salvation
which is pledged to us by these mysteries.
Through Christ our Lord.

EIGHTH SUNDAY IN ORDINARY TIME

Entrance Antiphon

The Lord became my protector.
He brought me out to a place of freedom;
he saved me because he delighted in me. Cf. Ps 18 (17): 19-20

COLLECT

Grant us, O Lord, we pray,
that the course of our world
may be directed by your peaceful rule
and that your Church may rejoice,
untroubled in her devotion.
Through our Lord Jesus Christ, your Son,
who lives and reigns with you
in the unity of the Holy Spirit,
one God, for ever and ever.

PRAYER AFTER COMMUNION

Nourished by your saving gifts,
we beseech your mercy, Lord,
that by this same Sacrament
with which you feed us in the present age,
you may make us partakers of life eternal.
Through Christ our Lord.

NINTH SUNDAY IN ORDINARY TIME

Entrance Antiphon

Turn to me and have mercy on me, O Lord,
for I am alone and poor.
See my lowliness and suffering
and take away all my sins, my God. Cf. Ps 25 (24): 16, 18

COLLECT

**O God, whose providence never fails in its design,
keep from us, we humbly beseech you,
all that might harm us
and grant all that works for our good.
Through our Lord Jesus Christ, your Son,
who lives and reigns with you
in the unity of the Holy Spirit,
one God, for ever and ever.**

PRAYER AFTER COMMUNION

**Govern by your Spirit, we pray, O Lord,
those you feed with the Body and Blood of your Son,
that, professing you not just in word or in speech,
but also in works and in truth,
we may merit to enter the Kingdom of Heaven.
Through Christ our Lord.**

TENTH SUNDAY IN ORDINARY TIME

Entrance Antiphon

The Lord is my light and my salvation; whom shall I fear?
The Lord is the stronghold of my life; whom should I dread?
When those who do evil draw near, they stumble and fall.
Cf. Ps 27 (26): 1-2

COLLECT

O God, from whom all good things come,
grant that we, who call on you in our need,
may at your prompting discern what is right,
and by your guidance do it.
Through our Lord Jesus Christ, your Son,
who lives and reigns with you
in the unity of the Holy Spirit,
one God, for ever and ever.

PRAYER AFTER COMMUNION

May your healing work, O Lord,
free us, we pray, from doing evil
and lead us to what is right.
Through Christ our Lord.

ELEVENTH SUNDAY IN ORDINARY TIME

Entrance Antiphon

O Lord, hear my voice, for I have called to you; be my help.
Do not abandon or forsake me, O God, my Savior!
Cf. Ps 27 (26): 7, 9

COLLECT

O God, strength of those who hope in you,
graciously hear our pleas,
and, since without you mortal frailty can do nothing,
grant us always the help of your grace,
that in following your commands
we may please you by our resolve and our deeds.
Through our Lord Jesus Christ, your Son,
who lives and reigns with you
in the unity of the Holy Spirit,
one God, for ever and ever.

PRAYER AFTER COMMUNION

As this reception of your Holy Communion, O Lord,
foreshadows the union of the faithful in you,
so may it bring about unity in your Church.
Through Christ our Lord.

TWELFTH SUNDAY IN ORDINARY TIME

Entrance Antiphon

The Lord is the strength of his people,
a saving refuge for the one he has anointed.
Save your people, Lord, and bless your heritage,
and govern them for ever. Cf. Ps 28 (27): 8-9

COLLECT

Grant, O Lord,
that we may always revere and love your holy name,
for you never deprive of your guidance
those you set firm on the foundation of your love.
Through our Lord Jesus Christ, your Son,
who lives and reigns with you
in the unity of the Holy Spirit,
one God, for ever and ever.

PRAYER AFTER COMMUNION

Renewed and nourished
by the Sacred Body and Precious Blood of your Son,
we ask of your mercy, O Lord,
that what we celebrate with constant devotion
may be our sure pledge of redemption.
Through Christ our Lord.

THIRTEENTH SUNDAY IN ORDINARY TIME

Entrance Antiphon

All peoples, clap your hands.
Cry to God with shouts of joy! Ps 47 (46): 2

COLLECT

O God, who through the grace of adoption
chose us to be children of light,
grant, we pray,
that we may not be wrapped in the darkness of error
but always be seen to stand in the bright light of truth.
Through our Lord Jesus Christ, your Son,
who lives and reigns with you
in the unity of the Holy Spirit,
one God, for ever and ever.

PRAYER AFTER COMMUNION

May this divine sacrifice we have offered and received
fill us with life, O Lord, we pray,
so that, bound to you in lasting charity,
we may bear fruit that lasts for ever.
Through Christ our Lord.

FOURTEENTH SUNDAY IN ORDINARY TIME

Entrance Antiphon

Your merciful love, O God,
we have received in the midst of your temple.
Your praise, O God, like your name,
reaches the ends of the earth;
your right hand is filled with saving justice. Cf. Ps 48 (47): 10-11

COLLECT

O God, who in the abasement of your Son
have raised up a fallen world,
fill your faithful with holy joy,
for on those you have rescued from slavery to sin
you bestow eternal gladness.
Through our Lord Jesus Christ, your Son,
who lives and reigns with you
in the unity of the Holy Spirit,
one God, for ever and ever.

PRAYER AFTER COMMUNION

Grant, we pray, O Lord,
that, having been replenished by such great gifts,
we may gain the prize of salvation
and never cease to praise you.
Through Christ our Lord.

FIFTEENTH SUNDAY IN ORDINARY TIME

Entrance Antiphon

As for me, in justice I shall behold your face;
I shall be filled with the vision of your glory. Cf. Ps 17 (16): 15

COLLECT

O God, who show the light of your truth
to those who go astray,
so that they may return to the right path,
give all who for the faith they profess
are accounted Christians
the grace to reject whatever is contrary
to the name of Christ
and to strive after all that does it honor.
Through our Lord Jesus Christ, your Son,
who lives and reigns with you
in the unity of the Holy Spirit,
one God, for ever and ever.

PRAYER AFTER COMMUNION

Having consumed these gifts, we pray, O Lord,
that, by our participation in this mystery,
its saving effects upon us may grow.
Through Christ our Lord.

SIXTEENTH SUNDAY IN ORDINARY TIME

Entrance Antiphon

See, I have God for my help.
The Lord sustains my soul.
I will sacrifice to you with willing heart,
and praise your name, O Lord, for it is good. Ps 54 (53): 6, 8

COLLECT

Show favor, O Lord, to your servants
and mercifully increase the gifts of your grace,
that, made fervent in hope, faith and charity,
they may be ever watchful in keeping your commands.
Through our Lord Jesus Christ, your Son,
who lives and reigns with you
in the unity of the Holy Spirit,
one God, for ever and ever.

PRAYER AFTER COMMUNION

Graciously be present to your people, we pray, O Lord,
and lead those you have imbued with heavenly mysteries
to pass from former ways to newness of life.
Through Christ our Lord.

SEVENTEENTH SUNDAY IN ORDINARY TIME

Entrance Antiphon

God is in his holy place,
God who unites those who dwell in his house;
he himself gives might and strength to his people.

Cf. Ps 68 (67): 6-7, 36

COLLECT

O God, protector of those who hope in you,
without whom nothing has firm foundation,
nothing is holy,
bestow in abundance your mercy upon us
and grant that, with you as our ruler and guide,
we may use the good things that pass
in such a way as to hold fast even now
to those that ever endure.
Through our Lord Jesus Christ, your Son,
who lives and reigns with you
in the unity of the Holy Spirit,
one God, for ever and ever.

PRAYER AFTER COMMUNION

We have consumed, O Lord, this divine Sacrament,
the perpetual memorial of the Passion of your Son;
grant, we pray, that this gift,
which he himself gave us with love beyond all telling,
may profit us for salvation.
Through Christ our Lord.

EIGHTEENTH SUNDAY IN ORDINARY TIME

Entrance Antiphon

O God, come to my assistance;
O Lord, make haste to help me!
You are my rescuer, my help;
O Lord, do not delay. Ps 70 (69): 2, 6

COLLECT

Draw near to your servants, O Lord,
and answer their prayers with unceasing kindness,
that, for those who glory in you as their Creator and guide,
you may restore what you have created
and keep safe what you have restored.
Through our Lord Jesus Christ, your Son,
who lives and reigns with you
in the unity of the Holy Spirit,
one God, for ever and ever.

PRAYER AFTER COMMUNION

Accompany with constant protection, O Lord,
those you renew with these heavenly gifts
and, in your never-failing care for them,
make them worthy of eternal redemption.
Through Christ our Lord.

NINETEENTH SUNDAY IN ORDINARY TIME

Entrance Antiphon

Look to your covenant, O Lord,
and forget not the life of your poor ones for ever.
Arise, O God, and defend your cause,
and forget not the cries of those who seek you.

Cf. Ps 74 (73): 20, 19, 22, 23

COLLECT

Almighty ever-living God,
whom, taught by the Holy Spirit,
we dare to call our Father,
bring, we pray, to perfection in our hearts
the spirit of adoption as your sons and daughters,
that we may merit to enter into the inheritance
which you have promised.
Through our Lord Jesus Christ, your Son,
who lives and reigns with you
in the unity of the Holy Spirit,
one God, for ever and ever.

PRAYER AFTER COMMUNION

May the communion in your Sacrament
that we have consumed, save us, O Lord,
and confirm us in the light of your truth.
Through Christ our Lord.

TWENTIETH SUNDAY IN ORDINARY TIME

Entrance Antiphon

Turn your eyes, O God, our shield;
and look on the face of your anointed one;
one day within your courts
is better than a thousand elsewhere. Ps 84 (83): 10-11

COLLECT

O God, who have prepared for those who love you
good things which no eye can see,
fill our hearts, we pray, with the warmth of your love,
so that, loving you in all things and above all things,
we may attain your promises,
which surpass every human desire.
Through our Lord Jesus Christ, your Son,
who lives and reigns with you
in the unity of the Holy Spirit,
one God, for ever and ever.

PRAYER AFTER COMMUNION

Made partakers of Christ through these Sacraments,
we humbly implore your mercy, Lord,
that, conformed to his image on earth,
we may merit also to be his coheirs in heaven.
Who lives and reigns for ever and ever.

TWENTY-FIRST SUNDAY IN ORDINARY TIME

Entrance Antiphon

Turn your ear, O Lord, and answer me;
save the servant who trusts in you, my God.
Have mercy on me, O Lord, for I cry to you all the day long.
Cf. Ps 86 (85): 1-3

COLLECT

O God, who cause the minds of the faithful
to unite in a single purpose,
grant your people to love what you command
and to desire what you promise,
that, amid the uncertainties of this world,
our hearts may be fixed on that place
where true gladness is found.
Through our Lord Jesus Christ, your Son,
who lives and reigns with you
in the unity of the Holy Spirit,
one God, for ever and ever.

PRAYER AFTER COMMUNION

Complete within us, O Lord, we pray,
the healing work of your mercy
and graciously perfect and sustain us,
so that in all things we may please you.
Through Christ our Lord.

TWENTY-SECOND SUNDAY IN ORDINARY TIME

Entrance Antiphon

Have mercy on me, O Lord, for I cry to you all the day long.
O Lord, you are good and forgiving,
full of mercy to all who call to you. Cf. Ps 86 (85): 3, 5

COLLECT

God of might, giver of every good gift,
put into our hearts the love of your name,
so that, by deepening our sense of reverence,
you may nurture in us what is good
and, by your watchful care,
keep safe what you have nurtured.
Through our Lord Jesus Christ, your Son,
who lives and reigns with you
in the unity of the Holy Spirit,
one God, for ever and ever.

PRAYER AFTER COMMUNION

Renewed by this bread from the heavenly table,
we beseech you, Lord,
that, being the food of charity,
it may confirm our hearts
and stir us to serve you in our neighbor.
Through Christ our Lord.

TWENTY-THIRD SUNDAY IN ORDINARY TIME

Entrance Antiphon

You are just, O Lord, and your judgment is right;
treat your servant in accord with your merciful love.
Ps 119 (118): 137, 124

COLLECT

O God, by whom we are redeemed and receive adoption,
look graciously upon your beloved sons and daughters,
that those who believe in Christ
may receive true freedom
and an everlasting inheritance.
Through our Lord Jesus Christ, your Son,
who lives and reigns with you
in the unity of the Holy Spirit,
one God, for ever and ever.

PRAYER AFTER COMMUNION

Grant that your faithful, O Lord,
whom you nourish and endow with life
through the food of your Word and heavenly Sacrament,
may so benefit from your beloved Son's great gifts
that we may merit an eternal share in his life.
Who lives and reigns for ever and ever.

TWENTY-FOURTH SUNDAY IN ORDINARY TIME

Entrance Antiphon

Give peace, O Lord, to those who wait for you,
that your prophets be found true.
Hear the prayers of your servant,
and of your people Israel. Cf. Sir 36: 18

COLLECT

Look upon us, O God,
Creator and ruler of all things,
and, that we may feel the working of your mercy,
grant that we may serve you with all our heart.
Through our Lord Jesus Christ, your Son,
who lives and reigns with you
in the unity of the Holy Spirit,
one God, for ever and ever.

PRAYER AFTER COMMUNION

May the working of this heavenly gift, O Lord, we pray,
take possession of our minds and bodies,
so that its effects, and not our own desires,
may always prevail in us.
Through Christ our Lord.

TWENTY-FIFTH SUNDAY IN ORDINARY TIME

Entrance Antiphon

I am the salvation of the people, says the Lord.
Should they cry to me in any distress,
I will hear them, and I will be their Lord for ever.

COLLECT

O God, who founded all the commands of your sacred Law
upon love of you and of our neighbor,
grant that, by keeping your precepts,
we may merit to attain eternal life.
Through our Lord Jesus Christ, your Son,
who lives and reigns with you
in the unity of the Holy Spirit,
one God, for ever and ever.

PRAYER AFTER COMMUNION

Graciously raise up, O Lord,
those you renew with this Sacrament,
that we may come to possess your redemption
both in mystery and in the manner of our life.
Through Christ our Lord.

TWENTY-SIXTH SUNDAY IN ORDINARY TIME

Entrance Antiphon

All that you have done to us, O Lord,
you have done with true judgment,
for we have sinned against you
and not obeyed your commandments.
But give glory to your name
and deal with us according to the bounty of your mercy.
Dn 3: 31, 29, 30, 43, 42

COLLECT

O God, who manifest your almighty power
above all by pardoning and showing mercy,
bestow, we pray, your grace abundantly upon us
and make those hastening to attain your promises
heirs to the treasures of heaven.
Through our Lord Jesus Christ, your Son,
who lives and reigns with you
in the unity of the Holy Spirit,
one God, for ever and ever.

PRAYER AFTER COMMUNION

May this heavenly mystery, O Lord,
restore us in mind and body,
that we may be coheirs in glory with Christ,
to whose suffering we are united
whenever we proclaim his Death.
Who lives and reigns for ever and ever.

TWENTY-SEVENTH SUNDAY IN ORDINARY TIME

Entrance Antiphon

Within your will, O Lord, all things are established,
and there is none that can resist your will.
For you have made all things, the heaven and the earth,
and all that is held within the circle of heaven;
you are the Lord of all. Cf. Est 4: 17

COLLECT

Almighty ever-living God,
who in the abundance of your kindness
surpass the merits and the desires of those
who entreat you,
pour out your mercy upon us
to pardon what conscience dreads
and to give what prayer does not dare to ask.
Through our Lord Jesus Christ, your Son,
who lives and reigns with you
in the unity of the Holy Spirit,
one God, for ever and ever.

PRAYER AFTER COMMUNION

Grant us, almighty God,
that we may be refreshed and nourished
by the Sacrament which we have received,
so as to be transformed into what we consume.
Through Christ our Lord.

TWENTY-EIGHTH SUNDAY IN ORDINARY TIME

Entrance Antiphon

If you, O Lord, should mark iniquities,
Lord, who could stand?
But with you is found forgiveness,
O God of Israel. Ps 130 (129): 3-4

COLLECT

May your grace, O Lord, we pray,
at all times go before us and follow after
and make us always determined
to carry out good works.
Through our Lord Jesus Christ, your Son,
who lives and reigns with you
in the unity of the Holy Spirit,
one God, for ever and ever.

PRAYER AFTER COMMUNION

We entreat your majesty most humbly, O Lord,
that, as you feed us with the nourishment
which comes from the most holy Body and Blood
of your Son,
so you may make us sharers of his divine nature.
Who lives and reigns for ever and ever.

TWENTY-NINTH SUNDAY IN ORDINARY TIME

Entrance Antiphon

To you I call; for you will surely heed me, O God;
turn your ear to me; hear my words.
Guard me as the apple of your eye;
in the shadow of your wings protect me. Cf. Ps 17 (16): 6, 8

COLLECT

Almighty ever-living God,
grant that we may always conform our will to yours
and serve your majesty in sincerity of heart.
Through our Lord Jesus Christ, your Son,
who lives and reigns with you
in the unity of the Holy Spirit,
one God, for ever and ever.

PRAYER AFTER COMMUNION

Grant, O Lord, we pray,
that, benefiting from participation in heavenly things,
we may be helped by what you give in this present age
and prepared for the gifts that are eternal.
Through Christ our Lord.

THIRTIETH SUNDAY IN ORDINARY TIME

Entrance Antiphon

Let the hearts that seek the Lord rejoice;
turn to the Lord and his strength;
constantly seek his face. Cf. Ps 105 (104): 3-4

COLLECT

Almighty ever-living God,
increase our faith, hope and charity,
and make us love what you command,
so that we may merit what you promise.
Through our Lord Jesus Christ, your Son,
who lives and reigns with you
in the unity of the Holy Spirit,
one God, for ever and ever.

PRAYER AFTER COMMUNION

May your Sacraments, O Lord, we pray,
perfect in us what lies within them,
that what we now celebrate in signs
we may one day possess in truth.
Through Christ our Lord.

THIRTY-FIRST SUNDAY IN ORDINARY TIME

Entrance Antiphon

Forsake me not, O Lord, my God;
be not far from me!
Make haste and come to my help,
O Lord, my strong salvation!
Cf. Ps 38 (37): 22-23

COLLECT

Almighty and merciful God,
by whose gift your faithful offer you
right and praiseworthy service,
grant, we pray,
that we may hasten without stumbling
to receive the things you have promised.
Through our Lord Jesus Christ, your Son,
who lives and reigns with you
in the unity of the Holy Spirit,
one God, for ever and ever.

PRAYER AFTER COMMUNION

May the working of your power, O Lord,
increase in us, we pray,
so that, renewed by these heavenly Sacraments,
we may be prepared by your gift
for receiving what they promise.
Through Christ our Lord.

THIRTY-SECOND SUNDAY IN ORDINARY TIME

Entrance Antiphon

Let my prayer come into your presence.
Incline your ear to my cry for help, O Lord. Cf. Ps 88 (87): 3

COLLECT

Almighty and merciful God,
graciously keep from us all adversity,
so that, unhindered in mind and body alike,
we may pursue in freedom of heart
the things that are yours.
Through our Lord Jesus Christ, your Son,
who lives and reigns with you
in the unity of the Holy Spirit,
one God, for ever and ever.

PRAYER AFTER COMMUNION

Nourished by this sacred gift, O Lord,
we give you thanks and beseech your mercy,
that, by the pouring forth of your Spirit,
the grace of integrity may endure
in those your heavenly power has entered.
Through Christ our Lord.

THIRTY-THIRD SUNDAY IN ORDINARY TIME

Entrance Antiphon

The Lord said: I think thoughts of peace and not of affliction.
You will call upon me, and I will answer you,
and I will lead back your captives from every place.
Jer 29: 11, 12, 14

COLLECT

Grant us, we pray, O Lord our God,
the constant gladness of being devoted to you,
for it is full and lasting happiness
to serve with constancy
the author of all that is good.
Through our Lord Jesus Christ, your Son,
who lives and reigns with you
in the unity of the Holy Spirit,
one God, for ever and ever.

PRAYER AFTER COMMUNION

We have partaken of the gifts of this sacred mystery,
humbly imploring, O Lord,
that what your Son commanded us to do
in memory of him
may bring us growth in charity.
Through Christ our Lord.

THIRTY-FOURTH WEEK IN ORDINARY TIME

On the last Sunday in Ordinary Time there occurs the Solemnity of Our Lord Jesus Christ, King of the Universe, p. 288.

Entrance Antiphon

The Lord speaks of peace to his people and his holy ones
and to those who turn to him. Cf. Ps 85 (84): 9

COLLECT

Stir up the will of your faithful, we pray, O Lord,
that, striving more eagerly
to bring your divine work to fruitful completion,
they may receive in greater measure
the healing remedies your kindness bestows.
Through our Lord Jesus Christ, your Son,
who lives and reigns with you
in the unity of the Holy Spirit,
one God, for ever and ever.

PRAYER AFTER COMMUNION

We pray, almighty God,
that those to whom you give the joy
of participating in divine mysteries
may never be parted from you.
Through Christ our Lord.

THE SOLEMNITIES OF THE LORD DURING ORDINARY TIME

First Sunday after Pentecost

THE MOST HOLY TRINITY

Solemnity

Entrance Antiphon

**Blest be God the Father,
and the Only Begotten Son of God,
and also the Holy Spirit,
for he has shown us his merciful love.**

The *Gloria in excelsis* (Glory to God in the highest) is said.

COLLECT

**God our Father, who by sending into the world
the Word of truth and the Spirit of sanctification
made known to the human race your wondrous mystery,
grant us, we pray, that in professing the true faith,
we may acknowledge the Trinity of eternal glory
and adore your Unity, powerful in majesty.
Through our Lord Jesus Christ, your Son,
who lives and reigns with you
in the unity of the Holy Spirit,
one God, for ever and ever.**

The Creed is said.

PRAYER AFTER COMMUNION

**May receiving this Sacrament, O Lord our God,
bring us health of body and soul,
as we confess your eternal holy Trinity
and undivided Unity.
Through Christ our Lord.**

[In the Dioceses of the United States]
Sunday after the Most Holy Trinity

THE MOST HOLY BODY AND BLOOD OF CHRIST (CORPUS CHRISTI)

Solemnity

Entrance Antiphon

He fed them with the finest wheat
and satisfied them with honey from the rock. Cf. Ps 81 (80): 17

The Gloria in excelsis (Glory to God in the highest) is said.

COLLECT

O God, who in this wonderful Sacrament
have left us a memorial of your Passion,
grant us, we pray,
so to revere the sacred mysteries of your Body and Blood
that we may always experience in ourselves
the fruits of your redemption.
Who live and reign with God the Father
in the unity of the Holy Spirit,
one God, for ever and ever.

The Creed is said.

PRAYER AFTER COMMUNION

Grant, O Lord, we pray,
that we may delight for all eternity
in that share in your divine life,
which is foreshadowed in the present age
by our reception of your precious Body and Blood.
Who live and reign for ever and ever.

It is desirable that a procession take place after the Mass in which the Host to be carried in the procession is consecrated. However, nothing prohibits a procession from taking place even after a public and lengthy period of adoration following the Mass. If a procession takes place after Mass, when the Communion of the faithful is over, the monstrance in which the consecrated host has been placed is set on the altar. When the Prayer after Communion has been said, the Concluding Rites are omitted and the procession forms.

Friday after the Second Sunday after Pentecost

THE MOST SACRED HEART OF JESUS

Solemnity

Entrance Antiphon **The designs of his Heart are from age to age,**
to rescue their souls from death,
and to keep them alive in famine. Ps 33 (32): 11, 19

The Gloria in excelsis (Glory to God in the highest) is said.

COLLECT

Grant, we pray, almighty God,
that we, who glory in the Heart of your beloved Son
and recall the wonders of his love for us,
may be made worthy to receive
an overflowing measure of grace
from that fount of heavenly gifts.
Through our Lord Jesus Christ, your Son,
who lives and reigns with you
in the unity of the Holy Spirit,
one God, for ever and ever.

Or:

O God, who in the Heart of your Son,
wounded by our sins,
bestow on us in mercy
the boundless treasures of your love,
grant, we pray,
that, in paying him the homage of our devotion,
we may also offer worthy reparation.
Through our Lord Jesus Christ, your Son,
who lives and reigns with you
in the unity of the Holy Spirit,
one God, for ever and ever.

The Creed is said.

PRAYER AFTER COMMUNION

May this sacrament of charity, O Lord,
make us fervent with the fire of holy love,
so that, drawn always to your Son,
we may learn to see him in our neighbor.
Through Christ our Lord.

Last Sunday in Ordinary Time

OUR LORD JESUS CHRIST, KING OF THE UNIVERSE

Solemnity

Entrance Antiphon

**How worthy is the Lamb who was slain,
to receive power and divinity,
and wisdom and strength and honor.
To him belong glory and power for ever and ever.** Rev 5: 12; 1: 6

The Gloria in excelsis (Glory to God in the highest) is said.

COLLECT

**Almighty ever-living God,
whose will is to restore all things
in your beloved Son, the King of the universe,
grant, we pray,
that the whole creation, set free from slavery,
may render your majesty service
and ceaselessly proclaim your praise.
Through our Lord Jesus Christ, your Son,
who lives and reigns with you
in the unity of the Holy Spirit,
one God, for ever and ever.**

The Creed is said.

PRAYER AFTER COMMUNION

**Having received the food of immortality,
we ask, O Lord,
that, glorying in obedience
to the commands of Christ, the King of the universe,
we may live with him eternally in his heavenly Kingdom.
Who lives and reigns for ever and ever.**

THE ORDER OF MASS

THE INTRODUCTORY RITES

1. When the people are gathered, the Priest approaches the altar with the ministers while the Entrance Chant is sung.

When he has arrived at the altar, after making a profound bow with the ministers, the Priest venerates the altar with a kiss and, if appropriate, incenses the cross and the altar. Then, with the ministers, he goes to the chair.

When the Entrance Chant is concluded, the Priest and the faithful, standing, sign themselves with the Sign of the Cross, while the Priest, facing the people, says:

In the name of the Father, and of the Son, and of the Holy Spirit.

The people reply:

Amen.

2. Then the Priest, extending his hands, greets the people, saying:

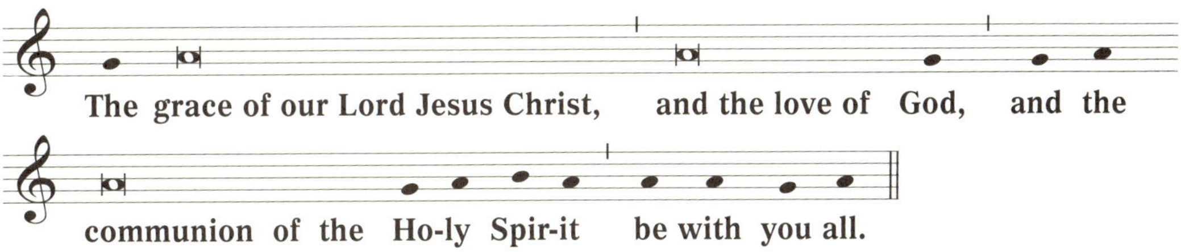

The grace of our Lord Jesus Christ,
and the love of God,
and the communion of the Holy Spirit
be with you all.

Or:

**Grace to you and peace from God our Father
and the Lord Jesus Christ.**

Or:

The Lord be with you.

The people reply:

And with your spirit.

In this first greeting, a Bishop, in place of The Lord be with you, says:

Peace be with you.

---

3. The Priest, or a Deacon, or another minister, may very briefly introduce the faithful to the Mass of the day.

Penitential Act[1]

4. Then follows the Penitential Act, to which the Priest invites the faithful, saying:

Brethren (brothers and sisters), let us acknowledge our sins,
and so prepare ourselves to celebrate the sacred mysteries.

A brief pause for silence follows. Then all recite together the formula of general confession:

I confess to almighty God
and to you, my brothers and sisters,
that I have greatly sinned,
in my thoughts and in my words,
in what I have done and in what I have failed to do,

And, striking their breast, they say:

through my fault, through my fault,
through my most grievous fault;

Then they continue:

therefore I ask blessed Mary ever-Virgin,
all the Angels and Saints,
and you, my brothers and sisters,
to pray for me to the Lord our God.

The absolution by the Priest follows:

May almighty God have mercy on us,
forgive us our sins,
and bring us to everlasting life.

[1] From time to time on Sundays, especially in Easter Time, instead of the customary Penitential Act, the blessing and sprinkling of water may take place (as in Appendix II, pp. 727-730) as a reminder of Baptism.

The people reply:

Amen.

Or:

5. The Priest invites the faithful to make the Penitential Act:

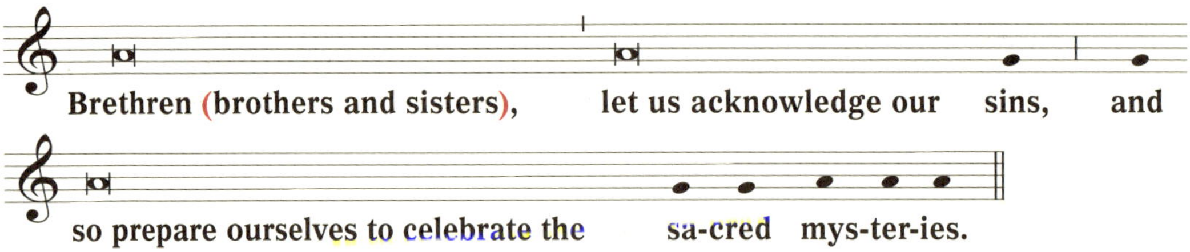

Brethren (brothers and sisters), let us acknowledge our sins, and so prepare ourselves to celebrate the sacred mysteries.

A brief pause for silence follows.

The Priest then says:

Have mercy on us, O Lord.

The people reply:

For we have sinned against you.

The Priest:

Show us, O Lord, your mercy.

The people:

And grant us your salvation.

The absolution by the Priest follows:

**May almighty God have mercy on us,
forgive us our sins,
and bring us to everlasting life.**

The people reply:

Amen.

Or:

6. The Priest invites the faithful to make the Penitential Act:

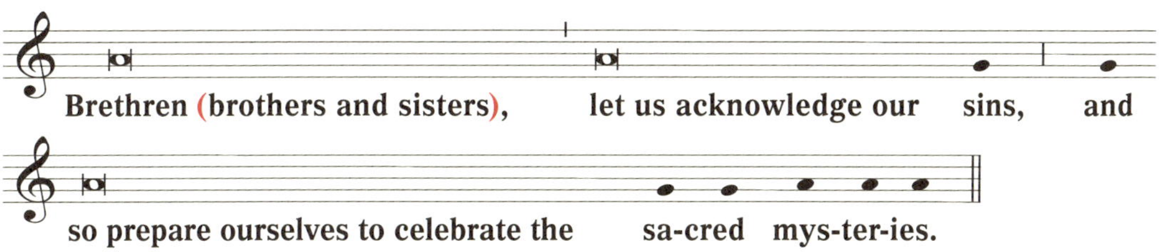

Brethren (brothers and sisters), let us acknowledge our sins, and so prepare ourselves to celebrate the sacred mysteries.

A brief pause for silence follows.

The Priest, or a Deacon or another minister, then says the following or other invocations[2] with Kyrie, eleison (Lord, have mercy):

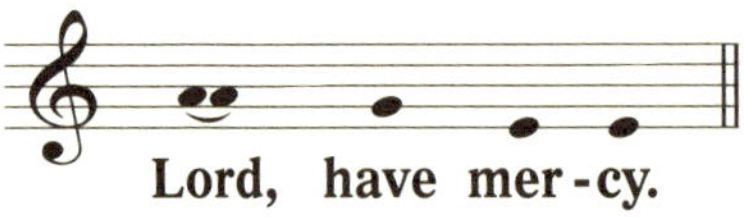

Or:

The people reply:

Or:

The Priest:

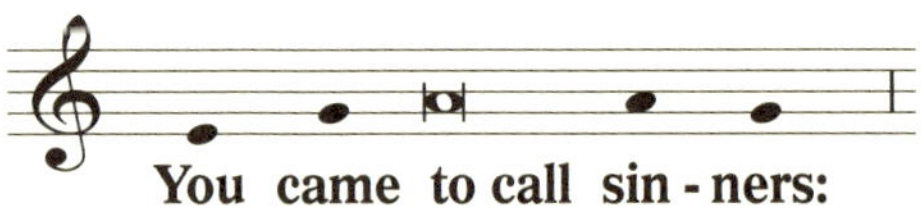

Or:

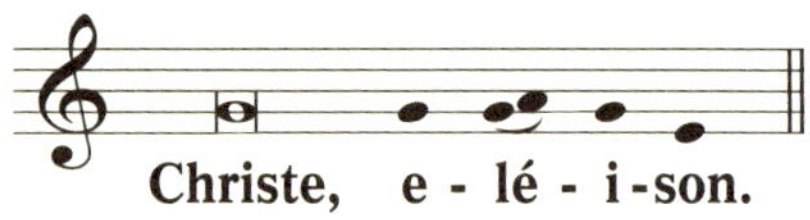

The people:

Or:

The Priest:

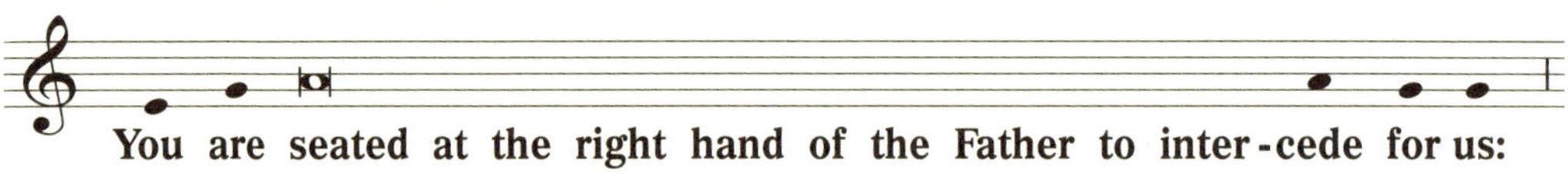

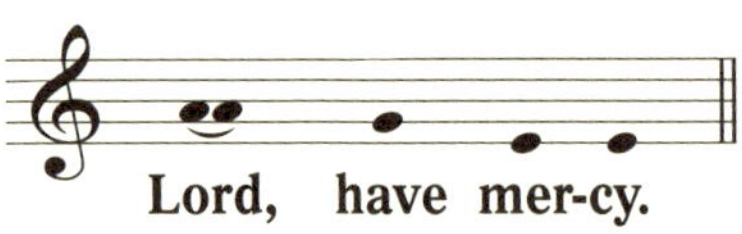

Or:

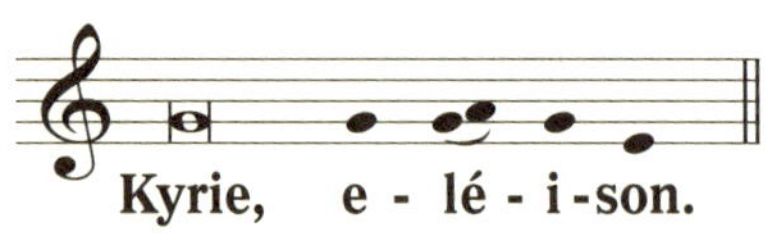

The people:

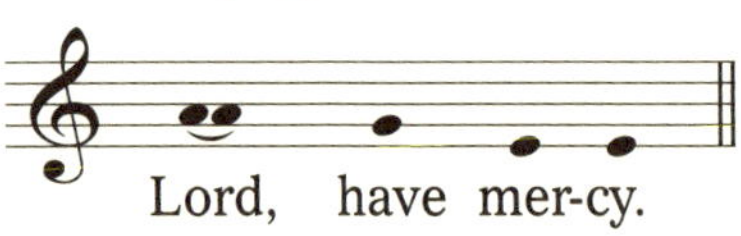

Or:

---

[2] Sample invocations are found in Appendix VI, pp. 744-750.

The absolution by the Priest follows:

The people reply:

The Priest, or a Deacon or another minister, then says the following or other invocations[3] with Kyrie, eleison (Lord, have mercy):

You were sent to heal the contrite of heart:

Lord, have mercy. Or: **Kyrie, eleison.**

The people reply:

Lord, have mercy. Or: Kyrie, eleison.

The Priest:

You came to call sinners:

Christ, have mercy. Or: **Christe, eleison.**

The people:

Christ, have mercy. Or: Christe, eleison.

The Priest:

You are seated at the right hand of the Father to intercede for us:

Lord, have mercy. Or: **Kyrie, eleison.**

The people:

Lord, have mercy. Or: Kyrie, eleison.

The absolution by the Priest follows:

May almighty God have mercy on us,
forgive us our sins,
and bring us to everlasting life.

The people reply:

Amen.

---

[3] Sample invocations are found in Appendix VI, pp. 744-750.

7. The Kyrie, eleison (Lord, have mercy) invocations follow, unless they have just occurred in a formula of the Penitential Act.

℣. **Lord, have mercy.** ℟. Lord, have mercy.
℣. **Christ, have mercy.** ℟. Christ, have mercy.
℣. **Lord, have mercy.** ℟. Lord, have mercy.

Or:

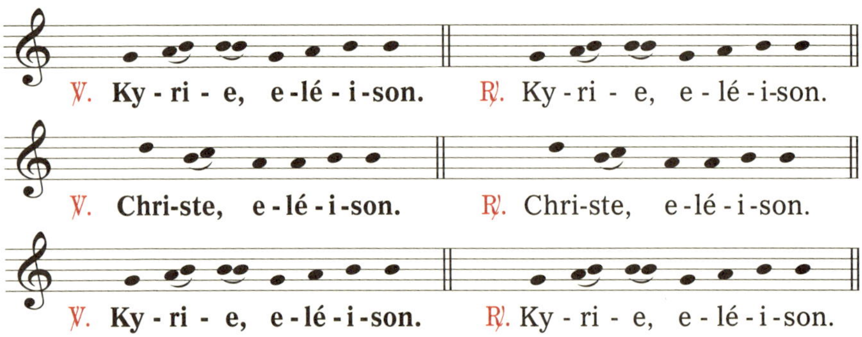

Or:

℣. **Kyrie, eleison.** ℟. Kyrie, eleison.
℣. **Christe, eleison.** ℟. Christe, eleison.
℣. **Kyrie, eleison.** ℟. Kyrie, eleison.

8. Then, when it is prescribed, this hymn is either sung or said:

**Glory to God in the highest,
and on earth peace to people of good will.**

**We praise you,
we bless you,
we adore you,
we glorify you,
we give you thanks for your great glory,
Lord God, heavenly King,
O God, almighty Father.**

**Lord Jesus Christ, Only Begotten Son,
Lord God, Lamb of God, Son of the Father,
you take away the sins of the world,
have mercy on us;
you take away the sins of the world,
receive our prayer;
you are seated at the right hand of the Father,
have mercy on us.**

**For you alone are the Holy One,
you alone are the Lord,
you alone are the Most High,
Jesus Christ,
with the Holy Spirit,
in the glory of God the Father.
Amen.**

9. When this hymn is concluded, the Priest, with hands joined, says:

Let us pray.

And all pray in silence with the Priest for a while.

Then the Priest, with hands extended, says the Collect prayer, at the end of which the people acclaim:

Amen.

THE LITURGY OF THE WORD

10. Then the reader goes to the ambo and reads the First Reading, while all sit and listen.

To indicate the end of the reading, the reader acclaims:

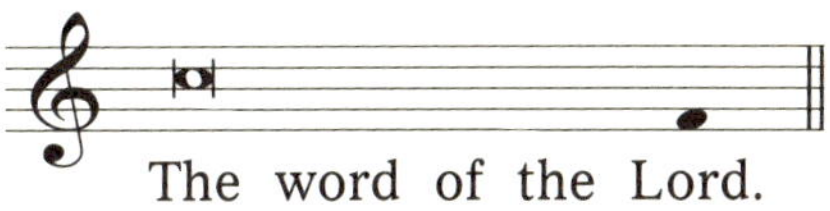

The word of the Lord.

All reply:

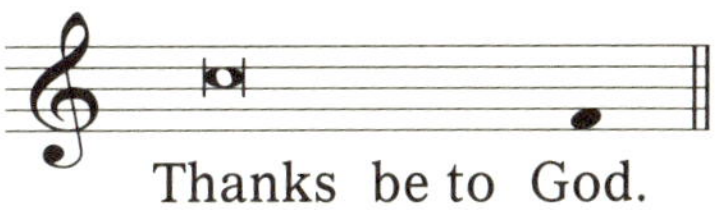

Thanks be to God.

11. The psalmist or cantor sings or says the Psalm, with the people making the response.

12. After this, if there is to be a Second Reading, a reader reads it from the ambo, as above.

To indicate the end of the reading, the reader acclaims:

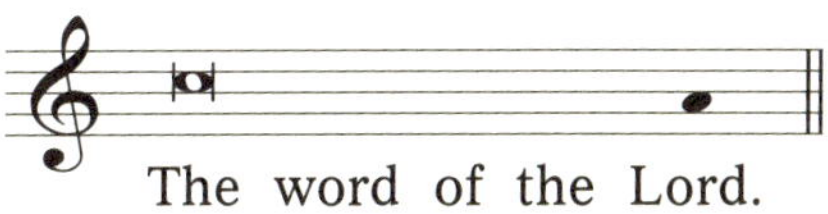

The word of the Lord.

All reply:

Thanks be to God.

13. There follows the Alleluia or another chant laid down by the rubrics, as the liturgical time requires.

14. Meanwhile, if incense is used, the Priest puts some into the thurible. After this, the Deacon who is to proclaim the Gospel, bowing profoundly before the Priest, asks for the blessing, saying in a low voice:

Your blessing, Father.

The Priest says in a low voice:

May the Lord be in your heart and on your lips,
that you may proclaim his Gospel worthily and well,
in the name of the Father, and of the Son, ✠ and of the Holy Spirit.

The Deacon signs himself with the Sign of the Cross and replies:

Amen.

If, however, a Deacon is not present, the Priest, bowing before the altar, says quietly:

Cleanse my heart and my lips, almighty God,
that I may worthily proclaim your holy Gospel.

15. The Deacon, or the Priest, then proceeds to the ambo, accompanied, if appropriate, by ministers with incense and candles. There he says:

The Lord be with you.

The people reply:

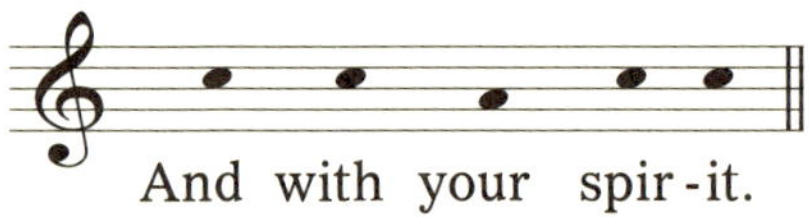

And with your spirit.

The Deacon, or the Priest:

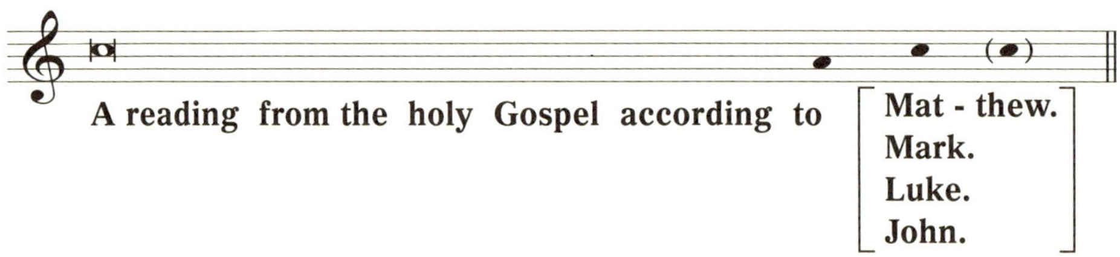

A reading from the holy Gospel according to N.

and, at the same time, he makes the Sign of the Cross on the book and on his forehead, lips, and breast.

The people acclaim:

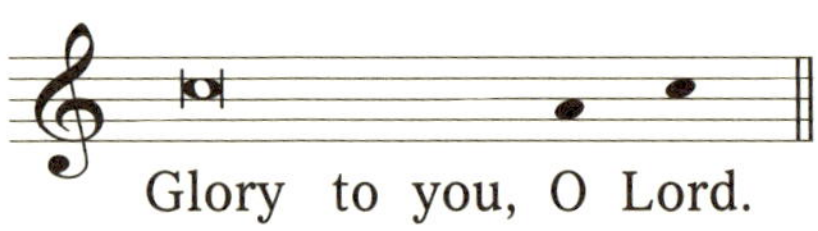

Glory to you, O Lord.

Then the Deacon, or the Priest, incenses the book, if incense is used, and proclaims the Gospel.

16. At the end of the Gospel, the Deacon, or the Priest, acclaims:

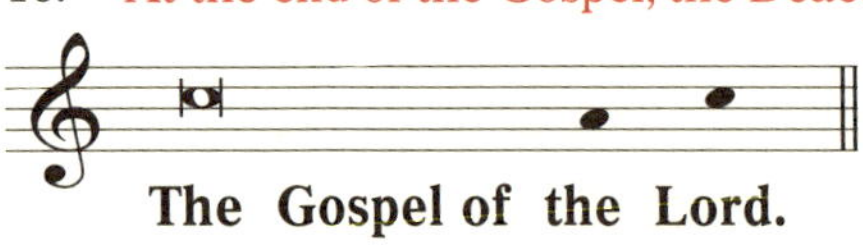

The Gospel of the Lord.

All reply:

Praise to you, Lord Jesus Christ.

Then he kisses the book, saying quietly:

Through the words of the Gospel
may our sins be wiped away.

17. Then follows the Homily, which is to be preached by a Priest or Deacon on all Sundays and Holydays of Obligation; on other days, it is recommended.

18. At the end of the Homily, the Symbol or Profession of Faith or Creed, when prescribed, is either sung or said:

At the words that follow, up to and including and became man, all bow.

For our sake he was cru-ci-fied un-der Pon-tius Pi-late, he
suffered death and was bur-ied, and rose a-gain on the third day
in accordance with the Scrip-tures. He as-cend-ed in-to heav-en
and is seated at the right hand of the Fa-ther. He will come a-gain
in glo-ry to judge the living and the dead and his kingdom will
have no end.
I be-lieve in the Ho-ly Spir-it, the Lord, the giv-er of life, who
pro-ceeds from the Father and the Son, who with the Fa-ther and
the Son is adored and glo-ri-fied, who has spoken through the
proph-ets. I be-lieve in one, ho-ly, ca-tho-lic and a-pos-tol-ic
Church. I con-fess one Bap-tism for the for-give-ness of sins
and I look for-ward to the res-ur-rec-tion of the dead and the life
of the world to come. A - men.

An alternate musical setting of the Creed may be found in Appendix I, pp. 722-723.

I believe in one God,
the Father almighty,
maker of heaven and earth,
of all things visible and invisible.

I believe in one Lord Jesus Christ,
the Only Begotten Son of God,
born of the Father before all ages.
God from God, Light from Light,
true God from true God,
begotten, not made, consubstantial with the Father;
through him all things were made.
For us men and for our salvation
he came down from heaven,

At the words that follow, up to and including and became man, all bow.

and by the Holy Spirit was incarnate of the Virgin Mary,
and became man.

For our sake he was crucified under Pontius Pilate,
he suffered death and was buried,
and rose again on the third day
in accordance with the Scriptures.
He ascended into heaven
and is seated at the right hand of the Father.
He will come again in glory
to judge the living and the dead
and his kingdom will have no end.

I believe in the Holy Spirit, the Lord, the giver of life,
who proceeds from the Father and the Son,
who with the Father and the Son is adored and glorified,
who has spoken through the prophets.

I believe in one, holy, catholic and apostolic Church.
I confess one Baptism for the forgiveness of sins
and I look forward to the resurrection of the dead
and the life of the world to come. Amen.

19. Instead of the Niceno-Constantinopolitan Creed, especially during Lent and Easter Time, the baptismal Symbol of the Roman Church, known as the Apostles' Creed, may be used.

I believe in God,
the Father almighty,
Creator of heaven and earth,
and in Jesus Christ, his only Son, our Lord,

At the words that follow, up to and including the Virgin Mary, all bow.

who was conceived by the Holy Spirit,
born of the Virgin Mary,
suffered under Pontius Pilate,
was crucified, died and was buried;
he descended into hell;
on the third day he rose again from the dead;
he ascended into heaven,
and is seated at the right hand of God the Father almighty;
from there he will come to judge the living and the dead.

I believe in the Holy Spirit,
the holy catholic Church,
the communion of saints,
the forgiveness of sins,
the resurrection of the body,
and life everlasting. Amen.

20. Then follows the Universal Prayer, that is, the Prayer of the Faithful or Bidding Prayers.

THE LITURGY OF THE EUCHARIST

21. When all this has been done, the Offertory Chant begins. Meanwhile, the ministers place the corporal, the purificator, the chalice, the pall, and the Missal on the altar.

22. It is desirable that the faithful express their participation by making an offering, bringing forward bread and wine for the celebration of the Eucharist and perhaps other gifts to relieve the needs of the Church and of the poor.

[For nos. 23–137, see the Roman Missal.]

138. Then the Priest may return to the chair. If appropriate, a sacred silence may be observed for a while, or a psalm or other canticle of praise or a hymn may be sung.

139. Then, standing at the altar or at the chair and facing the people, with hands joined, the Priest says:

Let us pray.

All pray in silence with the Priest for a while, unless silence has just been observed. Then the Priest, with hands extended, says the Prayer after Communion, at the end of which the people acclaim:

Amen.

THE CONCLUDING RITES

140. If they are necessary, any brief announcements to the people follow here.

141. Then the dismissal takes place. The Priest, facing the people and extending his hands, says:

The Lord be with you.

The people reply:

And with your spirit.

The Priest blesses the people, saying:

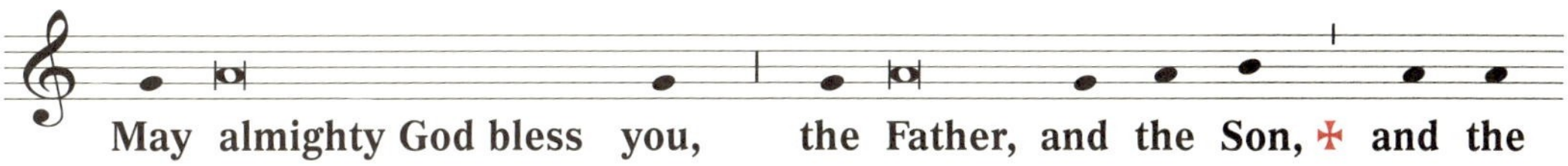

May almighty God bless you,
the Father, and the Son, ✠ and the Holy Spirit.

The people reply:

Amen.

142. On certain days or occasions, this formula of blessing is preceded, in accordance with the rubrics, by another more solemn formula of blessing or by a prayer over the people (cf. pp. 310ff.).

143. In a Pontifical Mass, the celebrant receives the miter and, extending his hands, says:

The Lord be with you.

All reply:

And with your spirit.

The celebrant says:

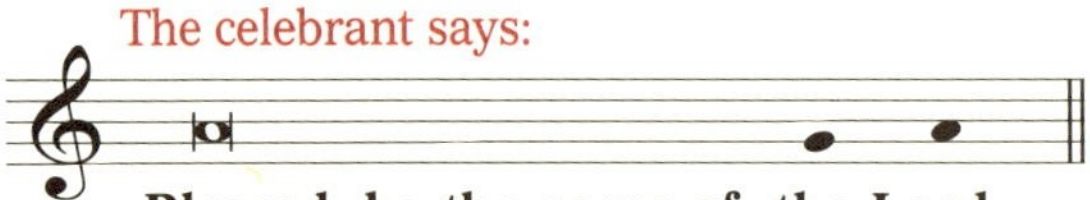

Blessed be the name of the Lord.

All reply:

Now and for ever.

The celebrant says:

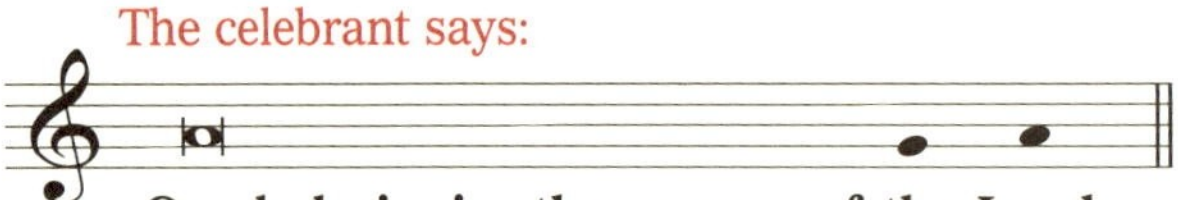

Our help is in the name of the Lord.

All reply:

Who made heaven and earth.

Then the celebrant receives the pastoral staff, if he uses it, and says:

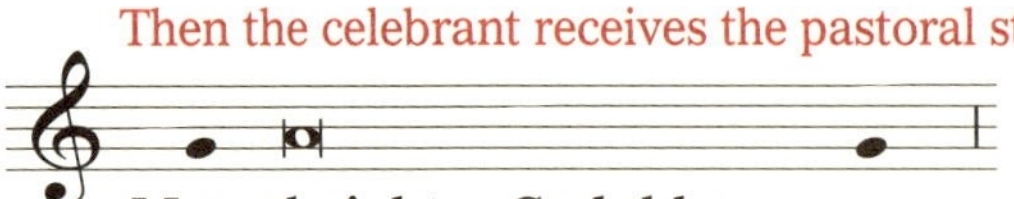

May almighty God bless you,

making the Sign of the Cross over the people three times, he adds:

the Father, ✠ and the Son, ✠ and the Holy ✠ Spirit.

All:

Amen.

---

144. Then the Deacon, or the Priest himself, with hands joined and facing the people, says:

Go forth, the Mass is ended.

Or:

Go and announce the Gospel of the Lord.

Or:

Go in peace, glorifying the Lord by your life.

Or:

Go in peace.

The people reply:

Thanks be to God.

145. Then the Priest venerates the altar as usual with a kiss, as at the beginning. After making a profound bow with the ministers, he withdraws.

146. If any liturgical action follows immediately, the rites of dismissal are omitted.

BLESSINGS AT THE END OF MASS AND PRAYERS OVER THE PEOPLE

SOLEMN BLESSINGS

The following blessings may be used, at the discretion of the Priest, at the end of the celebration of Mass, or of a Liturgy of the Word, or of the Office, or of the Sacraments.

The Deacon or, in his absence, the Priest himself, says the invitation: **Bow down for the blessing**. Then the Priest, with hands extended over the people, says the blessing, with all responding: Amen.

I. For Celebrations in the Different Liturgical Times

1. Advent

May the almighty and merciful God,
by whose grace you have placed your faith
in the First Coming of his Only Begotten Son
and yearn for his coming again,
sanctify you by the radiance of Christ's Advent
and enrich you with his blessing.
℟. Amen.

As you run the race of this present life,
may he make you firm in faith,
joyful in hope and active in charity.
℟. Amen.

So that, rejoicing now with devotion
at the Redeemer's coming in the flesh,
you may be endowed with the rich reward of eternal life
when he comes again in majesty.
℟. Amen.

And may the blessing of almighty God,
the Father, and the Son, ✠ and the Holy Spirit,
come down on you and remain with you for ever.
℟. Amen.

2. The Nativity of the Lord

May the God of infinite goodness,
who by the Incarnation of his Son has driven darkness from the world
and by that glorious Birth has illumined this most holy night (day),
drive far from you the darkness of vice
and illumine your hearts with the light of virtue.
℟. Amen.

May God, who willed that the great joy
of his Son's saving Birth
be announced to shepherds by the Angel,
fill your minds with the gladness he gives
and make you heralds of his Gospel.

℟. Amen.

And may God, who by the Incarnation
brought together the earthly and heavenly realm,
fill you with the gift of his peace and favor
and make you sharers with the Church in heaven.

℟. Amen.

And may the blessing of almighty God,
the Father, and the Son, ✠ and the Holy Spirit,
come down on you and remain with you for ever.

℟. Amen.

3. The Beginning of the Year

May God, the source and origin of all blessing,
grant you grace,
pour out his blessing in abundance,
and keep you safe from harm throughout the year.

℟. Amen.

May he give you integrity in the faith,
endurance in hope,
and perseverance in charity
with holy patience to the end.

℟. Amen.

May he order your days and your deeds in his peace,
grant your prayers in this and in every place,
and lead you happily to eternal life.

℟. Amen.

And may the blessing of almighty God,
the Father, and the Son, ✠ and the Holy Spirit,
come down on you and remain with you for ever.

℟. Amen.

4. The Epiphany of the Lord

**May God, who has called you
out of darkness into his wonderful light,
pour out in kindness his blessing upon you
and make your hearts firm
in faith, hope and charity.**
℟. Amen.

**And since in all confidence you follow Christ,
who today appeared in the world
as a light shining in darkness,
may God make you, too,
a light for your brothers and sisters.**
℟. Amen.

**And so when your pilgrimage is ended,
may you come to him
whom the Magi sought as they followed the star
and whom they found with great joy, the Light from Light,
who is Christ the Lord.**
℟. Amen.

**And may the blessing of almighty God,
the Father, and the Son, ✠ and the Holy Spirit,
come down on you and remain with you for ever.**
℟. Amen.

5. The Passion of the Lord

**May God, the Father of mercies,
who has given you an example of love
in the Passion of his Only Begotten Son,
grant that, by serving God and your neighbor,
you may lay hold of the wondrous gift of his blessing.**
℟. Amen.

**So that you may receive the reward of everlasting life from him,
through whose earthly Death
you believe that you escape eternal death.**
℟. Amen.

**And by following the example of his self-abasement,
may you possess a share in his Resurrection.**
℟. Amen.

And may the blessing of almighty God,
the Father, and the Son, ✠ and the Holy Spirit,
come down on you and remain with you for ever.

℟. Amen.

6. Easter Time

May God, who by the Resurrection of his Only Begotten Son
was pleased to confer on you
the gift of redemption and of adoption,
give you gladness by his blessing.

℟. Amen.

May he, by whose redeeming work
you have received the gift of everlasting freedom,
make you heirs to an eternal inheritance.

℟. Amen.

And may you, who have already risen with Christ
in Baptism through faith,
by living in a right manner on this earth,
be united with him in the homeland of heaven.

℟. Amen.

And may the blessing of almighty God,
the Father, and the Son, ✠ and the Holy Spirit,
come down on you and remain with you for ever.

℟. Amen.

7. The Ascension of the Lord

**May almighty God bless you,
for on this very day his Only Begotten Son
pierced the heights of heaven
and unlocked for you the way
to ascend to where he is.**
℟. Amen.

**May he grant that,
as Christ after his Resurrection
was seen plainly by his disciples,
so when he comes as Judge
he may show himself merciful to you for all eternity.**
℟. Amen.

**And may you, who believe he is seated
with the Father in his majesty,
know with joy the fulfillment of his promise
to stay with you until the end of time.**
℟. Amen.

**And may the blessing of almighty God,
the Father, and the Son, ✠ and the Holy Spirit,
come down on you and remain with you for ever.**
℟. Amen.

8. The Holy Spirit

**May God, the Father of lights,
who was pleased to enlighten the disciples' minds
by the outpouring of the Spirit, the Paraclete,
grant you gladness by his blessing
and make you always abound with the gifts of the same Spirit.**
℟. Amen.

**May the wondrous flame that appeared above the disciples,
powerfully cleanse your hearts from every evil
and pervade them with its purifying light.**
℟. Amen.

**And may God, who has been pleased to unite many tongues
in the profession of one faith,
give you perseverance in that same faith
and, by believing, may you journey from hope to clear vision.**
℟. Amen.

And may the blessing of almighty God,
the Father, and the Son, ✠ and the Holy Spirit,
come down on you and remain with you for ever.
℟. Amen.

9. Ordinary Time I

May the Lord bless you and keep you.
℟. Amen.

May he let his face shine upon you
and show you his mercy.
℟. Amen.

May he turn his countenance towards you
and give you his peace.
℟. Amen.

And may the blessing of almighty God,
the Father, and the Son, ✠ and the Holy Spirit,
come down on you and remain with you for ever.
℟. Amen.

10. Ordinary Time II

May the peace of God,
which surpasses all understanding,
keep your hearts and minds
in the knowledge and love of God,
and of his Son, our Lord Jesus Christ.
℟. Amen.

And may the blessing of almighty God,
the Father, and the Son, ✠ and the Holy Spirit,
come down on you and remain with you for ever.
℟. Amen.

11. Ordinary Time III

**May almighty God bless you in his kindness
and pour out saving wisdom upon you.**
℟. Amen.

**May he nourish you always with the teachings of the faith
and make you persevere in holy deeds.**
℟. Amen.

**May he turn your steps towards himself
and show you the path of charity and peace.**
℟. Amen.

**And may the blessing of almighty God,
the Father, and the Son, ✠ and the Holy Spirit,
come down on you and remain with you for ever.**
℟. Amen.

12. Ordinary Time IV

**May the God of all consolation order your days in his peace
and grant you the gifts of his blessing.**
℟. Amen.

**May he free you always from every distress
and confirm your hearts in his love.**
℟. Amen.

**So that on this life's journey
you may be effective in good works,
rich in the gifts of hope, faith and charity,
and may come happily to eternal life.**
℟. Amen.

**And may the blessing of almighty God,
the Father, and the Son, ✠ and the Holy Spirit,
come down on you and remain with you for ever.**
℟. Amen.

13. Ordinary Time V

**May almighty God always keep every adversity far from you
and in his kindness pour out upon you the gifts of his blessing.**
℟. Amen.

**May God keep your hearts attentive to his words,
that they may be filled with everlasting gladness.**
℟. Amen.

**And so, may you always understand what is good and right,
and be found ever hastening along
in the path of God's commands,
made coheirs with the citizens of heaven.**
℟. Amen.

**And may the blessing of almighty God,
the Father, and the Son, ✠ and the Holy Spirit,
come down on you and remain with you for ever.**
℟. Amen.

14. Ordinary Time VI

**May God bless you with every heavenly blessing,
make you always holy and pure in his sight,
pour out in abundance upon you the riches of his glory,
and teach you with the words of truth;
may he instruct you in the Gospel of salvation,
and ever endow you with fraternal charity.
Through Christ our Lord.**
℟. Amen.

**And may the blessing of almighty God,
the Father, and the Son, ✠ and the Holy Spirit,
come down on you and remain with you for ever.**
℟. Amen.

II. For Celebrations of the Saints

15. The Blessed Virgin Mary

May God, who through the childbearing of the Blessed Virgin Mary
willed in his great kindness to redeem the human race,
be pleased to enrich you with his blessing.
℟. Amen.

May you know always and everywhere the protection of her,
through whom you have been found worthy
to receive the author of life.
℟. Amen.

May you, who have devoutly gathered on this day,
carry away with you the gifts of spiritual joys
and heavenly rewards.
℟. Amen.

And may the blessing of almighty God,
the Father, and the Son, ✠ and the Holy Spirit,
come down on you and remain with you for ever.
℟. Amen.

16. Saints Peter and Paul, Apostles

May almighty God bless you,
for he has made you steadfast in Saint Peter's saving confession
and through it has set you on the solid rock of the Church's faith.
℟. Amen.

And having instructed you
by the tireless preaching of Saint Paul,
may God teach you constantly by his example
to win brothers and sisters for Christ.
℟. Amen.

So that by the keys of St. Peter and the words of St. Paul,
and by the support of their intercession,
God may bring us happily to that homeland
that Peter attained on a cross
and Paul by the blade of a sword.
℟. Amen.

And may the blessing of almighty God,
the Father, and the Son, ✠ and the Holy Spirit,
come down on you and remain with you for ever.
℟. Amen.

17. The Apostles

May God, who has granted you
to stand firm on apostolic foundations,
graciously bless you through the glorious merits
of the holy Apostles N. and N. (the holy Apostle N.).
℟. Amen.

And may he, who endowed you
with the teaching and example of the Apostles,
make you, under their protection,
witnesses to the truth before all.
℟. Amen.

So that through the intercession of the Apostles,
you may inherit the eternal homeland,
for by their teaching you possess firmness of faith.
℟. Amen.

And may the blessing of almighty God,
the Father, and the Son, ✠ and the Holy Spirit,
come down on you and remain with you for ever.
℟. Amen.

18. All Saints

May God, the glory and joy of the Saints,
who has caused you to be strengthened
by means of their outstanding prayers,
bless you with unending blessings.
℟. Amen.

Freed through their intercession from present ills
and formed by the example of their holy way of life,
may you be ever devoted
to serving God and your neighbor.
℟. Amen.

So that, together with all,
you may possess the joys of the homeland,
where Holy Church rejoices
that her children are admitted in perpetual peace
to the company of the citizens of heaven.
℟. Amen.

And may the blessing of almighty God,
the Father, and the Son, ✠ and the Holy Spirit,
come down on you and remain with you for ever.
℟. Amen.

III. Other Blessings

19. For the Dedication of a Church

May God, the Lord of heaven and earth,
who has gathered you today for the dedication of this church,
make you abound in heavenly blessings.
℟. Amen.

And may he, who has willed that all his scattered children
should be gathered together in his Son,
grant that you may become his temple
and the dwelling place of the Holy Spirit.
℟. Amen.

And so, when you are thoroughly cleansed,
may God dwell within you
and grant you to possess with all the Saints
the inheritance of eternal happiness.
℟. Amen.

And may the blessing of almighty God,
the Father, ✠ and the Son, ✠ and the Holy ✠ Spirit,
come down on you and remain with you for ever.
℟. Amen.

20. In Celebrations for the Dead

May the God of all consolation bless you,
for in his unfathomable goodness he created the human race,
and in the Resurrection of his Only Begotten Son
he has given believers the hope of rising again.
℟. Amen.

To us who are alive, may God grant pardon for our sins,
and to all the dead, a place of light and peace.
℟. Amen.

So may we all live happily for ever with Christ,
whom we believe truly rose from the dead.
℟. Amen.

And may the blessing of almighty God,
the Father, and the Son, ✠ and the Holy Spirit,
come down on you and remain with you for ever.
℟. Amen.

PRAYERS OVER THE PEOPLE

The following prayers may be used, at the discretion of the Priest, at the end of the celebration of Mass, or of a Liturgy of the Word, or of the Office, or of the Sacraments.

The Deacon or, in his absence, the Priest himself, says the invitation: **Bow down for the blessing**. Then the Priest, with hands outstretched over the people, says the prayer, with all responding: Amen.

After the prayer, the Priest always adds: **And may the blessing of almighty God, the Father, and the Son, ✠ and the Holy Spirit, come down on you and remain with you for ever.** ℟. Amen.

1. **Be gracious to your people, O Lord,
and do not withhold consolation on earth
from those you call to strive for heaven.
Through Christ our Lord.**

2. **Grant, O Lord, we pray,
that the Christian people
may understand the truths they profess
and love the heavenly liturgy
in which they participate.
Through Christ our Lord.**

3. **May your people receive your holy blessing,
O Lord, we pray,
and, by that gift,
spurn all that would harm them
and obtain what they desire.
Through Christ our Lord.**

4. **Turn your people to you with all their heart,
O Lord, we pray,
for you protect even those who go astray,
but when they serve you with undivided heart,
you sustain them with still greater care.
Through Christ our Lord.**

5. **Graciously enlighten your family, O Lord, we pray,
that by holding fast to what is pleasing to you,
they may be worthy to accomplish all that is good.
Through Christ our Lord.**

6. **Bestow pardon and peace, O Lord, we pray,
upon your faithful,
that they may be cleansed from every offense
and serve you with untroubled hearts.
Through Christ our Lord.**

7. **May your heavenly favor, O Lord, we pray,
increase in number the people subject to you
and make them always obedient to your commands.
Through Christ our Lord.**

8. **Be propitious to your people, O God,
that, freed from every evil,
they may serve you with all their heart
and ever stand firm under your protection.
Through Christ our Lord.**

9. **May your family always rejoice together, O God,
over the mysteries of redemption they have celebrated,
and grant its members the perseverance
to attain the effects that flow from them.
Through Christ our Lord.**

10. **Lord God, from the abundance of your mercies
provide for your servants and ensure their safety,
so that, strengthened by your blessings,
they may at all times abound in thanksgiving
and bless you with unending exultation.
Through Christ our Lord.**

11. **Keep your family, we pray, O Lord,
in your constant care,
so that, under your protection,
they may be free from all troubles
and by good works show dedication to your name.
Through Christ our Lord.**

12. **Purify your faithful, both in body and in mind,
O Lord, we pray,
so that, feeling the compunction you inspire,
they may be able to avoid harmful pleasures
and ever feed upon your delights.
Through Christ our Lord.**

13. May the effects of your sacred blessing, O Lord,
make themselves felt among your faithful,
to prepare with spiritual sustenance the minds of all,
that they may be strengthened by the power of your love
to carry out works of charity.
Through Christ our Lord.

14. The hearts of your faithful submitted to your name,
entreat your help, O Lord,
and since without you they can do nothing that is just,
grant by your abundant mercy
that they may both know what is right
and receive all that they need for their good.
Through Christ our Lord.

15. Hasten to the aid of your faithful people
who call upon you, O Lord, we pray,
and graciously give strength in their human weakness,
so that, being dedicated to you in complete sincerity,
they may find gladness in your remedies
both now and in the life to come.
Through Christ our Lord.

16. Look with favor on your family, O Lord,
and bestow your endless mercy on those who seek it:
and just as without your mercy,
they can do nothing truly worthy of you,
so through it,
may they merit to obey your saving commands.
Through Christ our Lord.

17. Bestow increase of heavenly grace
on your faithful, O Lord;
may they praise you with their lips,
with their souls, with their lives;
and since it is by your gift that we exist,
may our whole lives be yours.
Through Christ our Lord.

18. Direct your people, O Lord, we pray,
with heavenly instruction,
that by avoiding every evil
and pursuing all that is good,
they may earn not your anger
but your unending mercy.
Through Christ our Lord.

19. Be near to those who call on you, O Lord,
and graciously grant your protection
to all who place their hope in your mercy,
that they may remain faithful in holiness of life
and, having enough for their needs in this world,
they may be made full heirs of your promise for eternity.
Through Christ our Lord.

20. Bestow the grace of your kindness
upon your supplicant people, O Lord,
that, formed by you, their creator,
and restored by you, their sustainer,
through your constant action they may be saved.
Through Christ our Lord.

21. May your faithful people, O Lord, we pray,
always respond to the promptings of your love
and, moved by wholesome compunction,
may they do gladly what you command,
so as to receive the things you promise.
Through Christ our Lord.

22. May the weakness of your devoted people
stir your compassion, O Lord, we pray,
and let their faithful pleading win your mercy,
that what they do not presume upon by their merits
they may receive by your generous pardon.
Through Christ our Lord.

23. In defense of your children, O Lord, we pray,
stretch forth the right hand of your majesty,
so that, obeying your fatherly will,
they may have the unfailing protection
of your fatherly care.
Through Christ our Lord.

24. Look, O Lord, on the prayers of your family,
and grant them the assistance they humbly implore,
so that, strengthened by the help they need,
they may persevere in confessing your name.
Through Christ our Lord.

25. Keep your family safe, O Lord, we pray,
and grant them the abundance of your mercies,
that they may find growth
through the teachings and the gifts of heaven.
Through Christ our Lord.

26. May your faithful people rejoice, we pray, O Lord,
to be upheld by your right hand,
and, progressing in the Christian life,
may they delight in good things
both now and in the time to come.
Through Christ our Lord.

On Feasts of Saints

27. May the Christian people exult, O Lord,
at the glorification of the illustrious members
of your Son's Body,
and may they gain a share in the eternal lot
of the Saints on whose feast day
they reaffirm their devotion to you,
rejoicing with them for ever in your glory.
Through Christ our Lord.

28. Turn the hearts of your people
always to you, O Lord, we pray,
and, as you give them the help of such great patrons as these,
grant also the unfailing help of your protection.
Through Christ our Lord.

THE ORDER OF MASS

WITH THE PARTICIPATION OF A SINGLE MINISTER

THE INTRODUCTORY RITES

1. The Priest approaches the altar with the minister and after making a profound bow with the minister, venerates the altar with a kiss and goes to the chair.

Then the minister or the Priest himself recites the Entrance Antiphon and the Priest and the minister, standing, sign themselves with the Sign of the Cross, while the Priest, facing the minister, says:

In the name of the Father, and of the Son, and of the Holy Spirit.

The minister replies:

Amen.

2. Then the Priest, facing the minister and extending his hands, greets him, saying:

The Lord be with you.

The minister replies:

And with your spirit.

Other formulas of greeting may also be used, as found in the Order of Mass (pp. 291-292).

3. Then the Priest and the minister recite together the formula of general confession:

I confess to almighty God
and to you, my brother,
that I have greatly sinned,
in my thoughts and in my words,
in what I have done and in what I have failed to do,

And, striking their breast, they say:

through my fault, through my fault,
through my most grievous fault;

Then they continue:

therefore I ask blessed Mary ever-Virgin,
all the Angels and Saints,
and you, my brother,
to pray for me to the Lord our God.

The absolution by the Priest follows:

May almighty God have mercy on us,
forgive us our sins,
and bring us to everlasting life.

The minister replies:

Amen.

Other formulas for the Penitential Act may also be used, as found in the Order of Mass (pp. 293-297).

4. The Kyrie, eleison (Lord, have mercy) invocations follow, the Priest reciting them in alternation with the minister:

Priest: **Lord, have mercy.** Minister: Lord, have mercy.

Priest: **Christ, have mercy.** Minister: Christ, have mercy.

Priest: **Lord, have mercy.** Minister: Lord, have mercy.

Or:

Priest: **Kyrie, eleison.** Minister: Kyrie, eleison.

Priest: **Christe, eleison.** Minister: Christe, eleison.

Priest: **Kyrie, eleison.** Minister: Kyrie, eleison.

5. Then, when it is prescribed, the Priest and the minister recite together the hymn Gloria in excelsis (Glory to God in the highest).

6. When this hymn is concluded, the Priest, with hands joined, says:

Let us pray.

After a moment of prayer in silence, he extends his hands and says the Collect prayer, at the end of which the minister acclaims:

Amen.

THE LITURGY OF THE WORD

7. Then the minister or the Priest himself reads the First Reading, the Psalm and the Second Reading, if there is to be one, along with the other chant.

8. Then the Priest, bowing profoundly before the altar, says quietly:

Cleanse my heart and my lips, almighty God,
that I may worthily proclaim your holy Gospel.

9. After this, with hands joined, he says:

The Lord be with you.

The minister replies:

And with your spirit.

The Priest:

A reading from the holy Gospel according to N.

and, at the same time, he makes the Sign of the Cross on the book and on his forehead, lips, and breast.

The minister acclaims:

Glory to you, O Lord.

Then the Priest proclaims the Gospel, at the end of which he acclaims:

The Gospel of the Lord.

The minister replies:

Praise to you, Lord Jesus Christ.

Then the Priest kisses the book, saying quietly:

**Through the words of the Gospel
may our sins be wiped away.**

10. When it is prescribed, the Priest and the minister recite together the Symbol or Profession of Faith or Creed.

11. After this there may follow the Universal Prayer, that is, the Prayer of the Faithful or Bidding Prayers. In it the Priest says the introduction and conclusion and the minister the intentions.

THE LITURGY OF THE EUCHARIST

12. The minister places the corporal, the purificator and the chalice on the altar, unless this was already done at the beginning of Mass. The Priest goes to the middle of the altar.

[For nos. 13–30, see the Roman Missal.]

31. A sacred silence may be observed for a while.

32. Then, with hands joined, the Priest says:

Let us pray.

After a brief pause for silence, unless silence has just been observed, he extends his hands and says the Prayer after Communion, at the end of which the minister acclaims:

Amen.

THE CONCLUDING RITES

33. Then the Priest, facing the minister and extending his hands, says:

The Lord be with you.

The minister replies:

And with your spirit.

The Priest blesses the minister, saying:

May almighty God bless you,
the Father, and the Son, ✠ and the Holy Spirit.

The minister replies:

Amen.

34. Then the Priest venerates the altar with a kiss, and after making a profound bow with the minister, he withdraws.

PROPER OF SAINTS

1. The rank of the celebration, namely Solemnity, Feast, or Memorial, is indicated for each day. If no other indication is given, the celebration is an Optional Memorial.

2. For each Solemnity and Feast a complete proper Mass is provided. This is therefore said as printed.

3. As regards Memorials, the following are to be observed:

a) The proper texts proposed for certain days are always to be used.

b) Whenever there is a reference to a particular Common, the more appropriate texts should be chosen according to the principles explained at the beginning of the Commons. The page reference given in each case only indicates a text that is particularly suitable.

c) If, however, a reference is given to several Commons, one or other of them may be used, with due regard for pastoral concerns; it is always allowed to exchange texts among several Masses of the same Common.

For example, if a Saint is both a Martyr and a Bishop, either the Common of Martyrs or the Common of Pastors (for Bishops) may be used.

d) Moreover, as well as the Commons that refer to a particular category of Saint (e.g., of Martyrs, Virgins, Pastors, etc.), it is always permitted to use the texts from the Common of Holy Men and Women, which refers to Sainthood in general.

e) The Prayers over the Offerings and after Communion, unless they are proper, are taken either from the Common or from the current time of the liturgical year.

4. The Masses contained in this Proper of Saints are also used as Votive Masses, with the exception of Masses of the mysteries of the life of the Lord and of the Blessed Virgin Mary (cf. *General Instruction of the Roman Missal*, no. 375) and also of Masses of certain Saints for whom a special Votive Mass is provided. When Masses of the Proper of Saints are used as Votive Masses, words in the prayers indicating the heavenly birthday or the Solemnity or Feast are not used but are replaced by the word memorial or commemoration.

JANUARY

January 2
Saints Basil the Great and Gregory Nazianzen, Bishops and Doctors of the Church

Memorial

Entrance Antiphon

Let the peoples recount the wisdom of the Saints,
and let the Church proclaim their praise.
Their names will live on and on. Cf. Sir 44: 15, 14

COLLECT

O God, who were pleased to give light to your Church
by the example and teaching
of the Bishops Saints Basil and Gregory,
grant, we pray,
that in humility we may learn your truth
and practice it faithfully in charity.
Through our Lord Jesus Christ, your Son,
who lives and reigns with you
in the unity of the Holy Spirit,
one God, for ever and ever.

PRAYER AFTER COMMUNION

May partaking at the heavenly table, almighty God,
confirm and increase strength from on high
in all who celebrate the feast day
of Saints Basil and Gregory,
that we may preserve in integrity the gift of faith
and walk in the path of salvation you trace for us.
Through Christ our Lord.

January 3

The Most Holy Name of Jesus

Entrance Antiphon

At the name of Jesus, every knee should bend,
of those in heaven and on earth and under the earth,
and every tongue confess
that Jesus Christ is Lord, to the glory of God the Father.

Phil 2: 10-11

COLLECT

O God, who founded the salvation of the human race
on the Incarnation of your Word,
give your peoples the mercy they implore,
so that all may know there is no other name to be invoked
but the Name of your Only Begotten Son.
Who lives and reigns with you
in the unity of the Holy Spirit,
one God, for ever and ever.

PRAYER AFTER COMMUNION

May the sacrificial gifts offered to your majesty, O Lord,
to honor Christ's Name
and which we have now received,
fill us, we pray, with your abundant grace,
so that we may come to rejoice
that our names, too, are written in heaven.
Through Christ our Lord.

[In the Dioceses of the United States]

January 4

Saint Elizabeth Ann Seton, Religious

Memorial

Entrance Antiphon

Behold a wise woman who has built her house.
She feared the Lord and walked in the right path. Cf. Prv 14: 1-2

Or:

This is the generation
which seeks the face of the God of Jacob. Cf. Ps 24 (23): 6

COLLECT

O God, who crowned with the gift of true faith
Saint Elizabeth Ann Seton's burning zeal to find you,
grant by her intercession and example
that we may always seek you with diligent love
and find you in daily service with sincere faith.
Through our Lord Jesus Christ, your Son,
who lives and reigns with you
in the unity of the Holy Spirit,
one God, for ever and ever.

PRAYER AFTER COMMUNION

As we partake of the sacrament of our salvation,
while recalling the memory of Saint Elizabeth Ann Seton,
we humbly ask you, O Lord,
that we may be inflamed with a burning desire
for the heavenly table,
and by its power consecrate our life faithfully to you.
Through Christ our Lord.

[In the Dioceses of the United States]

January 5

Saint John Neumann, Bishop

Memorial

Entrance Antiphon

O Lord, my allotted portion and my cup,
you it is who hold fast my lot.
For me the measuring lines have fallen on pleasant sites;
fair to me indeed is my inheritance. Ps 16 (15): 5-6

COLLECT

O God, who called the Bishop Saint John Neumann,
renowned for his charity and pastoral service,
to shepherd your people in America,
grant by his intercession
that, as we foster the Christian education of youth
and are strengthened by the witness of brotherly love,
we may constantly increase the family of your Church.
Through our Lord Jesus Christ, your Son,
who lives and reigns with you
in the unity of the Holy Spirit,
one God, for ever and ever.

PRAYER AFTER COMMUNION

Refreshed by our participation in the memorial
of the Death and Resurrection of your Son,
we ask, O Lord,
that by the example of Saint John Neumann,
we may experience the power of this Sacrament
and remain constantly in the Church
by the bond of unity and truth.
Through Christ our Lord.

[In the Dioceses of the United States]

January 6

Saint André Bessette, Religious

From the Common of Holy Men and Women: For Religious (p. 563).

COLLECT

Lord our God, friend of the lowly,
who gave your servant, Saint André Bessette,
a great devotion to Saint Joseph
and a special commitment to the poor and afflicted,
help us through his intercession
to follow his example of prayer and love
and so come to share with him in your glory.
Through our Lord Jesus Christ, your Son,
who lives and reigns with you
  in the unity of the Holy Spirit,
one God, for ever and ever.

January 7

Saint Raymond of Penyafort, Priest

From the Common of Pastors: For One Pastor (p. 544).

COLLECT

O God, who adorned the Priest Saint Raymond
with the virtue of outstanding mercy and compassion
for sinners and for captives,
grant us, through his intercession,
that, released from slavery to sin,
we may carry out in freedom of spirit
what is pleasing to you.
Through our Lord Jesus Christ, your Son,
who lives and reigns with you
  in the unity of the Holy Spirit,
one God, for ever and ever.

January 13

Saint Hilary, Bishop and Doctor of the Church

From the Common of Pastors: For a Bishop (p. 541), or from the Common of Doctors of the Church (p. 551).

COLLECT

Grant, we pray, almighty God,
that we may rightly understand and truthfully profess
the divinity of your Son,
which the Bishop Saint Hilary taught with such constancy.
Through our Lord Jesus Christ, your Son,
who lives and reigns with you
in the unity of the Holy Spirit,
one God, for ever and ever.

January 17

Saint Anthony, Abbot

Memorial

Entrance Antiphon

The just will flourish like the palm tree,
and grow like a Lebanon cedar,
planted in the house of the Lord,
in the courts of the house of our God. Cf. Ps 92 (91): 13-14

COLLECT

O God, who brought the Abbot Saint Anthony
to serve you by a wondrous way of life in the desert,
grant, through his intercession,
that, denying ourselves,
we may always love you above all things.
Through our Lord Jesus Christ, your Son,
who lives and reigns with you
in the unity of the Holy Spirit,
one God, for ever and ever.

PRAYER AFTER COMMUNION

Nourished for our healing by your Sacraments, O Lord,
may we escape every snare of the enemy unharmed,
just as by your grace Saint Anthony won glorious victories
over the powers of darkness.
Through Christ our Lord.

January 20
Saint Fabian, Pope and Martyr

From the Common of Martyrs: For One Martyr (p. 531), or from the Common of Pastors: For a Pope (p. 539).

COLLECT

**O God, glory of your Priests,
grant, we pray,
that, helped by the intercession
of your Martyr Saint Fabian,
we may make progress by communion in the faith
and by worthy service.
Through our Lord Jesus Christ, your Son,
who lives and reigns with you
in the unity of the Holy Spirit,
one God, for ever and ever.**

Saint Sebastian, Martyr

From the Common of Martyrs: For One Martyr (p. 531).

COLLECT

**Grant us, we pray, O Lord, a spirit of fortitude,
so that, taught by the glorious example
of your Martyr Saint Sebastian,
we may learn to obey you rather than men.
Through our Lord Jesus Christ, your Son,
who lives and reigns with you
in the unity of the Holy Spirit,
one God, for ever and ever.**

January 21

Saint Agnes, Virgin and Martyr

Memorial

From the Common of Martyrs: For a Virgin Martyr (p. 537), or from the Common of Virgins: For One Virgin (p. 554).

COLLECT

Almighty ever-living God,
who choose what is weak in the world
to confound the strong,
mercifully grant,
that we, who celebrate the heavenly birthday
of your Martyr Saint Agnes,
may follow her constancy in the faith.
Through our Lord Jesus Christ, your Son,
who lives and reigns with you
in the unity of the Holy Spirit,
one God, for ever and ever.

[In the Dioceses of the United States]

January 22*
(*January 23, when January 22 falls on a Sunday)

Day of Prayer for the Legal Protection of Unborn Children

From the Masses and Prayers for Various Needs and Occasions: For Giving Thanks to God for the Gift of Human Life (no. 48/1), with white vestments (p. 660); or For the Preservation of Peace and Justice (no. 30), with violet vestments (p. 642).

[In the Dioceses of the United States]

January 23

Saint Vincent, Deacon and Martyr

From the Common of Martyrs: For One Martyr (p. 531).

COLLECT

Almighty ever-living God,
mercifully pour out your Spirit upon us,
so that our hearts may possess that strong love
by which the Martyr Saint Vincent
triumphed over all bodily torments.
Through our Lord Jesus Christ, your Son,
who lives and reigns with you
in the unity of the Holy Spirit,
one God, for ever and ever.

[In the Dioceses of the United States]

Saint Marianne Cope, Virgin

From the Common of Virgins: For One Virgin (p. 554), or from the Common of Holy Men and Women: For Those Who Practiced Works of Mercy (p. 564).

COLLECT

O God, who called us to serve your Son
in the least of our brothers and sisters,
grant, we pray, that by the example and intercession
of the Virgin Saint Marianne Cope,
we may burn with love for you and for those who suffer.
Through our Lord Jesus Christ, your Son,
who lives and reigns with you
in the unity of the Holy Spirit,
one God, for ever and ever.

January 24

Saint Francis de Sales, Bishop and Doctor of the Church

Memorial

From the Common of Pastors: For a Bishop (p. 541), or from the Common of Doctors of the Church (p. 551).

COLLECT

O God, who for the salvation of souls
willed that the Bishop Saint Francis de Sales
become all things to all,
graciously grant that, following his example,
we may always display the gentleness of your charity
in the service of our neighbor.
Through our Lord Jesus Christ, your Son,
who lives and reigns with you
in the unity of the Holy Spirit,
one God, for ever and ever.

PRAYER AFTER COMMUNION

Grant, we pray, almighty God,
that through the Sacrament we have received,
we may imitate on earth
the charity and meekness of Saint Francis de Sales
and so attain like him the glory of heaven.
Through Christ our Lord.

January 25
The Conversion of Saint Paul the Apostle
Feast

Entrance Antiphon

I know the one in whom I have believed
and I am sure that he, the just judge, the mighty,
will keep safe what is my due until that day. 2 Tm 1: 12; 4: 8

The Gloria in excelsis (Glory to God in the highest) is said.

COLLECT

O God, who taught the whole world
through the preaching of the blessed Apostle Paul,
draw us, we pray, nearer to you
through the example of him whose conversion
we celebrate today,
and so make us witnesses to your truth in the world.
Through our Lord Jesus Christ, your Son,
who lives and reigns with you
in the unity of the Holy Spirit,
one God, for ever and ever.

PRAYER AFTER COMMUNION

May the Sacrament we have received, O Lord our God,
stir up in us that fire of charity
with which the blessed Apostle Paul burned ardently
as he bore his concern for all the Churches.
Through Christ our Lord.

The Solemn Blessing formula on p. 318 may be used.

January 26
Saints Timothy and Titus, Bishops

Memorial

Entrance Antiphon

Tell among the nations his glory,
and his wonders among all the peoples,
for the Lord is great and highly to be praised. Ps 96 (95): 3-4

COLLECT

O God, who adorned Saints Timothy and Titus
with apostolic virtues,
grant, through the intercession of them both,
that, living justly and devoutly in this present age,
we may merit to reach our heavenly homeland.
Through our Lord Jesus Christ, your Son,
who lives and reigns with you
in the unity of the Holy Spirit,
one God, for ever and ever.

PRAYER AFTER COMMUNION

May the Sacrament we have received, O Lord our God,
nourish in us that faith
taught by the preaching of the Apostles
and kept safe by the labors of Saints Timothy and Titus.
Through Christ our Lord.

January 27
Saint Angela Merici, Virgin

From the Common of Virgins: For One Virgin (p. 554), or from the Common of Holy Men and Women: For Educators (p. 566).

COLLECT

May the Virgin Saint Angela never fail to commend us
to your compassion, O Lord, we pray,
that, following the lessons of her charity and prudence,
we may hold fast to your teaching
and express it in what we do.
Through our Lord Jesus Christ, your Son,
who lives and reigns with you
in the unity of the Holy Spirit,
one God, for ever and ever.

January 28

Saint Thomas Aquinas, Priest and Doctor of the Church

Memorial

From the Common of Doctors of the Church (p. 551), or from the Common of Pastors: For One Pastor (p. 544).

COLLECT

O God, who made Saint Thomas Aquinas
outstanding in his zeal for holiness
and his study of sacred doctrine,
grant us, we pray,
that we may understand what he taught
and imitate what he accomplished.
Through our Lord Jesus Christ, your Son,
who lives and reigns with you
in the unity of the Holy Spirit,
one God, for ever and ever.

January 31

Saint John Bosco, Priest

Memorial

From the Common of Pastors: For One Pastor (p. 544), or from the Common of Holy Men and Women: For Educators (p. 566).

COLLECT

O God, who raised up the Priest Saint John Bosco
as a father and teacher of the young,
grant, we pray,
that, aflame with the same fire of love,
we may seek out souls and serve you alone.
Through our Lord Jesus Christ, your Son,
who lives and reigns with you
in the unity of the Holy Spirit,
one God, for ever and ever.

FEBRUARY

February 2
THE PRESENTATION OF THE LORD

Feast

The Blessing of Candles and the Procession

First Form: The Procession

1. At an appropriate hour, a gathering takes place at a smaller church or other suitable place other than inside the church to which the procession will go. The faithful hold in their hands unlighted candles.

2. The Priest, wearing white vestments as for Mass, approaches with the ministers. Instead of the chasuble, the Priest may wear a cope, which he leaves aside after the procession is over.

3. While the candles are being lit, the following antiphon or another appropriate chant is sung.

Or:

4. When the chant is concluded, the Priest, facing the people, says: In the name of the Father, and of the Son, and of the Holy Spirit. Then the Priest greets the people in the usual way, and next he gives an introductory address, encouraging the faithful to celebrate the rite of this feast day actively and consciously. He may use these or similar words:

Dear brethren (brothers and sisters),
forty days have passed since we celebrated the joyful feast
of the Nativity of the Lord.
Today is the blessed day
when Jesus was presented in the Temple
by Mary and Joseph.

**Outwardly he was fulfilling the Law,
but in reality he was coming to meet his believing people.
Prompted by the Holy Spirit,
Simeon and Anna came to the Temple.
Enlightened by the same Spirit,
they recognized the Lord
and confessed him with exultation.
So let us also, gathered together by the Holy Spirit,
proceed to the house of God to encounter Christ.
There we shall find him
and recognize him in the breaking of the bread,
until he comes again, revealed in glory.**

5. After the address the Priest blesses the candles, saying, with hands extended:

Let us pray.

**O God, source and origin of all light,
who on this day showed to the just man Simeon
the Light for revelation to the Gentiles,
we humbly ask that,
in answer to your people's prayers,
you may be pleased to sanctify with your blessing ✠
these candles,
which we are eager to carry in praise of your name,
so that, treading the path of virtue,
we may reach that light which never fails.
Through Christ our Lord.**

℟. Amen.

Or:

**O God, true light, who create light eternal,
spreading it far and wide,
pour, we pray, into the hearts of the faithful
the brilliance of perpetual light,
so that all who are brightened in your holy temple
by the splendor of these candles
may happily reach the light of your glory.
Through Christ our Lord.**

℟. Amen.

He sprinkles the candles with holy water without saying anything, and puts incense into the thurible for the procession.

6. Then the Priest receives from the Deacon or a minister the lighted candle prepared for him and the procession begins, with the Deacon announcing (or, if there is no Deacon, the Priest himself):

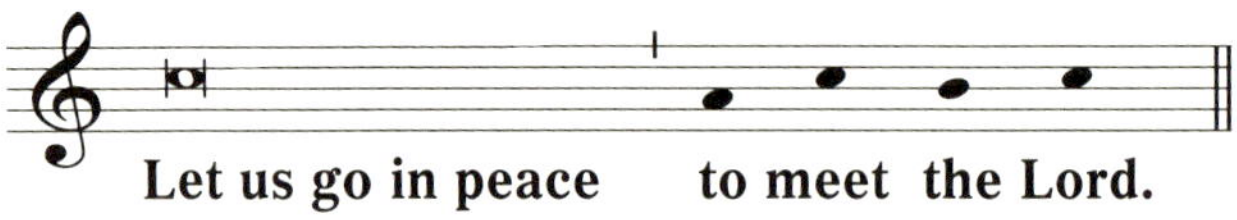

Or:

In this case, all respond:

7. All carry lighted candles. As the procession moves forward, one or other of the antiphons that follow is sung, namely the antiphon A light for revelation with the canticle (Lk 2: 29-32), or the antiphon Sion, adorn your bridal chamber or another appropriate chant.

I

Ant.

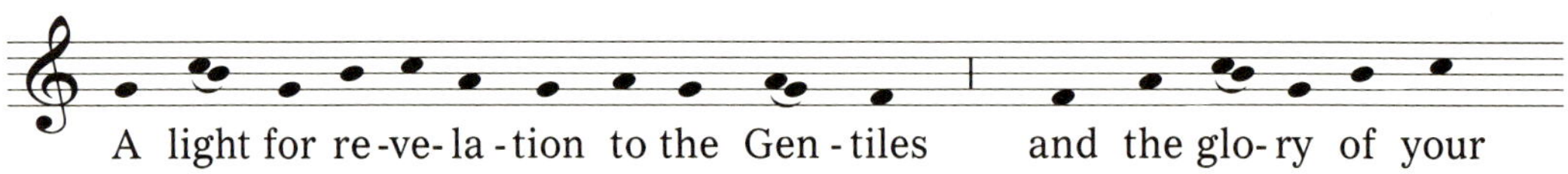

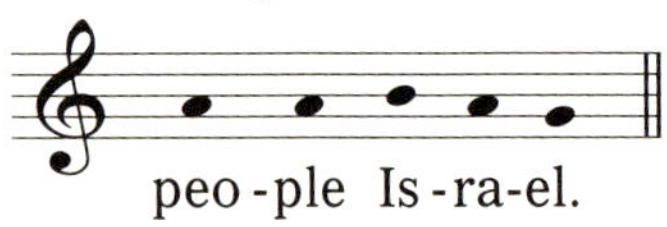

Lk 2: 29-32

Or:

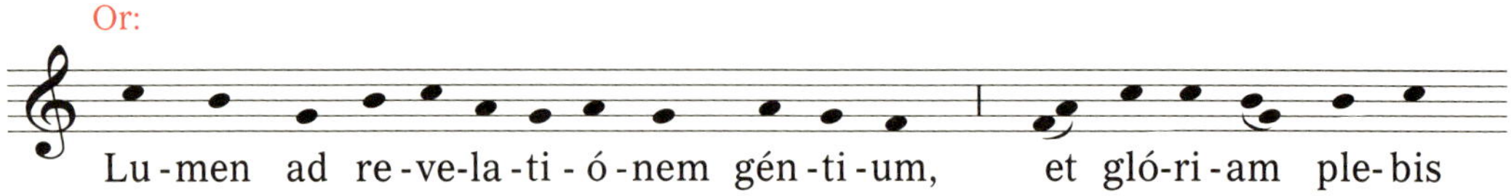

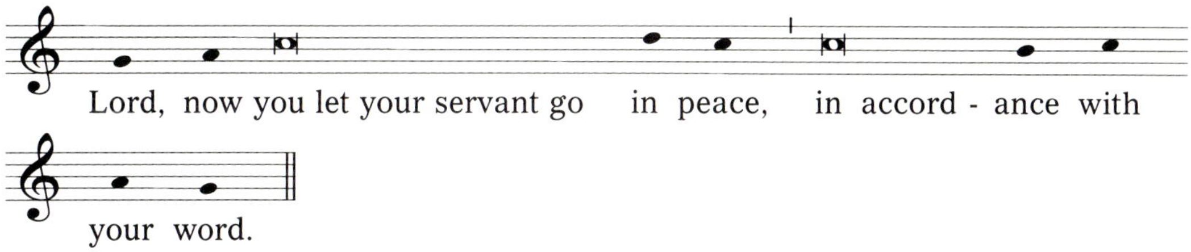

Ant.

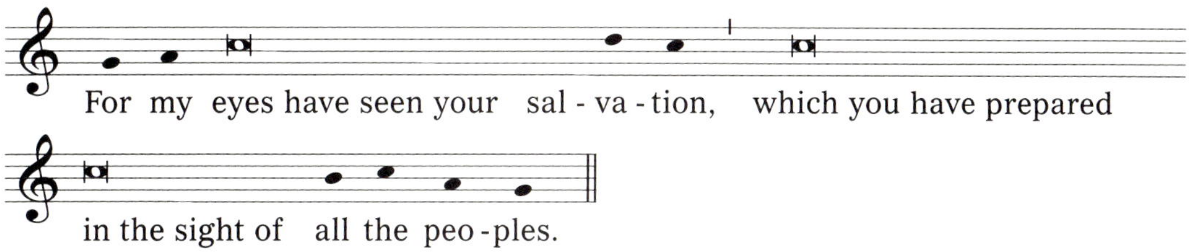

Ant.

Text without music:

Ant. A light for revelation to the Gentiles
and the glory of your people Israel.

Lord, now you let your servant go in peace,
in accordance with your word.

Ant. A light for revelation to the Gentiles . . .
For my eyes have seen your salvation.

Ant. A light for revelation to the Gentiles . . .
Which you have prepared in the sight of all the peoples.

Ant. A light for revelation to the Gentiles . . .

II

Ant. Sion, adorn your bridal chamber and welcome Christ the King; take Mary in your arms, who is the gate of heaven, for she herself is carrying the King of glory and new light. A Virgin she remains, though bringing in her hands the Son before the morning star begotten, whom Simeon, taking in his arms announced to the peoples as Lord of life and death and Savior of the world.

8. As the procession enters the church, the Entrance Antiphon of the Mass is sung. When the Priest has arrived at the altar, he venerates it and, if appropriate, incenses it. Then he goes to the chair, where he takes off the cope, if he used it in the procession, and puts on a chasuble. After the singing of the hymn Gloria in excelsis (Glory to God in the highest), he says the Collect as usual. The Mass continues in the usual manner.

Second Form: The Solemn Entrance

9. Whenever a procession cannot take place, the faithful gather in church, holding candles in their hands. The Priest, wearing white sacred vestments as for Mass, together with the ministers and a representative group of the faithful, goes to a suitable place, either in front of the church door or inside the church itself, where at least a large part of the faithful can conveniently participate in the rite.

10. When the Priest reaches the place appointed for the blessing of the candles, candles are lit while the antiphon Behold, our Lord (no. 3) or another appropriate chant is sung.

11. Then, after the greeting and address, the Priest blesses the candles, as above nos. 4-5; and then the procession to the altar takes place, with singing (nos. 6-7). For Mass, what is indicated in no. 8 above is observed.

At the Mass

Entrance Antiphon

Your merciful love, O God,
we have received in the midst of your temple.
Your praise, O God, like your name,
reaches the ends of the earth;
your right hand is filled with saving justice. Cf. Ps 48 (47): 10-11

The Gloria in excelsis (Glory to God in the highest) is said.

COLLECT

Almighty ever-living God,
we humbly implore your majesty
that, just as your Only Begotten Son
was presented on this day in the Temple
in the substance of our flesh,
so, by your grace,
we may be presented to you with minds made pure.
Through our Lord Jesus Christ, your Son,
who lives and reigns with you
in the unity of the Holy Spirit,
one God, for ever and ever.

When this Feast falls on a Sunday, the Creed is said.

PRAYER AFTER COMMUNION

By these holy gifts which we have received, O Lord,
bring your grace to perfection within us,
and, as you fulfilled Simeon's expectation
that he would not see death
until he had been privileged to welcome the Christ,
so may we, going forth to meet the Lord,
obtain the gift of eternal life.
Through Christ our Lord.

February 3

Saint Blaise, Bishop and Martyr

From the Common of Martyrs: For One Martyr (p. 531), or from the Common of Pastors: For a Bishop (p. 541).

COLLECT

**Hear, O Lord, the supplications your people make
under the patronage of the Martyr Saint Blaise,
and grant that they may rejoice in peace
in this present life,
and find help for life eternal.
Through our Lord Jesus Christ, your Son,
who lives and reigns with you
in the unity of the Holy Spirit,
one God, for ever and ever.**

Saint Ansgar, Bishop

From the Common of Pastors: For Missionaries (p. 548), or For a Bishop (p. 541).

COLLECT

**O God, who willed to send the Bishop Saint Ansgar
to enlighten many peoples,
grant us, through his intercession,
that we may always walk in the light of your truth.
Through our Lord Jesus Christ, your Son,
who lives and reigns with you
in the unity of the Holy Spirit,
one God, for ever and ever.**

February 5

Saint Agatha, Virgin and Martyr

Memorial

From the Common of Martyrs: For a Virgin Martyr (p. 537), or from the Common of Virgins: For One Virgin (p. 554).

COLLECT

**May the Virgin Martyr Saint Agatha
implore your compassion for us, O Lord, we pray,
for she found favor with you
by the courage of her martyrdom
and the merit of her chastity.
Through our Lord Jesus Christ, your Son,
who lives and reigns with you
in the unity of the Holy Spirit,
one God, for ever and ever.**

February 6

Saint Paul Miki and Companions, Martyrs

Memorial

From the Common of Martyrs: For Several Martyrs (p. 526).

COLLECT

**O God, strength of all the Saints,
who through the Cross were pleased to call
the Martyrs Saint Paul Miki and companions to life,
grant, we pray, that by their intercession
we may hold with courage even until death
to the faith that we profess.
Through our Lord Jesus Christ, your Son,
who lives and reigns with you
in the unity of the Holy Spirit,
one God, for ever and ever.**

February 8

Saint Jerome Emiliani

From the Common of Holy Men and Women: For Educators (p. 566).

COLLECT

**O God, Father of mercies,
who sent Saint Jerome Emiliani
as a helper and father to orphans,
grant, through his intercession,
that we may preserve faithfully the spirit of adoption,
by which we are called, and truly are, your children.
Through our Lord Jesus Christ, your Son,
who lives and reigns with you
in the unity of the Holy Spirit,
one God, for ever and ever.**

Saint Josephine Bakhita, Virgin

From the Common of Virgins: For One Virgin (p. 554).

COLLECT

**O God, who led Saint Josephine Bakhita
from abject slavery
to the dignity of being your daughter and a bride of Christ,
grant, we pray, that by her example
we may show constant love for the Lord Jesus crucified,
remaining steadfast in charity
and prompt to show compassion.
Through our Lord Jesus Christ, your Son,
who lives and reigns with you
in the unity of the Holy Spirit,
one God, for ever and ever.**

February 10

Saint Scholastica, Virgin

Memorial

From the Common of Virgins: For One Virgin (p. 554), or from the Common of Holy Men and Women: For a Nun (p. 562).

COLLECT

As we celebrate anew the Memorial
of the Virgin Saint Scholastica,
we pray, O Lord,
that, following her example,
we may serve you with pure love
and happily receive what comes from loving you.
Through our Lord Jesus Christ, your Son,
who lives and reigns with you
in the unity of the Holy Spirit,
one God, for ever and ever.

February 11

Our Lady of Lourdes

From the Common of the Blessed Virgin Mary (p. 518).

COLLECT

Grant us, O merciful God, protection in our weakness,
that we, who keep the Memorial
of the Immaculate Mother of God,
may, with the help of her intercession,
rise up from our iniquities.
Through our Lord Jesus Christ, your Son,
who lives and reigns with you
in the unity of the Holy Spirit,
one God, for ever and ever.

February 14
Saints Cyril, Monk, and Methodius, Bishop

Memorial

Entrance Antiphon These are holy men who became friends of God,
glorious heralds of divine truth.

COLLECT O God, who enlightened the Slavic peoples
through the brothers Saints Cyril and Methodius,
grant that our hearts may grasp the words of your teaching,
and perfect us as a people of one accord
in true faith and right confession.
Through our Lord Jesus Christ, your Son,
who lives and reigns with you
in the unity of the Holy Spirit,
one God, for ever and ever.

PRAYER AFTER COMMUNION O God, Father of all nations,
who make us sharers in the one Bread and the one Spirit
and heirs of the eternal banquet,
grant in your kindness
on this feast day of Saints Cyril and Methodius,
that the multitude of your children,
persevering in the same faith,
may be united in building up
the Kingdom of justice and peace.
Through Christ our Lord.

February 17
The Seven Holy Founders of the Servite Order

From the Common of Holy Men and Women: For Religious (p. 563).

COLLECT Impart to us, O Lord, in kindness
the filial devotion with which the holy brothers
venerated so devoutly the Mother of God
and led your people to yourself.
Through our Lord Jesus Christ, your Son,
who lives and reigns with you
in the unity of the Holy Spirit,
one God, for ever and ever.

February 21

Saint Peter Damian, Bishop and Doctor of the Church

From the Common of Doctors of the Church (p. 551), or from the Common of Pastors: For a Bishop (p. 541).

COLLECT

**Grant, we pray, almighty God,
that we may so follow the teaching and example
of the Bishop Saint Peter Damian,
that, putting nothing before Christ
and always ardent in the service of your Church,
we may be led to the joys of eternal light.
Through our Lord Jesus Christ, your Son,
who lives and reigns with you
in the unity of the Holy Spirit,
one God, for ever and ever.**

February 22

The Chair of Saint Peter the Apostle

Feast

Entrance Antiphon

**The Lord says to Simon Peter:
I have prayed for you that your faith may not fail,
and, once you have turned back, strengthen your brothers.**

Lk 22: 32

The Gloria in excelsis (Glory to God in the highest) is said.

COLLECT

**Grant, we pray, almighty God,
that no tempests may disturb us,
for you have set us fast
on the rock of the Apostle Peter's confession of faith.
Through our Lord Jesus Christ, your Son,
who lives and reigns with you
in the unity of the Holy Spirit,
one God, for ever and ever.**

PRAYER AFTER COMMUNION

O God, who at our celebration
of the feast day of the blessed Apostle Peter
have nourished us by communion
in the Body and Blood of Christ,
grant, we pray, that this redeeming exchange
may be for us a Sacrament of unity and peace.
Through Christ our Lord.

The Solemn Blessing formula on p. 318 may be used.

February 23

Saint Polycarp, Bishop and Martyr

Memorial

From the Common of Martyrs: For One Martyr (p. 531), or from the Common of Pastors: For a Bishop (p. 541).

COLLECT

God of all creation,
who were pleased to give the Bishop Saint Polycarp
a place in the company of the Martyrs,
grant, through his intercession,
that, sharing with him in the chalice of Christ,
we may rise through the Holy Spirit to eternal life.
Through our Lord Jesus Christ, your Son,
who lives and reigns with you
in the unity of the Holy Spirit,
one God, for ever and ever.

MARCH

[In the Dioceses of the United States]

March 3

Saint Katharine Drexel, Virgin

From the Common of Virgins: For One Virgin (p. 554).

COLLECT

God of love,
you called Saint Katharine Drexel
to teach the message of the Gospel
and to bring the life of the Eucharist
to the Native American and African American peoples;
by her prayers and example,
enable us to work for justice
among the poor and the oppressed,
and keep us undivided in love
in the eucharistic community of your Church.
Through our Lord Jesus Christ, your Son,
who lives and reigns with you
in the unity of the Holy Spirit,
one God, for ever and ever.

March 4

Saint Casimir

From the Common of Holy Men and Women: For One Saint (p. 559).

COLLECT

Almighty God, to serve you is to reign;
grant that, with the help of Saint Casimir's intercession,
we may constantly serve you in holiness and justice.
Through our Lord Jesus Christ, your Son,
who lives and reigns with you
in the unity of the Holy Spirit,
one God, for ever and ever.

March 7

Saints Perpetua and Felicity, Martyrs

Memorial

Entrance Antiphon

The souls of the Saints are rejoicing in heaven,
the Saints who followed the footsteps of Christ,
and since for love of him they shed their blood,
they now exult with Christ for ever.

COLLECT

O God, at the urging of whose love
the Martyrs Saints Perpetua and Felicity
defied their persecutors and overcame
the torment of death,
grant, we ask, by their prayers, that we may ever grow
in your love.
Through our Lord Jesus Christ, your Son,
who lives and reigns with you
in the unity of the Holy Spirit,
one God, for ever and ever.

PRAYER AFTER COMMUNION

As we draw everlasting joys, O Lord,
from our participation in this Sacrament
and from the Memorial of Saints Perpetua and Felicity,
we humbly implore,
that by your gift we may truly understand
what you grant us to enact in diligent service.
Through Christ our Lord.

March 8

Saint John of God, Religious

From the Common of Holy Men and Women: For Religious (p. 563), or For Those Who Practiced Works of Mercy (p. 564).

COLLECT

O God, who filled Saint John of God
with a spirit of compassion,
grant, we pray,
that, giving ourselves to works of charity,
we may merit to be found among the elect
in your Kingdom.
Through our Lord Jesus Christ, your Son,
who lives and reigns with you
in the unity of the Holy Spirit,
one God, for ever and ever.

March 9

Saint Frances of Rome, Religious

From the Common of Holy Men and Women: For Holy Women (p. 566), or For Religious (p. 563).

COLLECT

O God, who have given us in Saint Frances of Rome
a singular model of both married and monastic life,
grant us perseverance in your service,
that in every circumstance of life
we may see and follow you.
Through our Lord Jesus Christ, your Son,
who lives and reigns with you
in the unity of the Holy Spirit,
one God, for ever and ever.

March 17
Saint Patrick, Bishop

From the Common of Pastors: For Missionaries (p. 548), or For a Bishop (p. 541).

COLLECT

O God, who chose the Bishop Saint Patrick
to preach your glory to the peoples of Ireland,
grant, through his merits and intercession,
that those who glory in the name of Christian
may never cease to proclaim your wondrous deeds to all.
Through our Lord Jesus Christ, your Son,
who lives and reigns with you
in the unity of the Holy Spirit,
one God, for ever and ever.

March 18
Saint Cyril of Jerusalem, Bishop and Doctor of the Church

From the Common of Pastors: For a Bishop (p. 541), or from the Common Doctors of the Church (p. 551).

COLLECT

O God, who through the Bishop Saint Cyril of Jerusalem
led your Church in a wonderful way
to a deeper sense of the mysteries of salvation,
grant us, through his intercession,
that we may so acknowledge your Son
as to have life ever more abundantly.
Through our Lord Jesus Christ, your Son,
who lives and reigns with you
in the unity of the Holy Spirit,
one God, for ever and ever.

March 19

SAINT JOSEPH, SPOUSE OF THE BLESSED VIRGIN MARY

Solemnity

Entrance Antiphon

Behold, a faithful and prudent steward,
whom the Lord set over his household. Cf. Lk 12: 42

The Gloria in excelsis (Glory to God in the highest) is said.

COLLECT

Grant, we pray, almighty God,
that by Saint Joseph's intercession
your Church may constantly watch over
the unfolding of the mysteries of human salvation,
whose beginnings you entrusted to his faithful care.
Through our Lord Jesus Christ, your Son,
who lives and reigns with you
in the unity of the Holy Spirit,
one God, for ever and ever.

The Creed is said.

PRAYER AFTER COMMUNION

Defend with unfailing protection,
O Lord, we pray,
the family you have nourished
with food from this altar,
as they rejoice at the Solemnity of Saint Joseph,
and graciously keep safe your gifts among them.
Through Christ our Lord.

March 23
Saint Turibius of Mogrovejo, Bishop

From the Common of Pastors: For a Bishop (p. 541).

COLLECT

**O God, who gave increase to your Church
through the apostolic labors and zeal for truth
of the Bishop Saint Turibius,
grant that the people consecrated to you
may always receive new growth in faith and holiness.
Through our Lord Jesus Christ, your Son,
who lives and reigns with you
in the unity of the Holy Spirit,
one God, for ever and ever.**

March 25

THE ANNUNCIATION OF THE LORD

Solemnity

Whenever this Solemnity occurs during Holy Week, it is transferred to the Monday after the Second Sunday of Easter.

Entrance Antiphon

The Lord said, as he entered the world:
Behold, I come to do your will, O God. Heb 10: 5, 7

The Gloria in excelsis (Glory to God in the highest) is said.

COLLECT

O God, who willed that your Word
should take on the reality of human flesh
in the womb of the Virgin Mary,
grant, we pray,
that we, who confess our Redeemer to be God and man,
may merit to become partakers
even in his divine nature.
Who lives and reigns with you
in the unity of the Holy Spirit,
one God, for ever and ever.

The Creed is said. All kneel at the words and by the Holy Spirit was incarnate.

PRAYER AFTER COMMUNION

Confirm in our minds the mysteries of the true faith,
we pray, O Lord,
so that, confessing that he who was conceived
of the Virgin Mary
is true God and true man,
we may, through the saving power of his Resurrection,
merit to attain eternal joy.
Through Christ our Lord.

APRIL

April 2
Saint Francis of Paola, Hermit

From the Common of Holy Men and Women: For Religious (p. 563).

COLLECT

O God, exaltation of the lowly,
who raised Saint Francis of Paola to the glory
of your Saints,
grant, we pray, that by his merits and example
we may happily attain the rewards
promised to the humble.
Through our Lord Jesus Christ, your Son,
who lives and reigns with you
in the unity of the Holy Spirit,
one God, for ever and ever.

April 4
Saint Isidore, Bishop and Doctor of the Church

From the Common of Pastors: For a Bishop (p. 541), or from the Common of Doctors of the Church (p. 551).

COLLECT

Graciously hear the prayers, O Lord,
which we make in commemoration of Saint Isidore,
that your Church may be aided by his intercession,
just as she has been instructed by his heavenly teaching.
Through our Lord Jesus Christ, your Son,
who lives and reigns with you
in the unity of the Holy Spirit,
one God, for ever and ever.

April 5
Saint Vincent Ferrer, Priest

From the Common of Pastors: For Missionaries (p. 548).

COLLECT

O God, who raised up the Priest Saint Vincent Ferrer
to minister by the preaching of the Gospel,
grant, we pray,
that, when the Judge comes,
whom Saint Vincent proclaimed on earth,
we may be among those blessed
to behold him reigning in heaven.
Who lives and reigns with you
in the unity of the Holy Spirit,
one God, for ever and ever.

April 7
Saint John Baptist de la Salle, Priest

Memorial

From the Common of Pastors: For One Pastor (p. 544), or from the Common of Holy Men and Women: For Educators (p. 566).

COLLECT

O God, who chose Saint John Baptist de la Salle
to educate young Christians,
raise up, we pray, teachers in your Church
ready to devote themselves wholeheartedly
to the human and Christian formation of the young.
Through our Lord Jesus Christ, your Son,
who lives and reigns with you
in the unity of the Holy Spirit,
one God, for ever and ever.

April 11

Saint Stanislaus, Bishop and Martyr

Memorial

From the Common of Martyrs: For One Martyr (p. 531, or, during Easter Time, p. 535), or from the Common of Pastors: For a Bishop (p. 541).

COLLECT

O God, for whose honor the Bishop Saint Stanislaus
fell beneath the swords of his persecutors,
grant, we pray,
that we may persevere strong in faith even until death.
Through our Lord Jesus Christ, your Son,
who lives and reigns with you
in the unity of the Holy Spirit,
one God, for ever and ever.

April 13

Saint Martin I, Pope and Martyr

From the Common of Martyrs: For One Martyr (p. 531, or, during Easter Time, p. 535), or from the Common of Pastors: For a Pope (p. 539).

COLLECT

Grant, almighty God,
that we may withstand the trials of this world
with invincible firmness of purpose,
just as you did not allow your Martyr
Pope Saint Martin the First
to be daunted by threats or broken by suffering.
Through our Lord Jesus Christ, your Son,
who lives and reigns with you
in the unity of the Holy Spirit,
one God, for ever and ever.

April 21
Saint Anselm, Bishop and Doctor of the Church

From the Common of Pastors: For a Bishop (p. 541), or from the Common of Doctors of the Church (p. 551).

COLLECT

**O God, who led the Bishop Saint Anselm
to seek out and teach the depths of your wisdom,
grant, we pray,
that our faith in you may so aid our understanding,
that what we believe by your command
may give delight to our hearts.
Through our Lord Jesus Christ, your Son,
who lives and reigns with you
in the unity of the Holy Spirit,
one God, for ever and ever.**

April 23
Saint George, Martyr

From the Common of Martyrs: For One Martyr during Easter Time (p. 535).

COLLECT

**Extolling your might, O Lord,
we humbly implore you,
that, as Saint George imitated the Passion of the Lord,
so he may lend us ready help in our weakness.
Through our Lord Jesus Christ, your Son,
who lives and reigns with you
in the unity of the Holy Spirit,
one God, for ever and ever.**

Saint Adalbert, Bishop and Martyr

From the Common of Martyrs: For One Martyr during Easter Time (p. 535), or from the Common of Pastors: For a Bishop (p. 541).

COLLECT

O God, who bestowed the crown of martyrdom
on the Bishop Saint Adalbert,
as he burned with zeal for souls,
grant, we pray, by his prayers,
that the obedience of the flock
may never fail the shepherds,
nor the care of the shepherds be ever lacking to the flock.
Through our Lord Jesus Christ, your Son,
who lives and reigns with you
in the unity of the Holy Spirit,
one God, for ever and ever.

April 24

Saint Fidelis of Sigmaringen, Priest and Martyr

From the Common of Martyrs: For One Martyr during Easter Time (p. 535), or from the Common of Pastors: For One Pastor (p. 544).

COLLECT

O God, who were pleased to award
the palm of martyrdom to Saint Fidelis
as, burning with love for you, he propagated the faith,
grant, we pray, through his intercession,
that, grounded in charity,
we may merit to know with him
the power of the Resurrection of Christ.
Who lives and reigns with you
in the unity of the Holy Spirit,
one God, for ever and ever.

April 25
Saint Mark, Evangelist

Feast

Entrance Antiphon Go into all the world,
and proclaim the Gospel to every creature, alleluia. Mk 16: 15

The Gloria in excelsis (Glory to God in the highest) is said.

COLLECT O God, who raised up Saint Mark, your Evangelist,
and endowed him with the grace to preach the Gospel,
grant, we pray,
that we may so profit from his teaching
as to follow faithfully in the footsteps of Christ.
Who lives and reigns with you
in the unity of the Holy Spirit,
one God, for ever and ever.

PRAYER AFTER COMMUNION Grant, we pray, almighty God,
that what we have received from your holy altar
may sanctify us and make us strong
in the faith of the Gospel which Saint Mark proclaimed.
Through Christ our Lord.

April 28

Saint Peter Chanel, Priest and Martyr

From the Common of Martyrs: For One Martyr during Easter Time (p. 535), or from the Common of Pastors: For Missionaries (p. 548).

COLLECT

O God, who for the spreading of your Church
crowned Saint Peter Chanel with martyrdom,
grant that, in these days of paschal joy,
we may so celebrate the mysteries
of Christ's Death and Resurrection
as to bear worthy witness to newness of life.
Through our Lord Jesus Christ, your Son,
who lives and reigns with you
in the unity of the Holy Spirit,
one God, for ever and ever.

Saint Louis Grignion de Montfort, Priest

From the Common of Pastors: For One Pastor (p. 544).

COLLECT

O God, who willed to direct the steps
of the Priest Saint Louis
along the way of salvation and of the love of Christ,
in the company of the Blessed Virgin,
grant us, by his example,
that, meditating on the mysteries of your love,
we may strive tirelessly for the building up of your Church.
Through our Lord Jesus Christ, your Son,
who lives and reigns with you
in the unity of the Holy Spirit,
one God, for ever and ever.

Or:

Almighty and eternal God,
who made the Priest Saint Louis
an outstanding witness and teacher
of total devotion to Christ your Son
through the hands of his Blessed Mother,
grant us that, following the same spiritual path,
we may constantly spread your Kingdom.
Through our Lord Jesus Christ, your Son,
who lives and reigns with you
in the unity of the Holy Spirit,
one God, for ever and ever.

April 29

Saint Catherine of Siena, Virgin and Doctor of the Church

Memorial

Entrance Antiphon Here is a wise virgin, from among the number of the prudent, who went forth with lighted lamp to meet Christ, alleluia.

COLLECT

O God, who set Saint Catherine of Siena on fire
with divine love
in her contemplation of the Lord's Passion
and her service of your Church,
grant, through her intercession,
that your people,
participating in the mystery of Christ,
may ever exult in the revelation of his glory.
Who lives and reigns with you
in the unity of the Holy Spirit,
one God, for ever and ever.

PRAYER AFTER COMMUNION

May the heavenly table
at which we have been fed, O Lord,
confer eternal life upon us,
as even in this world
it nourished the life of Saint Catherine.
Through Christ our Lord.

April 30

Saint Pius V, Pope

From the Common of Pastors: For a Pope (p. 539).

COLLECT

O God, who in your providence
raised up Pope Saint Pius the Fifth in your Church
that the faith might be safeguarded
and more fitting worship be offered to you,
grant, through his intercession,
that we may participate in your mysteries
with lively faith and fruitful charity.
Through our Lord Jesus Christ, your Son,
who lives and reigns with you
in the unity of the Holy Spirit,
one God, for ever and ever.

MAY

May 1
Saint Joseph the Worker

Entrance Antiphon

Blessed are all who fear the Lord and walk in his ways!
By the labor of your hands you shall eat;
blessed are you, and blessed will you be, alleluia.
Ps 128 (127): 1-2

COLLECT

O God, Creator of all things,
who laid down for the human race the law of work,
graciously grant
that by the example of Saint Joseph
and under his patronage
we may complete the works you set us to do
and attain the rewards you promise.
Through our Lord Jesus Christ, your Son,
who lives and reigns with you
in the unity of the Holy Spirit,
one God, for ever and ever.

PRAYER AFTER COMMUNION

Having fed upon heavenly delights,
we humbly ask you, O Lord,
that, by Saint Joseph's example,
cherishing in our hearts the signs of your love,
we may ever enjoy the fruit of perpetual peace.
Through Christ our Lord.

May 2

Saint Athanasius, Bishop and Doctor of the Church

Memorial

Entrance Antiphon

In the midst of the Church he opened his mouth,
and the Lord filled him
with the spirit of wisdom and understanding
and clothed him in a robe of glory, alleluia. Cf. Sir 15: 5

COLLECT

Almighty ever-living God,
who raised up the Bishop Saint Athanasius
as an outstanding champion of your Son's divinity,
mercifully grant,
that, rejoicing in his teaching and his protection,
we may never cease to grow
in knowledge and love of you.
Through our Lord Jesus Christ, your Son,
who lives and reigns with you
in the unity of the Holy Spirit,
one God, for ever and ever.

PRAYER AFTER COMMUNION

Grant us, we pray, almighty God,
that the true divinity of your Only Begotten Son,
which we firmly profess with Saint Athanasius,
may, through this Sacrament,
ever give us life and protection.
Through Christ our Lord.

May 3
Saints Philip and James, Apostles

Feast

Entrance Antiphon

These are the holy men
whom the Lord chose in his own perfect love;
to them he gave eternal glory, alleluia.

The Gloria in excelsis (Glory to God in the highest) is said.

COLLECT

O God, who gladden us each year
with the feast day of the Apostles Philip and James,
grant us, through their prayers,
a share in the Passion and Resurrection
of your Only Begotten Son,
so that we may merit to behold you for eternity.
Through our Lord Jesus Christ, your Son,
who lives and reigns with you
in the unity of the Holy Spirit,
one God, for ever and ever.

PRAYER AFTER COMMUNION

Purify our minds, we pray, O Lord,
by these holy gifts we have received,
so that, contemplating you in your Son
together with the Apostles Philip and James,
we may be worthy to possess eternal life.
Through Christ our Lord.

The Solemn Blessing formula on p. 319 may be used.

[In the Dioceses of the United States]

May 10

Saint Damien de Veuster, Priest

From the Common of Pastors: For Missionaries (p. 548).

COLLECT

Father of mercy,
who gave us in Saint Damien
a shining witness of love for the poorest
and most abandoned,
grant that, by his intercession,
as faithful witnesses of the heart of your Son Jesus,
we too may be servants of the most needy and rejected.
Through our Lord Jesus Christ, your Son,
who lives and reigns with you
in the unity of the Holy Spirit,
one God, for ever and ever.

May 12

Saints Nereus and Achilleus, Martyrs

From the Common of Martyrs: For Several Martyrs (p. 526 or, during Easter Time, p. 532).

COLLECT

Grant, we pray, almighty God,
that we, who know the great courage
of the glorious Martyrs Nereus and Achilleus
in confessing you,
may experience their loving intercession for us
in your presence.
Through our Lord Jesus Christ, your Son,
who lives and reigns with you
in the unity of the Holy Spirit,
one God, for ever and ever.

May 12
Saint Pancras, Martyr

From the Common of Martyrs: For One Martyr (p. 531 or, during Easter Time, p. 535).

COLLECT

May your Church rejoice, O God,
confident in the intercession of the Martyr Saint Pancras,
and by his glorious prayers
may she persevere in devotion to you
and stand ever firm.
Through our Lord Jesus Christ, your Son,
who lives and reigns with you
in the unity of the Holy Spirit,
one God, for ever and ever.

May 13
Our Lady of Fatima

From the Common of the Blessed Virgin Mary (p. 518).

COLLECT

O God, who chose the Mother of your Son
to be our Mother also,
grant us that, persevering in penance and prayer
for the salvation of the world,
we may further more effectively each day
the reign of Christ.
Who lives and reigns with you
in the unity of the Holy Spirit,
one God, for ever and ever.

May 14

SAINT MATTHIAS, APOSTLE

Feast

Entrance Antiphon

**It was not you who chose me, says the Lord,
but I who chose you and appointed you to go and bear fruit,
fruit that will last (E.T. alleluia).** Jn 15: 16

The Gloria in excelsis (Glory to God in the highest) is said.

COLLECT

**O God, who assigned Saint Matthias
a place in the college of Apostles,
grant us, through his intercession,
that, rejoicing at how your love has been allotted to us,
we may merit to be numbered among the elect.
Through our Lord Jesus Christ, your Son,
who lives and reigns with you
in the unity of the Holy Spirit,
one God, for ever and ever.**

PRAYER AFTER COMMUNION

**Never cease, O Lord, we pray,
to fill your family with divine gifts,
and, through blessed Matthias' intercession for us,
graciously admit us to a share in the lot
of the Saints in light.
Through Christ our Lord.**

The Solemn Blessing formula on p. 319 may be used.

[In the Dioceses of the United States]

May 15

Saint Isidore

From the Common of Holy Men and Women: For One Saint (p. 559).

COLLECT

**Lord God, to whom belongs all creation,
and who call us to serve you
by caring for the gifts that surround us,
inspire us by the example of Saint Isidore
to share our food with the hungry
and to work for the salvation of all people.
Through our Lord Jesus Christ, your Son,
who lives and reigns with you
in the unity of the Holy Spirit,
one God, for ever and ever.**

May 18

Saint John I, Pope and Martyr

From the Common of Martyrs: For One Martyr (p. 531 or, during Easter Time, p. 535), or from the Common of Pastors: For a Pope (p. 539).

COLLECT

**O God, who reward faithful souls
and who have consecrated this day
by the martyrdom of Pope Saint John the First,
graciously hear the prayers of your people
and grant that we, who venerate his merits,
may imitate his constancy in the faith.
Through our Lord Jesus Christ, your Son,
who lives and reigns with you
in the unity of the Holy Spirit,
one God, for ever and ever.**

May 20
Saint Bernardine of Siena, Priest

From the Common of Pastors: For Missionaries (p. 548), or from the Common of Holy Men and Women: For Religious (p. 563).

COLLECT

**O God, who gave the Priest Saint Bernardine of Siena
a great love for the holy Name of Jesus,
grant, through his merits and prayers,
that we may ever be set aflame
with the spirit of your love.
Through our Lord Jesus Christ, your Son,
who lives and reigns with you
in the unity of the Holy Spirit,
one God, for ever and ever.**

May 21
Saint Christopher Magallanes, Priest, and Companions, Martyrs

From the Common of Martyrs: For Several Martyrs (p. 526 or, during Easter Time, p. 532).

COLLECT

**Almighty and eternal God,
who made the Priest Saint Christopher Magallanes
and his companions
faithful to Christ the King even to the point of martyrdom,
grant us, through their intercession,
that, persevering in confession of the true faith,
we may always hold fast to the commandments
of your love.
Through our Lord Jesus Christ, your Son,
who lives and reigns with you
in the unity of the Holy Spirit,
one God, for ever and ever.**

May 22

Saint Rita of Cascia, Religious

From the Common of Holy Men and Women: For Religious (p. 563).

COLLECT

**Bestow on us, we pray, O Lord,
the wisdom and strength of the Cross,
with which you were pleased to endow Saint Rita,
so that, suffering in every tribulation with Christ,
we may participate ever more deeply
in his Paschal Mystery.
Who lives and reigns with you
in the unity of the Holy Spirit,
one God, for ever and ever.**

May 25

Saint Bede the Venerable, Priest and Doctor of the Church

From the Common of Doctors of the Church (p. 551), or from the Common of Holy Men and Women: For a Monk (p. 561).

COLLECT

**O God, who bring light to your Church
through the learning of the Priest Saint Bede,
mercifully grant that your servants
may always be enlightened by his wisdom
and helped by his merits.
Through our Lord Jesus Christ, your Son,
who lives and reigns with you
in the unity of the Holy Spirit,
one God, for ever and ever.**

Saint Gregory VII, Pope

From the Common of Pastors: For a Pope (p. 539).

COLLECT

Give to your Church, we pray, O Lord,
that spirit of fortitude and zeal for justice
which you made to shine forth
  in Pope Saint Gregory the Seventh,
so that, rejecting evil, she may be free
to carry out in charity whatever is right.
Through our Lord Jesus Christ, your Son,
who lives and reigns with you
  in the unity of the Holy Spirit,
one God, for ever and ever.

Saint Mary Magdalene de' Pazzi, Virgin

From the Common of Virgins: For One Virgin (p. 554), or from the Common of Holy Men and Women: For Religious (p. 563).

COLLECT

O God, lover of virginity,
who adorned with heavenly gifts
the Virgin Saint Mary Magdalene de' Pazzi,
setting her on fire with your love,
grant, we pray, that we, who honor her today,
may imitate her example of purity and love.
Through our Lord Jesus Christ, your Son,
who lives and reigns with you
  in the unity of the Holy Spirit,
one God, for ever and ever.

May 26

Saint Philip Neri, Priest

Memorial

Entrance Antiphon

The love of God has been poured into our hearts
through the Spirit of God dwelling within us (E.T. alleluia).
Rom 5: 5; cf. 8: 11

COLLECT

O God, who never cease to bestow the glory of holiness
on the faithful servants you raise up for yourself,
graciously grant
that the Holy Spirit may kindle in us that fire
with which he wonderfully filled
the heart of Saint Philip Neri.
Through our Lord Jesus Christ, your Son,
who lives and reigns with you
in the unity of the Holy Spirit,
one God, for ever and ever.

PRAYER AFTER COMMUNION

Having fed upon these heavenly delights,
we pray, O Lord,
that in imitation of Saint Philip
we may always long for that food by which we truly live.
Through Christ our Lord.

May 27
Saint Augustine of Canterbury, Bishop

From the Common of Pastors: For Missionaries (p. 548), or For a Bishop (p. 541).

COLLECT

O God, who by the preaching
of the Bishop Saint Augustine of Canterbury
led the English peoples to the Gospel,
grant, we pray, that the fruits of his labors
may remain ever abundant in your Church.
Through our Lord Jesus Christ, your Son,
who lives and reigns with you
in the unity of the Holy Spirit,
one God, for ever and ever.

May 31
THE VISITATION OF THE BLESSED VIRGIN MARY

Feast

Entrance Antiphon

Come and hear, all who fear God;
I will tell what the Lord did for my soul (E.T. alleluia).

Cf. Ps 66 (65): 16

The Gloria in excelsis (Glory to God in the highest) is said.

COLLECT

Almighty ever-living God,
who, while the Blessed Virgin Mary was carrying
your Son in her womb,
inspired her to visit Elizabeth,
grant us, we pray,
that, faithful to the promptings of the Spirit,
we may magnify your greatness
with the Virgin Mary at all times.
Through our Lord Jesus Christ, your Son,
who lives and reigns with you
in the unity of the Holy Spirit,
one God, for ever and ever.

PRAYER AFTER COMMUNION

May your Church proclaim your greatness, O God,
for you have done great things for your faithful,
and, as Saint John the Baptist leapt with joy
when he first sensed the hidden presence of Christ,
so may your Church rejoice
to receive in this Sacrament the same ever-living Lord.
Who lives and reigns for ever and ever.

The Solemn Blessing formula on p. 318 may be used.

Saturday after the Second Sunday after Pentecost
The Immaculate Heart of the Blessed Virgin Mary

Memorial

Entrance Antiphon

My heart will rejoice in your salvation.
I will sing to the Lord, who has been bountiful with me.
Ps 13 (12): 6

COLLECT

O God, who prepared a fit dwelling place
for the Holy Spirit
in the Heart of the Blessed Virgin Mary,
graciously grant that through her intercession
we may be a worthy temple of your glory.
Through our Lord Jesus Christ, your Son,
who lives and reigns with you
in the unity of the Holy Spirit,
one God, for ever and ever.

PRAYER AFTER COMMUNION

Having been made partakers of eternal redemption,
we pray, O Lord,
that we, who commemorate the Mother of your Son,
may glory in the fullness of your grace
and experience its continued increase for our salvation.
Through Christ our Lord.

JUNE

June 1
Saint Justin, Martyr

Memorial

Entrance Antiphon

The wicked have told me lies, but not so is your law:
I spoke of your decrees before kings,
and was not confounded (E.T. alleluia). Cf. Ps 119 (118): 85, 46

COLLECT

O God, who through the folly of the Cross
wondrously taught Saint Justin the Martyr
the surpassing knowledge of Jesus Christ,
grant us, through his intercession,
that, having rejected deception and error,
we may become steadfast in the faith.
Through our Lord Jesus Christ, your Son,
who lives and reigns with you
in the unity of the Holy Spirit,
one God, for ever and ever.

PRAYER AFTER COMMUNION

Refreshed by heavenly food,
we humbly implore you, O Lord,
that, attentive to the teaching of Saint Justin the Martyr,
we may abide at all times in thanksgiving
for the gifts we have received.
Through Christ our Lord.

June 2
Saints Marcellinus and Peter, Martyrs

From the Common of Martyrs: For Several Martyrs (p. 526 or, during Easter Time, p. 532).

COLLECT

**O God, who surround us with protection
through the glorious confession
of the Martyrs Saints Marcellinus and Peter,
grant that we may profit by imitating them
and be upheld by their prayer.
Through our Lord Jesus Christ, your Son,
who lives and reigns with you
in the unity of the Holy Spirit,
one God, for ever and ever.**

June 3

Saint Charles Lwanga and Companions, Martyrs

Memorial

Entrance Antiphon

As gold in the furnace, the Lord put his chosen to the test;
as sacrificial offerings, he took them to himself;
and in due time they will be honored,
and grace and peace will be with the elect of God (E.T. alleluia).

Cf. Wis 3: 6-7, 9

COLLECT

O God, who have made the blood of Martyrs
the seed of Christians,
mercifully grant that the field which is your Church,
watered by the blood
shed by Saint Charles Lwanga and his companions,
may be fertile and always yield you an abundant harvest.
Through our Lord Jesus Christ, your Son,
who lives and reigns with you
in the unity of the Holy Spirit,
one God, for ever and ever.

PRAYER AFTER COMMUNION

We have received this divine Sacrament, O Lord,
as we celebrate the victory of your holy Martyrs;
may what helped them to endure torment, we pray,
make us, in the face of trials,
steadfast in faith and in charity.
Through Christ our Lord.

June 5
Saint Boniface, Bishop and Martyr

Memorial

From the Common of Martyrs: For One Martyr (p. 531 or, during Easter Time, p. 535) or from the Common of Pastors: For Missionaries (p. 548).

COLLECT

**May the Martyr Saint Boniface be our advocate, O Lord,
that we may firmly hold the faith
he taught with his lips and sealed in his blood
and confidently profess it by our deeds.
Through our Lord Jesus Christ, your Son,
who lives and reigns with you
in the unity of the Holy Spirit,
one God, for ever and ever.**

June 6
Saint Norbert, Bishop

From the Common of Pastors: For a Bishop (p. 541), or from the Common of Holy Men and Women: For Religious (p. 563).

COLLECT

**O God, who made the Bishop Saint Norbert
a servant of your Church
outstanding in his prayer and pastoral zeal,
grant, we ask, that by the help of his intercession,
the flock of the faithful
may always find shepherds after your own heart
and be fed in the pastures of salvation.
Through our Lord Jesus Christ, your Son,
who lives and reigns with you
in the unity of the Holy Spirit,
one God, for ever and ever.**

June 9

Saint Ephrem, Deacon and Doctor of the Church

From the Common of Doctors of the Church (p. 551).

COLLECT

**Pour into our hearts O Lord, we pray, the Holy Spirit,
at whose prompting the Deacon Saint Ephrem
exulted in singing of your mysteries
and from whom he received the strength
to serve you alone.
Through our Lord Jesus Christ, your Son,
who lives and reigns with you
in the unity of the Holy Spirit,
one God, for ever and ever.**

June 11

Saint Barnabas, Apostle

Memorial

Entrance Antiphon

Blessed is this holy man,
who was worthy to be numbered among the Apostles,
for he was a good man,
filled with the Holy Spirit and with faith (E.T. alleluia).
Cf. Acts 11: 24

COLLECT

**O God, who decreed that Saint Barnabas,
a man filled with faith and the Holy Spirit,
should be set apart to convert the nations,
grant that the Gospel of Christ,
which he strenuously preached,
may be faithfully proclaimed by word and by deed.
Through our Lord Jesus Christ, your Son,
who lives and reigns with you
in the unity of the Holy Spirit,
one God, for ever and ever.**

PRAYER AFTER COMMUNION

**As we receive the pledge of eternal life,
we humbly implore you, Lord,
that what we celebrate in sacramental signs
on the Memorial of the blessed Apostle Barnabas
we may one day behold unveiled.
Through Christ our Lord.**

June 13

Saint Anthony of Padua, Priest and Doctor of the Church

Memorial

From the Common of Pastors: For One Pastor (p. 544), or from the Common of Doctors of the Church (p. 551), or from the Common of Holy Men and Women: For Religious (p. 563).

COLLECT

**Almighty ever-living God,
who gave Saint Anthony of Padua to your people
as an outstanding preacher
and an intercessor in their need,
grant that, with his assistance,
as we follow the teachings of the Christian life,
we may know your help in every trial.
Through our Lord Jesus Christ, your Son,
who lives and reigns with you
in the unity of the Holy Spirit,
one God, for ever and ever.**

June 19

Saint Romuald, Abbot

From the Common of Holy Men and Women: For an Abbot (p. 560).

COLLECT

**O God, who through Saint Romuald renewed
the manner of life of hermits in your Church,
grant that, denying ourselves and following Christ,
we may merit to reach the heavenly realms on high.
Through our Lord Jesus Christ, your Son,
who lives and reigns with you
in the unity of the Holy Spirit,
one God, for ever and ever.**

June 21

Saint Aloysius Gonzaga, Religious

Memorial

Entrance Antiphon

The clean of hands and pure of heart
shall climb the mountain of the Lord
and stand in his holy place. Cf. Ps 24 (23): 4, 3

COLLECT

O God, giver of heavenly gifts,
who in Saint Aloysius Gonzaga
joined penitence to a wonderful innocence of life,
grant, through his merits and intercession,
that, though we have failed to follow him in innocence,
we may imitate him in penitence.
Through our Lord Jesus Christ, your Son,
who lives and reigns with you
in the unity of the Holy Spirit,
one God, for ever and ever.

PRAYER AFTER COMMUNION

Bring us who have been fed
with the food of Angels, O Lord,
to serve you in purity of life,
and, following the example of Saint Aloysius,
whom we honor today,
may we persevere in constant thanksgiving.
Through Christ our Lord.

June 22
Saint Paulinus of Nola, Bishop

From the Common of Pastors: For a Bishop (p. 541).

COLLECT

O God, who made the Bishop Saint Paulinus of Nola
outstanding for love of poverty and for pastoral care,
graciously grant that, as we celebrate his merits,
we may imitate the example of his charity.
Through our Lord Jesus Christ, your Son,
who lives and reigns with you
in the unity of the Holy Spirit,
one God, for ever and ever.

Saints John Fisher, Bishop, and Thomas More, Martyrs

From the Common of Martyrs: For Several Martyrs (p. 526).

COLLECT

O God, who in martyrdom
have brought true faith to its highest expression,
graciously grant
that, strengthened through the intercession
of Saints John Fisher and Thomas More,
we may confirm by the witness of our life
the faith we profess with our lips.
Through our Lord Jesus Christ, your Son,
who lives and reigns with you
in the unity of the Holy Spirit,
one God, for ever and ever.

June 24

THE NATIVITY OF SAINT JOHN THE BAPTIST

Solemnity

At the Vigil Mass

This Mass is used on the evening of June 23, either before or after First Vespers (Evening Prayer I) of the Solemnity.

Entrance Antiphon

**He will be great in the sight of the Lord
and will be filled with the Holy Spirit,
even from his mother's womb;
and many will rejoice at his birth.** Lk 1: 15, 14

The Gloria in excelsis (Glory to God in the highest) is said.

COLLECT

**Grant, we pray, almighty God,
that your family may walk in the way of salvation
and, attentive to what Saint John the Precursor urged,
may come safely to the One he foretold,
our Lord Jesus Christ.
Who lives and reigns with you
in the unity of the Holy Spirit,
one God, for ever and ever.**

The Creed is said.

PRAYER AFTER COMMUNION

**May the marvelous prayer of Saint John the Baptist
accompany us who have eaten our fill
at this sacrificial feast, O Lord,
and, since Saint John proclaimed your Son
to be the Lamb who would take away our sins,
may he implore now for us your favor.
Through Christ our Lord.**

At the Mass during the Day

Entrance Antiphon

A man was sent from God, whose name was John.
He came to testify to the light,
to prepare a people fit for the Lord. Jn 1: 6-7; Lk 1: 17

The Gloria in excelsis (Glory to God in the highest) is said.

COLLECT

O God, who raised up Saint John the Baptist
to make ready a nation fit for Christ the Lord,
give your people, we pray,
the grace of spiritual joys
and direct the hearts of all the faithful
into the way of salvation and peace.
Through our Lord Jesus Christ, your Son,
who lives and reigns with you
in the unity of the Holy Spirit,
one God, for ever and ever.

The Creed is said.

PRAYER AFTER COMMUNION

Having feasted at the banquet of the heavenly Lamb,
we pray, O Lord,
that, finding joy in the nativity of Saint John the Baptist,
your Church may know as the author of her rebirth
the Christ whose coming John foretold.
Who lives and reigns for ever and ever.

June 27

Saint Cyril of Alexandria, Bishop and Doctor of the Church

From the Common of Pastors: For a Bishop (p. 541), or from the Common of Doctors of the Church (p. 551).

COLLECT

**O God, who made the Bishop Saint Cyril of Alexandria
an invincible champion of the divine motherhood
of the most Blessed Virgin Mary,
grant, we pray,
that we, who believe she is truly the Mother of God,
may be saved through the Incarnation of Christ your Son.
Who lives and reigns with you
in the unity of the Holy Spirit,
one God, for ever and ever.**

June 28

Saint Irenaeus, Bishop and Martyr

Memorial

Entrance Antiphon

The law of truth was in his mouth;
no dishonesty was found on his lips.
He walked with me in integrity and peace,
and turned many away from evil.
Mal 2: 6

COLLECT

O God, who called the Bishop Saint Irenaeus
to confirm true doctrine and the peace of the Church,
grant, we pray, through his intercession,
that, being renewed in faith and charity,
we may always be intent on fostering unity and concord.
Through our Lord Jesus Christ, your Son,
who lives and reigns with you
in the unity of the Holy Spirit,
one God, for ever and ever.

PRAYER AFTER COMMUNION

Through these sacred mysteries, we pray, O Lord,
give us in your compassion an increase of that faith
which brought glory to the Bishop Saint Irenaeus
as he maintained it even until death,
and may the same faith bring to us, who truly follow it,
justification in your sight.
Through Christ our Lord.

June 29

SAINTS PETER AND PAUL, APOSTLES

Solemnity

At the Vigil Mass

This Mass is used on the evening of June 28, either before or after First Vespers (Evening Prayer I) of the Solemnity.

Entrance Antiphon **Peter the Apostle, and Paul the teacher of the Gentiles, these have taught us your law, O Lord.**

The Gloria in excelsis (Glory to God in the highest) is said.

COLLECT

**Grant, we pray, O Lord our God,
that we may be sustained
by the intercession of the blessed Apostles Peter and Paul,
that, as through them you gave your Church
the foundations of her heavenly office,
so through them you may help her to eternal salvation.
Through our Lord Jesus Christ, your Son,
who lives and reigns with you
in the unity of the Holy Spirit,
one God, for ever and ever.**

The Creed is said.

PRAYER AFTER COMMUNION

**By this heavenly Sacrament, O Lord, we pray,
strengthen your faithful,
whom you have enlightened with the teaching
of the Apostles.
Through Christ our Lord.**

The Solemn Blessing formula on p. 318 may be used.

At the Mass during the Day

Entrance Antiphon

**These are the ones who, living in the flesh,
planted the Church with their blood;
they drank the chalice of the Lord
and became the friends of God.**

The Gloria in excelsis (Glory to God in the highest) is said.

COLLECT

**O God, who on the Solemnity
of the Apostles Peter and Paul,
give us the noble and holy joy of this day,
grant, we pray, that your Church
may in all things follow the teaching
of those through whom she received
the beginnings of right religion.
Through our Lord Jesus Christ, your Son,
who lives and reigns with you
in the unity of the Holy Spirit,
one God, for ever and ever.**

The Creed is said.

PRAYER AFTER COMMUNION

**Grant us, O Lord,
who have been renewed by this Sacrament,
so to live in the Church,
that, persevering in the breaking of the Bread
and in the teaching of the Apostles,
we may be one heart and one soul,
made steadfast in your love.
Through Christ our Lord.**

The Solemn Blessing formula on p. 318 may be used.

For a Votive Mass of Saint Peter or of Saint Paul, cf. below, pp. 682-683, or p. 683.

June 30
The First Martyrs of the Holy Roman Church

From the Common of Martyrs: For Several Martyrs (p. 526).

COLLECT

O God, who consecrated
the abundant first fruits of the Roman Church
by the blood of the Martyrs,
grant, we pray, that with firm courage
we may together draw strength from so great a struggle
and ever rejoice at the triumph of faithful love.
Through our Lord Jesus Christ, your Son,
who lives and reigns with you
in the unity of the Holy Spirit,
one God, for ever and ever.

JULY

[In the Dioceses of the United States]

July 1

Saint Junípero Serra, Priest

From the Common of Pastors: For Missionaries (p. 548), or For One Pastor (p. 544).

COLLECT

O God, who by your ineffable mercy
have been pleased through the labors
of your Priest Saint Junípero Serra
to count many American peoples within your Church,
grant by his intercession
that we may so join our hearts to you in love,
as to carry always and everywhere before all people
the image of your Only Begotten Son.
Who lives and reigns with you
in the unity of the Holy Spirit,
one God, for ever and ever.

July 3
SAINT THOMAS, APOSTLE

Feast

Entrance Antiphon

You are my God, and I confess you;
you are my God, and I exalt you;
I will thank you, for you became my savior.

Cf. Ps 118 (117): 28, 21

The Gloria in excelsis (Glory to God in the highest) is said.

COLLECT

Grant, almighty God,
that we may glory in the Feast
of the blessed Apostle Thomas,
so that we may always be sustained by his intercession
and, believing, may have life
in the name of Jesus Christ your Son,
whom Thomas acknowledged as the Lord.
Who lives and reigns with you
in the unity of the Holy Spirit,
one God, for ever and ever.

PRAYER AFTER COMMUNION

O God, as we truly receive in this Sacrament
the Body of your Only Begotten Son,
grant, we pray, that we may recognize him
with the Apostle Thomas by faith
as our Lord and our God
and proclaim him by our deeds and by our life.
Who lives and reigns for ever and ever.

The Solemn Blessing formula, p. 319, may be used.

[In the Dioceses of the United States]

July 4

Independence Day

Entrance Antiphon

**Give peace, O Lord, to those who wait for you;
hear the prayers of your servants
and guide us in the way of justice.** Cf. Sir 36: 18-19

The Gloria in excelsis (Glory to God in the highest) is said.

COLLECT

**God of justice, Father of truth,
who guide creation in wisdom and goodness
to fulfillment in Christ your Son,
open our hearts to the truth of his Gospel,
that your peace may rule in our hearts
and your justice guide our lives.
Through our Lord Jesus Christ, your Son,
who lives and reigns with you
in the unity of the Holy Spirit,
one God, for ever and ever.**

Or:

**Father of all nations and ages,
we recall the day when our country
claimed its place among the family of nations;
for what has been achieved we give you thanks,
for the work that still remains we ask your help,
and as you have called us from many peoples
to be one nation,
grant that, under your providence,
our country may share your blessings
with all the peoples of the earth.
Through our Lord Jesus Christ, your Son,
who lives and reigns with you
in the unity of the Holy Spirit,
one God, for ever and ever.**

PRAYER AFTER COMMUNION

**By showing us in this Eucharist, O Lord,
a glimpse of the unity and joy
of your people in heaven,
deepen our unity and intensify our joy,
that all who believe in you
may work together to build the city of lasting peace.
Through Christ our Lord.**

Or:

**May the love we share in this Eucharist, heavenly Father,
flow in rich blessing throughout our land
and by your grace may we as a nation
place our trust in you
and seek to do your will.
Through Christ our Lord.**

SOLEMN BLESSING

**May God the Father who has called us
to be one human family
fill your hearts with deep longing
for peace and harmony.**
℟. Amen.

**May the Son of God who came to share our life
and make us children of the one Father
enable you to grow in wisdom and grace
before God and the human family.**
℟. Amen.

**And may the Holy Spirit who is the bond of love
between the Father and the Son
unite in love all here present;
may he be the bond of love among you,
our nation, and all peoples.**
℟. Amen.

**And may the blessing of almighty God,
the Father, and the Son, ✠ and the Holy Spirit,
come down on you and remain with you for ever.**
℟. Amen.

July 5

Saint Anthony Zaccaria, Priest

From the Common of Pastors: For One Pastor (p. 544), or from the Common of Holy Men and Women: For Educators (p. 566), or For Religious (p. 563).

COLLECT

Grant, O Lord, that in the spirit of the Apostle Paul
we may pursue the surpassing knowledge of Jesus Christ,
for, having learned it,
Saint Anthony Zaccaria
constantly preached your saving word in the Church.
Through our Lord Jesus Christ, your Son,
who lives and reigns with you
in the unity of the Holy Spirit,
one God, for ever and ever.

[In the Dioceses of the United States]

Saint Elizabeth of Portugal

From the Common of Holy Men and Women: For Those Who Practiced Works of Mercy (p. 564).

COLLECT

O God, author of peace and lover of charity,
who adorned Saint Elizabeth of Portugal
with a marvelous grace for reconciling those in conflict,
grant, through her intercession,
that we may become peacemakers,
and so be called children of God.
Through our Lord Jesus Christ, your Son,
who lives and reigns with you
in the unity of the Holy Spirit,
one God, for ever and ever.

July 6

Saint Maria Goretti, Virgin and Martyr

From the Common of Martyrs: For a Virgin Martyr (p. 537), or from the Common of Virgins: For One Virgin (p. 554).

COLLECT

**O God, author of innocence and lover of chastity,
who bestowed the grace of martyrdom
on your handmaid, the Virgin Saint Maria Goretti,
in her youth,
grant, we pray, through her intercession,
that, as you gave her a crown for her steadfastness,
so we, too, may be firm
in obeying your commandments.
Through our Lord Jesus Christ, your Son,
who lives and reigns with you
in the unity of the Holy Spirit,
one God, for ever and ever.**

July 9

Saint Augustine Zhao Rong, Priest, and Companions, Martyrs

From the Common of Martyrs: For Several Martyrs (p. 526).

COLLECT

**O God, who in your wonderful providence
have strengthened your Church
through the confession of the Martyrs
Saint Augustine Zhao and companions,
grant that your people,
faithful to the mission entrusted to it,
may enjoy ever greater freedom
and witness to the truth before the world.
Through our Lord Jesus Christ, your Son,
who lives and reigns with you
in the unity of the Holy Spirit,
one God, for ever and ever.**

July 11

Saint Benedict, Abbot

Memorial

Entrance Antiphon

There was a man of venerable life,
Benedict, blessed by grace and by name,
who, leaving home and patrimony
and desiring to please God alone,
sought out the habit of holy living.

COLLECT

O God, who made the Abbot Saint Benedict
an outstanding master in the school of divine service,
grant, we pray,
that, putting nothing before love of you,
we may hasten with a loving heart
in the way of your commands.
Through our Lord Jesus Christ, your Son,
who lives and reigns with you
in the unity of the Holy Spirit,
one God, for ever and ever.

PRAYER AFTER COMMUNION

Having received this pledge of eternal life,
we humbly beseech you, O Lord,
that, attentive to the teaching of Saint Benedict,
we may faithfully serve your designs
and love one another with fervent charity.
Through Christ our Lord.

July 13

Saint Henry

From the Common of Holy Men and Women: For One Saint (p. 559).

COLLECT

**O God, whose abundant grace prepared Saint Henry
to be raised by you in a wonderful way
from the cares of earthly rule to heavenly realms,
grant, we pray, through his intercession,
that amid the uncertainties of this world
we may hasten towards you with minds made pure.
Through our Lord Jesus Christ, your Son,
who lives and reigns with you
in the unity of the Holy Spirit,
one God, for ever and ever.**

[In the Dioceses of the United States]

July 14

Saint Kateri Tekakwitha, Virgin

Memorial

From the Common of Virgins: For One Virgin (p. 554).

COLLECT

**O God, who desired the Virgin Saint Kateri Tekakwitha
to flower among Native Americans
in a life of innocence,
grant, through her intercession,
that when all are gathered into your Church
from every nation, tribe and tongue,
they may magnify you
in a single canticle of praise.
Through our Lord Jesus Christ, your Son,
who lives and reigns with you
in the unity of the Holy Spirit,
one God, for ever and ever.**

July 15

Saint Bonaventure, Bishop and Doctor of the Church

Memorial

From the Common of Pastors: For a Bishop (p. 541) or from the Common of Doctors of the Church (p. 551).

COLLECT

**Grant, we pray, almighty God,
that, just as we celebrate the heavenly birthday
of the Bishop Saint Bonaventure,
we may benefit from his great learning
and constantly imitate the ardor of his charity.
Through our Lord Jesus Christ, your Son,
who lives and reigns with you
in the unity of the Holy Spirit,
one God, for ever and ever.**

July 16

Our Lady of Mount Carmel

From the Common of the Blessed Virgin Mary (p. 518).

COLLECT

**May the venerable intercession
of the glorious Virgin Mary
come to our aid, we pray, O Lord,
so that, fortified by her protection,
we may reach the mountain which is Christ.
Who lives and reigns with you
in the unity of the Holy Spirit,
one God, for ever and ever.**

[In the Dioceses of the United States]

July 18

Saint Camillus de Lellis, Priest

From the Common of Holy Men and Women: For Those Who Practiced Works of Mercy (p. 564).

COLLECT

**O God, who adorned the Priest Saint Camillus
with a singular grace of charity towards the sick,
pour out upon us, by his merits,
a spirit of love for you,
so that, serving you in our neighbor,
we may, at the hour of our death,
pass safely over to you.
Through our Lord Jesus Christ, your Son,
who lives and reigns with you
in the unity of the Holy Spirit,
one God, for ever and ever.**

July 20

Saint Apollinaris, Bishop and Martyr

From the Common of Martyrs: For One Martyr (p. 531), or from the Common of Pastors: For a Bishop (p. 541).

COLLECT

**Direct your faithful, Lord, in the way of eternal salvation,
which the Bishop Saint Apollinaris showed
by his teaching and martyrdom,
and grant, through his intercession,
that we may so persevere in keeping your commandments
as to merit being crowned with him.
Through our Lord Jesus Christ, your Son,
who lives and reigns with you
in the unity of the Holy Spirit,
one God, for ever and ever.**

July 21

Saint Lawrence of Brindisi, Priest and Doctor of the Church

From the Common of Pastors: For One Pastor (p. 544), or from the Common of Doctors of the Church (p. 551), or from the Common of Holy Men and Women: For Religious (p. 563).

COLLECT

**O God, who for the glory of your name
and the salvation of souls
bestowed on the Priest Saint Lawrence of Brindisi
a spirit of counsel and fortitude,
grant, we pray, that in the same spirit,
we may know what must be done
and, through his intercession,
bring it to completion.
Through our Lord Jesus Christ, your Son,
who lives and reigns with you
in the unity of the Holy Spirit,
one God, for ever and ever.**

July 22
Saint Mary Magdalene

Feast

Entrance Antiphon

The Lord said to Mary Magdalene:
Go to my brothers and tell them:
I am going to my Father and your Father,
to my God and your God. Jn 20: 17

The Gloria in excelsis (Glory to God in the highest) is said.

COLLECT

O God, whose Only Begotten Son
entrusted Mary Magdalene before all others
with announcing the great joy of the Resurrection,
grant, we pray,
that through her intercession and example
we may proclaim the living Christ
and come to see him reigning in your glory.
Who lives and reigns with you
in the unity of the Holy Spirit,
one God, for ever and ever.

PRAYER AFTER COMMUNION

May the holy reception of your mysteries, Lord,
instill in us that persevering love
with which Saint Mary Magdalene
clung resolutely to Christ her Master.
Who lives and reigns for ever and ever.

July 23

Saint Bridget, Religious

From the Common of Holy Men and Women: For Holy Women (p. 566) or For Religious (p. 563).

COLLECT

**O God, who guided Saint Bridget of Sweden
along different paths of life
and wondrously taught her the wisdom of the Cross
as she contemplated the Passion of your Son,
grant us, we pray,
that, walking worthily in our vocation,
we may seek you in all things.
Through our Lord Jesus Christ, your Son,
who lives and reigns with you
in the unity of the Holy Spirit,
one God, for ever and ever.**

July 24

Saint Sharbel Makhlūf, Priest

From the Common of Pastors: For One Pastor (p. 544), or from the Common of Holy Men and Women: For a Monk (p. 561).

COLLECT

**O God, who called the Priest Saint Sharbel Makhlūf
to the solitary combat of the desert
and imbued him with all manner of devotion,
grant us, we pray,
that, being made imitators of the Lord's Passion,
we may merit to be co-heirs of his Kingdom.
Who lives and reigns with you
in the unity of the Holy Spirit,
one God, for ever and ever.**

July 25

Saint James, Apostle

Feast

Entrance Antiphon

As he walked by the Sea of Galilee,
Jesus saw James the son of Zebedee and John his brother
mending their nets and he called them. Cf. Mt 4: 18, 21

The Gloria in excelsis (Glory to God in the highest) is said.

COLLECT

Almighty ever-living God,
who consecrated the first fruits of your Apostles
by the blood of Saint James,
grant, we pray,
that your Church may be strengthened
by his confession of faith
and constantly sustained by his protection.
Through our Lord Jesus Christ, your Son,
who lives and reigns with you
in the unity of the Holy Spirit,
one God, for ever and ever.

PRAYER AFTER COMMUNION

Help us, O Lord, we pray,
through the intercession of the blessed Apostle James,
on whose feast day we have received with joy
your holy gifts.
Through Christ our Lord.

The Solemn Blessing formula, p. 319, may be used.

July 26

Saints Joachim and Anne, Parents of the Blessed Virgin Mary

Memorial

Entrance Antiphon

Let us praise Joachim and Anne, to whom, in their generation, the Lord gave him who was a blessing for all the nations.

Cf. Sir 44: 1, 25

COLLECT

O Lord, God of our Fathers,
who bestowed on Saints Joachim and Anne this grace,
that of them should be born the Mother
of your incarnate Son,
grant, through the prayers of both,
that we may attain the salvation
you have promised to your people.
Through our Lord Jesus Christ, your Son,
who lives and reigns with you
in the unity of the Holy Spirit,
one God, for ever and ever.

PRAYER AFTER COMMUNION

O God, who willed that your Only Begotten Son
should be born from among humanity
so that by a wonderful mystery
humanity might be born again from you,
we pray that, in your kindness,
you may sanctify by the spirit of adoption
those you have fed with the Bread you give your children.
Through Christ our Lord.

July 29
Saint Martha

Memorial

Entrance Antiphon

Jesus entered a village,
where a woman named Martha welcomed him into her home.
Cf. Lk 10: 38

COLLECT

Almighty ever-living God,
whose Son was pleased to be welcomed
in Saint Martha's house as a guest,
grant, we pray,
that through her intercession,
serving Christ faithfully in our brothers and sisters,
we may merit to be received by you
in the halls of heaven.
Through our Lord Jesus Christ, your Son,
who lives and reigns with you
in the unity of the Holy Spirit,
one God, for ever and ever.

PRAYER AFTER COMMUNION

May the holy reception of the Body and Blood
of your Only Begotten Son, O Lord,
turn us away from the cares of this fallen world,
so that, following the example of Saint Martha,
we may grow in sincere love for you on earth
and rejoice to behold you for eternity in heaven.
Through Christ our Lord.

July 30

Saint Peter Chrysologus, Bishop and Doctor of the Church

From the Common of Pastors: For a Bishop (p. 541), or from the Common of Doctors of the Church (p. 551).

COLLECT

O God, who made the Bishop Saint Peter Chrysologus
an outstanding preacher of your incarnate Word,
grant, through his intercession,
that we may constantly ponder in our hearts
the mysteries of your salvation
and faithfully express them in what we do.
Through our Lord Jesus Christ, your Son,
who lives and reigns with you
in the unity of the Holy Spirit,
one God, for ever and ever.

July 31

Saint Ignatius of Loyola, Priest

Memorial

Entrance Antiphon

**At the name of Jesus, every knee should bend,
of those in heaven and on earth and under the earth,
and every tongue confess that Jesus Christ is Lord,
to the glory of God the Father.** Cf. Phil 2: 10-11

COLLECT

**O God, who raised up Saint Ignatius of Loyola
in your Church
to further the greater glory of your name,
grant that by his help we may imitate him
in fighting the good fight on earth
and merit to receive with him a crown in heaven.
Through our Lord Jesus Christ, your Son,
who lives and reigns with you
in the unity of the Holy Spirit,
one God, for ever and ever.**

PRAYER AFTER COMMUNION

**May the sacrifice of praise
that we have offered with thanksgiving
in honor of Saint Ignatius, O Lord,
bring us to exalt your majesty without end.
Through Christ our Lord.**

AUGUST

August 1
Saint Alphonsus Liguori, Bishop and Doctor of the Church

Memorial

From the Common of Pastors: For a Bishop (p. 541), or from the Common of Doctors of the Church (p. 551).

COLLECT

O God, who constantly raise up in your Church
new examples of virtue,
grant that we may follow so closely in the footsteps
of the Bishop Saint Alphonsus in his zeal for souls
as to attain the same rewards that are his in heaven.
Through our Lord Jesus Christ, your Son,
who lives and reigns with you
in the unity of the Holy Spirit,
one God, for ever and ever.

PRAYER AFTER COMMUNION

O God, who gave us Saint Alphonsus
to be a faithful steward and preacher of this great mystery,
grant that your faithful
may receive it often and, receiving it,
praise you without end.
Through Christ our Lord.

August 2
Saint Eusebius of Vercelli, Bishop

From the Common of Pastors: For a Bishop (p. 541).

COLLECT

Lead us, Lord God, to imitate the constancy
of Saint Eusebius
in affirming the divinity of your Son,
so that, by preserving the faith he taught as your Bishop,
we may merit a share in the very life of your Son.
Who lives and reigns with you
in the unity of the Holy Spirit,
one God, for ever and ever.

Saint Peter Julian Eymard, Priest

From the Common of Holy Men and Women: For Religious (p. 563), or from the Common of Pastors: For One Pastor (p. 544).

COLLECT

O God, who adorned Saint Peter Julian Eymard
with a wonderful love for the sacred mysteries
of the Body and Blood of your Son,
graciously grant
that we, too, may be worthy to receive
the delights he drew from this divine banquet.
Through our Lord Jesus Christ, your Son,
who lives and reigns with you
in the unity of the Holy Spirit,
one God, for ever and ever.

August 4

Saint John Vianney, Priest

Memorial

From the Common of Pastors: For One Pastor (p. 544).

COLLECT

**Almighty and merciful God,
who made the Priest Saint John Vianney
wonderful in his pastoral zeal,
grant, we pray,
that through his intercession and example
we may in charity win brothers and sisters for Christ
and attain with them eternal glory.
Through our Lord Jesus Christ, your Son,
who lives and reigns with you
in the unity of the Holy Spirit,
one God, for ever and ever.**

August 5
The Dedication of the Basilica of Saint Mary Major

From the Common of the Blessed Virgin Mary (p. 518).

COLLECT

**Pardon the faults of your servants, we pray, O Lord,
that we, who cannot please you by our own deeds,
may be saved through the intercession
of the Mother of your Son and our Lord.
Who lives and reigns with you
in the unity of the Holy Spirit,
one God, for ever and ever.**

August 6

The Transfiguration of the Lord

Feast

Entrance Antiphon

In a resplendent cloud the Holy Spirit appeared.
The Father's voice was heard: This is my beloved Son,
with whom I am well pleased. Listen to him. Cf. Mt 17: 5

The Gloria in excelsis (Glory to God in the highest) is said.

COLLECT

O God, who in the glorious Transfiguration
of your Only Begotten Son
confirmed the mysteries of faith by the witness
of the Fathers
and wonderfully prefigured our full adoption to sonship,
grant, we pray, to your servants,
that, listening to the voice of your beloved Son,
we may merit to become co-heirs with him.
Who lives and reigns with you
in the unity of the Holy Spirit,
one God, for ever and ever.

When this Feast falls on a Sunday, the Creed is said.

PRAYER AFTER COMMUNION

May the heavenly nourishment we have received,
O Lord, we pray,
transform us into the likeness of your Son,
whose radiant splendor you willed to make manifest
in his glorious Transfiguration.
Who lives and reigns for ever and ever.

August 7

Saint Sixtus II, Pope, and Companions, Martyrs

From the Common of Martyrs: For Several Martyrs (p. 526).

COLLECT

By the power of the Holy Spirit,
we pray, almighty God,
make us docile in believing the faith
and courageous in confessing it,
just as you granted Saint Sixtus and his companions
that they might lay down their lives
for the sake of your word and in witness to Jesus.
Who lives and reigns with you
in the unity of the Holy Spirit,
one God, for ever and ever.

Saint Cajetan, Priest

From the Common of Pastors: For One Pastor (p. 544), or from the Common of Holy Men and Women: For Religious (p. 563).

COLLECT

O God, who endowed the Priest Saint Cajetan
with the grace of imitating
the apostolic way of life,
grant us, through his example and intercession,
to trust in you at all times
and to seek unceasingly your Kingdom.
Through our Lord Jesus Christ, your Son,
who lives and reigns with you
in the unity of the Holy Spirit,
one God, for ever and ever.

August 8
Saint Dominic, Priest

Memorial

Entrance Antiphon

In the midst of the Church he opened his mouth,
and the Lord filled him with the spirit
of wisdom and understanding
and clothed him in a robe of glory. Cf. Sir 15: 5

COLLECT

May Saint Dominic come to the help of your Church
by his merits and teaching, O Lord,
and may he, who was an outstanding preacher
of your truth,
be a devoted intercessor on our behalf.
Through our Lord Jesus Christ, your Son,
who lives and reigns with you
in the unity of the Holy Spirit,
one God, for ever and ever.

PRAYER AFTER COMMUNION

May your Church, O Lord,
receive with wholehearted reverence
the power of this heavenly Sacrament,
by which we have been nourished
on the commemoration of Saint Dominic,
and may your Church,
having flourished by means of his preaching,
be helped through his intercession.
Through Christ our Lord.

August 9

Saint Teresa Benedicta of the Cross, Virgin and Martyr

From the Common of Martyrs: For a Virgin Martyr (p. 537), or from the Common of Virgins: For One Virgin (p. 554).

COLLECT

God of our Fathers,
who brought the Martyr Saint Teresa Benedicta
of the Cross
to know your crucified Son
and to imitate him even until death,
grant, through her intercession,
that the whole human race may acknowledge Christ
as its Savior
and through him come to behold you for eternity.
Who lives and reigns with you
in the unity of the Holy Spirit,
one God, for ever and ever.

August 10
SAINT LAWRENCE, DEACON AND MARTYR

Feast

Entrance Antiphon

This is the blessed Lawrence,
who gave himself up for the treasure of the Church:
for this he earned the suffering of martyrdom
to ascend with joy to the Lord Jesus Christ.

The Gloria in excelsis (Glory to God in the highest) is said.

COLLECT

O God, giver of that ardor of love for you
by which Saint Lawrence was outstandingly faithful
in service
and glorious in martyrdom,
grant that we may love what he loved
and put into practice what he taught.
Through our Lord Jesus Christ, your Son,
who lives and reigns with you
in the unity of the Holy Spirit,
one God, for ever and ever.

PRAYER AFTER COMMUNION

Nourished by these sacred gifts,
we humbly implore you, Lord,
that the homage of dutiful service,
which we render on the feast of Saint Lawrence,
may bring us an increase of your saving grace.
Through Christ our Lord.

August 11

Saint Clare, Virgin

Memorial

From the Common of Virgins: For One Virgin (p. 554), or from the Common of Holy Men and Women: For a Nun (p. 562).

COLLECT

**O God, who in your mercy led Saint Clare
to a love of poverty,
grant, through her intercession,
that, following Christ in poverty of spirit,
we may merit to contemplate you
one day in the heavenly Kingdom.
Through our Lord Jesus Christ, your Son,
who lives and reigns with you
in the unity of the Holy Spirit,
one God, for ever and ever.**

August 12

Saint Jane Frances de Chantal, Religious

From the Common of Holy Men and Women: For Religious (p. 563).

COLLECT

**O God, who made Saint Jane Frances de Chantal
radiant with outstanding merits in different walks of life,
grant us, through her intercession,
that, walking faithfully in our vocation,
we may constantly be examples of shining light.
Through our Lord Jesus Christ, your Son,
who lives and reigns with you
in the unity of the Holy Spirit,
one God, for ever and ever.**

August 13
Saints Pontian, Pope, and Hippolytus, Priest, Martyrs

From the Common of Martyrs: For Several Martyrs (p. 526), or from the Common of Pastors: For Several Pastors (p. 543).

COLLECT

**May the precious long-suffering of the just,
O Lord, we pray,
bring us a great increase of love for you
and always prompt in our hearts
constancy in the holy faith.
Through our Lord Jesus Christ, your Son,
who lives and reigns with you
in the unity of the Holy Spirit,
one God, for ever and ever.**

August 14
Saint Maximilian Mary Kolbe, Priest and Martyr

Memorial

Entrance Antiphon

Come, you blessed of my Father, says the Lord.
Amen, I say to you:
Whatever you did for one of the least of my brethren,
you did it for me. Mt 25: 34, 40

COLLECT

**O God, who filled the Priest and Martyr
Saint Maximilian Kolbe
with a burning love for the Immaculate Virgin Mary
and with zeal for souls and love of neighbor,
graciously grant, through his intercession,
that, striving for your glory by eagerly serving others,
we may be conformed, even until death, to your Son.
Who lives and reigns with you
in the unity of the Holy Spirit,
one God, for ever and ever.**

PRAYER AFTER COMMUNION

**We pray, O Lord,
that, renewed by the Body and Blood of your Son,
we may be inflamed with the same fire of charity
that Saint Maximilian received from this holy banquet.
Through Christ our Lord.**

August 15

THE ASSUMPTION OF THE BLESSED VIRGIN MARY

Solemnity

At the Vigil Mass

This Mass is used on the evening of August 14, either before or after First Vespers (Evening Prayer I) of the Solemnity.

Entrance Antiphon

**Glorious things are spoken of you, O Mary,
who today were exalted above the choirs of Angels
into eternal triumph with Christ.**

The Gloria in excelsis (Glory to God in the highest) is said.

COLLECT

**O God, who, looking on the lowliness
of the Blessed Virgin Mary,
raised her to this grace,
that your Only Begotten Son was born of her
according to the flesh
and that she was crowned this day with surpassing glory,
grant through her prayers,
that, saved by the mystery of your redemption,
we may merit to be exalted by you on high.
Through our Lord Jesus Christ, your Son,
who lives and reigns with you
in the unity of the Holy Spirit,
one God, for ever and ever.**

The Creed is said.

PRAYER AFTER COMMUNION

**Having partaken of this heavenly table,
we beseech your mercy, Lord our God,
that we, who honor the Assumption
of the Mother of God,
may be freed from every threat of harm.
Through Christ our Lord.**

The Solemn Blessing formula, p. 318, may be used.

At the Mass during the Day

Entrance Antiphon

A great sign appeared in heaven:
a woman clothed with the sun, and the moon beneath her feet,
and on her head a crown of twelve stars. Cf. Rev 12: 1

Or:

Let us all rejoice in the Lord,
as we celebrate the feast day in honor of the Virgin Mary,
at whose Assumption the Angels rejoice
and praise the Son of God.

The Gloria in excelsis (Glory to God in the highest) is said.

COLLECT

Almighty ever-living God,
who assumed the Immaculate Virgin Mary,
the Mother of your Son,
body and soul into heavenly glory,
grant, we pray,
that, always attentive to the things that are above,
we may merit to be sharers of her glory.
Through our Lord Jesus Christ, your Son,
who lives and reigns with you
in the unity of the Holy Spirit,
one God, for ever and ever.

The Creed is said.

PRAYER AFTER COMMUNION

Having received the Sacrament of salvation,
we ask you to grant, O Lord,
that, through the intercession
of the Blessed Virgin Mary,
whom you assumed into heaven,
we may be brought to the glory of the resurrection.
Through Christ our Lord.

The Solemn Blessing formula, p. 318, may be used.

August 16
Saint Stephen of Hungary

From the Common of Holy Men and Women: For One Saint (p. 559).

COLLECT

**Grant your Church, we pray, almighty God,
that she may have Saint Stephen of Hungary,
who fostered her growth while a king on earth,
as her glorious defender in heaven.
Through our Lord Jesus Christ, your Son,
who lives and reigns with you
in the unity of the Holy Spirit,
one God, for ever and ever.**

August 19
Saint John Eudes, Priest

From the Common of Pastors: For One Pastor (p. 544), or from the Common of Holy Men and Women: For Religious (p. 563).

COLLECT

**O God, who wonderfully chose the Priest Saint John Eudes
to proclaim the unfathomable riches of Christ,
grant us, by his example and teachings,
that, growing in knowledge of you,
we may live faithfully by the light of the Gospel.
Through our Lord Jesus Christ, your Son,
who lives and reigns with you
in the unity of the Holy Spirit,
one God, for ever and ever.**

August 20

Saint Bernard, Abbot and Doctor of the Church

Memorial

Entrance Antiphon

Filled by the Lord with a spirit of understanding,
blessed Bernard ministered streams of clear teaching
to the people of God.

COLLECT

O God, who made of the Abbot Saint Bernard
a man consumed with zeal for your house
and a light shining and burning in your Church,
grant, through his intercession,
that we may be on fire with the same spirit
and walk always as children of light.
Through our Lord Jesus Christ, your Son,
who lives and reigns with you
in the unity of the Holy Spirit,
one God, for ever and ever.

PRAYER AFTER COMMUNION

May the food we have received, O Lord,
as we honor Saint Bernard,
work its effect in us,
so that, strengthened by his example
and instructed by his teaching,
we may be caught up in love of your incarnate Word.
Who lives and reigns for ever and ever.

August 21
Saint Pius X, Pope

Memorial

From the Common of Pastors: For a Pope (p. 539).

COLLECT

O God, who to safeguard the Catholic faith
and to restore all things in Christ,
filled Pope Saint Pius the Tenth
with heavenly wisdom and apostolic fortitude,
graciously grant
that, following his teaching and example,
we may gain an eternal prize.
Through our Lord Jesus Christ, your Son,
who lives and reigns with you
in the unity of the Holy Spirit,
one God, for ever and ever.

PRAYER AFTER COMMUNION

Celebrating the Memorial of Pope Saint Pius,
we pray, O Lord our God,
that by the power of this heavenly table
we may be made constant in the faith
and be of one accord in your love.
Through Christ our Lord.

August 22

The Queenship of the Blessed Virgin Mary

Memorial

Entrance Antiphon At your right stands the queen in robes of gold,
finely arrayed. Cf. Ps 45 (44): 10

COLLECT O God, who made the Mother of your Son
to be our Mother and our Queen,
graciously grant that, sustained by her intercession,
we may attain in the heavenly Kingdom
the glory promised to your children.
Through our Lord Jesus Christ, your Son,
who lives and reigns with you
in the unity of the Holy Spirit,
one God, for ever and ever.

PRAYER AFTER COMMUNION Having received this heavenly Sacrament,
we humbly pray, O Lord,
that we, who reverently celebrate the Memorial
of the Blessed Virgin Mary,
may merit to be partakers at your eternal banquet.
Through Christ our Lord.

August 23

Saint Rose of Lima, Virgin

From the Common of Virgins: For One Virgin (p. 554).

COLLECT O God, you set Saint Rose of Lima on fire with your love,
so that, secluded from the world
in the austerity of a life of penance,
she might give herself to you alone;
grant, we pray, that through her intercession,
we may tread the paths of life on earth
and drink at the stream of your delights in heaven.
Through our Lord Jesus Christ, your Son,
who lives and reigns with you
in the unity of the Holy Spirit,
one God, for ever and ever.

August 24
SAINT BARTHOLOMEW, APOSTLE

Feast

Entrance Antiphon

Proclaim the salvation of God day by day;
tell among the nations his glory. Cf. Ps 96 (95): 2-3

The Gloria in excelsis (Glory to God in the highest) is said.

COLLECT

Strengthen in us, O Lord, the faith,
by which the blessed Apostle Bartholomew
clung wholeheartedly to your Son,
and grant that through the help of his prayers
your Church may become for all the nations
the sacrament of salvation.
Through our Lord Jesus Christ, your Son,
who lives and reigns with you
in the unity of the Holy Spirit,
one God, for ever and ever.

PRAYER AFTER COMMUNION

As we celebrate the feast day
of the blessed Apostle Bartholomew,
we have received the pledge of eternal salvation, O Lord,
and we pray that it may be of help to us,
both now and for the life to come.
Through Christ our Lord.

The Solemn Blessing formula, p. 319, may be used.

August 25
Saint Louis

From the Common of Holy Men and Women: For One Saint (p. 559).

COLLECT

**O God, who brought Saint Louis
from the cares of earthly rule
to the glory of a heavenly realm,
grant, we pray, through his intercession,
that, by fulfilling our duties on earth,
we may seek out your eternal Kingdom.
Through our Lord Jesus Christ, your Son,
who lives and reigns with you
in the unity of the Holy Spirit,
one God, for ever and ever.**

Saint Joseph Calasanz, Priest

From the Common of Holy Men and Women: For Educators (p. 566), or from the Common of Pastors: For One Pastor (p. 544).

COLLECT

**O God, who adorned the Priest Saint Joseph Calasanz
with such charity and patience
that he labored tirelessly
to educate children and endow them with every virtue,
grant, we pray, that we, who venerate him
as a teacher of wisdom,
may constantly imitate him,
for he was a co-worker of your truth.
Through our Lord Jesus Christ, your Son,
who lives and reigns with you
in the unity of the Holy Spirit,
one God, for ever and ever.**

August 27

Saint Monica

Memorial

From the Common of Holy Men and Women: For Holy Women (p. 566).

COLLECT

**O God, who console the sorrowful
and who mercifully accepted
the motherly tears of Saint Monica
for the conversion of her son Augustine,
grant us, through the intercession of them both,
that we may bitterly regret our sins
and find the grace of your pardon.
Through our Lord Jesus Christ, your Son,
who lives and reigns with you
in the unity of the Holy Spirit,
one God, for ever and ever.**

August 28

Saint Augustine, Bishop and Doctor of the Church

Memorial

Entrance Antiphon

In the midst of the Church he opened his mouth,
and the Lord filled him
with the spirit of wisdom and understanding
and clothed him in a robe of glory. Cf. Sir 15: 5

COLLECT

Renew in your Church, we pray, O Lord,
the spirit with which you endowed
your Bishop Saint Augustine
that, filled with the same spirit,
we may thirst for you,
the sole fount of true wisdom,
and seek you, the author of heavenly love.
Through our Lord Jesus Christ, your Son,
who lives and reigns with you
in the unity of the Holy Spirit,
one God, for ever and ever.

PRAYER AFTER COMMUNION

May partaking of Christ's table
sanctify us, we pray, O Lord,
that, being made members of his Body,
we may become what we have received.
Through Christ our Lord.

August 29
The Passion of Saint John the Baptist

Memorial

Entrance Antiphon

I spoke, O Lord, of your decrees before kings,
and was not confounded;
I pondered your commands and loved them greatly.

Cf. Ps 119 (118): 46-47

COLLECT

O God, who willed that Saint John the Baptist
should go ahead of your Son
both in his birth and in his death,
grant that, as he died a Martyr for truth and justice,
we, too, may fight hard
for the confession of what you teach.
Through our Lord Jesus Christ, your Son,
who lives and reigns with you
in the unity of the Holy Spirit,
one God, for ever and ever.

PRAYER AFTER COMMUNION

Grant, O Lord,
as we celebrate the heavenly birth
of Saint John the Baptist,
that we may revere, for what it signifies,
the saving Sacrament we have received
and, even more, may rejoice
at its clear effects in us.
Through Christ our Lord.

SEPTEMBER

September 3
Saint Gregory the Great, Pope and Doctor of the Church

Memorial

Entrance Antiphon

Blessed Gregory, raised upon the throne of Peter,
sought always the beauty of the Lord
and lived in celebration of that love.

COLLECT

O God, who care for your people with gentleness
and rule them in love,
through the intercession of Pope Saint Gregory,
endow, we pray, with a spirit of wisdom
those to whom you have given authority to govern,
that the flourishing of a holy flock
may become the eternal joy of the shepherds.
Through our Lord Jesus Christ, your Son,
who lives and reigns with you
in the unity of the Holy Spirit,
one God, for ever and ever.

PRAYER AFTER COMMUNION

Through Christ the teacher, O Lord,
instruct those you feed with Christ, the living Bread,
that on the feast day of Saint Gregory
they may learn your truth
and express it in works of charity.
Through Christ our Lord.

September 8
THE NATIVITY OF THE BLESSED VIRGIN MARY

Feast

Entrance Antiphon

Let us celebrate with joy the Nativity
of the Blessed Virgin Mary,
for from her arose the sun of justice, Christ our God.

The Gloria in excelsis (Glory to God in the highest) is said.

COLLECT

Impart to your servants, we pray, O Lord,
the gift of heavenly grace,
that the feast of the Nativity of the Blessed Virgin
may bring deeper peace
to those for whom the birth of her Son
was the dawning of salvation.
Through our Lord Jesus Christ, your Son,
who lives and reigns with you
in the unity of the Holy Spirit,
one God, for ever and ever.

PRAYER AFTER COMMUNION

May your Church exult, O Lord,
for you have renewed her with these sacred mysteries,
as she rejoices in the Nativity of the Blessed Virgin Mary,
which was the hope and the daybreak of salvation
for all the world.
Through Christ our Lord.

The Solemn Blessing formula, p. 318, may be used.

[In the Dioceses of the United States]

September 9

Saint Peter Claver, Priest

Memorial

From the Common of Pastors: For One Pastor (p. 544), or from the Common of Holy Men and Women: For Those Who Practiced Works of Mercy (p. 564).

COLLECT

O God, who made Saint Peter Claver a slave of slaves
and strengthened him
with wonderful charity and patience
as he came to their help,
grant, through his intercession,
that, seeking the things of Jesus Christ,
we may love our neighbor in deeds and in truth.
Through our Lord Jesus Christ, your Son,
who lives and reigns with you
in the unity of the Holy Spirit,
one God, for ever and ever.

September 12

The Most Holy Name of Mary

Entrance Antiphon

Blessed are you, O Virgin Mary, by the Lord God Most High,
above all women on the earth;
for he has so exalted your name
that your praise shall be undying on our lips. Cf. Jdt 13: 18-19

COLLECT

Grant, we pray, almighty God,
that, for all who celebrate the glorious Name
of the Blessed Virgin Mary,
she may obtain your merciful favor.
Through our Lord Jesus Christ, your Son,
who lives and reigns with you
in the unity of the Holy Spirit,
one God, for ever and ever.

PRAYER AFTER COMMUNION

May we obtain the grace of your blessing, O Lord,
through the intercession of Mary, the Mother of God,
that from her, whose holy Name we venerate,
we may obtain help in our every need.
Through Christ our Lord.

September 13

Saint John Chrysostom, Bishop and Doctor of the Church

Memorial

Entrance Antiphon

Those who are wise will shine brightly
like the splendor of the firmament
and those who lead the many to justice
shall be like the stars for ever. Cf. Dn 12: 3

COLLECT

O God, strength of those who hope in you,
who willed that the Bishop Saint John Chrysostom
should be illustrious by his wonderful eloquence
and his experience of suffering,
grant us, we pray,
that, instructed by his teachings,
we may be strengthened through the example
of his invincible patience.
Through our Lord Jesus Christ, your Son,
who lives and reigns with you
in the unity of the Holy Spirit,
one God, for ever and ever.

PRAYER AFTER COMMUNION

Grant, O merciful God,
that these mysteries we have received
as we commemorate Saint John Chrysostom,
may confirm us in your love
and enable us to be faithful in confessing your truth.
Through Christ our Lord.

September 14

THE EXALTATION OF THE HOLY CROSS

Feast

Entrance Antiphon

We should glory in the Cross of our Lord Jesus Christ,
in whom is our salvation, life and resurrection,
through whom we are saved and delivered. Cf. Gal 6: 14

The Gloria in excelsis (Glory to God in the highest) is said.

COLLECT

O God, who willed that your Only Begotten Son
should undergo the Cross to save the human race,
grant, we pray,
that we, who have known his mystery on earth,
may merit the grace of his redemption in heaven.
Through our Lord Jesus Christ, your Son,
who lives and reigns with you
in the unity of the Holy Spirit,
one God, for ever and ever.

When this Feast falls on a Sunday, the Creed is said.

PRAYER AFTER COMMUNION

Having been nourished by your holy banquet,
we beseech you, Lord Jesus Christ,
to bring those you have redeemed
by the wood of your life-giving Cross
to the glory of the resurrection.
Who live and reign for ever and ever.

September 15
Our Lady of Sorrows

Memorial

Entrance Antiphon

Simeon said to Mary: Behold, this child is destined
for the ruin and rising of many in Israel,
and to be a sign of contradiction;
and your own soul a sword will pierce. Cf. Lk 2: 34-35

COLLECT

O God, who willed
that, when your Son was lifted high on the Cross,
his Mother should stand close by and share his suffering,
grant that your Church,
participating with the Virgin Mary in the Passion of Christ,
may merit a share in his Resurrection.
Who lives and reigns with you
in the unity of the Holy Spirit,
one God, for ever and ever.

PRAYER AFTER COMMUNION

Having received the Sacrament of eternal redemption,
we humbly ask, O Lord,
that, honoring how the Blessed Virgin Mary
suffered with her Son,
we may complete in ourselves for the Church's sake
what is lacking in the sufferings of Christ.
Who lives and reigns for ever and ever.

September 16

Saints Cornelius, Pope, and Cyprian, Bishop, Martyrs

Memorial

From the Common of Martyrs: For Several Martyrs (p. 526), or from the Common of Pastors: For a Bishop (p. 541).

COLLECT

**O God, who gave Saints Cornelius and Cyprian
to your people
as diligent shepherds and valiant Martyrs,
grant that through their intercession
we may be strengthened in faith and constancy
and spend ourselves without reserve
for the unity of the Church.
Through our Lord Jesus Christ, your Son,
who lives and reigns with you
in the unity of the Holy Spirit,
one God, for ever and ever.**

PRAYER AFTER COMMUNION

**Through these mysteries which we have received,
we humbly beseech you, O Lord,
that by the example of the Martyrs
Saints Cornelius and Cyprian
we may be strengthened with the fortitude
of your Spirit
to bear witness to the truth of the Gospel.
Through Christ our Lord.**

September 17
Saint Robert Bellarmine, Bishop and Doctor of the Church

From the Common of Pastors: For a Bishop (p. 541), or from the Common of Doctors of the Church (p. 551).

COLLECT

O God, who adorned the Bishop Saint Robert Bellarmine
with wonderful learning and virtue
to vindicate the faith of your Church,
grant, through his intercession,
that in the integrity of that same faith
your people may always find joy.
Through our Lord Jesus Christ, your Son,
who lives and reigns with you
in the unity of the Holy Spirit,
one God, for ever and ever.

September 19
Saint Januarius, Bishop and Martyr

From the Common of Martyrs: For One Martyr (p. 531), or from the Common of Pastors: For a Bishop (p. 541).

COLLECT

O God, who grant us to venerate
the memory of the Martyr Saint Januarius,
give us, we pray, the joy of his company
in blessed happiness for all eternity.
Through our Lord Jesus Christ, your Son,
who lives and reigns with you
in the unity of the Holy Spirit,
one God, for ever and ever.

September 20

Saints Andrew Kim Tae-gŏn, Priest, and Paul Chŏng Ha-sang, and Companions, Martyrs

Memorial

Entrance Antiphon

The blood of the holy Martyrs
was poured out for Christ upon the earth;
therefore they have gained everlasting rewards.

COLLECT

O God, who have been pleased to increase
your adopted children in all the world,
and who made the blood of the Martyrs
Saint Andrew Kim Tae-gŏn and his companions
a most fruitful seed of Christians,
grant that we may be defended by their help
and profit always from their example.
Through our Lord Jesus Christ, your Son,
who lives and reigns with you
in the unity of the Holy Spirit,
one God, for ever and ever.

PRAYER AFTER COMMUNION

Nourished with the food of the valiant
as we celebrate the blessed Martyrs,
we humbly ask you, O Lord,
that, clinging faithfully to Christ,
we may labor in the Church for the salvation of all.
Through Christ our Lord.

September 21
SAINT MATTHEW, APOSTLE AND EVANGELIST

Feast

Entrance Antiphon

**Go and make disciples of all nations, baptizing them
and teaching them to observe all that I have commanded you,
says the Lord.** Cf. Mt 28: 19-20

The Gloria in excelsis (Glory to God in the highest) is said.

COLLECT

**O God, who with untold mercy
were pleased to choose as an Apostle
Saint Matthew, the tax collector,
grant that, sustained by his example and intercession,
we may merit to hold firm in following you.
Through our Lord Jesus Christ, your Son,
who lives and reigns with you
in the unity of the Holy Spirit,
one God, for ever and ever.**

PRAYER AFTER COMMUNION

**Sharing in that saving joy, O Lord,
with which Saint Matthew welcomed
the Savior as a guest in his home, we pray:
grant that we may always be renewed
by the food we receive from Christ,
who came to call not the just, but sinners to salvation.
Who lives and reigns for ever and ever.**

The Solemn Blessing formula, p. 319, may be used.

September 23

Saint Pius of Pietrelcina, Priest

Memorial

From the Common of Pastors: For One Pastor (p. 544), or from the Common of Holy Men and Women: For Religious (p. 563).

COLLECT

**Almighty ever-living God, who, by a singular grace,
gave the Priest Saint Pius a share
in the Cross of your Son
and, by means of his ministry,
renewed the wonders of your mercy,
grant that through his intercession
we may be united constantly to the sufferings of Christ,
and so brought happily to the glory of the resurrection.
Through our Lord Jesus Christ, your Son,
who lives and reigns with you
in the unity of the Holy Spirit,
one God, for ever and ever.**

September 26

Saints Cosmas and Damian, Martyrs

From the Common of Martyrs: For Several Martyrs (p. 526).

COLLECT

**May you be magnified, O Lord,
by the revered memory
of your Saints Cosmas and Damian,
for with providence beyond words
you have conferred on them everlasting glory,
and on us, your unfailing help.
Through our Lord Jesus Christ, your Son,
who lives and reigns with you
in the unity of the Holy Spirit,
one God, for ever and ever.**

PRAYER AFTER COMMUNION

**Preserve in us your gift, O Lord,
and may what we have received at your hands
as we commemorate the Martyrs
Saints Cosmas and Damian,
bring us healing, salvation and peace.
Through Christ our Lord.**

September 27

Saint Vincent de Paul, Priest

Memorial

Entrance Antiphon

The Spirit of the Lord is upon me, for he has anointed me
and sent me to preach the good news to the poor,
to heal the broken-hearted. Cf. Lk 4: 18

COLLECT

O God, who for the relief of the poor
and the formation of the clergy
endowed the Priest Saint Vincent de Paul
with apostolic virtues,
grant, we pray, that, afire with that same spirit,
we may love what he loved
and put into practice what he taught.
Through our Lord Jesus Christ, your Son,
who lives and reigns with you
in the unity of the Holy Spirit,
one God, for ever and ever.

PRAYER AFTER COMMUNION

Renewed by this heavenly Sacrament, O Lord,
we implore
that, just as we are prompted by Saint Vincent's example
to imitate your Son in his preaching of the Gospel
to the poor,
so, too, we may be sustained by his prayers.
Through Christ our Lord.

September 28
Saint Wenceslaus, Martyr

From the Common of Martyrs: For One Martyr (p. 531).

COLLECT

O God, who taught the Martyr Saint Wenceslaus
to place the heavenly Kingdom before an earthly one,
grant through his prayers that, denying ourselves,
we may hold fast to you with all our heart.
Through our Lord Jesus Christ, your Son,
who lives and reigns with you
in the unity of the Holy Spirit,
one God, for ever and ever.

Saint Lawrence Ruiz and Companions, Martyrs

From the Common of Martyrs: For Several Martyrs (p. 526).

COLLECT

Grant us, we pray, Lord God,
the same perseverance shown by your Martyrs
Saint Lawrence Ruiz and his companions
in serving you and their neighbor,
since those persecuted for the sake of righteousness
are blessed in your Kingdom.
Through our Lord Jesus Christ, your Son,
who lives and reigns with you
in the unity of the Holy Spirit,
one God, for ever and ever.

September 29

SAINTS MICHAEL, GABRIEL AND RAPHAEL, ARCHANGELS

Feast

Entrance Antiphon

**Bless the Lord, all you his angels, mighty in power,
fulfilling his word, and heeding his voice.** Cf. Ps 103 (102): 20

The Gloria in excelsis (Glory to God in the highest) is said.

COLLECT

**O God, who dispose in marvelous order
ministries both angelic and human,
graciously grant
that our life on earth may be defended
by those who watch over us
as they minister perpetually to you in heaven.
Through our Lord Jesus Christ, your Son,
who lives and reigns with you
in the unity of the Holy Spirit,
one God, for ever and ever.**

PRAYER AFTER COMMUNION

**Having been nourished with heavenly Bread,
we beseech you humbly, O Lord,
that, drawing from it new strength,
under the faithful protection of your Angels,
we may advance boldly along the way of salvation.
Through Christ our Lord.**

September 30

Saint Jerome, Priest and Doctor of the Church

Memorial

Entrance Antiphon

Blessed indeed is he
who ponders the law of the Lord day and night:
he will yield his fruit in due season. Cf. Ps 1: 2-3

COLLECT

O God, who gave the Priest Saint Jerome
a living and tender love for Sacred Scripture,
grant that your people
may be ever more fruitfully nourished by your Word
and find in it the fount of life.
Through our Lord Jesus Christ, your Son,
who lives and reigns with you
in the unity of the Holy Spirit,
one God, for ever and ever.

PRAYER AFTER COMMUNION

May these holy gifts we have received, O Lord,
as we rejoice in celebrating Saint Jerome,
stir up the hearts of your faithful
so that, attentive to sacred teachings,
they may understand the path they are to follow
and, by following it, obtain life everlasting.
Through Christ our Lord.

OCTOBER

October 1
Saint Thérèse of the Child Jesus, Virgin and Doctor of the Church

Memorial

Entrance Antiphon

The Lord led her and taught her,
and kept her as the apple of his eye.
Like an eagle spreading its wings
he took her up and bore her on his shoulders.
The Lord alone was her guide. Cf. Dt 32: 10-12

COLLECT

O God, who open your Kingdom
to those who are humble and to little ones,
lead us to follow trustingly in the little way
of Saint Thérèse,
so that through her intercession
we may see your eternal glory revealed.
Through our Lord Jesus Christ, your Son,
who lives and reigns with you
in the unity of the Holy Spirit,
one God, for ever and ever.

PRAYER AFTER COMMUNION

May the Sacrament we have received, O Lord,
kindle in us the force of that love
with which Saint Thérèse dedicated herself to you
and longed to obtain your mercy for all.
Through Christ our Lord.

October 2
The Holy Guardian Angels

Memorial

Entrance Antiphon

Angels of the Lord, bless the Lord,
praise and exalt him above all for ever. Cf. Dn 3: 58

COLLECT

O God, who in your unfathomable providence
are pleased to send your holy Angels to guard us,
hear our supplication as we cry to you,
that we may always be defended by their protection
and rejoice eternally in their company.
Through our Lord Jesus Christ, your Son,
who lives and reigns with you
in the unity of the Holy Spirit,
one God, for ever and ever.

PRAYER AFTER COMMUNION

As you are pleased to nourish us for eternal life
with so great a Sacrament, O Lord,
direct us by the ministry of Angels
into the way of salvation and peace.
Through Christ our Lord.

October 4

Saint Francis of Assisi

Memorial

Entrance Antiphon

Francis, the man of God, left his home behind,
abandoned his inheritance and became poor and penniless,
but the Lord raised him up.

COLLECT

O God, by whose gift Saint Francis
was conformed to Christ in poverty and humility,
grant that, by walking in Francis' footsteps,
we may follow your Son,
and, through joyful charity,
come to be united with you.
Through our Lord Jesus Christ, your Son,
who lives and reigns with you
in the unity of the Holy Spirit,
one God, for ever and ever.

PRAYER AFTER COMMUNION

Grant us, we pray, O Lord,
through these holy gifts which we have received,
that, imitating the charity and apostolic zeal
of Saint Francis,
we may experience the effects of your love
and spread them everywhere for the salvation of all.
Through Christ our Lord.

[In the Dioceses of the United States]

October 5

Blessed Francis Xavier Seelos, Priest

From the Common of Pastors: For Missionaries (p. 548).

COLLECT

O God, who made your Priest Blessed Francis Xavier Seelos
outstanding in love,
that he might proclaim the mysteries of redemption
and comfort those in affliction,
grant, by his intercession,
that we may work zealously for your glory
and for the salvation of mankind.
Through our Lord Jesus Christ, your Son,
who lives and reigns with you in the unity of the Holy Spirit,
one God, for ever and ever.

October 6
Saint Bruno, Priest

From the Common of Holy Men and Women: For a Monk (p. 561), or from the Common of Pastors: For One Pastor (p. 544).

COLLECT

O God, who called Saint Bruno to serve you in solitude,
grant, through his intercession,
that amid the changes of this world
we may constantly look to you alone.
Through our Lord Jesus Christ, your Son,
who lives and reigns with you
in the unity of the Holy Spirit,
one God, for ever and ever.

[In the Dioceses of the United States]
Blessed Marie Rose Durocher, Virgin

From the Common of Virgins: For One Virgin (p. 554).

COLLECT

Lord, who enkindled in the heart
of Blessed Marie Rose Durocher
the flame of ardent charity
and a great desire to cooperate
in the mission of the Church as a teacher,
grant us that same active love,
so that, in responding to the needs of the world today,
we may lead our brothers and sisters
to the blessedness of eternal life.
Through our Lord Jesus Christ, your Son,
who lives and reigns with you
in the unity of the Holy Spirit,
one God, for ever and ever.

October 7

Our Lady of the Rosary

Memorial

Entrance Antiphon

Hail Mary, full of grace, the Lord is with you.
Blessed are you among women
and blessed is the fruit of your womb. Cf. Lk 1: 28, 42

COLLECT

Pour forth, we beseech you, O Lord,
your grace into our hearts,
that we, to whom the Incarnation of Christ your Son
was made known by the message of an Angel,
may, through the intercession of the Blessed Virgin Mary,
by his Passion and Cross
be brought to the glory of his Resurrection.
Who lives and reigns with you
in the unity of the Holy Spirit,
one God, for ever and ever.

PRAYER AFTER COMMUNION

We pray, O Lord our God,
that, just as we proclaim in this Sacrament
the Death and Resurrection of your Son,
so, being made partakers in his suffering,
we may also merit a share
in his consolation and his glory.
Who lives and reigns for ever and ever.

October 9

Saint Denis, Bishop, and Companions, Martyrs

From the Common of Martyrs: For Several Martyrs (p. 526).

COLLECT

**O God, who sent Saint Denis and his companions
to preach your glory to the nations
and strengthened them for their mission
with the virtue of constancy in suffering,
grant, we pray, that we may imitate them
in disdaining prosperity in this world
and in being undaunted by any trial.
Through our Lord Jesus Christ, your Son,
who lives and reigns with you
in the unity of the Holy Spirit,
one God, for ever and ever.**

Saint John Leonardi, Priest

From the Common of Pastors: For Missionaries (p. 548), or from the Common of Holy Men and Women: For Those Who Practiced Works of Mercy (p. 564).

COLLECT

**O God, giver of all good things,
who through the Priest Saint John Leonardi
caused the Gospel to be announced to the nations,
grant, through his intercession,
that the true faith may always and everywhere prosper.
Through our Lord Jesus Christ, your Son,
who lives and reigns with you
in the unity of the Holy Spirit,
one God, for ever and ever.**

October 11

Saint John XXIII, Pope

From the Common of Pastors: For a Pope (p. 539).

October 14

Saint Callistus I, Pope and Martyr

From the Common of Martyrs: For One Martyr (p. 531), or from the Common of Pastors: For a Pope (p. 539).

COLLECT

O God, who raised up Pope Saint Callistus the First
to serve the Church
and attend devoutly to Christ's faithful departed,
strengthen us, we pray, by his witness to the faith,
so that, rescued from the slavery of corruption,
we may merit an incorruptible inheritance.
Through our Lord Jesus Christ, your Son,
who lives and reigns with you
in the unity of the Holy Spirit,
one God, for ever and ever.

October 15

Saint Teresa of Jesus, Virgin and Doctor of the Church

Memorial

Entrance Antiphon

Like the deer that yearns for running streams,
so my soul is yearning for you, my God;
my soul is thirsting for God, the living God. Cf. Ps 42 (41): 2-3

COLLECT

O God, who through your Spirit
raised up Saint Teresa of Jesus
to show the Church the way to seek perfection,
grant that we may always be nourished
by the food of her heavenly teaching
and fired with longing for true holiness.
Through our Lord Jesus Christ, your Son,
who lives and reigns with you
in the unity of the Holy Spirit,
one God, for ever and ever.

PRAYER AFTER COMMUNION

Grant, O Lord our God,
that your obedient family,
whom you have fed with the Bread of heaven,
may follow the example of Saint Teresa
and rejoice to sing of your mercies for all eternity.
Through Christ our Lord.

October 16
Saint Hedwig, Religious

From the Common of Holy Men and Women: For Religious (p. 563), or For Holy Women (p. 566).

COLLECT

Grant, we pray, almighty God,
that the revered intercession of Saint Hedwig
may bring us heavenly aid,
just as her wonderful life
is an example of humility for all.
Through our Lord Jesus Christ, your Son,
who lives and reigns with you
in the unity of the Holy Spirit,
one God, for ever and ever.

Saint Margaret Mary Alacoque, Virgin

From the Common of Virgins: For One Virgin (p. 554).

COLLECT

Pour out on us, we pray, O Lord,
the spirit with which you so remarkably endowed
Saint Margaret Mary,
so that we may come to know
that love of Christ which surpasses all understanding
and be utterly filled with your fullness.
Through our Lord Jesus Christ, your Son,
who lives and reigns with you
in the unity of the Holy Spirit,
one God, for ever and ever.

October 17

Saint Ignatius of Antioch, Bishop and Martyr

Memorial

Entrance Antiphon

I am crucified with Christ, yet I live;
no longer I, but Christ lives in me.
I live by faith in the Son of God,
who has loved me and given himself up for me.

Cf. Gal 2: 19-20

COLLECT

Almighty ever-living God,
who adorn the sacred body of your Church
with the confessions of holy Martyrs,
grant, we pray,
that, just as the glorious passion
of Saint Ignatius of Antioch,
which we celebrate today,
brought him eternal splendor,
so it may be for us unending protection.
Through our Lord Jesus Christ, your Son,
who lives and reigns with you
in the unity of the Holy Spirit,
one God, for ever and ever.

PRAYER AFTER COMMUNION

May the heavenly Bread we have received, O Lord,
on the feast day of Saint Ignatius
renew us, we pray,
and make us Christians in name and in deed.
Through Christ our Lord.

October 18
Saint Luke, Evangelist

Feast

Entrance Antiphon

How beautiful upon the mountains are the feet of him
who brings glad tidings of peace,
bearing good news, announcing salvation! Is 52: 7

The Gloria in excelsis (Glory to God in the highest) is said.

COLLECT

Lord God, who chose Saint Luke
to reveal by his preaching and writings
the mystery of your love for the poor,
grant that those who already glory in your name
may persevere as one heart and one soul
and that all nations may merit to see your salvation.
Through our Lord Jesus Christ, your Son,
who lives and reigns with you
in the unity of the Holy Spirit,
one God, for ever and ever.

PRAYER AFTER COMMUNION

Grant, we pray, almighty God,
that what we have received from your holy altar
may sanctify us and make us strong
in the faith of the Gospel which Saint Luke proclaimed.
Through Christ our Lord.

[In the Dioceses of the United States]

October 19

Saints John de Brébeuf and Isaac Jogues, Priests, and Companions, Martyrs

Memorial

From the Common of Martyrs: For Missionary Martyrs (p. 536).

COLLECT

O God, who chose to manifest
the blessed hope of your eternal Kingdom
by the toil of Saints John de Brébeuf,
Isaac Jogues and their companions
and by the shedding of their blood,
graciously grant that through their intercession
the faith of Christians may be strengthened day by day.
Through our Lord Jesus Christ, your Son,
who lives and reigns with you
in the unity of the Holy Spirit,
one God, for ever and ever.

[In the Dioceses of the United States]

October 20

Saint Paul of the Cross, Priest

Entrance Antiphon

I resolved to know nothing while I was with you
except for Jesus Christ, and him crucified. Cf. 1 Cor 2: 2

COLLECT

May the Priest Saint Paul,
whose only love was the Cross,
obtain for us your grace, O Lord,
so that, urged on more strongly by his example,
we may each embrace our own cross with courage.
Through our Lord Jesus Christ, your Son,
who lives and reigns with you
in the unity of the Holy Spirit,
one God, for ever and ever.

PRAYER AFTER COMMUNION

**O God, who in Saint Paul
have wonderfully made known the mystery of the Cross,
graciously grant
that, drawing strength from this sacrifice,
we may cling faithfully to Christ
and labor in the Church for the salvation of all.
Through Christ our Lord.**

October 22

Saint John Paul II, Pope

From the Common of Pastors: For a Pope (p. 539).

COLLECT

**O God, who are rich in mercy,
and who willed that Saint John Paul the Second
should preside as Pope over your universal Church,
grant, we pray, that instructed by his teaching,
we may open our hearts to the saving grace of Christ,
the sole Redeemer of mankind.
Who lives and reigns with you
in the unity of the Holy Spirit,
one God, for ever and ever.**

October 23

Saint John of Capistrano, Priest

From the Common of Pastors: For Missionaries (p. 548), or from the Common of Holy Men and Women: For Religious (p. 563).

COLLECT

O God, who raised up Saint John of Capistrano
to comfort your faithful people in tribulation,
place us, we pray, under your safe protection
and keep your Church in everlasting peace.
Through our Lord Jesus Christ, your Son,
who lives and reigns with you
in the unity of the Holy Spirit,
one God, for ever and ever.

October 24

Saint Anthony Mary Claret, Bishop

From the Common of Pastors: For Missionaries (p. 548), or For a Bishop (p. 541).

COLLECT

O God, who for the evangelization of peoples
strengthened the Bishop Saint Anthony Mary Claret
with admirable charity and long-suffering,
grant, through his intercession,
that, seeking the things that are yours,
we may earnestly devote ourselves
to winning our brothers and sisters for Christ.
Who lives and reigns with you
in the unity of the Holy Spirit,
one God, for ever and ever.

October 28
Saints Simon and Jude, Apostles

Feast

Entrance Antiphon These are the holy men
whom the Lord chose in his own perfect love;
to them he gave eternal glory.

The Gloria in excelsis (Glory to God in the highest) is said.

COLLECT O God, who by the blessed Apostles
have brought us to acknowledge your name,
graciously grant,
through the intercession of Saints Simon and Jude,
that the Church may constantly grow
by increase of the peoples who believe in you.
Through our Lord Jesus Christ, your Son,
who lives and reigns with you
in the unity of the Holy Spirit,
one God, for ever and ever.

PRAYER AFTER COMMUNION Having received this Sacrament, O Lord,
we humbly implore you in the Holy Spirit,
that what we do to honor the glorious passion
of the Apostles Simon and Jude
may keep us ever in your love.
Through Christ our Lord.

The Solemn Blessing formula, p. 319, may be used.

NOVEMBER

November 1
ALL SAINTS

Solemnity

Entrance Antiphon

Let us all rejoice in the Lord,
as we celebrate the feast day in honor of all the Saints,
at whose festival the Angels rejoice
and praise the Son of God.

The Gloria in excelsis (Glory to God in the highest) is said.

COLLECT

Almighty ever-living God,
by whose gift we venerate in one celebration
the merits of all the Saints,
bestow on us, we pray,
through the prayers of so many intercessors,
an abundance of the reconciliation with you
for which we earnestly long.
Through our Lord Jesus Christ, your Son,
who lives and reigns with you
in the unity of the Holy Spirit,
one God, for ever and ever.

The Creed is said.

PRAYER AFTER COMMUNION

As we adore you, O God, who alone are holy
and wonderful in all your Saints,
we implore your grace,
so that, coming to perfect holiness
in the fullness of your love,
we may pass from this pilgrim table
to the banquet of our heavenly homeland.
Through Christ our Lord.

The Solemn Blessing formula, p. 319, may be used.

For the Votive Mass of All Saints, cf. below, p. 685.

November 2

THE COMMEMORATION OF ALL THE FAITHFUL DEPARTED

(All Souls' Day)

The Masses that follow may be used at the discretion of the celebrant.[1]

Even when November 2 falls on a Sunday, the Mass celebrated is that of the Commemoration of All the Faithful Departed.

1

Entrance Antiphon

Just as Jesus died and has risen again,
so through Jesus God will bring with him
those who have fallen asleep;
and as in Adam all die,
so also in Christ will all be brought to life.

Cf. 1 Thes 4: 14; 1 Cor 15: 22

COLLECT

Listen kindly to our prayers, O Lord,
and, as our faith in your Son,
raised from the dead, is deepened,
so may our hope of resurrection for your departed servants
also find new strength.
Through our Lord Jesus Christ, your Son,
who lives and reigns with you
in the unity of the Holy Spirit,
one God, for ever and ever.

PRAYER AFTER COMMUNION

Grant we pray, O Lord, that your departed servants,
for whom we have celebrated this paschal Sacrament,
may pass over to a dwelling place of light and peace.
Through Christ our Lord.

The Solemn Blessing formula, p. 320, may be used.

---

[1] On this day, any Priest may celebrate three Masses, observing, nevertheless, what was established by Benedict XV in the Apostolic Constitution, *Incruentum altaris sacrificium*, August 10, 1915: *Acta Apostolicae Sedis* 7 (1915), pp. 401-404.

2

Entrance Antiphon

Eternal rest grant unto them, O Lord,
and let perpetual light shine upon them. Cf. 4 Esdr 2: 34-35

COLLECT

O God, glory of the faithful and life of the just,
by the Death and Resurrection of whose Son
we have been redeemed,
look mercifully on your departed servants,
that, just as they professed the mystery of our resurrection,
so they may merit to receive the joys of eternal happiness.
Through our Lord Jesus Christ, your Son,
who lives and reigns with you
in the unity of the Holy Spirit,
one God, for ever and ever.

PRAYER AFTER COMMUNION

Having received the Sacrament
of your Only Begotten Son,
who was sacrificed for us and rose in glory,
we humbly implore you, O Lord,
for your departed servants,
that, cleansed by the paschal mysteries,
they may glory in the gift of the resurrection to come.
Through Christ our Lord.

The Solemn Blessing formula, p. 320, may be used.

3

Entrance Antiphon

God, who raised Jesus from the dead,
will give life also to your mortal bodies,
through his Spirit that dwells in you. Cf. Rom 8: 11

COLLECT

O God, who willed that your Only Begotten Son,
having conquered death,
should pass over into the realm of heaven,
grant, we pray, to your departed servants
that, with the mortality of this life overcome,
they may gaze eternally on you,
their Creator and Redeemer.
Through our Lord Jesus Christ, your Son,
who lives and reigns with you
in the unity of the Holy Spirit,
one God, for ever and ever.

PRAYER AFTER COMMUNION

Through these sacrificial gifts
which we have received, O Lord,
bestow on your departed servants your great mercy
and, to those you have endowed with the grace of Baptism,
grant also the fullness of eternal joy.
Through Christ our Lord.

The Solemn Blessing formula, p. 320, may be used.

November 3
Saint Martin de Porres, Religious

From the Common of Holy Men and Women: For Religious (p. 563).

COLLECT

O God, who led Saint Martin de Porres
by the path of humility to heavenly glory,
grant that we may so follow his radiant example
in this life
as to merit to be exalted with him in heaven.
Through our Lord Jesus Christ, your Son,
who lives and reigns with you
in the unity of the Holy Spirit,
one God, for ever and ever.

November 4
Saint Charles Borromeo, Bishop

Memorial

From the Common of Pastors: For a Bishop (p. 541).

COLLECT

Preserve in the midst of your people,
we ask, O Lord, the spirit with which you filled
the Bishop Saint Charles Borromeo,
that your Church may be constantly renewed
and, by conforming herself to the likeness of Christ,
may show his face to the world.
Who lives and reigns with you
in the unity of the Holy Spirit,
one God, for ever and ever.

PRAYER AFTER COMMUNION

May the sacred mysteries of which we have partaken,
O Lord, we pray, give us that determination
which made Saint Charles faithful in ministry
and fervent in charity.
Through Christ our Lord.

November 9

THE DEDICATION OF THE LATERAN BASILICA

Feast

In the basilica itself, the Mass of the Common of the Dedication of a Church is used (p. 515).

Entrance Antiphon

I saw the holy city, a new Jerusalem,
coming down out of heaven from God,
prepared like a bride adorned for her husband. Cf. Rev 21: 2

Or:

Behold God's dwelling with the human race.
He will dwell with them and they will be his people,
and God himself with them will be their God. Cf. Rev 21: 3

The Gloria in excelsis (Glory to God in the highest) is said.

COLLECT

O God, who from living and chosen stones
prepare an eternal dwelling for your majesty,
increase in your Church the spirit of grace
you have bestowed,
so that by new growth your faithful people
may build up the heavenly Jerusalem.
Through our Lord Jesus Christ, your Son,
who lives and reigns with you
in the unity of the Holy Spirit,
one God, for ever and ever.

Or:

O God, who were pleased to call your Church the Bride,
grant that the people that serves your name
may revere you, love you and follow you,
and may be led by you
to attain your promises in heaven.
Through our Lord Jesus Christ, your Son,
who lives and reigns with you
in the unity of the Holy Spirit,
one God, for ever and ever.

When this Feast falls on a Sunday, the Creed is said.

PRAYER AFTER COMMUNION

O God, who chose to foreshadow for us
the heavenly Jerusalem
through the sign of your Church on earth,
grant, we pray,
that, by our partaking of this Sacrament,
we may be made the temple of your grace
and may enter the dwelling place of your glory.
Through Christ our Lord.

The Solemn Blessing formula, p. 320, may be used.

November 10

Saint Leo the Great, Pope and Doctor of the Church

Memorial

Entrance Antiphon

The Lord established for him a covenant of peace,
and made him the prince,
that he might have the dignity of the priesthood for ever.

Cf. Sir 45: 30

COLLECT

O God, who never allow the gates of hell
to prevail against your Church,
firmly founded on the apostolic rock,
grant her, we pray,
that through the intercession of Pope Saint Leo,
she may stand firm in your truth
and know the protection of lasting peace.
Through our Lord Jesus Christ, your Son,
who lives and reigns with you
in the unity of the Holy Spirit,
one God, for ever and ever.

PRAYER AFTER COMMUNION

Be pleased, O Lord, we pray,
to govern the Church you have nourished
by this holy meal,
so that, firmly directed,
she may enjoy ever greater freedom
and persevere in integrity of religion.
Through Christ our Lord.

November 11

Saint Martin of Tours, Bishop

Memorial

Entrance Antiphon

I shall raise up for myself a faithful priest
who will act in accord with my heart and my mind,
says the Lord. Cf. 1 Sm 2: 35

COLLECT

O God, who are glorified in the Bishop Saint Martin
both by his life and death,
make new, we pray,
the wonders of your grace in our hearts,
that neither death nor life
may separate us from your love.
Through our Lord Jesus Christ, your Son,
who lives and reigns with you
in the unity of the Holy Spirit,
one God, for ever and ever.

PRAYER AFTER COMMUNION

Grant to us who have been restored
by this Sacrament of unity, O Lord,
perfect harmony with your will in all things,
that, just as Saint Martin submitted himself
entirely to you,
so we, too, may glory in being truly yours.
Through Christ our Lord.

November 12

Saint Josaphat, Bishop and Martyr

Memorial

Entrance Antiphon

Because of the Lord's covenant and the ancestral laws,
the Saints of God persevered in loving brotherhood,
for there was always one spirit in them, and one faith.

COLLECT

Stir up in your Church, we pray, O Lord,
the Spirit that filled Saint Josaphat
as he laid down his life for the sheep,
so that through his intercession
we, too, may be strengthened by the same Spirit
and not be afraid to lay down our life for others.
Through our Lord Jesus Christ, your Son,
who lives and reigns with you
in the unity of the Holy Spirit,
one God, for ever and ever.

PRAYER AFTER COMMUNION

May this heavenly table, O Lord,
bestow on us a spirit of fortitude and peace,
so that, following Saint Josaphat's example,
we may willingly spend our lives
working for the honor and unity of the Church.
Through Christ our Lord.

[In the Dioceses of the United States]

November 13

Saint Frances Xavier Cabrini, Virgin

From the Common of Virgins: For One Virgin (p. 554), or from the Common of Holy Men and Women: For Those Who Practiced Works of Mercy (p. 564).

COLLECT

**God our Father,
who called Saint Frances Xavier Cabrini from Italy
to serve the immigrants of America,
by her example,
teach us to have concern for the stranger,
the sick, and all those in need,
and by her prayers help us to see Christ
in all the men and women we meet.
Through our Lord Jesus Christ, your Son,
who lives and reigns with you
in the unity of the Holy Spirit,
one God, for ever and ever.**

November 15

Saint Albert the Great, Bishop and Doctor of the Church

From the Common of Pastors: For a Bishop (p. 541), or from the Common of Doctors of the Church (p. 551).

COLLECT

**O God, who made the Bishop Saint Albert great
by his joining of human wisdom to divine faith,
grant, we pray, that we may so adhere
to the truths he taught,
that through progress in learning
we may come to a deeper knowledge and love of you.
Through our Lord Jesus Christ, your Son,
who lives and reigns with you
in the unity of the Holy Spirit,
one God, for ever and ever.**

November 16
Saint Margaret of Scotland

From the Common of Holy Men and Women: For Those Who Practiced Works of Mercy (p. 564).

COLLECT

O God, who made Saint Margaret of Scotland wonderful
in her outstanding charity towards the poor,
grant that through her intercession and example
we may reflect among all humanity
the image of your divine goodness.
Through our Lord Jesus Christ, your Son,
who lives and reigns with you
in the unity of the Holy Spirit,
one God, for ever and ever.

Saint Gertrude, Virgin

From the Common of Virgins: For One Virgin (p. 554), or from the Common of Holy Men and Women: For a Nun (p. 562).

COLLECT

O God, who prepared a delightful dwelling for yourself
in the heart of the Virgin Saint Gertrude,
graciously bring light, through her intercession,
to the darkness of our hearts,
that we may joyfully experience you present
and at work within us.
Through our Lord Jesus Christ, your Son,
who lives and reigns with you
in the unity of the Holy Spirit,
one God, for ever and ever.

November 17

Saint Elizabeth of Hungary, Religious

Memorial

From the Common of Holy Men and Women: For Those Who Practiced Works of Mercy (p. 564).

COLLECT

**O God, by whose gift Saint Elizabeth of Hungary
recognized and revered Christ in the poor,
grant, through her intercession,
that we may serve with unfailing charity
the needy and those afflicted.
Through our Lord Jesus Christ, your Son,
who lives and reigns with you
in the unity of the Holy Spirit,
one God, for ever and ever.**

November 18

The Dedication of the Basilicas of Saints Peter and Paul, Apostles

Entrance Antiphon

**You will make them princes over all the earth;
they will remember your name through all generations.
Thus the peoples will praise you for ever, from age to age.**

Cf. Ps 45 (44): 17-18

COLLECT

**Defend your Church, O Lord,
by the protection of the holy Apostles,
that, as she received from them
the beginnings of her knowledge of things divine,
so through them she may receive,
even to the end of the world,
an increase in heavenly grace.
Through our Lord Jesus Christ, your Son,
who lives and reigns with you
in the unity of the Holy Spirit,
one God, for ever and ever.**

PRAYER AFTER COMMUNION

**May your people, we pray, O Lord,
nourished by the Bread of heaven,
rejoice in commemorating the Apostles Peter and Paul,
for it is through your gift
that we are governed under their patronage.
Through Christ our Lord.**

[In the Dioceses of the United States]

Saint Rose Philippine Duchesne, Virgin

From the Common of Virgins: For One Virgin (p. 554).

COLLECT

**Almighty God, who filled the heart
of Saint Rose Philippine Duchesne
with charity and missionary zeal,
and gave her the desire
to make you known among all peoples,
grant us to follow her way
and fill us with that same love and zeal
to extend your Kingdom to the ends of the earth.
Through our Lord Jesus Christ, your Son,
who lives and reigns with you
in the unity of the Holy Spirit,
one God, for ever and ever.**

November 21

The Presentation of the Blessed Virgin Mary

Memorial

From the Common of the Blessed Virgin Mary (p. 518).

COLLECT

**As we venerate the glorious memory
of the most holy Virgin Mary,
grant, we pray, O Lord, through her intercession,
that we, too, may merit to receive
from the fullness of your grace.
Through our Lord Jesus Christ, your Son,
who lives and reigns with you
in the unity of the Holy Spirit,
one God, for ever and ever.**

November 22

Saint Cecilia, Virgin and Martyr

Memorial

From the Common of Martyrs: For a Virgin Martyr (p. 537), or from the Common of Virgins: For One Virgin (p. 554).

COLLECT

O God, who gladden us each year
with the feast day of your handmaid Saint Cecilia,
grant, we pray,
that what has been devoutly handed down
concerning her
may offer us examples to imitate
and proclaim the wonders worked in his servants
by Christ your Son.
Who lives and reigns with you
in the unity of the Holy Spirit,
one God, for ever and ever.

November 23

Saint Clement I, Pope and Martyr

From the Common of Martyrs: For One Martyr (p. 531), or from the Common of Pastors: For a Pope (p. 539).

COLLECT

Almighty ever-living God,
who are wonderful in the virtue of all your Saints,
grant us joy in the yearly commemoration
of Saint Clement,
who, as a Martyr and High Priest of your Son,
bore out by his witness what he celebrated in mystery
and confirmed by example what he preached with his lips.
Through our Lord Jesus Christ, your Son,
who lives and reigns with you
in the unity of the Holy Spirit,
one God, for ever and ever.

Saint Columban, Abbot

From the Common of Pastors: For Missionaries (p. 548), or from the Common of Holy Men and Women: For an Abbot (p. 560).

COLLECT

O God, who in Saint Columban
wonderfully joined the work of evangelization
to zeal for the monastic life,
grant, we pray,
that through his intercession and example
we may strive to seek you above all things
and to bring increase to your faithful people.
Through our Lord Jesus Christ, your Son,
who lives and reigns with you
in the unity of the Holy Spirit,
one God, for ever and ever.

[In the Dioceses of the United States]

Blessed Miguel Agustín Pro, Priest and Martyr

From the Common of Martyrs: For One Martyr (p. 531), or from the Common of Pastors: For One Pastor (p. 544).

COLLECT

Our God and Father,
who conferred upon your servant
Blessed Miguel Agustín Pro
the grace of ardently seeking your greater glory
and the salvation of others,
grant, through his intercession and example,
that by faithfully and joyfully performing our daily duties
and effectively assisting those around us,
we may serve you with zeal
and ever seek your glory.
Through our Lord Jesus Christ, your Son,
who lives and reigns with you
in the unity of the Holy Spirit,
one God, for ever and ever.

November 24

Saint Andrew Dũng-Lạc, Priest, and Companions, Martyrs

Memorial

Entrance Antiphon

May we never boast, except in the Cross of our Lord Jesus Christ.
For the word of the Cross is the power of God
to us who have been saved. Cf. Gal 6: 14; cf. 1 Cor 1: 18

COLLECT

O God, source and origin of all fatherhood,
who kept the Martyrs Saint Andrew Dũng-Lạc
and his companions
faithful to the Cross of your Son,
even to the shedding of their blood,
grant, through their intercession,
that, spreading your love among our brothers and sisters,
we may be your children both in name and in truth.
Through our Lord Jesus Christ, your Son,
who lives and reigns with you
in the unity of the Holy Spirit,
one God, for ever and ever.

PRAYER AFTER COMMUNION

Renewed by the one Bread
as we commemorate the holy Martyrs,
we humbly beseech you, O Lord,
that, abiding as one in your love,
we may merit by endurance an eternal prize.
Through Christ our Lord.

November 25
Saint Catherine of Alexandria, Virgin and Martyr

From the Common of Martyrs: For a Virgin Martyr (p. 537), or from the Common of Virgins: For One Virgin (p. 554).

COLLECT

Almighty ever-living God,
who gave Saint Catherine of Alexandria to your people
as a Virgin and an invincible Martyr,
grant that through her intercession
we may be strengthened in faith and constancy
and spend ourselves without reserve
for the unity of the Church.
Through our Lord Jesus Christ, your Son,
who lives and reigns with you
in the unity of the Holy Spirit,
one God, for ever and ever.

November 30
SAINT ANDREW, APOSTLE

Feast

Entrance Antiphon

Beside the Sea of Galilee,
the Lord saw two brothers, Peter and Andrew,
and he said to them:
Come after me and I will make you fishers of men.

Cf. Mt 4: 18-19

The Gloria in excelsis (Glory to God in the highest) is said.

COLLECT

We humbly implore your majesty, O Lord,
that, just as the blessed Apostle Andrew
was for your Church a preacher and pastor,
so he may be for us a constant intercessor before you.
Through our Lord Jesus Christ, your Son,
who lives and reigns with you
in the unity of the Holy Spirit,
one God, for ever and ever.

PRAYER AFTER COMMUNION

May communion in your Sacrament strengthen us,
O Lord,
so that by the example of the blessed Apostle Andrew
we, who carry in our body the Death of Christ,
may merit to live with him in glory.
Who lives and reigns for ever and ever.

The Solemn Blessing formula, p. 319, may be used.

[In the Dioceses of the United States]

Fourth Thursday in November

Thanksgiving Day

Entrance Antiphon

Sing and make music to the Lord in your hearts,
always thanking God the Father for all things
in the name of our Lord Jesus Christ.

Eph 5: 19-20

COLLECT

Father all-powerful,
your gifts of love are countless
and your goodness infinite;
as we come before you on Thanksgiving Day
with gratitude for your kindness,
open our hearts to have concern
for every man, woman, and child,
so that we may share your gifts in loving service.
Through our Lord Jesus Christ, your Son,
who lives and reigns with you
in the unity of the Holy Spirit,
one God, for ever and ever.

PRAYER AFTER COMMUNION

In this celebration, O Lord our God,
you have shown us the depths of your love
for all your children;
help us, we pray, to reach out in love to all your people,
so that we may share with them
the good things of time and eternity.
Through Christ our Lord.

DECEMBER

December 3
Saint Francis Xavier, Priest

Memorial

Entrance Antiphon

I will praise you, Lord, among the nations;
I will tell of your name to my kin. Ps 18 (17): 50; 22 (21): 23

COLLECT

O God, who through the preaching
of Saint Francis Xavier
won many peoples to yourself,
grant that the hearts of the faithful
may burn with the same zeal for the faith
and that Holy Church may everywhere rejoice
in an abundance of offspring.
Through our Lord Jesus Christ, your Son,
who lives and reigns with you
in the unity of the Holy Spirit,
one God, for ever and ever.

PRAYER AFTER COMMUNION

May your mysteries, O God,
kindle in us that fire of charity
with which Saint Francis Xavier burned
for the salvation of souls,
so that, walking ever more worthily in our vocation,
we may obtain with him the reward you promise
to those who labor well in your harvest.
Through Christ our Lord.

December 4

Saint John Damascene, Priest and Doctor of the Church

From the Common of Pastors: For One Pastor (p. 544), or from the Common of Doctors of the Church (p. 551).

COLLECT

**Grant, we pray, O Lord,
that we may be helped by the prayers
of the Priest Saint John Damascene,
so that the true faith,
which he excelled in teaching,
may always be our light and our strength.
Through our Lord Jesus Christ, your Son,
who lives and reigns with you
in the unity of the Holy Spirit,
one God, for ever and ever.**

December 6

Saint Nicholas, Bishop

From the Common of Pastors: For a Bishop (p. 541).

COLLECT

**We humbly implore your mercy, Lord:
protect us in all dangers
through the prayers of the Bishop Saint Nicholas,
that the way of salvation may lie open before us.
Through our Lord Jesus Christ, your Son,
who lives and reigns with you
in the unity of the Holy Spirit,
one God, for ever and ever.**

December 7

Saint Ambrose, Bishop and Doctor of the Church

Memorial

Entrance Antiphon

In the midst of the Church he opened his mouth,
and the Lord filled him
with the spirit of wisdom and understanding
and clothed him in a robe of glory. Cf. Sir 15: 5

COLLECT

O God, who made the Bishop Saint Ambrose
a teacher of the Catholic faith
and a model of apostolic courage,
raise up in your Church men after your own heart
to govern her with courage and wisdom.
Through our Lord Jesus Christ, your Son,
who lives and reigns with you
in the unity of the Holy Spirit,
one God, for ever and ever.

PRAYER AFTER COMMUNION

Lead us who have been strengthened
by the power of this Sacrament, O Lord,
so to profit from the teaching of Saint Ambrose
that, hastening fearlessly along your paths,
we may be prepared for the delights
of the eternal banquet.
Through Christ our Lord.

December 8

THE IMMACULATE CONCEPTION OF THE BLESSED VIRGIN MARY

PATRONAL FEASTDAY OF THE UNITED STATES OF AMERICA

Solemnity

Entrance Antiphon

I rejoice heartily in the Lord,
in my God is the joy of my soul;
for he has clothed me with a robe of salvation,
and wrapped me in a mantle of justice,
like a bride adorned with her jewels. Is 61: 10

The Gloria in excelsis (Glory to God in the highest) is said.

COLLECT

O God, who by the Immaculate Conception
of the Blessed Virgin
prepared a worthy dwelling for your Son,
grant, we pray,
that, as you preserved her from every stain
by virtue of the Death of your Son, which you foresaw,
so, through her intercession,
we, too, may be cleansed and admitted to your presence.
Through our Lord Jesus Christ, your Son,
who lives and reigns with you
in the unity of the Holy Spirit,
one God, for ever and ever.

The Creed is said.

PRAYER AFTER COMMUNION

May the Sacrament we have received,
O Lord our God,
heal in us the wounds of that fault
from which in a singular way
you preserved Blessed Mary
in her Immaculate Conception.
Through Christ our Lord.

The Solemn Blessing formula, p. 318, may be used.

December 9

Saint Juan Diego Cuauhtlatoatzin

From the Common of Holy Men and Women: For One Saint (p. 559).

COLLECT

O God, who by means of Saint Juan Diego showed
the love of the most holy Virgin Mary for your people,
grant, through his intercession,
that, by following the counsels
our Mother gave at Guadalupe,
we may be ever constant in fulfilling your will.
Through our Lord Jesus Christ, your Son,
who lives and reigns with you
in the unity of the Holy Spirit,
one God, for ever and ever.

December 11

Saint Damasus I, Pope

From the Common of Pastors: For a Pope (p. 539).

COLLECT

Grant, we pray, O Lord,
that we may constantly exalt the merits of your Martyrs,
whom Pope Saint Damasus so venerated and loved.
Through our Lord Jesus Christ, your Son,
who lives and reigns with you
in the unity of the Holy Spirit,
one God, for ever and ever.

[In the Dioceses of the United States]

December 12

Our Lady of Guadalupe

Feast

Entrance Antiphon

A great sign appeared in the sky, a woman clothed with the sun,
with the moon under her feet,
and on her head a crown of twelve stars.

Rev 12: 1

The Gloria in excelsis (Glory to God in the highest) is said.

COLLECT

O God, Father of mercies,
who placed your people under the singular protection
of your Son's most holy Mother,
grant that all who invoke the Blessed Virgin of Guadalupe,
may seek with ever more lively faith
the progress of peoples in the ways of justice and of peace.
Through our Lord Jesus Christ, your Son,
who lives and reigns with you
in the unity of the Holy Spirit,
one God, for ever and ever.

PRAYER AFTER COMMUNION

Lord God, may the Body and Blood of your Son,
which we receive in this sacrament,
reconcile us always in your love;
and may we who rejoice in Our Lady of Guadalupe
live united and at peace in this world
until the day of the Lord dawns in glory.
Through Christ our Lord.

December 13

Saint Lucy, Virgin and Martyr

Memorial

From the Common of Martyrs: For a Virgin Martyr (p. 537), or from the Common of Virgins: For One Virgin (p. 554).

COLLECT

May the glorious intercession
of the Virgin and Martyr Saint Lucy
give us new heart, we pray, O Lord,
so that we may celebrate her heavenly birthday
in this present age
and so behold things eternal.
Through our Lord Jesus Christ, your Son,
who lives and reigns with you
in the unity of the Holy Spirit,
one God, for ever and ever.

December 14

Saint John of the Cross, Priest and Doctor of the Church

Memorial

Entrance Antiphon

May I never boast,
except in the Cross of our Lord Jesus Christ,
through which the world has been crucified to me,
and I to the world. Gal 6: 14

COLLECT

O God, who gave the Priest Saint John
an outstanding dedication to perfect self-denial
and love of the Cross,
grant that, by imitating him closely at all times,
we may come to contemplate eternally your glory.
Through our Lord Jesus Christ, your Son,
who lives and reigns with you
in the unity of the Holy Spirit,
one God, for ever and ever.

PRAYER AFTER COMMUNION

O God, who in Saint John
have wonderfully made known the mystery of the Cross,
graciously grant
that, drawing strength from this sacrifice,
we may cling faithfully to Christ
and labor in the Church for the salvation of all.
Through Christ our Lord.

December 21

Saint Peter Canisius, Priest and Doctor of the Church

From the Common of Pastors: For One Pastor (p. 544), or from the Common of Doctors of the Church (p. 551).

COLLECT

O God, who for the defense of the Catholic faith
made the Priest Saint Peter Canisius
strong in virtue and in learning,
grant, through his intercession,
that those who seek the truth
may joyfully find you, their God,
and that your faithful people
may persevere in confessing you.
Through our Lord Jesus Christ, your Son,
who lives and reigns with you
in the unity of the Holy Spirit,
one God, for ever and ever.

December 23

Saint John of Kanty, Priest

From the Common of Pastors: For One Pastor (p. 544), or from the Common of Holy Men and Women: For Those Who Practiced Works of Mercy (p. 564).

COLLECT

Grant, we pray, almighty God,
that by the example of the Priest Saint John of Kanty
we may advance in the knowledge of holy things
and, by showing compassion to all,
may gain forgiveness in your sight.
Through our Lord Jesus Christ, your Son,
who lives and reigns with you
in the unity of the Holy Spirit,
one God, for ever and ever.

December 26
SAINT STEPHEN, THE FIRST MARTYR

Feast

Entrance Antiphon The gates of heaven were opened for blessed Stephen,
who was found to be first among the number of the Martyrs
and therefore is crowned triumphant in heaven.

The Gloria in excelsis (Glory to God in the highest) is said.

COLLECT Grant, Lord, we pray,
that we may imitate what we worship,
and so learn to love even our enemies,
for we celebrate the heavenly birthday
of a man who knew how to pray even for his persecutors.
Through our Lord Jesus Christ, your Son,
who lives and reigns with you
in the unity of the Holy Spirit,
one God, for ever and ever.

PRAYER AFTER COMMUNION For the many mercies which surround us
we give thanks to you, O Lord,
who save us through the Nativity of your Son
and gladden us with the celebration
of the blessed Martyr Stephen.
Through Christ our Lord.

December 27
SAINT JOHN, APOSTLE AND EVANGELIST

Feast

Entrance Antiphon

**This is John, who reclined on the Lord's breast at supper,
the blessed Apostle, to whom celestial secrets were revealed
and who spread the words of life through all the world.**

Or:

**In the midst of the Church he opened his mouth,
and the Lord filled him
with the spirit of wisdom and understanding
and clothed him in a robe of glory.** Cf. Sir 15: 5

The Gloria in excelsis (Glory to God in the highest) is said.

COLLECT

**O God, who through the blessed Apostle John
have unlocked for us the secrets of your Word,
grant, we pray,
that we may grasp with proper understanding
what he has so marvelously brought to our ears.
Through our Lord Jesus Christ, your Son,
who lives and reigns with you
in the unity of the Holy Spirit,
one God, for ever and ever.**

PRAYER AFTER COMMUNION

**Grant, we pray, almighty God,
that the Word made flesh,
proclaimed by the blessed Apostle John,
may, through this mystery which we have celebrated,
ever dwell among us.
Through Christ our Lord.**

December 28

THE HOLY INNOCENTS, MARTYRS

Feast

Entrance Antiphon

The innocents were slaughtered as infants for Christ;
spotless, they follow the Lamb
and sing for ever: Glory to you, O Lord.

The Gloria in excelsis (Glory to God in the highest) is said.

COLLECT

O God, whom the Holy Innocents confessed
and proclaimed on this day,
not by speaking but by dying,
grant, we pray,
that the faith in you which we confess with our lips
may also speak through our manner of life.
Through our Lord Jesus Christ, your Son,
who lives and reigns with you
in the unity of the Holy Spirit,
one God, for ever and ever.

PRAYER AFTER COMMUNION

Grant, O Lord, abundant salvation to your faithful
as they receive your holy gifts
on the feast day of these, your Saints,
who, though still unable to profess your Son in speech,
were crowned with heavenly grace
on account of his birth.
Who lives and reigns for ever and ever.

December 29
Saint Thomas Becket, Bishop and Martyr

From the Common of Martyrs: For One Martyr (p. 531), or from the Common of Pastors: For a Bishop (p. 541).

COLLECT

**O God, who gave the Martyr Saint Thomas Becket
the courage to give up his life for the sake of justice,
grant, through his intercession,
that, renouncing our life
for the sake of Christ in this world,
we may find it in heaven.
Through our Lord Jesus Christ, your Son,
who lives and reigns with you
in the unity of the Holy Spirit,
one God, for ever and ever.**

December 31
Saint Sylvester I, Pope

From the Common of Pastors: For a Pope (p. 539).

COLLECT

**Come, O Lord, to the help of your people,
sustained by the intercession of Pope Saint Sylvester,
so that, running the course of this present life
under your guidance,
we may happily attain life without end.
Through our Lord Jesus Christ, your Son,
who lives and reigns with you
in the unity of the Holy Spirit,
one God, for ever and ever.**

COMMONS

1. For convenience, the individual Commons each offer several Masses with all the elements, namely antiphons and prayers, included.

   It is permitted for the Priest, as appropriate, to exchange antiphons and prayers of the same Common, choosing those texts which seem more suitable for pastoral reasons.

   In addition, for Masses of Memorials, the Prayers over the Offerings and the Prayers after Communion may also be taken from the weekdays of the current liturgical time as well as from these Commons.

2. In the Common of Martyrs and in the Common of Holy Men and Women, all the prayers that are given for men may also be used for women, with the necessary change of gender.

3. In the individual Commons, texts in the singular may always be used for several Saints, with the necessary change to the plural. Similarly, texts in the plural may be used for an individual, with the necessary change to the singular.

4. Masses that are designated for specific times or circumstances should only be used for these.

COMMON OF THE DEDICATION OF A CHURCH

The formularies of the Mass for the Dedication of a Church and of the Mass for the Dedication of an Altar are to be found among the Ritual Masses in the Roman Missal.

ON THE ANNIVERSARY OF THE DEDICATION

I. In the Church that was Dedicated

Entrance Antiphon

Wonderful are you, O God in your holy place.
The God of Israel himself gives his people strength and courage.
Blessed be God (E.T. alleluia)! Ps 68 (67): 36

The Gloria in excelsis (Glory to God in the highest) is said.

COLLECT

O God, who year by year renew for us the day
when this your holy temple was consecrated,
hear the prayers of your people
and grant that in this place
for you there may always be pure worship
and for us, fullness of redemption.
Through our Lord Jesus Christ, your Son,
who lives and reigns with you
in the unity of the Holy Spirit,
one God, for ever and ever.

The Creed is said.

PRAYER AFTER COMMUNION

**May the people consecrated to you, O Lord, we pray,
receive the fruits and joy of your blessing,
that the festive homage
they have offered you today in the body
may redound upon them as a spiritual gift.
Through Christ our Lord.**

BLESSING AT THE END OF MASS

**May God, the Lord of heaven and earth,
who has gathered you today
in memory of the dedication of this church,
make you abound in heavenly blessings.**

℟. Amen.

**And may he, who has willed that all his scattered children
be gathered together in his Son,
grant that you may become his temple
and the dwelling place of the Holy Spirit.**

℟. Amen.

**Thus, may you be made thoroughly clean,
so that God may dwell within you
and you may possess with all the Saints
the inheritance of eternal happiness.**

℟. Amen.

**And may the blessing of almighty God,
the Father, and the Son, ✠ and the Holy Spirit,
come down on you and remain with you for ever.**

℟. Amen.

II. Outside the Church that was Dedicated

Entrance Antiphon

I saw the holy city, a new Jerusalem,
coming down out of heaven from God
prepared like a bride adorned for her husband (E.T. alleluia).

Cf. Rev 21: 2

Or:

Behold God's dwelling with the human race.
He will dwell with them
and they will be his people,
and God himself with them will be their God (E.T. alleluia).

Cf. Rev 21: 3

The Gloria in excelsis (Glory to God in the highest) is said.

COLLECT

O God, who from living and chosen stones
prepare an eternal dwelling for your majesty,
increase in your Church the grace you have bestowed,
so that by unceasing growth
your faithful people may build up the heavenly Jerusalem.
Through our Lord Jesus Christ, your Son,
who lives and reigns with you
in the unity of the Holy Spirit,
one God, for ever and ever.

Or:

O God, who were pleased to call your Church the Bride,
grant that the people that serves your name
may revere you, love you and follow you,
and may be led by you
to attain your promises in heaven.
Through our Lord Jesus Christ, your Son,
who lives and reigns with you
in the unity of the Holy Spirit,
one God, for ever and ever.

PRAYER AFTER COMMUNION

O God, who chose to foreshadow for us
the heavenly Jerusalem
through the sign of your Church on earth,
grant, we pray,
that, by our partaking of this Sacrament,
we may be made the temple of your grace
and may enter the dwelling place of your glory.
Through Christ our Lord.

COMMON OF THE BLESSED VIRGIN MARY

These Masses are also used for celebrating the Memorial of the Blessed Virgin Mary on Saturday, and in Votive Masses of the Blessed Virgin Mary. In all the prayers, where the word "commemoration" is found, "memorial" may also be used, as appropriate.

I. In Ordinary Time

These formularies may be used in accordance with the norms, even in Lent, should a celebration of the Blessed Virgin Mary occur that is duly inscribed in a proper calendar.

1

Entrance Antiphon

Hail, Holy Mother, who gave birth to the King
who rules heaven and earth for ever.

COLLECT

Grant, Lord God, that we, your servants,
may rejoice in unfailing health of mind and body,
and, through the glorious intercession
of Blessed Mary ever-Virgin,
may we be set free from present sorrow
and come to enjoy eternal happiness.
Through our Lord Jesus Christ, your Son,
who lives and reigns with you
in the unity of the Holy Spirit,
one God, for ever and ever.

PRAYER AFTER COMMUNION

As we receive this heavenly Sacrament,
we beseech, O Lord, your mercy,
that we, who rejoice in commemorating
the Blessed Virgin Mary,
may by imitating her
serve worthily the mystery of our redemption.
Through Christ our Lord.

2

Entrance Antiphon

Blessed are you, O Virgin Mary,
who bore the Creator of all things.
You became the Mother of your Maker,
and you remain for ever Virgin.

COLLECT

Grant us, O merciful God,
protection in our weakness,
that we, who keep the Memorial
of the holy Mother of God,
may, with the help of her intercession,
rise up from our iniquities.
Through our Lord Jesus Christ, your Son,
who lives and reigns with you
in the unity of the Holy Spirit,
one God, for ever and ever.

PRAYER AFTER COMMUNION

Having been made partakers of eternal redemption,
we pray, O Lord,
that we, who commemorate the Mother of your Son,
may glory in the fullness of your grace
and experience its continued increase for our salvation.
Through Christ our Lord.

3

Entrance Antiphon

Blessed are you, O Virgin Mary, by the Lord God Most High,
above all women on the earth;
for he has so exalted your name
that your praise shall be undying on our lips. Cf. Jdt 13: 18-19

COLLECT

As we venerate the glorious memory
of the most holy Virgin Mary,
grant, we pray, O Lord, through her intercession,
that we, too, may merit to receive
from the fullness of your grace.
Through our Lord Jesus Christ, your Son,
who lives and reigns with you
in the unity of the Holy Spirit,
one God, for ever and ever.

PRAYER AFTER COMMUNION

Renewed with this heavenly food,
we humbly implore you, Lord,
that, having received your Son, born of the tender Virgin,
under sacramental signs,
we may profess him in words
and hold fast to him in deeds.
Who lives and reigns for ever and ever.

4

Entrance Antiphon

All the richest of the people long to see your face:
behind her, her maiden companions are escorted to the King;
her attendants are escorted to you amid gladness and joy.
Cf. Ps 45 (44): 13, 15, 10

COLLECT

Pardon the faults of your servants, we pray, O Lord,
that we, who cannot please you by our own deeds,
may be saved through the intercession
of the Mother of your Son and our Lord.
Who lives and reigns with you
in the unity of the Holy Spirit,
one God, for ever and ever.

PRAYER AFTER COMMUNION

Having received the Sacrament of salvation and of faith,
we humbly beseech you, O Lord,
that we, who devoutly honor the Blessed Virgin Mary,
may be worthy to share with her in the charity of heaven.
Through Christ our Lord.

5

Entrance Antiphon

Hail, Mary, full of grace, the Lord is with you.
Blessed are you among women,
and blessed is the fruit of your womb. Cf. Lk 1: 28, 42

COLLECT

O God, who chose the Blessed Virgin Mary,
foremost among the poor and humble,
to be the Mother of the Savior,
grant, we pray, that, following her example,
we may offer you the homage of sincere faith
and place in you all our hope of salvation.
Through our Lord Jesus Christ, your Son,
who lives and reigns with you
in the unity of the Holy Spirit,
one God, for ever and ever.

PRAYER AFTER COMMUNION

Grant to your Church, O Lord,
that, strengthened by the power of this Sacrament,
she may eagerly walk in the pathways of the Gospel,
until she reaches the blessed vision of peace,
which the Virgin Mary, your lowly handmaid,
already enjoys eternally in glory.
Through Christ our Lord.

6

Entrance Antiphon

The rod of Jesse has blossomed;
the Virgin has brought forth one who is both God and man.
God has restored peace,
reconciling in himself the depths and the heights.

COLLECT

May the venerable intercession
of Blessed Mary ever-Virgin
come to our aid, we pray, O Lord,
and free us from every danger,
so that we may rejoice in your peace.
Through our Lord Jesus Christ, your Son,
who lives and reigns with you
in the unity of the Holy Spirit,
one God, for ever and ever.

PRAYER AFTER COMMUNION

Having nourished us with heavenly food, O Lord,
grant that, according to the example
of the Blessed Virgin Mary,
we may serve you in purity of life
and magnify you, with her, in wholehearted praise.
Through Christ our Lord.

7

Entrance Antiphon

Mary said: My spirit rejoices in God my Savior,
because the Lord has looked on his lowly handmaid.
Cf. Lk 1: 47-48

COLLECT

O God, who were pleased to choose Blessed Mary
as the virginal chamber where your Word would dwell,
grant, we pray, that under her protection,
we may participate joyfully in her commemoration.
Through our Lord Jesus Christ, your Son,
who lives and reigns with you
in the unity of the Holy Spirit,
one God, for ever and ever.

PRAYER AFTER COMMUNION

Having been made partakers of this spiritual food,
we pray, O Lord our God,
that, steadily imitating the Blessed Virgin Mary,
we may always be found intent on service of the Church
and may know the joys of doing your will.
Through Christ our Lord.

8

Entrance Antiphon

Happy are you, holy Virgin Mary, and most worthy of all praise,
for from you arose the sun of justice, Christ our God,
through whom we have been saved and redeemed.

COLLECT

Grant, we pray, almighty God, that your faithful,
who rejoice under the patronage
of the most holy Virgin Mary,
may be freed by her motherly intercession
from all evils on earth
and merit the attainment of eternal joys in heaven.
Through our Lord Jesus Christ, your Son,
who lives and reigns with you
in the unity of the Holy Spirit,
one God, for ever and ever.

PRAYER AFTER COMMUNION

Renewed by the Sacrament of salvation,
we humbly beseech you, Lord,
that we, who have honored in veneration
the memory of the Blessed Virgin Mary, Mother of God,
may merit to experience in perpetuity
the fruits of your redemption.
Through Christ our Lord.

II. In Advent

Entrance Antiphon

Drop down dew from above, you heavens,
and let the clouds rain down the Just One;
let the earth be opened and bring forth a Savior. Cf. Is 45: 8

Or:

The angel said to Mary: You have found favor with God.
Behold, you will conceive and bear a son,
and he will be called Son of the Most High. Cf. Lk 1: 30-32

COLLECT

O God, who willed that at the message of an Angel
your Word should take flesh
in the womb of the Blessed Virgin Mary,
grant that we, who pray to you
and believe her to be truly the Mother of God,
may be helped by her interceding before you.
Through our Lord Jesus Christ, your Son,
who lives and reigns with you
in the unity of the Holy Spirit,
one God, for ever and ever.

Or:

O God, who, fulfilling the promise made to our Fathers,
chose the Blessed Virgin Mary
to become the Mother of the Savior,
grant that we may follow her example,
for her humility was pleasing to you
and her obedience profitable to us.
Through our Lord Jesus Christ, your Son,
who lives and reigns with you
in the unity of the Holy Spirit,
one God, for ever and ever.

PRAYER AFTER COMMUNION

May the mysteries we have received,
O Lord our God,
always show forth your mercy in us,
that we, who commemorate in faith
the Mother of your Son,
may be saved by his Incarnation.
Who lives and reigns for ever and ever.

III. In Christmas Time

Entrance Antiphon

In childbirth she brought forth the King, whose name is eternal.
She keeps a mother's joy with a virgin's honor.
None like her was seen before, and none thereafter.

Or:

O Virgin Mother of God,
he whom the whole world cannot contain
cloistered himself within your womb, made man for us.

COLLECT

O God, who through the fruitful virginity of Blessed Mary
bestowed on the human race
the grace of eternal salvation,
grant, we pray,
that we may experience the intercession of her,
through whom we were found worthy to receive
the author of life,
our Lord Jesus Christ, your Son.
Who lives and reigns with you
in the unity of the Holy Spirit,
one God, for ever and ever.

Or:

O God, who willed that your Word,
begotten from all eternity,
should come forth from the womb
of the Blessed Virgin Mary,
grant, we pray, through her intercession,
that he may light up our darkness
with the splendor of his presence,
and from his fullness give us joy and peace.
Who lives and reigns with you
in the unity of the Holy Spirit,
one God, for ever and ever.

PRAYER AFTER COMMUNION

Renewed by the Body and Blood of your incarnate Word,
we pray, O Lord, that these divine mysteries,
which we have joyfully received
as we commemorate the Blessed Virgin Mary,
may make us sharers for eternity
in the divinity of your Son.
Who lives and reigns for ever and ever.

IV. In Easter Time

Entrance Antiphon

You have changed my mourning into dancing, O Lord,
and have girded me with joy, alleluia. Cf. Ps 30 (29): 12

COLLECT

O God, who have been pleased to gladden the world
by the Resurrection of your Son our Lord Jesus Christ,
grant, we pray,
that through his Mother, the Virgin Mary,
we may receive the joys of everlasting life.
Through our Lord Jesus Christ, your Son,
who lives and reigns with you
in the unity of the Holy Spirit,
one God, for ever and ever.

PRAYER AFTER COMMUNION

Renewed by this paschal Sacrament,
we pray, O Lord,
that we, who honor the memory
of the Mother of your Son,
may show forth in our mortal flesh the life of Jesus.
Who lives and reigns for ever and ever.

During Easter Time, the Mass of Our Lady, Queen of Apostles, may also be used, p. 678.

COMMON OF MARTYRS

I. Outside Easter Time

A. For Several Martyrs

1

Entrance Antiphon

The souls of the Saints are rejoicing in heaven,
the Saints who followed the footsteps of Christ,
and since for love of him they shed their blood,
they now exult with Christ for ever.

Or:

Holy men shed their glorious blood for the Lord;
they loved Christ in their life,
they imitated him in their death,
and therefore were crowned in triumph.

COLLECT

Grant a joyful outcome to our prayers, O Lord,
so that we, who each year
devoutly honor the day of the passion
of the holy Martyrs N. and N.,
may also imitate the constancy of their faith.
Through our Lord Jesus Christ, your Son,
who lives and reigns with you
in the unity of the Holy Spirit,
one God, for ever and ever.

PRAYER AFTER COMMUNION

O God, who in your holy Martyrs
have wonderfully made known the mystery of the Cross,
graciously grant
that, drawing strength from this sacrifice,
we may cling faithfully to Christ
and labor in the Church for the salvation of all.
Through Christ our Lord.

2

Entrance Antiphon

Many are the trials of the just,
but from them all the Lord will rescue them.
The Lord will keep guard over all their bones;
not one of their bones shall be broken. Cf. Ps 34 (33): 20-21

Or:

These are they who come out of the great ordeal
and have washed their robes in the blood of the Lamb.
For God's sake they handed their bodies over for punishment,
and they have earned unfading crowns. Cf. Rev 7: 14; Dn 3: 95

COLLECT

Almighty ever-living God,
who gave Saints N. and N.
the grace of suffering for Christ,
come, in your divine mercy, we pray,
to the help of our own weakness,
that, as your Saints did not hesitate to die for your sake,
we, too, may live bravely in confessing you.
Through our Lord Jesus Christ, your Son,
who lives and reigns with you
in the unity of the Holy Spirit,
one God, for ever and ever.

PRAYER AFTER COMMUNION

Grant us, O Lord, we pray,
that, being nourished by the Bread of heaven
and made one Body in Christ,
we may never be separated from his love
and, after the example of your holy Martyrs N. and N.,
may bravely overcome all things
for the sake of him who loved us.
Who lives and reigns for ever and ever.

3

Entrance Antiphon

From the Lord comes the salvation of the just;
he is their stronghold in time of distress. Cf. Ps 37 (36): 39

Or:

As gold in the furnace, the Lord put his chosen to the test;
as sacrificial offerings he took them to himself;
and in due time they will be honored,
and grace and peace will be with the elect of God.
Cf. Wis 3: 6-7, 9

COLLECT

May the sight of the great number
of your holy Martyrs gladden us, O Lord,
making our faith stronger
and bringing us consolation by the prayers of them all.
Through our Lord Jesus Christ, your Son,
who lives and reigns with you
in the unity of the Holy Spirit,
one God, for ever and ever.

Or:

May the prayer of the blessed Martyrs N. and N.,
being pleasing to you, O Lord,
commend us, we pray,
and confirm us in the profession of your truth.
Through our Lord Jesus Christ, your Son,
who lives and reigns with you
in the unity of the Holy Spirit,
one God, for ever and ever.

PRAYER AFTER COMMUNION

Preserve in us your gift, O Lord,
and may what we have received at your hands
for the feast day of the blessed Martyrs N. and N.
bring us salvation and peace.
Through Christ our Lord.

4

Entrance Antiphon

When the just cried out, the Lord heard them
and rescued them in all their distress. Cf. Ps 34 (33): 18

Or:

Because of the Lord's covenant and the ancestral laws,
the Saints of God persevered in loving brotherhood,
for there was always one spirit in them, and one faith.

COLLECT

O God, who gladden us each year
with the feast day of blessed N. and N.,
grant in your mercy
that we, who honor their heavenly birthday,
may also imitate their courage in suffering.
Through our Lord Jesus Christ, your Son,
who lives and reigns with you
in the unity of the Holy Spirit,
one God, for ever and ever.

Or:

O God, who bestowed on Saints N. and N.
the grace of coming to such surpassing glory,
grant to your servants, we pray,
through your Martyrs' merits,
pardon for their sins and freedom from every trial.
Through our Lord Jesus Christ, your Son,
who lives and reigns with you
in the unity of the Holy Spirit,
one God, for ever and ever.

PRAYER AFTER COMMUNION

Through this heavenly Sacrament, O Lord,
grant us manifold grace
on the celebration of the blessed Martyrs N. and N.,
that from so great a struggle
we may learn to be united in unwavering patience
and to exult in the victory they won for love of you.
Through Christ our Lord.

5

Entrance Antiphon

The blood of the holy Martyrs
was poured out for Christ upon the earth;
therefore they have gained everlasting rewards.

Or:

The souls of the just are in the hand of God
and no torment shall touch them.
They seemed, in the view of the foolish, to be dead,
but they are in peace. Cf. Wis 3: 1-2, 3

COLLECT

Grant us in your compassion, O Lord, we pray,
an increase of that faith
which brought glory to your holy Martyrs N. and N.
as they maintained it even to the shedding of their blood,
and may the same faith bring to us, who truly follow it,
justification in your sight.
Through our Lord Jesus Christ, your Son,
who lives and reigns with you
in the unity of the Holy Spirit,
one God, for ever and ever.

PRAYER AFTER COMMUNION

Having been fed, O Lord,
on the commemoration of your blessed Martyrs N. and N.,
with the precious Body and Blood
of your Only Begotten Son,
we humbly pray:
grant that by steadfast charity we may abide in you,
draw life from you, and to you be drawn.
Through Christ our Lord.

B. For One Martyr

1

Entrance Antiphon

This holy man fought to the death for the law of his God
and did not fear the words of the godless,
for he was built on solid rock.

Or:

The Lord granted him a stern struggle,
that he might know that wisdom is mightier than all else.
Cf. Wis 10: 12

COLLECT

Almighty and merciful God,
who brought your Martyr blessed N.
to overcome the torments of his (her) passion,
grant that we, who celebrate the day of his (her) triumph,
may remain invincible under your protection
against the snares of the enemy.
Through our Lord Jesus Christ, your Son,
who lives and reigns with you
in the unity of the Holy Spirit,
one God, for ever and ever.

PRAYER AFTER COMMUNION

May the sacred mysteries of which we have partaken,
O Lord, we pray,
give us that determination
which made your blessed Martyr N.
faithful in your service
and victorious in suffering.
Through Christ our Lord.

2

Entrance Antiphon

This truly is a Martyr,
who shed his (her) blood for the name of Christ,
who did not fear the threats of judges
but attained the heavenly kingdom.

Or:

He (She) counted all as loss in order to know Christ
and to have a share in his sufferings,
conforming himself (herself) to his death. Cf. Phil 3: 8, 10

COLLECT

Almighty ever-living God,
by whose gift blessed N. fought
for righteousness' sake even until death,
grant, we pray, through his (her) intercession,
that we may bear every adversity for the sake of your love
and hasten with all our strength towards you
who alone are life.
Through our Lord Jesus Christ, your Son,
who lives and reigns with you
in the unity of the Holy Spirit,
one God, for ever and ever.

PRAYER AFTER COMMUNION

Made new by these sacred mysteries, we pray, O Lord,
that, imitating the wondrous constancy of blessed N.,
we may merit an eternal reward for suffering endured.
Through Christ our Lord.

II. During Easter Time

A. For Several Martyrs

1

Entrance Antiphon

Come, you blessed of my Father;
receive the kingdom prepared for you
from the foundation of the world, alleluia. Cf. Mt 25: 34

Or:

These who are clothed in white robes
are they who survived the time of great distress
and have washed their robes in the blood of the Lamb, alleluia.
Cf. Rev 7: 13-14

COLLECT

By the power of the Holy Spirit
we pray, almighty God:
make us docile in believing the faith
and courageous in confessing it,
just as you granted the blessed Martyrs N. and N.
that they might lay down their lives
for the sake of your word and in witness to Jesus.
Who lives and reigns with you
in the unity of the Holy Spirit,
one God, for ever and ever.

Or:

O God, from whom faith draws perseverance
and weakness strength,
grant, through the example and prayers
of the Martyrs N. and N.,
that we may share in the Passion and Resurrection
of your Only Begotten Son,
so that with the Martyrs
we may attain perfect joy in your presence.
Through our Lord Jesus Christ, your Son,
who lives and reigns with you
in the unity of the Holy Spirit,
one God, for ever and ever.

PRAYER AFTER COMMUNION

As we celebrate by this divine banquet
the heavenly victory of the blessed Martyrs N. and N.,
we beseech you, Lord, to bestow victory
on those who eat here below of the Bread of life
and to allow them to eat as victors
from the tree of life in paradise.
Through Christ our Lord.

2

Entrance Antiphon

These are the Saints who were victorious
because of the blood of the Lamb,
and in the face of death refused to cling to life;
therefore they reign with Christ for ever, alleluia. Cf. Rev 12: 11

Or:

Rejoice, you Saints, in the presence of the Lamb;
a kingdom has been prepared for you
from the foundation of the world, alleluia. Cf. Mt 25: 34

COLLECT

May the glorious feast day
of your blessed Martyrs N. and N.
gladden us, we pray, O Lord,
for, as they boldly confessed the Passion and Resurrection
of your Only Begotten Son,
you led them to shed their costly blood in a glorious death.
Through our Lord Jesus Christ, your Son,
who lives and reigns with you
in the unity of the Holy Spirit,
one God, for ever and ever.

PRAYER AFTER COMMUNION

Renewed by the sustenance of the one Bread, O Lord,
on the commemoration of the blessed Martyrs N. and N.,
we humbly pray
that you may confirm us ever in your charity
and make us walk in newness of life.
Through Christ our Lord.

B. For One Martyr

Entrance Antiphon

Perpetual light will shine on your Saints, O Lord,
and life without end for ever, alleluia. Cf. 4 Esdr 2: 35

Or:

This is the one who was not deserted by God
on the day of struggle
and now wears a crown of victory
for faithfulness to the Lord's commands, alleluia.

COLLECT

O God, who were pleased to give light to your Church
by adorning blessed N. with the victory of martyrdom,
graciously grant
that, as he (she) imitated the Lord's Passion,
so we may, by following in his (her) footsteps,
be worthy to attain eternal joys.
Through our Lord Jesus Christ, your Son,
who lives and reigns with you
in the unity of the Holy Spirit,
one God, for ever and ever.

PRAYER AFTER COMMUNION

We have received your heavenly gifts,
rejoicing at this feast day, O Lord;
grant, we pray, that we, who in this divine banquet
proclaim the Death of your Son,
may merit to be partakers with the holy Martyrs
in his Resurrection and his glory.
Who lives and reigns for ever and ever.

III. For Missionary Martyrs

A. For Several Missionary Martyrs

Entrance Antiphon

May we never boast,
except in the Cross of our Lord Jesus Christ.
For the word of the Cross is the power of God
to us who have been saved (E.T. alleluia). Cf. Gal 6: 14; 1 Cor 1: 18

COLLECT

We humbly beseech the mercy of your majesty,
almighty and merciful God,
that, as you have poured the knowledge
of your Only Begotten Son into the hearts of the peoples
by the preaching of the blessed Martyrs N. and N.,
so, through their intercession,
we may be made steadfast in the faith.
Through our Lord Jesus Christ, your Son,
who lives and reigns with you
in the unity of the Holy Spirit,
one God, for ever and ever.

PPRAYER AFTER COMMUNION

Having fed upon heavenly delights,
we humbly ask you, O Lord,
that by the example of blessed N. and N.
we may bear in our hearts
the marks of your Son's charity and suffering
and ever enjoy the fruit of perpetual peace.
Through Christ our Lord.

B. For One Missionary Martyr

Entrance Antiphon

This Saint went as far as death,
handing over his life to destruction
for the work of Christ (E.T. alleluia). Cf. Phil 2: 30

COLLECT

Grant, we pray, almighty God,
that we may follow with due devotion
the faith of blessed N.,
who, for spreading the faith,
merited the crown of martyrdom.
Through our Lord Jesus Christ, your Son,
who lives and reigns with you
in the unity of the Holy Spirit,
one God, for ever and ever.

PRAYER AFTER COMMUNION

As we celebrate the heavenly banquet,
we beseech you, Lord,
that, in following such a great example of faith,
we may be encouraged by the remembrance
of the blessed Martyr N.
and led on by his (her) gracious intercession.
Through Christ our Lord.

IV. For a Virgin Martyr

Entrance Antiphon

Behold, now she follows the Lamb who was crucified for us,
powerful in virginity, modesty her offering,
a sacrifice on the altar of chastity (E.T. alleluia).

Or:

Blessed is the virgin
who by denying herself and taking up her cross
imitated the Lord, the spouse of virgins
and prince of martyrs (E.T. alleluia).

COLLECT

O God, who gladden us today
with the annual commemoration of blessed N.,
graciously grant
that we may be helped by her merits,
just as our lives are lit up by the splendor
of her example of chastity and fortitude.
Through our Lord Jesus Christ, your Son,
who lives and reigns with you
in the unity of the Holy Spirit,
one God, for ever and ever.

PRAYER AFTER COMMUNION

O God, who bestowed on blessed N.
a crown among the Saints
for her twofold triumph of virginity and martyrdom,
grant, we pray, through the power of this Sacrament,
that, bravely overcoming every evil,
we may attain the glory of heaven.
Through Christ our Lord.

V. For a Holy Woman Martyr

Entrance Antiphon

For the Kingdom of Heaven belongs to these women,
who despised life in the world,
and have reached the rewards of the kingdom
and washed their robes in the blood of the Lamb (E.T. alleluia).

COLLECT

O God, by whose gift strength is made perfect in weakness,
grant to all who honor the glory of blessed N.
that she, who drew from you the strength to triumph,
may likewise always obtain from you
the grace of victory for us.
Through our Lord Jesus Christ, your Son,
who lives and reigns with you
in the unity of the Holy Spirit,
one God, for ever and ever.

PRAYER AFTER COMMUNION

As we draw everlasting joys, O Lord,
from our participation in this Sacrament
and from the commemoration of blessed N.,
we humbly implore
that by your gift we may truly understand
what you grant us to enact in diligent service.
Through Christ our Lord.

COMMON OF PASTORS

I. For a Pope or for a Bishop

1

Entrance Antiphon

The Lord chose him for himself as high priest,
and, opening his treasure house,
made him rich in all good things (E.T. alleluia).

Or:

Behold a great priest, who in his days pleased God;
therefore, in accordance with his promise,
the Lord gave him growth for the good of his people
(E.T. alleluia). Cf. Sir 50: 1; 44: 16, 22

COLLECT

For a Pope:

Almighty ever-living God,
who chose blessed N. to preside over your whole people
and benefit them by word and example,
keep safe, we pray, by his intercession,
the shepherds of your Church
along with the flocks entrusted to their care,
and direct them in the way of eternal salvation.
Through our Lord Jesus Christ, your Son,
who lives and reigns with you
in the unity of the Holy Spirit,
one God, for ever and ever.

For a Bishop:

O God, who in blessed N.
were pleased to provide for your Church
the example of a good shepherd,
mercifully grant that through his intercession
we may merit an eternal place in your pastures.
Through our Lord Jesus Christ, your Son,
who lives and reigns with you
in the unity of the Holy Spirit,
one God, for ever and ever.

PRAYER AFTER COMMUNION

May the Sacraments we have received, O Lord our God,
stir up in us that fire of charity
with which blessed N. burned ardently
as he gave himself unceasingly for your Church.
Through Christ our Lord.

2

Entrance Antiphon

The Lord established for him a covenant of peace,
and made him the prince,
that he might have the dignity of the priesthood for ever
(E.T. alleluia). Cf. Sir 45: 30

COLLECT

For a Pope:

O God, who gave blessed N.
to be shepherd of the whole Church
and made him resplendent
with wondrous virtue and teaching,
grant that we, who venerate the merits of such a Bishop,
may shine with good deeds before others
and burn with love before you.
Through our Lord Jesus Christ, your Son,
who lives and reigns with you
in the unity of the Holy Spirit,
one God, for ever and ever.

For a Pope:

O God, who made blessed N. the Vicar of Peter
and committed to him the care of the universal Church,
by his intercession keep your beloved flock ever safe,
so that with integrity of faith and perfect charity
your Church may journey to her heavenly homeland.
Through our Lord Jesus Christ, your Son,
who lives and reigns with you
in the unity of the Holy Spirit,
one God, for ever and ever.

For a Bishop:

Grant, we pray, almighty God,
that we may venerate fittingly
the memory of the Bishop blessed N.,
and, as you willed that his word and example
should benefit those over whom he presided,
so may we always experience
the support of his intercession before you.
Through our Lord Jesus Christ, your Son,
who lives and reigns with you
in the unity of the Holy Spirit,
one God, for ever and ever.

PRAYER AFTER COMMUNION

May the power of the gifts we have received, Lord God,
on this feast day of blessed N.
fill us with its effects,
both to sustain our mortal life
and to gain us the joy of unending happiness.
Through Christ our Lord.

II. For a Bishop

1

Entrance Antiphon

I will look after my sheep, says the Lord,
and I will appoint a shepherd to pasture them,
and I, the Lord, will be their God (E.T. alleluia).
Cf. Ez 34: 11, 23-24

Or:

This is the steward, faithful and prudent,
whom the Lord set over his household
to give them their allowance of food at the proper time
(E.T. alleluia).
Cf. Lk 12: 42

COLLECT

Almighty ever-living God,
who chose blessed N.
to preside as Bishop over your holy people,
we pray that, by his merits,
you may bestow on us the grace of your loving kindness.
Through our Lord Jesus Christ, your Son,
who lives and reigns with you
in the unity of the Holy Spirit,
one God, for ever and ever.

Or:

Almighty and eternal God,
who gave your holy Church blessed N. as Bishop,
grant that what he taught
  when moved by the divine Spirit
may always stay firm in our hearts;
and as by your gift we embrace him as our patron,
may we also have him as our defender
to entreat your mercy.
Through our Lord Jesus Christ, your Son,
who lives and reigns with you
  in the unity of the Holy Spirit,
one God, for ever and ever.

PRAYER AFTER COMMUNION

Renewed by the sacred mysteries,
we humbly pray, O Lord,
that, following the example of blessed N.,
we may strive to profess what he believed
and to practice what he taught.
Through Christ our Lord.

2

Entrance Antiphon

I shall raise up for myself a faithful priest
who will act in accord with my heart and my mind,
says the Lord (E.T. alleluia). Cf. 1 Sm 2: 35

Or:

This is the steward, faithful and prudent,
whom the Lord set over his household,
to give them their allowance of food at the proper time
  (E.T. alleluia). Cf. Lk 12: 42

COLLECT

O God, who wonderfully numbered
among your holy shepherds blessed N.,
a man aflame with divine charity
and outstanding for that faith that overcomes the world,
grant, we pray, that through his intercession
we, too, persevering in faith and charity,
may merit to be sharers of his glory.
Through our Lord Jesus Christ, your Son,
who lives and reigns with you
  in the unity of the Holy Spirit,
one God, for ever and ever.

Or:

Lord God, who graciously imbued
blessed N. with heavenly doctrine,
grant, through his intercession,
that we may keep that same teaching faithfully
and express it in what we do.
Through our Lord Jesus Christ, your Son,
who lives and reigns with you
in the unity of the Holy Spirit,
one God, for ever and ever.

PRAYER AFTER COMMUNION

Replenished by the sacred Body and the precious Blood
of your Son,
we pray, O Lord our God,
that what we celebrate with loving devotion,
may be our sure pledge of redemption.
Through Christ our Lord.

III. For Pastors

A. For Several Pastors

Entrance Antiphon

I will appoint over you shepherds after my own heart,
who will shepherd you wisely and prudently (E.T. alleluia).
Jer 3: 15

Or:

Priests of God, bless the Lord;
praise the Lord, all who are holy and humble of heart
(E.T. alleluia). Cf. Dn 3: 84, 87

COLLECT

O God, who to pasture your people
filled (the Bishops) blessed N. and N.
with a spirit of truth and of love,
grant that, as we celebrate their feast day with honor,
we may benefit by imitating them
and be given relief through their intercession.
Through our Lord Jesus Christ, your Son,
who lives and reigns with you
in the unity of the Holy Spirit,
one God, for ever and ever.

PRAYER AFTER COMMUNION

We have received this heavenly Sacrament, O Lord,
as we commemorate your Saints N. and N.;
grant, we pray, that what we celebrate in time
we may attain with eternal joy.
Through Christ our Lord.

B. For One Pastor

1

Entrance Antiphon

Your priests, O Lord, shall be clothed with justice;
your holy ones shall ring out their joy (E.T. alleluia).
Cf. Ps 132 (131): 9

COLLECT

We humbly ask you, almighty God,
that at the intercession of (the Bishop) blessed N.
you may multiply your gifts among us
and order our days in peace.
Through our Lord Jesus Christ, your Son,
who lives and reigns with you
in the unity of the Holy Spirit,
one God, for ever and ever.

PRAYER AFTER COMMUNION

May partaking at the heavenly table, almighty God,
confirm and increase strength from on high
in all who celebrate the feast day of blessed N.,
that we may preserve in integrity the gift of faith
and walk in the path of salvation you trace for us.
Through Christ our Lord.

2

Entrance Antiphon

The Spirit of the Lord is upon me,
for he has anointed me
and sent me to preach the good news to the poor,
to heal the broken-hearted (E.T. alleluia). Cf. Lk 4: 18

Or:

The Lord chose him as a priest for himself,
to offer him a sacrifice of praise (E.T. alleluia). Cf. Sir 45: 20

COLLECT

O God, light of the faithful and shepherd of souls,
who set (the Bishop) blessed N. in the Church
to feed your sheep by his words
and form them by his example,
grant that through his intercession
we may keep the faith he taught by his words
and follow the way he showed by his example.
Through our Lord Jesus Christ, your Son,
who lives and reigns with you
in the unity of the Holy Spirit,
one God, for ever and ever.

PRAYER AFTER COMMUNION

May the mysteries we have received, O Lord,
prepare us, we pray, for the eternal joys
that, as a faithful steward, blessed N. came to deserve.
Through Christ our Lord.

Or:

Make us, who have been nourished
by this sacred meal, almighty God,
always follow the example of blessed N.
in serving you with constant devotion
and assisting all with untiring charity.
Through Christ our Lord.

IV. For Founders of Churches

A. For One Founder

Entrance Antiphon

Thus says the Lord: My words, which I have put
into your mouth,
will remain for ever on your lips
and your gifts will be accepted on my altar (E.T. alleluia).
Cf. Is 59: 21; 56: 7

COLLECT

Almighty and merciful God,
who were pleased to enlighten our forebears
by the preaching of blessed N.,
grant, we pray,
that, glorying in the name of Christian,
we may show continually in our deeds
the faith that we profess.
Through our Lord Jesus Christ, your Son,
who lives and reigns with you
in the unity of the Holy Spirit,
one God, for ever and ever.

Or:

Look, O Lord, upon your family,
which (the Bishop) blessed N.
engendered by the Word of truth
and fed with the Sacrament of life,
that your grace, which has made them faithful
through his ministry,
may through his prayers make them fervent in charity.
Through our Lord Jesus Christ, your Son,
who lives and reigns with you
in the unity of the Holy Spirit,
one God, for ever and ever.

PRAYER AFTER COMMUNION

As we rejoice at the feast day of blessed N.,
we have received the pledge of eternal redemption,
O Lord,
and we pray that it may be of help to us,
both now and for the life to come.
Through Christ our Lord.

B. For Several Founders

Entrance Antiphon

These are the holy men
whom the Lord chose in his own perfect love;
to them he gave eternal glory;
their teaching is a light for the Church (E.T. alleluia).

COLLECT

O Lord, who through the apostolic ministry
of Saints N. and N.
gave your Church the beginnings of religion,
look on her with kindness
and grant her, we pray, through their intercession,
constant increase in Christian devotion.
Through our Lord Jesus Christ, your Son,
who lives and reigns with you
in the unity of the Holy Spirit,
one God, for ever and ever.

Or:

O God, who called our forebears
by the preaching of (the Bishops) blessed N. and N.
into the wonderful light of the Gospel,
grant that through their intercession
we may grow in grace and in the knowledge
of our Lord Jesus Christ, your Son.
Who lives and reigns with you
in the unity of the Holy Spirit,
one God, for ever and ever.

PRAYER AFTER COMMUNION

May the Savior we have welcomed at this altar, O Lord,
gladden us on the feast day of Saints N. and N.,
on which, with longing for your favor,
we honor the precious beginnings of our faith
and proclaim your wonders in your Saints.
Through Christ our Lord.

V. For Missionaries

For Missionary Martyrs, pp. 536-537.

1

Entrance Antiphon

O chosen people, proclaim the mighty works of him
who called you out of darkness into his wonderful light
(E.T. alleluia).

Or:

I will praise you, Lord, among the nations;
I will tell of your name to my kin (E.T. alleluia).

Ps 18 (17): 50; 22 (21): 23

COLLECT

O God, who through (the Bishop) blessed N.
brought peoples without faith
from darkness to the light of truth,
grant us, through his intercession,
that we may stand firm in faith
and remain constant in the hope
of the Gospel he preached.
Through our Lord Jesus Christ, your Son,
who lives and reigns with you
in the unity of the Holy Spirit,
one God, for ever and ever.

Or:

Almighty ever-living God,
who have made sacred this day's rejoicing
at the glorification of blessed N.,
graciously grant
that we may strive always to keep
and to put into practice the faith
which, with unquenchable zeal, he strove to proclaim.
Through our Lord Jesus Christ, your Son,
who lives and reigns with you
in the unity of the Holy Spirit,
one God, for ever and ever.

PRAYER AFTER COMMUNION

By the power of this mystery, O Lord,
confirm your servants in the true faith,
that they may everywhere profess in word and deed
the faith for which blessed N. never ceased to labor
and for which he spent his whole life.
Through Christ our Lord.

2

Entrance Antiphon

How beautiful upon the mountains are the feet
of him who brings glad tidings of peace,
bearing good news, announcing salvation (E.T. alleluia).
Cf. Is 52: 7

COLLECT

O God, who gave increase to your Church
through the zeal for religion
and apostolic labors of blessed N.,
grant, through his intercession,
that she may always receive
new growth in faith and in holiness.
Through our Lord Jesus Christ, your Son,
who lives and reigns with you
in the unity of the Holy Spirit,
one God, for ever and ever.

PRAYER AFTER COMMUNION

May the Sacrament we have received, O Lord our God,
nourish in us that faith
taught by the preaching of the Apostles
and kept safe by the labors of blessed N.
Through Christ our Lord.

3

Entrance Antiphon

Tell among the nations his glory,
and his wonders among all the peoples,
for the Lord is great and highly to be praised (E.T. alleluia).
Ps 96 (95): 3-4

COLLECT

O God, by whose untold mercy
blessed N. preached the good news
of the unfathomable riches of Christ,
grant that through his intercession
we may grow in knowledge of you
and, bearing fruit in every good work,
faithfully walk in your presence,
in accord with the truth of the Gospel.
Through our Lord Jesus Christ, your Son,
who lives and reigns with you
in the unity of the Holy Spirit,
one God, for ever and ever.

PRAYER AFTER COMMUNION

May your holy gifts which we have received
fill us with life, O Lord,
so that we, who rejoice in commemorating blessed N.,
may also profit from his example of apostolic virtue.
Through Christ our Lord.

COMMON OF DOCTORS OF THE CHURCH

1

Entrance Antiphon

In the midst of the Church he opened his mouth,
and the Lord filled him
with the spirit of wisdom and understanding
and clothed him in a robe of glory (E.T. alleluia). Cf. Sir 15: 5

Or:

The mouth of the just man utters wisdom,
and his tongue tells forth what is just;
the law of his God is in his heart (E.T. alleluia).
Ps 37 (36): 30-31

COLLECT

Almighty and eternal God,
who gave your holy Church blessed N.
as Doctor (and Bishop),
grant that what he taught
when moved by the divine Spirit
may always stay firm in our hearts;
and, as by your gift we embrace him as our patron,
may we also have him as our defender
to entreat your mercy.
Through our Lord Jesus Christ, your Son,
who lives and reigns with you
in the unity of the Holy Spirit,
one God, for ever and ever.

PRAYER AFTER COMMUNION

Through Christ the teacher, O Lord,
instruct those you feed with Christ, the living Bread,
that on the feast day of blessed N.
they may learn your truth
and express it in works of charity.
Through Christ our Lord.

2

Entrance Antiphon

Those who are wise will shine brightly
like the splendor of the firmament
and those who lead the many to justice
shall be like the stars for ever (E.T. alleluia). Cf. Dn 12: 3

Or:

Let the peoples recount the wisdom of the Saints,
and let the Church proclaim their praise.
Their names will live on and on (E.T. alleluia).
Cf. Sir 44: 15, 14

COLLECT

Lord God, who graciously imbued blessed N.
with heavenly doctrine,
grant, through his intercession,
that we may keep that same teaching faithfully
and express it in what we do.
Through our Lord Jesus Christ, your Son,
who lives and reigns with you
in the unity of the Holy Spirit,
one God, for ever and ever.

PRAYER AFTER COMMUNION

Refreshed by heavenly food,
we humbly implore you, O Lord,
that, attentive to the teaching of blessed N.,
we may abide at all times in thanksgiving
for the gifts we have received.
Through Christ our Lord.

COMMON OF VIRGINS

For a Virgin Martyr, p. 537.

I. For Several Virgins

Entrance Antiphon

Let the virgins praise the name of the Lord,
for his name alone is exalted;
his splendor is above heaven and earth (E.T. alleluia).
Cf. Ps 148: 12-14

Or:

The virgins to the King are escorted amid gladness and joy;
they are led within the temple to the Lord and King
(E.T. alleluia). Cf. Ps 45 (44): 16

COLLECT

Bestow your mercy upon us, Lord, we pray,
that, as we rejoice with loving devotion
on the feast day of the Virgins blessed N. and N.,
so by your gift we may know
the eternal delight of their company.
Through our Lord Jesus Christ, your Son,
who lives and reigns with you
in the unity of the Holy Spirit,
one God, for ever and ever.

PRAYER AFTER COMMUNION

May the mysteries we have received, O Lord,
on this feast day of the Virgins blessed N. and N.
constantly bestir and enlighten us, we pray,
so that we may stand ready for the coming of your Son
and be admitted to his wedding feast on high.
Through Christ our Lord.

II. For One Virgin

1

Entrance Antiphon

Here is a wise virgin, from among the number of the prudent,
who went forth with lighted lamp to meet Christ (E.T. alleluia).

Or:

How beautiful you are, O virgin of Christ,
who were worthy to receive the Lord's crown,
the crown of perpetual virginity (E.T. alleluia).

COLLECT

Hear us, God our Savior,
that, as we rejoice in commemorating the Virgin
blessed N.,
we may be instructed by her loving devotion.
Through our Lord Jesus Christ, your Son,
who lives and reigns with you
in the unity of the Holy Spirit,
one God, for ever and ever.

PRAYER AFTER COMMUNION

Renewed by partaking of this divine gift,
we pray, O Lord our God,
that by the example of the blessed N.,
bearing in our body the Death of Jesus,
we may strive to hold fast to you alone.
Through Christ our Lord.

2

Entrance Antiphon

Let us rejoice and exult for joy:
for the Lord of all has shown his love
for a holy and glorious virgin (E.T. alleluia).

Or:

Here is a wise virgin whom the Lord found watching;
when they took up their lamps
she brought oil with her
and when the Lord came
she went in with him to the wedding feast (E.T. alleluia).

COLLECT

Lord God, who gave the holy Virgin N.
gift upon gift from heaven,
grant, we pray,
that, imitating her virtues on earth,
we may delight with her in the joys of eternity.
Through our Lord Jesus Christ, your Son,
who lives and reigns with you
in the unity of the Holy Spirit,
one God, for ever and ever.

Or, for a Virgin foundress:

Grant, O Lord our God,
that the Virgin blessed N., your faithful spouse,
may stir up in our hearts the flame of divine love,
which she inspired in other virgins
to the enduring glory of your Church.
Through our Lord Jesus Christ, your Son,
who lives and reigns with you
in the unity of the Holy Spirit,
one God, for ever and ever.

PRAYER AFTER COMMUNION

May the holy reception of the Body and Blood
of your Only Begotten Son, O Lord,
turn us away from the cares of this fleeting world,
so that, following the example of blessed N.,
we may grow in sincere love for you on earth
and rejoice to behold you for eternity in heaven.
Through Christ our Lord.

3

Entrance Antiphon

Come, bride of Christ, receive the crown,
which the Lord has prepared for you for eternity (E.T. alleluia).

Or:

For love of the Lord Jesus Christ,
she despised the kingdom of the world
and all worldly things (E.T. alleluia).

COLLECT

O God, who declare that you abide in hearts that are pure,
grant that through the intercession of the Virgin
blessed N.
we may be so fashioned by your grace,
that we become a dwelling pleasing to you.
Through our Lord Jesus Christ, your Son,
who lives and reigns with you
in the unity of the Holy Spirit,
one God, for ever and ever.

Or:

Hear our prayers, we ask, O Lord,
that we, who devoutly honor the virtue of the Virgin
blessed N.,
may be worthy to abide in love of you
and to grow in it always until the end.
Through our Lord Jesus Christ, your Son,
who lives and reigns with you
in the unity of the Holy Spirit,
one God, for ever and ever.

PRAYER AFTER COMMUNION

Renewed by heavenly Bread,
we humbly beseech your mercy, O Lord,
that we, who rejoice in commemorating blessed N.,
may obtain pardon for our offenses,
health for our bodies,
and grace and eternal glory for our souls.
Through Christ our Lord.

COMMON OF HOLY MEN AND WOMEN

The following Masses, if indicated for a particular category of Saints, are used for Saints of that category. Other Masses, however, may be used for all categories of Saints.

I. For All Categories of Saints

A. For Several Saints

1

Entrance Antiphon

May all your works thank you, O Lord,
and all your Holy ones bless you.
They shall speak of the glory of your reign,
and declare your mighty deeds (E.T. alleluia).

Cf. Ps 145 (144): 10-11

COLLECT

Almighty and eternal God,
who by glorifying the Saints,
bestow on us fresh proofs of your love,
graciously grant
that, commended by their intercession
and spurred on by their example,
we may be faithful in imitating your Only Begotten Son.
Who lives and reigns with you
in the unity of the Holy Spirit,
one God, for ever and ever.

PRAYER AFTER COMMUNION

Almighty ever-living God,
Father of all consolation and peace,
grant your family,
gathered to praise your name in celebration of the Saints,
that through the mysteries of your Only Begotten Son,
which they have here received,
they may obtain the pledge of eternal redemption.
Through Christ our Lord.

2

Entrance Antiphon

The just will rejoice in the Lord and hope in him,
and all upright hearts will be praised (E.T. alleluia).

Cf. Ps 64 (63): 11

COLLECT

O God, who see that in our weakness we fail,
mercifully restore us to your love
by the example of your Saints.
Through our Lord Jesus Christ, your Son,
who lives and reigns with you
in the unity of the Holy Spirit,
one God, for ever and ever.

PRAYER AFTER COMMUNION

On the heavenly birthday of your Saints, we pray, O Lord,
that we, who are nourished by the gift of this Sacrament,
may delight for all eternity
in the good things with which even now
by your grace you nurture us.
Through Christ our Lord.

3

Entrance Antiphon

The just will flourish like the palm tree,
and grow like a Lebanon cedar,
planted in the house of the Lord,
in the courts of the house of our God (E.T. alleluia).

Cf. Ps 92 (91): 13-14

COLLECT

May the prayer and integrity of the Saints,
O Lord, we pray,
obtain help for your faithful,
that they may gain a share in the eternal inheritance
of those whom they celebrate with devotion.
Through our Lord Jesus Christ, your Son,
who lives and reigns with you
in the unity of the Holy Spirit,
one God, for ever and ever.

PRAYER AFTER COMMUNION

May the communion in your Sacrament
that we have consumed,
save us, O Lord,
and confirm us in the light of your truth.
Through Christ our Lord.

4

Entrance Antiphon

Blessed is the man who trusts in the Lord,
whose hope is the Lord.
He is like a tree planted beside the waters
that stretches out its roots to the stream:
it fears not the heat when it comes (E.T. alleluia). Jer 17: 7-8

COLLECT

Grant, we pray, almighty God,
that the example of your Saints may spur us on
to a better life,
so that we, who celebrate the memory of blessed N. and N.,
may also imitate without ceasing their deeds.
Through our Lord Jesus Christ, your Son,
who lives and reigns with you
in the unity of the Holy Spirit,
one God, for ever and ever.

PRAYER AFTER COMMUNION

We pray, O Lord our God,
that the divine mysteries
which we celebrate in commemoration of your Saints,
may bring about in us salvation and eternal peace.
Through Christ our Lord.

B. For One Saint

1

Entrance Antiphon

In your strength, O Lord, the just one rejoices;
how greatly your salvation makes him glad!
You have granted him his soul's desire (E.T. alleluia).
Cf. Ps 21 (20): 2-3

COLLECT

O God, who in your Saints have given an example
and brought us protection in our weakness
to help us tread the path of salvation,
mercifully grant
that we, who honor the heavenly birthday of blessed N.,
may, through his (her) example, make our way to you.
Through our Lord Jesus Christ, your Son,
who lives and reigns with you
in the unity of the Holy Spirit,
one God, for ever and ever.

PRAYER AFTER COMMUNION

May the Sacrament we have received, O Lord,
in commemoration of blessed N.,
sanctify our minds and hearts,
that we may merit to be made sharers
in the divine nature.
Through Christ our Lord.

2

Entrance Antiphon

The law of truth was in his mouth;
no dishonesty was found on his lips.
He walked with me in integrity and peace,
and turned many away from evil (E.T. alleluia). Mal 2: 6

COLLECT

O God, who alone are holy
and without whom no one is good,
command, we pray, through the intercession of blessed N.,
that we be numbered among those
who do not deserve to be deprived of your glory.
Through our Lord Jesus Christ, your Son,
who lives and reigns with you
in the unity of the Holy Spirit,
one God, for ever and ever.

PRAYER AFTER COMMUNION

Nourished by these sacred gifts,
we humbly implore you, Lord,
that the homage of dutiful service,
which we render on the feast day of blessed N.,
may bring us an increase of your saving grace.
Through Christ our Lord.

II. For Monks and Religious

A. For an Abbot

Entrance Antiphon

The just will flourish like the palm tree,
and grow like a Lebanon cedar,
planted in the house of the Lord,
in the courts of the house of our God (E.T. alleluia).
Cf. Ps 92 (91): 13-14

Or:

The mouth of the just man utters wisdom,
and his tongue tells forth what is right.
The law of his God is in his heart (E.T. alleluia). Ps 37 (36): 30-31

COLLECT

Grant us, O Lord,
that amid the uncertainties of this world
we may cling with all our heart to the things of heaven,
for through the Abbot blessed N.
you have given us a model of evangelical perfection.
Through our Lord Jesus Christ, your Son,
who lives and reigns with you
in the unity of the Holy Spirit,
one God, for ever and ever.

PRAYER AFTER COMMUNION

By the power of this Sacrament which we have received,
renew our hearts, O Lord,
so that by the example of the Abbot blessed N.,
being wise in the things above
and not in the things of earth here below,
we may merit to appear in glory with Christ.
Who lives and reigns for ever and ever.

B. For a Monk

Entrance Antiphon

Where brothers unite to glorify God,
there the Lord will give blessing (E.T. alleluia).

Or:

Let my mouth be filled with your praise, that I may sing aloud;
my lips shall shout for joy, when I sing to you (E.T. alleluia).
Cf. Ps 71 (70): 8, 23

COLLECT

O God, who in your kindness
called your servant blessed N. to the following of Christ,
grant, we pray, through his intercession,
that, denying ourselves,
we may hold fast to you with all our heart.
Through our Lord Jesus Christ, your Son,
who lives and reigns with you
in the unity of the Holy Spirit,
one God, for ever and ever.

PRAYER AFTER COMMUNION

Grant our request, we pray, O Lord our God,
that, defended by the protection of blessed N.,
we may live by this Sacrament of your wisdom
in serenity and moderation.
Through Christ our Lord.

C. For a Nun

Entrance Antiphon

I am like a growing olive tree in the house of God.
I trust in the mercy of God, for ever and ever (E.T. alleluia).
Cf. Ps 52 (51): 10

Or:

I despised the kingdom of the world and all worldly finery
for love of my Lord, Jesus Christ,
whom I have seen, whom I have loved,
in whom I have believed, in whom has been my delight
(E.T. alleluia).

COLLECT

O God, who called your handmaid blessed N.
to seek you before all else,
grant that, serving you,
through her example and intercession,
with a pure and humble heart,
we may come at last to your eternal glory.
Through our Lord Jesus Christ, your Son,
who lives and reigns with you
in the unity of the Holy Spirit,
one God, for ever and ever.

PRAYER AFTER COMMUNION

Renewed, O Lord, at the wellsprings of salvation,
we humbly entreat you
that through the intercession of blessed N.,
holding more closely day by day to Christ,
we may merit to be coheirs in his Kingdom of grace.
Who lives and reigns for ever and ever.

D. For Religious

1

Entrance Antiphon

O Lord, it is you who are my portion and cup;
you yourself who secure my portion (E.T. alleluia).
Cf. Ps 16 (15): 5

Or, for a Woman Religious:

The Lord has taken her as his bride for ever
in faithfulness and mercy (E.T. alleluia). Cf. Hos 2: 21-22

COLLECT

O God, by whose gift blessed N.
persevered in imitating Christ, poor and lowly,
grant us through his (her) intercession
that, faithfully walking in our own vocation,
we may reach the perfection
you have set before us in your Son.
Who lives and reigns with you
in the unity of the Holy Spirit,
one God, for ever and ever.

PRAYER AFTER COMMUNION

By the power of this Sacrament, Lord, we pray,
lead us always in your love,
through the example of blessed N.,
and bring to fulfillment the good work
you have begun in us
until the day of Christ Jesus.
Who lives and reigns for ever and ever.

2

Entrance Antiphon

These are the holy ones,
who have received blessings from the Lord,
and mercy from the God who saves them,
such is the people who seek the Lord (E.T. alleluia).
Cf. Ps 24 (23): 5-6

Or:

Let the hearts that seek the Lord rejoice;
turn to the Lord and his strength;
constantly seek his face (E.T. alleluia). Ps 105 (104): 3-4

COLLECT

O God, who called blessed N.
to seek your Kingdom in this world
through the pursuit of perfect charity,
grant, we pray, through his (her) intercession
that we may advance with joyful spirit
along the way of love.
Through our Lord Jesus Christ, your Son,
who lives and reigns with you
in the unity of the Holy Spirit,
one God, for ever and ever.

PRAYER AFTER COMMUNION

We pray, almighty God,
that we, who are fortified by the power of this Sacrament,
may learn through the example of blessed N.
to seek you always above all things
and to bear in this world the likeness of the New Man.
Through Christ our Lord.

III. For Those Who Practiced Works of Mercy

Entrance Antiphon

Come, you blessed of my Father, says the Lord:
I was sick, and you visited me.
Amen, I say to you: Whatever you did
for one of the least of my brethren
you did it for me (E.T. alleluia). Cf. Mt 25: 34, 36, 40

Or:

Open-handed, he gives to the poor;
his justice stands firm for ever.
His might shall be exalted in glory (E.T. alleluia).
Ps 112 (111): 9

COLLECT

O God, who have taught your Church
to keep all the heavenly commandments
by love of you as God and love of neighbor;
grant that, practicing the works of charity
after the example of blessed N.,
we may be worthy to be numbered
among the blessed in your Kingdom.
Through our Lord Jesus Christ, your Son,
who lives and reigns with you
in the unity of the Holy Spirit,
one God, for ever and ever.

PRAYER AFTER COMMUNION

Grant, we pray, O Lord,
that we, who are renewed by these sacred mysteries,
may follow the example of blessed N.,
who honored you with tireless devotion
and, by surpassing charity, was of service to your people.
Through Christ our Lord.

Or:

Having fed upon the delights
of the Sacrament of salvation, O Lord,
we humbly implore your faithful love,
that, imitating, by your grace, the charity of blessed N.,
we may also be made partakers with him (her) in glory.
Through Christ our Lord.

IV. For Educators

Entrance Antiphon

Let the children come to me; do not prevent them,
for the kingdom of God belongs to such as these (E.T. alleluia).
Cf. Mk 10: 14

Or:

Whoever obeys and teaches the commandments of the Lord
will be called great in the Kingdom of Heaven,
says the Lord (E.T. alleluia). Cf. Mt 5: 19

COLLECT

O God, who raised up blessed N. in your Church
to show others the way of salvation,
grant us, by his (her) example,
so to follow Christ the master,
that we may come with our neighbor into your presence.
Through our Lord Jesus Christ, your Son,
who lives and reigns with you
in the unity of the Holy Spirit,
one God, for ever and ever.

PRAYER AFTER COMMUNION

May this holy meal give us strength, almighty God,
so that, by the example of blessed N.,
we may show in our hearts and by our deeds
both fraternal charity and the light of truth.
Through Christ our Lord.

V. For Holy Women

For a Holy Woman Martyr, p. 538.

1

Entrance Antiphon

The woman who fears the Lord will herself be praised.
Her children have called her most blessed,
her husband has sung her praises (E.T. alleluia).
Cf. Prv 31: 30, 28

Or:

She reaches out her hands to the needy
and extends her arms to the poor.
She did not eat her food in idleness (E.T. alleluia).
Cf. Prv 31: 20, 27

COLLECT

O God, who gladden us each year
  with the feast day of blessed N.,
grant, we pray, that we, who are called to honor her,
may also follow her example of holy living.
Through our Lord Jesus Christ, your Son,
who lives and reigns with you
  in the unity of the Holy Spirit,
one God, for ever and ever.

Or, for several:

Grant, we pray, almighty God,
that the revered intercession of blessed N. and N.
may bring us heavenly aid,
just as their wonderful lives
point the way to salvation for us all.
Through our Lord Jesus Christ, your Son,
who lives and reigns with you
  in the unity of the Holy Spirit,
one God, for ever and ever.

PRAYER AFTER COMMUNION

May the working of this divine Sacrament
enlighten and inflame us, almighty God,
on this feast day of blessed N.,
that we may be ever fervent with holy desires
and abound in good works.
Through Christ our Lord.

2

Entrance Antiphon

Behold a wise woman who has built her house.
She feared the Lord and walked in the right path (E.T. alleluia).
Cf. Prv 14: 1-2

COLLECT

O God, the exaltation of the lowly,
who willed that blessed N. should excel
in the beauty of her charity and patience,
grant, through her merits and intercession,
that, carrying our cross each day,
we may always persevere in love for you.
Through our Lord Jesus Christ, your Son,
who lives and reigns with you
in the unity of the Holy Spirit,
one God, for ever and ever.

Or:

Pour out upon us, Lord,
the spirit of knowledge and love of you,
with which you filled your handmaid blessed N.,
so that, serving you sincerely in imitation of her,
we may be pleasing to you
by our faith and our works.
Through our Lord Jesus Christ, your Son,
who lives and reigns with you
in the unity of the Holy Spirit,
one God, for ever and ever.

PRAYER AFTER COMMUNION

We are replenished, O Lord, with the gifts
we have received on the feast day of blessed N.;
grant, we pray,
that we may be purified by their effects
and strengthened by the help they bring.
Through Christ our Lord.

RITUAL MASSES

Ritual Masses are prohibited on the Sundays of Advent, Lent, and Easter, on Solemnities, on days within the Octave of Easter, on the Commemoration of All the Faithful Departed (All Souls' Day), on Ash Wednesday and on the weekdays of Holy Week. The norms given in the ritual books and in connection with the Masses themselves are to be observed.

I. FOR THE CONFERRAL OF THE SACRAMENTS OF CHRISTIAN INITIATION

All the prayers given for a man may be adapted for a woman, with the necessary change of gender, or adapted for several individuals, with the necessary change to the plural.

1. For the Election or Enrollment of Names

The rite of "election" or "enrollment of names" for catechumens who are to be admitted to the Sacraments of Christian Initiation at the Easter Vigil should be celebrated during the Mass of the First Sunday of Lent (p. 63). If, for pastoral reasons, it is celebrated apart from this Sunday, the Mass that follows may be used with the color violet on any day except those listed in nos. 1-4 of the Table of Liturgical Days in the Roman Missal. The Mass of the Friday of the Fourth Week of Lent may also be used (p. 89).

Entrance Antiphon

Let the hearts that seek the Lord rejoice;
turn to the Lord and his strength;
constantly seek his face. Cf. Ps 105 (104): 3-4

COLLECT

O God, who though you are ever the cause
of the salvation of the human race
now gladden your people with grace
in still greater measure,
look mercifully, we pray, upon your chosen ones,
that your compassionate and protecting help
may defend both those yet to be born anew
and those already reborn.
Through our Lord Jesus Christ, your Son,
who lives and reigns with you
in the unity of the Holy Spirit,
one God, for ever and ever.

PRAYER AFTER COMMUNION

May this Sacrament we have received
purify us, we pray, O Lord,
and grant your servants freedom from all blame,
that those bound by a guilty conscience
may glory in the fullness of heavenly remedy.
Through Christ our Lord.

2. For the Celebration of the Scrutinies

These Masses may be used with the color violet when the Scrutinies for the catechumens who are to be admitted to the Sacraments of Christian Initiation at the Easter Vigil are celebrated at the time proper for them, namely, on the Third, Fourth, and Fifth Sundays of Lent. If, however, for pastoral reasons, the Scrutinies cannot take place on these Sundays, other appropriate weekdays may be chosen in Lent, or, whenever Baptism is to be conferred outside the Easter Vigil, also at other times of the year. Nevertheless, in the first Mass of the Scrutinies, the Gospel of the Samaritan Woman is always read, in the second, that of the Man born blind, in the third, that of Lazarus, as given respectively for the Third, Fourth, and Fifth Sundays of Lent.

A

For the First Scrutiny

Entrance Antiphon

When I prove my holiness among you,
I will gather you from all the foreign lands
and I will pour clean water upon you
and cleanse you from all your impurities,
and I will give you a new spirit, says the Lord. Ez 36: 23-26

Or:

Come to the waters, you who are thirsty, says the Lord;
you who have no money, come and drink joyfully. Cf. Is 55: 1

COLLECT

Grant, we pray, O Lord,
that these chosen ones may come worthily and wisely
to the confession of your praise,
so that in accordance with that first dignity
which they lost by original sin
they may be fashioned anew through your glory.
Through our Lord Jesus Christ, your Son,
who lives and reigns with you
in the unity of the Holy Spirit,
one God, for ever and ever.

PRAYER AFTER COMMUNION

Give help, O Lord, we pray,
by the grace of your redemption
and be pleased to protect and prepare
those you are to initiate
through the Sacraments of eternal life.
Through Christ our Lord.

B

For the Second Scrutiny

Entrance Antiphon

My eyes are always on the Lord,
for he rescues my feet from the snare.
Turn to me and have mercy on me, for I am alone and poor.
Cf. Ps 25 (24): 15-16

COLLECT

Almighty ever-living God,
give to your Church an increase in spiritual joy,
so that those once born of earth
may be reborn as citizens of heaven.
Through our Lord Jesus Christ, your Son,
who lives and reigns with you
in the unity of the Holy Spirit,
one God, for ever and ever.

PRAYER AFTER COMMUNION

Sustain your family always in your kindness,
O Lord, we pray,
correct them, set them in order,
graciously protect them under your rule,
and in your unfailing goodness
direct them along the way of salvation.
Through Christ our Lord.

C

For the Third Scrutiny

Entrance Antiphon

The waves of death rose about me;
the pains of the netherworld surrounded me.
In my anguish I called to the Lord;
and from his holy temple he heard my voice. Cf. Ps 18 (17): 5-7

COLLECT

Grant, O Lord, to these chosen ones
that, instructed in the holy mysteries,
they may receive new life at the font of Baptism
and be numbered among the members of your Church.
Through our Lord Jesus Christ, your Son,
who lives and reigns with you
in the unity of the Holy Spirit,
one God, for ever and ever.

PRAYER AFTER COMMUNION

May your people be as one, O Lord, we pray,
and in wholehearted submission to you
may they obtain this grace:
that, safe from all distress,
they may readily live out their joy at being saved
and remember in loving prayer those to be reborn.
Through Christ our Lord.

3. For the Conferral of Baptism

The Sacraments of Christian Initiation are usually conferred on adults during the Vigil of the Holy Night of Easter. If, however, they are celebrated apart from the Paschal Solemnity because of necessity, this Mass may be used with the color white or a festive color on days when Ritual Masses are permitted.

This Mass may also be said for the conferral of the Baptism of infants, under the same conditions.

In this Mass, the Penitential Act, the Kyrie and the Creed are omitted. The Gloria in excelsis (Glory to God in the highest), however, is said.

A

Entrance Antiphon

Put on the new man,
created in the image of God
in righteousness and holiness of truth (E.T. alleluia). Cf. Eph 4: 24

COLLECT

O God, who bring us to participate in the mystery
of the Passion and Resurrection of your Son,
grant, we pray,
that, strengthened by the spirit of adoption
as your children,
we may always walk in newness of life.
Through our Lord Jesus Christ, your Son,
who lives and reigns with you
in the unity of the Holy Spirit,
one God, for ever and ever.

PRAYER AFTER COMMUNION

Grant, O Lord, we pray,
that, nourished with the Sacrament
of your Son's Body and Blood,
we may grow in the communion of his Spirit
and in love for one another,
and so, through ardent charity,
reach the full stature of the Body of Christ.
Who lives and reigns for ever and ever.

B

Entrance Antiphon

God has saved us through the bath
that gives rebirth and renewal in the Holy Spirit,
that, justified by his grace, we may become heirs
with the hope of eternal life (E.T. alleluia). Ti 3: 5, 7

COLLECT

O God, who bring us to rebirth by the word of life,
grant that, accepting it with a sincere heart,
we may be eager to live by the truth
and may bear abundant fruits of fraternal charity.
Through our Lord Jesus Christ, your Son,
who lives and reigns with you
in the unity of the Holy Spirit,
one God, for ever and ever.

PRAYER AFTER COMMUNION

Grant, O Lord,
that by the power of this Sacrament
we, who have proclaimed in celebration
the glorious mystery
of your Son's Death and Resurrection,
may also profess it by our manner of life.
Through Christ our Lord.

4. For the Conferral of Confirmation

This Mass is used, with the color red or white, or a festive color, at the conferral of Confirmation on days when Ritual Masses are permitted. The Gloria in excelsis (Glory to God in the highest) is said. The Creed, however, is omitted.

A

Entrance Antiphon

Thus says the Lord:
I will pour clean water upon you
and I will give you a new heart;
a new spirit I will put within you (E.T. alleluia). Ez 36: 25-26

COLLECT

Grant, we pray, almighty and merciful God,
that the Holy Spirit, coming near
and dwelling graciously within us,
may make of us a perfect temple of his glory.
Through our Lord Jesus Christ, your Son,
who lives and reigns with you
in the unity of the Holy Spirit,
one God, for ever and ever.

Or:

Fulfill for us your gracious promise, O Lord, we pray,
so that by his coming
the Holy Spirit may make us witnesses before the world
to the Gospel of our Lord Jesus Christ.
Who lives and reigns with you
in the unity of the Holy Spirit,
one God, for ever and ever.

Other prayers to be used at choice (p. 580).

PRAYER AFTER COMMUNION

Accompany with your blessing
from this day forward, O Lord,
those who have been anointed with the Holy Spirit
and nourished by the Sacrament of your Son,
so that, with all trials overcome,
they may gladden your Church by their holiness
and, through their works and their charity,
foster her growth in the world.
Through Christ our Lord.

SOLEMN BLESSING AT THE END OF MASS

The Bishop, with hands extended over the newly confirmed, says:

May God the Father almighty bless you,
whom he has made his adopted sons and daughters
reborn from water and the Holy Spirit,
and may he keep you worthy of his fatherly love.
℟. Amen.

May his Only Begotten Son,
who promised that the Spirit of truth
would abide in his Church,
bless you and confirm you by his power
in the confession of the true faith.
℟. Amen.

May the Holy Spirit,
who kindles the fire of charity in the hearts of disciples,
bless you and lead you blameless and gathered as one
into the joy of the Kingdom of God.
℟. Amen.

And he blesses all the people, adding:

And may almighty God bless all of you,
who are gathered here,
the Father, ✠ and the Son, ✠ and the Holy ✠ Spirit.
℟. Amen.

Or:

PRAYER OVER THE PEOPLE

The Bishop, with hands extended over the newly confirmed and the people, says:

Confirm, O God,
what you have brought about in us,
and preserve in the hearts of your faithful
the gifts of the Holy Spirit:
may they never be ashamed
to confess Christ crucified before the world
and by devoted charity
may they ever fulfill his commands.
Who lives and reigns for ever and ever.
℟. Amen.

And may the blessing of almighty God,
the Father, ✠ and the Son, ✠ and the Holy ✠ Spirit,
come down on you and remain with you for ever.
℟. Amen.

B

Entrance Antiphon

The love of God has been poured into our hearts
through the Spirit of God dwelling within us (E.T. **alleluia**).
Rom 5: 5; cf. 8: 11

COLLECT

Graciously pour out your Holy Spirit upon us,
we pray, O Lord,
so that, walking in oneness of faith
and strengthened by the power of his love,
we may come to the measure of the full stature of Christ.
Who lives and reigns with you
in the unity of the Holy Spirit,
one God, for ever and ever.

Other prayers to be used at choice (p. 580).

PRAYER AFTER COMMUNION

Instruct, O Lord, in the fullness of the Law
those you have endowed with the gifts of your Spirit
and nourished by the Body of your Only Begotten Son,
that they may constantly show to the world
the freedom of your adopted children
and, by the holiness of their lives,
exercise the prophetic mission of your people.
Through Christ our Lord.

Solemn Blessing or Prayer over the People (pp. 578-579).

C

Other Prayers to Be Used if Appropriate

COLLECT

May the Paraclete who proceeds from you,
we pray, O Lord,
enlighten our minds and lead us into all truth,
just as your Son has promised.
Who lives and reigns with you
in the unity of the Holy Spirit,
one God, for ever and ever.

PRAYER AFTER COMMUNION

Pour on us, O Lord, the Spirit of your love,
and, in your kindness,
make those you have nourished
by this one heavenly Bread
one in mind and heart.
Through Christ our Lord.

II. FOR THE CONFERRAL OF THE ANOINTING OF THE SICK

Whenever Holy Anointing is conferred during Mass, on days when Ritual Masses are permitted, the Mass for the Sick (p. 654) may be used with the color white.

All the prayers given for a man may be adapted for a woman, with the necessary change of gender; in addition, those expressed in the plural may be used for individuals, with the necessary change to the singular.

At the end of Mass, a formula of blessing chosen from those that follow may be used.

May God the Father bless you.
℟. Amen.

May the Son of God heal you.
℟. Amen.

May the Holy Spirit shed light upon you.
℟. Amen.

May God guard your body and save your soul.
℟. Amen.

May he enlighten your heart and lead you to life on high.
℟. Amen.

And may almighty God bless all of you,
who are gathered here,
the Father, and the Son, ✠ and the Holy Spirit.
℟. Amen.

Or:

May the Lord Jesus Christ be with you to defend you.
℟. Amen.

May he go before you to lead you
and behind you to guard you.
℟. Amen.

May he look upon you, keep you safe and bless you.
℟. Amen.

And may almighty God bless all of you,
who are gathered here,
the Father, and the Son, ✠ and the Holy Spirit.
℟. Amen.

III. FOR THE ADMINISTERING OF VIATICUM

This Mass may be used with the color white on days when Ritual Masses are permitted.

All the prayers given for a man may be adapted for a woman, with the necessary change of gender; in addition, those expressed in the plural form may be used for individuals, with the necessary change to the singular.

Entrance Antiphon

He fed them with the finest wheat,
and satisfied them with honey from the rock (E.T. **alleluia**).
Cf. Ps 81 (80): 17

Or:

Truly the Lord has borne our infirmities,
and he has carried our sorrows (E.T. **alleluia**). Cf. Is 53: 4

COLLECT

O God, whose Son is for us the way, the truth and the life,
look lovingly upon your servant N.
and grant that, trusting in your promises
and strengthened by the Body of your Son,
he (**she**) **may journey in peace to your Kingdom.**
Through our Lord Jesus Christ, your Son,
who lives and reigns with you
in the unity of the Holy Spirit,
one God, for ever and ever.

PRAYER AFTER COMMUNION

O Lord, eternal health and salvation
of those who believe in you,
grant, we pray, that your servant N.,
renewed by heavenly food and drink,
may safely reach your Kingdom of light and life.
Through Christ our Lord.

V. FOR THE CELEBRATION OF MARRIAGE

Whenever Marriage is celebrated during Mass, this Ritual Mass is used, with the color white or a festive color.

However, on those days listed in nos. 1-4 of the Table of Liturgical Days, the Mass of the day is used, retaining the Nuptial Blessing in the Mass and, if appropriate, the proper formula for the final blessing.

If, however, during Christmas Time and Ordinary Time, the parish community participates in a Sunday Mass during which Marriage is celebrated, the Mass of the Sunday is used.

Although complete Mass formularies are given here for the sake of convenience, all texts, especially the prayers and the Nuptial Blessing, may be exchanged, if appropriate, with others.

A

Entrance Antiphon

May the Lord send you help from the holy place
and give you support from Sion.
May he grant you your hearts' desire
and fulfill every one of your designs (E.T. alleluia).

Cf. Ps 20 (19): 3, 5

The Penitential Act is omitted. The Gloria in excelsis (Glory to God in the highest) is said.

COLLECT

Be attentive to our prayers, O Lord,
and in your kindness uphold
what you have established
for the increase of the human race,
so that the union you have created
may be kept safe by your assistance.
Through our Lord Jesus Christ, your Son,
who lives and reigns with you
in the unity of the Holy Spirit,
one God, for ever and ever.

Or:

O God, who in creating the human race
willed that man and wife should be one,
join, we pray, in a bond of inseparable love
these your servants who are to be united
in the covenant of Marriage,
so that, as you make their love fruitful,
they may become, by your grace,
witnesses to charity itself.
Through our Lord Jesus Christ, your Son,
who lives and reigns with you
in the unity of the Holy Spirit,
one God, for ever and ever.

NUPTIAL BLESSING

After the Our Father, the prayer Deliver us is omitted. The Priest, standing and facing the bride and bridegroom, invokes upon them God's blessing, and this is never omitted.

In the invitation, if one or both of the spouses will not be receiving Communion, the words in parentheses are omitted. In the prayer, the words in parentheses may be omitted if it seems that circumstances suggest it, for example, if the bride and bridegroom are advanced in years.

The bride and bridegroom approach the altar or, if appropriate, they remain at their place and kneel.

The Priest, with hands joined, calls upon those present to pray, saying:

Dear brothers and sisters,
let us humbly pray to the Lord
that on these his servants, now married in Christ,
he may mercifully pour out
the blessing of his grace
and make of one heart in love
(by the Sacrament of Christ's Body and Blood)
those he has joined by a holy covenant.

And all pray in silence for a while.

Then the Priest, with hands extended over the bride and bridegroom, continues:

O God, who by your mighty power
created all things out of nothing,
and, when you had set in place
the beginnings of the universe,
formed man and woman in your own image,
making the woman an inseparable helpmate to the man,
that they might no longer be two, but one flesh,
and taught that what you were pleased to make one
must never be divided;

O God, who consecrated the bond of Marriage
by so great a mystery
that in the wedding covenant you foreshadowed
the Sacrament of Christ and his Church;

O God, by whom woman is joined to man
and the companionship they had in the beginning
is endowed with the one blessing
not forfeited by original sin
nor washed away by the flood.

Look now with favor on these your servants,
joined together in Marriage,
who ask to be strengthened by your blessing.
Send down on them the grace of the Holy Spirit
and pour your love into their hearts,
that they may remain faithful in the Marriage covenant.

May the grace of love and peace
abide in your daughter N.,
and let her always follow the example
of those holy women
whose praises are sung in the Scriptures.
May her husband entrust his heart to her,
so that, acknowledging her as his equal
and his joint heir to the life of grace,
he may show her due honor
and cherish her always
with the love that Christ has for his Church.

And now, Lord, we implore you:
may these your servants
hold fast to the faith and keep your commandments;
made one in the flesh,
may they be blameless in all they do;
and with the strength that comes from the Gospel,
may they bear true witness to Christ before all;
(may they be blessed with children,
and prove themselves virtuous parents,
who live to see their children's children).

And grant that,
reaching at last together the fullness of years
for which they hope,
they may come to the life of the blessed
in the Kingdom of Heaven.
Through Christ our Lord.

℟. Amen.

The prayer Lord Jesus Christ is omitted, and The peace of the Lord is said immediately.

Then the bride and bridegroom and all present offer one another a sign, in keeping with local customs, that expresses peace, communion and charity.

PRAYER AFTER COMMUNION

By the power of this sacrifice, O Lord,
accompany with your loving favor
what in your providence you have instituted,
so as to make of one heart in love
those you have already joined in this holy union
(and replenished with the one Bread and the one Chalice).
Through Christ our Lord.

SOLEMN BLESSING AT THE END OF MASS

The Priest, with hands extended over the bride and bridegroom, says:

May God the eternal Father
keep you of one heart in love for one another,
that the peace of Christ may dwell in you
and abide always in your home.

℟. Amen.

May you be blessed in your children,
have solace in your friends
and enjoy true peace with everyone.

℟. Amen.

May you be witnesses in the world to God's charity,
so that the afflicted and needy
who have known your kindness
may one day receive you thankfully
into the eternal dwelling of God.

℟. Amen.

And he blesses all the people, adding:

And may almighty God bless all of you,
who are gathered here,
the Father, and the Son, ✠ and the Holy Spirit.

℟. Amen.

B

Entrance Antiphon

At dawn, O Lord, fill us with your merciful love,
and we shall exult and rejoice all our days.
Let the favor of the Lord our God be upon us
and upon the work of our hands (E.T. alleluia).

Cf. Ps 90 (89): 14, 17

The Penitential Act is omitted. The Gloria in excelsis (Glory to God in the highest) is said.

COLLECT

Be attentive to our prayers, O Lord,
and in your kindness
pour out your grace on these your servants (N. and N.),
that, coming together before your altar,
they may be confirmed in love for one another.
Through our Lord Jesus Christ, your Son,
who lives and reigns with you
in the unity of the Holy Spirit,
one God, for ever and ever.

Or:

O God, who consecrated the bond of Marriage
by so great a mystery
that in the wedding covenant you foreshadow
the Sacrament of Christ and his Church,
grant, we pray, to these your servants,
that what they receive in faith
they may live out in deeds.
Through our Lord Jesus Christ, your Son,
who lives and reigns with you
in the unity of the Holy Spirit,
one God, for ever and ever.

NUPTIAL BLESSING

After the Our Father, the prayer Deliver us is omitted. The Priest, standing and facing the bride and bridegroom, invokes upon them God's blessing, and this is never omitted.

In the invitation, if one or both of the spouses will not be receiving Communion, the words in parentheses are omitted. In the prayer, the words in parentheses may be omitted if it seems that circumstances suggest it, for example, if the bride and bridegroom are advanced in years.

The bride and bridegroom approach the altar or, if appropriate, they remain at their place and kneel.

The Priest, with hands joined, calls upon those present to pray, saying:

Let us pray to the Lord for this bride and groom,
who come to the altar as they begin their married life,
that (partaking of the Body and Blood of Christ)
they may always be bound together
by love for one another.

And all pray in silence for a while.

Then the Priest, with hands extended over the bride and bridegroom, continues:

Holy Father,
who formed man in your own image,
male and female you created them,
so that as husband and wife, united in body and heart,
they might fulfill their calling in the world;

O God, who, to reveal the great design
you formed in your love,
willed that the love of spouses for each other
should foreshadow the covenant
you graciously made with your people,
so that, by fulfillment of the sacramental sign,
the mystical marriage of Christ with his Church
might become manifest
in the union of husband and wife among your faithful;

Graciously stretch out your right hand
over these your servants (N. and N.), we pray,
and pour into their hearts the power of the Holy Spirit.

Grant, O Lord,
that, as they enter upon this sacramental union,
they may share with one another the gifts of your love
and, by being for each other a sign of your presence,
become one heart and one mind.

May they also sustain, O Lord, by their deeds
the home they are forming
(and prepare their children
to become members of your heavenly household
by raising them in the way of the Gospel).

Graciously crown with your blessings your daughter N.,
so that, by being a good wife (and mother),
she may bring warmth to her home
with a love that is pure
and adorn it with welcoming graciousness.

Bestow a heavenly blessing also, O Lord,
on N., your servant,
that he may be a worthy, good and
faithful husband (and a provident father).

Grant, holy Father,
that, desiring to approach your table
as a couple joined in Marriage in your presence,
they may one day have the joy
of taking part in your great banquet in heaven.
Through Christ our Lord.

℟. Amen.

The prayer Lord Jesus Christ is omitted, and The peace of the Lord is said immediately.

Then the bride and bridegroom and all present offer a sign, in keeping with local customs, that expresses peace, communion and charity.

PRAYER AFTER COMMUNION

Having been made partakers at your table,
we pray, O Lord,
that those who are united by the Sacrament of Marriage
may always hold fast to you
and proclaim your name to the world.
Through Christ our Lord.

SOLEMN BLESSING AT THE END OF MASS

The Priest, with hands extended over the bride and bridegroom, says:

May God the all-powerful Father grant you his joy
and bless you in your children.

℟. Amen.

May the Only Begotten Son of God
stand by you with compassion in good times and in bad.

℟. Amen.

May the Holy Spirit of God
always pour forth his love into your hearts.

℟. Amen.

And he blesses all the people, adding:

And may almighty God bless all of you,
who are gathered here,
the Father, and the Son, ✠ and the Holy Spirit.

℟. Amen.

C

Entrance Antiphon

I will bless you day after day, O Lord,
and praise your name for ever and ever,
for you are kind to all
and compassionate to all your creatures (E.T. alleluia).

Cf. Ps 145 (144): 2, 9

The Penitential Act is omitted. The Gloria in excelsis (Glory to God in the highest) is said.

COLLECT

Grant, we pray, almighty God,
that these your servants,
now to be joined by the Sacrament of Matrimony,
may grow in the faith they profess
and enrich your Church with faithful offspring.
Through our Lord Jesus Christ, your Son,
who lives and reigns with you
  in the unity of the Holy Spirit,
one God, for ever and ever.

Or:

O God, who since the beginning of the world
have blessed the increase of offspring,
show favor to our supplications
and pour forth the help of your blessing
on these your servants (N. and N.),
so that in the union of Marriage
they may be bound together
in mutual affection,
in likeness of mind,
and in shared holiness.
Through our Lord Jesus Christ, your Son,
who lives and reigns with you
  in the unity of the Holy Spirit,
one God, for ever and ever.

NUPTIAL BLESSING

After the Our Father, the prayer Deliver us is omitted. The Priest, standing and facing the bride and bridegroom, invokes upon them God's blessing, and this is never omitted.

In the invitation, if one or both of the spouses will not be receiving Communion, the words in parentheses are omitted. In the prayer, the words in parentheses may be omitted if it seems that circumstances suggest it, for example, if the bride and bridegroom are advanced in years.

The bride and bridegroom approach the altar or, if appropriate, they remain at their place and kneel.

The Priest, with hands joined, calls upon those present to pray, saying:

Let us humbly invoke by our prayers,
dear brothers and sisters,
God's blessing upon this bride and groom,
that in his kindness he may favor with his help
those on whom he has bestowed
the Sacrament of Matrimony.

All pray in silence for a while.

Then the Priest, with hands extended over the bride and bridegroom, continues:

Holy Father, maker of the whole world,
who created man and woman in your own image
and willed that their union be crowned with your blessing,
we humbly beseech you for these your servants,
who are joined today in the Sacrament of Matrimony.

May your abundant blessing, Lord,
come down upon this bride, N.,
and upon N., her companion for life,
and may the power of your Holy Spirit
set their hearts aflame from on high,
so that, living out together the gift of Matrimony,
they may (adorn their family with children
and) enrich the Church.

**In happiness may they praise you, O Lord,
in sorrow may they seek you out;
may they have the joy of your presence
to assist them in their toil,
and know that you are near
to comfort them in their need;
let them pray to you in the holy assembly
and bear witness to you in the world,
and after a happy old age,
together with the circle of friends that surrounds them,
may they come to the Kingdom of Heaven.
Through Christ our Lord.**

℟. Amen.

The prayer Lord Jesus Christ is omitted and The peace of the Lord is said immediately.

Then the bride and bridegroom and all present offer one another a sign, in keeping with local customs, that expresses peace, communion and charity.

PRAYER AFTER COMMUNION

Grant, we pray, almighty God,
that the power of the Sacrament we have received
may find growth in these your servants
and that the effects of the sacrifice we have offered
may be felt by us all.
Through Christ our Lord.

SOLEMN BLESSING AT THE END OF MASS

The Priest, with hands extended over the bride and bridegroom, says:

May the Lord Jesus,
who graced the marriage at Cana by his presence,
bless you and your loved ones.
℟. Amen.

May he, who loved the Church to the end,
unceasingly pour his love into your hearts.
℟. Amen.

May the Lord grant
that, bearing witness to faith in his Resurrection,
you may await with joy the blessed hope to come.
℟. Amen.

And he blesses all the people, adding:

And may almighty God bless all of you,
who are gathered here,
the Father, and the Son, ✠ and the Holy Spirit.
℟. Amen.

Masses for the Anniversaries of Marriage are found among the Masses for Various Needs (pp. 617-619).

MASSES AND PRAYERS FOR VARIOUS NEEDS AND OCCASIONS

1. This section groups together Masses and prayers for various intentions, which may be used in many situations, and for various needs and occasions.

The texts found in the first two parts may be used either in a Mass with the people or in a Mass without the people. The texts collected in the third part may, in general, be used in Masses celebrated without the people, unless at times a pastoral reason suggests otherwise.

2. In case of some grave need, a corresponding Mass may be said on the instructions of the local Ordinary or with his permission, on any day except on Solemnities, the Sundays of Advent, Lent, and Easter, days within the Octave of Easter, the Commemoration of All the Faithful Departed (All Souls' Day), Ash Wednesday, and on the weekdays of Holy Week.

If, however, some real necessity or pastoral advantage requires it, in the judgment of the rector of the church or the Priest celebrant himself, an appropriate Mass or a Collect may be used in a celebration with the people even if on that day there occurs an Obligatory Memorial or a weekday of Advent up to and including December 16, or a weekday of Christmas Time from January 2 or a weekday of Easter Time after the Octave of Easter.

During Easter Time, Alleluia is added to the Entrance Antiphon and Communion Antiphon, unless this would be not in accord with the sense.

3. In a Mass for a weekday in Ordinary Time, the Priest may always use all the prayers of this series, or even only the Collect, observing what is indicated in no. 1.

4. As for the Eucharistic Prayer which may be used with formularies of the Masses for Various Needs, see Appendix to the Order of Mass in the Roman Missal.

5. In certain Masses, the liturgical texts given for a man may be adapted for a woman, with the necessary change of gender; in addition, those expressed in the plural may be used for individuals, with the necessary change to the singular.

6. These Masses may be said with the color proper to the day or the liturgical time or with the color violet if they have a penitential character, see e.g., nos. 31, 33, 38 (cf. the *General Instruction*, no. 347).

I. FOR HOLY CHURCH

1. For the Church

A

Entrance Antiphon

God has made known to us the mystery of his will,
to bring together all things in Christ,
all things in heaven and on earth in him. Cf. Eph 1: 9-10

COLLECT

O God, who in your wonderful providence
decreed that Christ's Kingdom
should be extended throughout the earth
and that all should become partakers
of his saving redemption,
grant, we pray, that your Church
may be the universal sacrament of salvation
and that Christ may be revealed to all
as the hope of the nations and their Savior.
Who lives and reigns with you
in the unity of the Holy Spirit,
one God, for ever and ever.

PRAYER AFTER COMMUNION

O God, who constantly feed and strengthen the Church
with your Sacraments,
grant to us,
who have been nourished at the heavenly table,
that, by obeying your teachings of love,
we may become for the human family
a life-giving leaven and a means to salvation.
Through Christ our Lord.

B

Entrance Antiphon

I had a vision of a great multitude, which no one could count,
from every nation, race, people, and tongue. Rev 7: 9

COLLECT

O God, in the covenant of your Christ
you never cease to gather to yourself from all nations
a people growing together in unity through the Spirit;
grant, we pray, that your Church,
faithful to the mission entrusted to her,
may continually go forward with the human family
and always be the leaven and the soul of human society,
to renew it in Christ and transform it
into the family of God.
Through our Lord Jesus Christ, your Son,
who lives and reigns with you
in the unity of the Holy Spirit,
one God, for ever and ever.

PRAYER AFTER COMMUNION

Nourished by the Sacrament of your Son,
we implore you, Lord,
to make fruitful the work of your Church,
for by it you constantly reveal
the fullness of the mystery of salvation to the poor,
whom you have called to an honored place
in your eternal Kingdom.
Through Christ our Lord.

C

Entrance Antiphon

Where two or three are gathered together in my name,
there am I in the midst of them. Mt 18: 20

Or:

Though many, we are one body in Christ
and individually parts of one another. Rom 12: 5

COLLECT

Grant, we pray, almighty God,
that your Church may always remain that holy people,
formed as one by the unity of Father, Son and Holy Spirit,
which manifests to the world
the Sacrament of your holiness and unity
and leads it to the perfection of your charity.
Through our Lord Jesus Christ, your Son,
who lives and reigns with you
in the unity of the Holy Spirit,
one God, for ever and ever.

PRAYER AFTER COMMUNION

O God, who by this wonderful Sacrament
give courage and comfort to the Church,
grant that through these holy gifts
your people may hold fast to Christ,
so that, by the tasks they carry out in this present age,
they may in freedom build up your eternal Kingdom.
Through Christ our Lord.

D

Entrance Antiphon

Father, I pray for those who will believe in me,
that they may be one in us,
so that the world may believe it was you who sent me.
Cf. Jn 17: 20-21

COLLECT

Almighty ever-living God,
who in Christ revealed your glory to all the nations,
watch over the works of your mercy,
that Holy Church, spread throughout the whole world,
may persevere with steadfast faith
in confessing your name.
Through our Lord Jesus Christ, your Son,
who lives and reigns with you
in the unity of the Holy Spirit,
one God, for ever and ever.

PRAYER AFTER COMMUNION

Be pleased, O Lord, we pray,
to govern the Church you have nourished
by this holy meal,
so that, firmly directed,
she may enjoy ever greater freedom
and persevere in integrity of religion.
Through Christ our Lord.

E

For the Particular Church

Entrance Antiphon

To Jesus Christ who loves us
and has washed us clean of our sins by his Blood,
who has made us into a kingdom, priests for his God and Father.
To him be glory and power for ever and ever. Amen. Rev 1: 5-6

COLLECT

O God, who in each pilgrim Church throughout the world
make visible the one, holy, catholic and apostolic Church,
graciously grant
that your faithful may be so united to their shepherd
and gathered together in the Holy Spirit
through the Gospel and the Eucharist,
as to worthily embody the universality of your people
and become a sign and instrument in the world
of the presence of Christ.
Who lives and reigns with you
in the unity of the Holy Spirit,
one God, for ever and ever.

PRAYER AFTER COMMUNION

In this your Church, O Lord,
may integrity of faith, holiness of life,
fraternal charity and pure religion
flourish and abide until the end,
and, as you do not fail to feed her
with the Body of your Son and with your word,
so also never cease, we pray,
to guide her under your protection.
Through Christ our Lord.

2. For the Pope

Especially on the Anniversary of Election

This Mass is said, with the color white, on the anniversary of the election of the Pope in places wherever special celebrations are held, provided they do not occur on a Sunday of Advent, Lent or Easter, on a Solemnity, on Ash Wednesday, or on a weekday of Holy Week.

Entrance Antiphon

You are Peter, and upon this rock I will build my Church,
and the gates of the netherworld shall not prevail against it.
To you I will give the keys to the Kingdom of Heaven.

Mt 16: 18-19

COLLECT

O God, who in your providential design
willed that your Church be built
upon blessed Peter, whom you set over the other Apostles,
look with favor, we pray, on N. our Pope
and grant that he, whom you have made Peter's successor,
may be for your people a visible source and foundation
of unity in faith and of communion.
Through our Lord Jesus Christ, your Son,
who lives and reigns with you
in the unity of the Holy Spirit,
one God, for ever and ever.

Or:

O God, shepherd and ruler of all the faithful,
look favorably on your servant N.,
whom you have set at the head of your Church
as her shepherd;
grant, we pray, that by word and example
he may be of service to those over whom he presides
so that, together with the flock entrusted to his care,
he may come to everlasting life.
Through our Lord Jesus Christ, your Son,
who lives and reigns with you
in the unity of the Holy Spirit,
one God, for ever and ever.

Or:

O God, who chose your servant N.
in succession to the Apostle Peter
as shepherd of the whole flock,
look favorably on the supplications of your people
and grant that, as Vicar of Christ on earth,
he may confirm his brethren
and that the whole Church
may be in communion with him
in the bond of unity, love and peace,
so that in you, the shepherd of souls,
all may know the truth and attain life eternal.
Through our Lord Jesus Christ, your Son,
who lives and reigns with you
in the unity of the Holy Spirit,
one God, for ever and ever.

PRAYER AFTER COMMUNION

Having been made sharers at the heavenly table,
we humbly entreat you, Lord:
by the power of this mystery,
strengthen your Church in unity and charity
and, as you have entrusted your servant N.
with the office of shepherd,
grant him always salvation and protection,
together with the flock entrusted to his care.
Through Christ our Lord.

3. For the Bishop

Especially on the Anniversary of Ordination

This Mass is said on the anniversary of the Ordination of the Bishop wherever special celebrations are held, provided they do not occur on a Sunday of Advent, Lent or Easter, on a Solemnity, on Ash Wednesday, or on a weekday of Holy Week.

Entrance Antiphon

I will look after my sheep, says the Lord,
and I will appoint a shepherd to pasture them,
and I, the Lord, will be their God. Ez 34: 11, 23, 24

COLLECT

O God, eternal shepherd of the faithful,
who tend your Church in countless ways
and rule over her in love,
grant, we pray, that N., your servant,
whom you have set over your people,
may preside in the place of Christ
over the flock whose shepherd he is,
and be faithful as a teacher of doctrine,
a Priest of sacred worship
and as one who serves them by governing.
Through our Lord Jesus Christ, your Son,
who lives and reigns with you
in the unity of the Holy Spirit,
one God, for ever and ever.

Or:

O God, shepherd and ruler of all the faithful,
look favorably on your servant,
whom you have set at the head
of your Church of N. as her shepherd;
grant, we pray, that by word and example
he may be of service to those over whom he presides,
so that, together with the flock entrusted to his care,
he may come to everlasting life.
Through our Lord Jesus Christ, your Son,
who lives and reigns with you
in the unity of the Holy Spirit,
one God, for ever and ever.

Or:

O Lord, who for the feeding of your flock
have set your servant N. over it
as a successor to the Apostles,
grant him, we pray,
a spirit of counsel and fortitude,
a spirit of knowledge and piety,
so that, by faithfully governing the people
entrusted to him,
he may build up in the world the sacrament of the Church.
Through our Lord Jesus Christ, your Son,
who lives and reigns with you
in the unity of the Holy Spirit,
one God, for ever and ever.

PRAYER AFTER COMMUNION

By the power of this Sacrament, O Lord,
increase the gifts of your grace
in N., your servant and our Bishop,
that he may serve you worthily in the pastoral ministry
and receive the eternal rewards of a faithful steward.
Through Christ our Lord.

4. For the Election of a Pope or a Bishop

Entrance Antiphon

I will raise up for myself a faithful priest,
who shall do according to my heart and mind;
I will establish a lasting house for him
and he shall walk before me all his days. 1 Sm 2: 35

COLLECT

O God, eternal shepherd,
who govern your flock with unfailing care,
grant in your boundless fatherly love
a pastor for your Church
who will please you by his holiness
and to us show watchful care.
Through our Lord Jesus Christ, your Son,
who lives and reigns with you
in the unity of the Holy Spirit,
one God, for ever and ever.

PRAYER AFTER COMMUNION

As we have been renewed, O Lord,
with the supreme Sacrament of salvation,
the Body and Blood of your Only Begotten Son,
may the wondrous grace of your majesty
gladden us with the gift of a shepherd
who will instruct your people by his virtues
and imbue the minds of the faithful
with the truth of the Gospel.
Through Christ our Lord.

5. For a Council or a Synod

Entrance Antiphon

And over all things put on love,
which is the bond of perfection,
and let the peace of Christ rule in your hearts. Cf. Col 3: 14-15

COLLECT

O Lord, ruler and guardian of your Church,
pour out, we pray, upon your servants
a spirit of truth, understanding and peace,
that they may strive with all their heart
to know what is pleasing to you
and then pursue it with all their strength.
Through our Lord Jesus Christ, your Son,
who lives and reigns with you
in the unity of the Holy Spirit,
one God, for ever and ever.

Or:

O God, who care for your peoples with gentleness
and rule them in love,
endow with a spirit of wisdom
those to whom you have handed on authority to govern,
that your people may be led to know the truth more fully
and to grow in holiness according to your will.
Through our Lord Jesus Christ, your Son,
who lives and reigns with you
in the unity of the Holy Spirit,
one God, for ever and ever.

PRAYER AFTER COMMUNION

Grant, we pray, O merciful God,
that the holy gifts we have received
may confirm your servants in the truth
and prompt them to seek the honor of your name.
Through Christ our Lord.

6. For Priests

Entrance Antiphon

The Spirit of the Lord is upon me, for he has anointed me
and sent me to preach good news to the poor,
to heal the broken-hearted
and to let the oppressed go free. Cf. Lk 4: 18

COLLECT

O God, who made your Only Begotten Son
eternal High Priest,
grant that those he has chosen
as ministers and stewards of your mysteries
may be found faithful in carrying out
the ministry they have received.
Through our Lord Jesus Christ, your Son,
who lives and reigns with you
in the unity of the Holy Spirit,
one God, for ever and ever.

Or:

Lord our God, who in governing your people
make use of the ministry of Priests,
grant to these men
a persevering obedience to your will,
so that by their ministry and life
they may gain glory for you in Christ.
Who lives and reigns with you
in the unity of the Holy Spirit,
one God, for ever and ever.

PRAYER AFTER COMMUNION

May the divine sacrifice
we have offered and received, O Lord,
give new life to your Priests and to all your servants,
that, united to you in unfailing love,
they may receive the grace
of giving worthy service to your majesty.
Through Christ our Lord.

7. For the Priest Himself

A

Especially for a Priest with the Care of Souls

Entrance Antiphon

I have become a servant of the Church
according to God's commission given to me for you.
We proclaim Christ, that we may present everyone
perfect in Christ Jesus. Cf. Col 1: 25, 28

COLLECT

O God, who have willed that I preside over your family
not by any merit of mine
but out of the abundance of your untold grace alone,
grant that I may carry out worthily
the ministry of the priestly office
and, under your governance in all things,
may direct the people entrusted to my care.
Through our Lord Jesus Christ, your Son,
who lives and reigns with you
in the unity of the Holy Spirit,
one God, for ever and ever.

PRAYER AFTER COMMUNION

Almighty ever-living God,
source and perfection of every virtue,
grant, we pray, that by participation in this mystery
I may do what is right and preach what is true,
so that by my deeds and by my words
I may offer to the faithful instruction in your grace.
Through Christ our Lord.

B

Entrance Antiphon

I say to the Lord: You are my Lord.
My goodness lies in you alone.
O Lord it is you who are my portion and cup;
you yourself who secure my lot. Ps 16 (15): 2, 5

COLLECT

Incline your merciful ear to my prayers,
O God of all compassion,
and enlighten my heart by the grace of the Holy Spirit,
that I may worthily celebrate your mysteries,
faithfully serve your Church
and love you with eternal charity.
Through our Lord Jesus Christ, your Son,
who lives and reigns with you
in the unity of the Holy Spirit,
one God, for ever and ever.

PRAYER AFTER COMMUNION

As you strengthen me with the Bread of heaven,
and gladden me with the chalice of the new covenant,
bring me, holy Father, to serve you faithfully
and to spend my life boldly and zealously
for the salvation of all humanity.
Through Christ our Lord.

C

On the Anniversary of His Ordination

Entrance Antiphon

It was not you who chose me, says the Lord,
but I who chose you and appointed you to go out and bear fruit,
fruit that will last. Cf. Jn 15: 16

COLLECT

Holy Father, who, by no merit of my own, chose me
for communion with the eternal priesthood of your Christ
and for the ministry of your Church,
grant that I may be an ardent
yet gentle preacher of the Gospel
and a faithful steward of your mysteries.
Through our Lord Jesus Christ, your Son,
who lives and reigns with you
in the unity of the Holy Spirit,
one God, for ever and ever.

PRAYER AFTER COMMUNION

For the glory of your name, O Lord,
I have joyfully celebrated the mystery of faith
to mark the anniversary of my priestly ordination,
so that I may be in truth
what I have handled mystically in this sacrifice.
Through Christ our Lord.

8. For Ministers of the Church

Entrance Antiphon

There are different graces but the same Spirit,
different ministries but the same Lord,
different works but the same God,
who accomplishes everything in everyone. Cf. 1 Cor 12: 4-6

COLLECT

O God, who have taught the ministers of your Church
to seek not to be served,
but to serve their brothers and sisters,
grant, we pray,
that they may be effective in action, gentle in ministry,
and constant in prayer.
Through our Lord Jesus Christ, your Son,
who lives and reigns with you
in the unity of the Holy Spirit,
one God, for ever and ever.

PRAYER AFTER COMMUNION

Grant, O Lord, to your servants,
whom you have replenished with heavenly food and drink,
that, for the sake of your glory
and the salvation of believers,
they may be found faithful as ministers of the Gospel,
of the Sacraments and of charity.
Through Christ our Lord.

9. For Vocations to Holy Orders

Entrance Antiphon

Ask the Lord of the harvest
to send out laborers for his harvest,
says Jesus to his disciples. Mt 9: 38

COLLECT

O God, who willed to provide shepherds for your people,
pour out in your Church a spirit of piety and fortitude,
to raise up worthy ministers for your altars
and make them ardent yet gentle heralds of your Gospel.
Through our Lord Jesus Christ, your Son,
who lives and reigns with you
in the unity of the Holy Spirit,
one God, for ever and ever.

PRAYER AFTER COMMUNION

Renewed with the Bread of the heavenly table,
we entreat you, O Lord,
that through this Sacrament of charity
the seeds you sow with great abundance
in the field of your Church
may come to maturity,
so that many may make it their choice in life
to serve you in their brothers and sisters.
Through Christ our Lord.

10. For the Laity

Entrance Antiphon

The Kingdom of Heaven is like yeast that a woman took
and mixed with three measures of wheat flour,
until the whole batch was leavened. Mt 13: 33

COLLECT

O God, who have sent the power of the Gospel
like leaven into the world,
grant that your faithful,
whom you have called to live amid the world
and its affairs,
may be fervent with the Christian spirit
and, through the tasks they carry out in this present age,
may constantly build up your Kingdom.
Through our Lord Jesus Christ, your Son,
who lives and reigns with you
in the unity of the Holy Spirit,
one God, for ever and ever.

PRAYER AFTER COMMUNION

As we draw upon the fullness of your grace,
we pray, O Lord,
that your faithful,
who by your will are engaged in the things of this world,
may be strengthened
by the power of the Eucharistic Banquet,
to be tireless witnesses to the truth of the Gospel
and may ever make your Church present and active
amid the affairs of this age.
Through Christ our Lord.

11. On the Anniversaries of Marriage

On the main anniversaries of marriage, as for example, on the twenty-fifth, fiftieth, or sixtieth anniversary, whenever Masses for Various Needs are permitted, the Mass for Giving Thanks to God (p. 662) may be used with the prayers given below.

The same prayers may also be used, if appropriate, at Mass on a weekday in Ordinary Time. In these celebrations, a special remembrance of the Sacrament of Marriage may appropriately be made, using the forms which are indicated in the Roman Ritual (*Order of Celebrating Matrimony*, nos. 237-251).

A

On Any Anniversary

COLLECT

**O God, Creator of all things,
who in the beginning made man and woman
that they might form the marriage bond,
bless and strengthen the union of your servants N. and N.,
that they may show forth an ever more perfect image
of the union of Christ with his Church.
Through our Lord Jesus Christ, your Son,
who lives and reigns with you
in the unity of the Holy Spirit,
one God, for ever and ever.**

PRAYER AFTER COMMUNION

**Open wide in joy and love, O Lord,
the hearts of these your servants,
who have been refreshed
with food and drink from on high,
that their home may be a place of decency and peace
and welcome everyone with love.
Through Christ our Lord.**

B

On the Twenty-Fifth Anniversary

COLLECT

O Lord, who have joined these your servants N. and N.
in the unbreakable bond of marriage
and have been pleased to sustain them
in communion of spirit amid toil and joy,
increase, we pray, and purify their love,
so that (together with their children) they may rejoice
in the sanctification they bring to each other.
Through our Lord Jesus Christ, your Son,
who lives and reigns with you
in the unity of the Holy Spirit,
one God, for ever and ever.

PRAYER AFTER COMMUNION

O God, who have graciously welcomed
this married couple, N. and N.
(together with their children and friends)
to the table of your family,
grant that they may continue to grow
in strong and eager communion with each other,
so that by your gift they may be united,
until they reach the heavenly banquet.
Through Christ our Lord.

C

On the Fiftieth Anniversary

COLLECT

O God, almighty Father,
for the sake of the good works they have done
through their long life together,
look kindly on this husband and wife N. and N.
(with the children they have brought to life and faith)
and, as you sealed the beginnings of their love
by a wonderful Sacrament,
so bless their fruitful old age.
Through our Lord Jesus Christ, your Son,
who lives and reigns with you
in the unity of the Holy Spirit,
one God, for ever and ever.

PRAYER AFTER COMMUNION

Having tasted the delights of your table,
we entreat you, O Lord,
to keep this married couple N. and N.
safe and holy in the years ahead,
until you welcome them both,
in the fullness of their days,
to your heavenly banquet.
Through Christ our Lord.

12. For the Family

Entrance Antiphon

Honor your father and mother.
This is the first commandment with a promise,
that it may go well with you
and that you may have a long life on earth. Eph 6: 2-3

COLLECT

O God, in whose eternal design
family life has its firm foundation,
look with compassion on the prayers of your servants
and grant that, following the example
of the Holy Family of your Only Begotten Son
in practicing the virtues of family life
and in the bonds of charity,
we may, in the joy of your house,
delight one day in eternal rewards.
Through our Lord Jesus Christ, your Son,
who lives and reigns with you
in the unity of the Holy Spirit,
one God, for ever and ever.

PRAYER AFTER COMMUNION

Bring those you refresh with this heavenly Sacrament,
most merciful Father,
to imitate constantly the example
of the Holy Family of your Only Begotten Son,
so that, after the trials of this world,
they may share their company for ever.
Through Christ our Lord.

13. For Religious

A

Entrance Antiphon

Trust in the Lord and do good,
and you will dwell in the land and be secure.
Find your delight in the Lord,
and he will grant your heart's desire. Ps 37 (36): 3-4

COLLECT

O God, who inspire and bring to fulfillment
every good intention,
direct your servants into the way of eternal salvation,
and, as they have left all things
to devote themselves entirely to you,
grant that, following Christ
and renouncing the things of this world,
they may faithfully serve you and their neighbor
in a spirit of poverty and in humility of heart.
Through our Lord Jesus Christ, your Son,
who lives and reigns with you
in the unity of the Holy Spirit,
one God, for ever and ever.

PRAYER AFTER COMMUNION

Grant, O Lord, that your servants,
gathered in your love and partaking of the one Bread,
may be of one heart in prompting each other
in the pursuit of charity and good works,
so that through a holy way of life
they may always and everywhere
be true witnesses to Christ.
Who lives and reigns for ever and ever.

B

On the Twenty-Fifth or Fiftieth Anniversary of Religious Profession

Entrance Antiphon

Behold, I come, O Lord, that I may do your will.
I have vowed it, and your law lies deep within me.

Cf. Ps 40 (39): 8-9

COLLECT

O Lord, faithful God,
grant, we pray, that we may give you thanks
for your kindness towards our brother (sister) N.,
who today is eager to renew the gift received from you;
strengthen in him (her) a spirit of perfect charity,
so that each day
he (she) may more fervently serve your glory
and the work of your salvation.
Through our Lord Jesus Christ, your Son,
who lives and reigns with you
in the unity of the Holy Spirit,
one God, for ever and ever.

PRAYER AFTER COMMUNION

We have partaken, O Lord,
of the Body and Blood of your Son,
which you have given us on this joyful anniversary;
grant, we pray, that our brother (sister) N.,
refreshed with heavenly food and drink,
may proceed happily on the journey towards you
already long begun.
Through Christ our Lord.

14. For Vocations to Religious Life

Entrance Antiphon

If you would be perfect,
go, sell what you have, give to the poor,
and follow me, says the Lord. Mt 19: 21

COLLECT

Holy Father, who,
though urging all the faithful to perfect charity,
never cease to prompt many to follow more closely
in the footsteps of your Son,
grant, we pray,
that those you have chosen for this special calling
may, by their way of life,
show to the Church and the world
a clear sign of your Kingdom.
Through our Lord Jesus Christ, your Son,
who lives and reigns with you
in the unity of the Holy Spirit,
one God, for ever and ever.

Or, to be said by a religious Priest:

Look with favor on your family, O Lord,
and increase it always with new offspring,
so that it may lead its sons (daughters)
towards their goal of perfect charity
and work effectively for the salvation of all.
Through our Lord Jesus Christ, your Son,
who lives and reigns with you
in the unity of the Holy Spirit,
one God, for ever and ever.

PRAYER AFTER COMMUNION

Strengthen your servants, O Lord,
with this spiritual food and drink,
so that, always faithful to the call of the Gospel,
they may make present everywhere
the living image of your Son.
Who lives and reigns for ever and ever.

Or, to be said by a religious Priest:

By the power of this Sacrament
give us, Lord, we pray,
perseverance in obeying your will,
that we may bear witness to your love before the world
and seek with courage those good things
which alone will last for ever.
Through Christ our Lord.

15. For Promoting Harmony

Entrance Antiphon

The community of believers was of one heart and mind.
The Apostles bore witness to the Resurrection of the Lord Jesus,
and great favor was accorded them all, alleluia. Acts 4: 32-33

COLLECT

O God, who are perfect unity and true charity,
grant your faithful one heart and one mind,
that the body of your Church,
which rests on the confession of the truth,
may flourish in harmony
and be made strong in enduring unity.
Through our Lord Jesus Christ, your Son,
who lives and reigns with you
in the unity of the Holy Spirit,
one God, for ever and ever.

Or:

O God, who have taught your Church
to keep all the heavenly commandments
by loving you and loving our neighbor,
grant us a spirit of peace and grace,
so that your entire family
may be devoted to you wholeheartedly
and united in purity of intent.
Through our Lord Jesus Christ, your Son,
who lives and reigns with you
in the unity of the Holy Spirit,
one God, for ever and ever.

PRAYER AFTER COMMUNION

We have received, O Lord, the Sacrament of unity;
grant us, we pray,
that, living in your house in holy accord,
we may possess the peace we hand on
and preserve the peace we have received.
Through Christ our Lord.

16. For Reconciliation

The words in this Mass printed within parentheses are said on the occasion of a special penitential time.

Entrance Antiphon

I am the salvation of the people, says the Lord.
Should they cry to me in any distress,
I will hear them, and I will be their Lord for ever.

COLLECT

God of mercy and reconciliation,
who offer your people special days of salvation
so that they may recognize you
as Creator and Father of all,
mercifully come to our help, we pray,
(throughout this acceptable time,)
so that, receiving gladly from you the message of peace,
we may serve your will to restore all things in Christ.
Who lives and reigns with you
in the unity of the Holy Spirit,
one God, for ever and ever.

Or, especially during the Easter Time:

O God, author of true freedom,
whose will it is to shape all men and women
into a single people released from slavery,
(and who offer us a time of grace and blessing,)
grant to your Church, we pray,
that, as she receives new growth in freedom,
she may appear more clearly to the world
as the universal sacrament of salvation,
manifesting and making present
the mystery of your love for all.
Through our Lord Jesus Christ, your Son,
who lives and reigns with you
in the unity of the Holy Spirit,
one God, for ever and ever.

PRAYER AFTER COMMUNION

May the Sacrament of your Son, which we have received,
increase our strength, we pray, O Lord,
that from this mystery of unity
we may drink deeply of love's power
and everywhere promote your peace.
Through Christ our Lord.

17. For the Unity of Christians

This Mass may be used whenever there are special celebrations for the unity of Christians, provided it does not occur on a Sunday of Advent, Lent or Easter, or on any Solemnity.

A

Entrance Antiphon

I am the Good Shepherd,
and I know my sheep and mine know me, says the Lord,
just as the Father knows me and I know the Father;
and I lay down my life for the sheep. Jn 10: 14-15

COLLECT

Almighty ever-living God,
who gather what is scattered
and keep together what you have gathered,
look kindly on the flock of your Son,
that those whom one Baptism has consecrated
may be joined together by integrity of faith
and united in the bond of charity.
Through our Lord Jesus Christ, your Son,
who lives and reigns with you
in the unity of the Holy Spirit,
one God, for ever and ever.

Or:

We humbly ask you, Lord, lover of the human family,
to pour out more fully upon us the grace of your Spirit,
and grant that, walking worthily in the vocation
to which you have called us,
we may bear witness to the truth before others
and seek with confidence
the unity of all believers in the bond of peace.
Through our Lord Jesus Christ, your Son,
who lives and reigns with you
in the unity of the Holy Spirit,
one God, for ever and ever.

PRAYER AFTER COMMUNION

As this reception of your Holy Communion, O Lord,
foreshadows the union of the faithful in you,
so may it bring about unity in your Church.
Through Christ our Lord.

B

Entrance Antiphon

Save us, O Lord our God,
and gather us from the nations,
to give thanks to your holy name
and make it our glory to praise you. Ps 106 (105): 47

COLLECT

O God, who have united many nations
in confessing your name,
grant us, we pray,
the grace to will and to do what you command,
that the people called to your Kingdom
may be one in the faith of their hearts
and the homage of their deeds.
Through our Lord Jesus Christ, your Son,
who lives and reigns with you
in the unity of the Holy Spirit,
one God, for ever and ever.

Or:

Attend with favor to the prayers of your people,
we ask, O Lord,
and grant that the hearts of believers
may be united in your praise and in repentance together,
so that, with division among Christians overcome,
we may hasten with joy to your eternal Kingdom
in the perfect communion of the Church.
Through our Lord Jesus Christ, your Son,
who lives and reigns with you
in the unity of the Holy Spirit,
one God, for ever and ever.

PRAYER AFTER COMMUNION

Pour out on us, O Lord, the Spirit of your love
and, in your kindness,
make those who believe in you
one in mind and heart
by the power of this sacrifice.
Through Christ our Lord.

C

Entrance Antiphon

One body and one Spirit,
as you were also called to the one hope of your call;
one Lord, one faith, one baptism;
one God and Father of all,
who is over all and through all and in us all. Eph 4: 4-6

COLLECT

Look with favor on your people, Lord, we pray,
and pour out upon them the gifts of your Spirit,
that they may grow constantly in love of the truth
and devote themselves with zeal
to perfect unity among Christians.
Through our Lord Jesus Christ, your Son,
who lives and reigns with you
in the unity of the Holy Spirit,
one God, for ever and ever.

Or:

Make known in us, O Lord,
the abundance of your mercy
and, in the power of your Spirit,
remove the divisions between Christians,
that your Church may appear more clearly
as a sign raised high among the nations
and that the world, enlightened by your Spirit,
may believe in the Christ whom you have sent.
Who lives and reigns with you
in the unity of the Holy Spirit,
one God, for ever and ever.

PRAYER AFTER COMMUNION

Receiving the Sacrament of your Christ,
we pray, O Lord, that you may renew in your Church
the sanctifying grace you have given
and that all who glory in the name of Christian
may come to serve you in unity of faith.
Through Christ our Lord.

18. For the Evangelization of Peoples

This Mass may be used even on Sundays of Ordinary Time, whenever there are special celebrations for the work of the missions, provided it does not occur on a Sunday of Advent, Lent or Easter, or on any Solemnity.

A

Entrance Antiphon

O God, be gracious and bless us,
and let your face shed its light upon us, and have mercy.
So will your ways be known upon earth
and all nations learn your salvation. Cf. Ps 67 (66): 2-3

COLLECT

O God, whose will it is that all should be saved
and come to the knowledge of the truth,
look upon your abundant harvest
and be pleased to send workers to gather it,
that the Gospel may be preached to all creation
and that your people, gathered by the word of life
and sustained by the power of the Sacraments,
may advance in the path of salvation and love.
Through our Lord Jesus Christ, your Son,
who lives and reigns with you
in the unity of the Holy Spirit,
one God, for ever and ever.

Or:

O God, who sent your Son into the world as the true light,
pour out, we pray, the Spirit he promised
to sow seeds of truth constantly in people's hearts
and to awaken in them obedience to the faith,
so that, being born to new life through Baptism,
all may become part of your one people.
Through our Lord Jesus Christ, your Son,
who lives and reigns with you
in the unity of the Holy Spirit,
one God, for ever and ever.

PRAYER AFTER COMMUNION

Nourished by these redeeming gifts,
we pray, O Lord,
that through this help to eternal salvation
true faith may ever increase.
Through Christ our Lord.

B

Entrance Antiphon

Tell among the nations his glory,
and his wonders among all the peoples,
for the Lord is great and highly to be praised. Ps 96 (95): 3-4

COLLECT

O God, you have willed that your Church
be the sacrament of salvation for all nations,
so that Christ's saving work
  may continue to the end of the ages;
stir up, we pray, the hearts of your faithful
and grant that they may feel a more urgent call
to work for the salvation of every creature,
so that from all the peoples on earth
one family and one people of your own
may arise and increase.
Through our Lord Jesus Christ, your Son,
who lives and reigns with you
  in the unity of the Holy Spirit,
one God, for ever and ever.

PRAYER AFTER COMMUNION

May our participation at your table sanctify us,
O Lord, we pray,
and grant that through the Sacrament of your Church
all nations may receive in rejoicing
the salvation accomplished on the Cross
by your Only Begotten Son.
Who lives and reigns for ever and ever.

19. For Persecuted Christians

Entrance Antiphon

Look to your covenant, O Lord,
and do not forget the life of your poor ones for ever.
Arise, O Lord, and defend your cause,
and forget not the cries of those who seek you!
Cf. Ps 74 (73): 20, 19, 22, 23

Or:

Peter thus was being kept in prison,
but prayer was made without ceasing
by the Church to God for him. Acts 12: 5

COLLECT

O God, who in your inscrutable providence
will that the Church be united
to the sufferings of your Son,
grant, we pray,
to your faithful who suffer for your name's sake
a spirit of patience and charity,
that they may be found true and faithful witnesses
to the promises you have made.
Through our Lord Jesus Christ, your Son,
who lives and reigns with you
in the unity of the Holy Spirit,
one God, for ever and ever.

PRAYER AFTER COMMUNION

By the power of this Sacrament, O Lord,
confirm your servants in the truth
and grant to your faithful who suffer tribulation
that, as they follow your Son in bearing their cross,
they may, in every trial, glory in the name of Christian.
Through Christ our Lord.

20. For a Spiritual or Pastoral Gathering

Entrance Antiphon

Thus says the Lord:
Where two or three are gathered together in my name,
there am I in the midst of them. Cf. Mt 18: 19, 20

Or:

And over all things put on love,
which is the bond of perfection.
And let the peace of Christ rule in your hearts,
the peace into which you were also called in one body.
Col 3: 14-15

COLLECT

Pour out on us, O Lord, we pray,
a spirit of truth, understanding and peace,
that we may know with all our hearts
what is pleasing to you
and, with one accord,
pursue what we have come to know.
Through our Lord Jesus Christ, your Son,
who lives and reigns with you
in the unity of the Holy Spirit,
one God, for ever and ever.

Or:

O God, whose Son promised
to all those gathered in his name
that he would be there in their midst,
grant, we pray,
that we may be aware of his presence among us
and, in truth and charity, experience in our hearts
an abundance of grace, mercy and peace.
Through our Lord Jesus Christ, your Son,
who lives and reigns with you
in the unity of the Holy Spirit,
one God, for ever and ever.

PRAYER AFTER COMMUNION

Grant us, O merciful God,
that the holy gifts we have received
may confirm us in our resolve to do your will
and make us everywhere witnesses to your truth.
Through Christ our Lord.

II. FOR CIVIL NEEDS

21. For the Nation or State

COLLECT

O God, who arrange all things
according to a wonderful design,
graciously receive the prayers
we pour out to you for our country (state),
that, through the wisdom of its leaders
and the integrity of its citizens,
harmony and justice may be assured
and lasting prosperity come with peace.
Through our Lord Jesus Christ, your Son,
who lives and reigns with you
in the unity of the Holy Spirit,
one God, for ever and ever.

22. For Those in Public Office

COLLECT

Almighty ever-living God,
in whose hand lies every human heart
and the rights of peoples,
look with favor, we pray,
on those who govern with authority over us,
that throughout the whole world
the prosperity of peoples,
the assurance of peace,
and freedom of religion
may through your gift be made secure.
Through our Lord Jesus Christ, your Son,
who lives and reigns with you
in the unity of the Holy Spirit,
one God, for ever and ever.

23. For a Governing Assembly

COLLECT

O God, who arrange all things in wondrous order
and govern in marvelous ways,
look with favor on the assembled, for whom we now pray,
and mercifully pour out upon them
the spirit of your wisdom,
that they may decide everything for the well-being and peace of all
and may never turn aside from your will.
Through our Lord Jesus Christ, your Son,
who lives and reigns with you
in the unity of the Holy Spirit,
one God, for ever and ever.

24. For the Head of State or Ruler

COLLECT

O God, to whom every human power is subject,
grant to your servant (our president, sovereign) N.
success in the exercise of his (her) high office,
so that, always revering you and striving to please you,
he (she) may constantly secure and preserve
for the people entrusted to his (her) care
the freedom that comes from civil peace.
Through our Lord Jesus Christ, your Son,
who lives and reigns with you
in the unity of the Holy Spirit,
one God, for ever and ever.

25. At the Beginning of the Civil Year

This Mass may not be used on the Solemnity of Mary, the Holy Mother of God, on January 1.

Entrance Antiphon

You crown the year with your bounty,
and abundance flows in your pathways. Cf. Ps 65 (64): 12

Or:

Behold, I am with you always, says the Lord,
even to the end of the age. Mt 28: 20

COLLECT

O God, who are without beginning or end,
the source of all creation,
grant us so to live this new year,
whose beginning we dedicate to you,
that we may abound in good things
and be resplendent with works of holiness.
Through our Lord Jesus Christ, your Son,
who lives and reigns with you
in the unity of the Holy Spirit,
one God, for ever and ever.

PRAYER AFTER COMMUNION

O Lord, draw near to the peoples
who have known the sacred mysteries,
that throughout this year no dangers may afflict
those who always trust in your protection.
Through Christ our Lord.

26. For the Sanctification of Human Labor

A

Entrance Antiphon

In the beginning, when God created the heavens and the earth,
God created man in his image;
God looked at everything he had made,
and he found it very good. Gn 1: 1, 27, 31

Or:

May your favor, O Lord, be upon us,
and may you give success to the work of our hands.
Cf. Ps 90 (89): 17

COLLECT

O God, Creator of all things,
who have commanded the human race
to bear the burden of labor,
grant that the work we are beginning
may bring progress in this life
and, by your favor,
advance the spread of the Kingdom of Christ.
Who lives and reigns with you
in the unity of the Holy Spirit,
one God, for ever and ever.

Or:

O God, who through human labor
never cease to perfect and govern
the vast work of creation,
listen to the supplications of your people
and grant that all men and women
may find work that befits their dignity,
joins them more closely to one another
and enables them to serve their neighbor.
Through our Lord Jesus Christ, your Son,
who lives and reigns with you
in the unity of the Holy Spirit,
one God, for ever and ever.

Other Prayers, p. 638.

PRAYER AFTER COMMUNION

Having been made partakers of this table
of unity and charity,
we beseech your mercy, Lord,
that through the work you have given us to do
we may sustain our life on earth
and trustingly build up your Kingdom.
Through Christ our Lord.

B

Other Prayers

COLLECT

O God, who willed to subject
the forces of nature to human labor,
mercifully grant
that, undertaking in a Christian spirit what we are to do,
we may merit to join our brothers and sisters
in practicing sincere charity
and in advancing the fulfillment
of your divine work of creation.
Through our Lord Jesus Christ, your Son,
who lives and reigns with you
in the unity of the Holy Spirit,
one God, for ever and ever.

PRAYER AFTER COMMUNION

Govern with temporal assistance, we pray, O Lord,
those you graciously renew with these eternal mysteries.
Through Christ our Lord.

27. At Seedtime

A

Entrance Antiphon

May your favor, O Lord, be upon us,
and may you give success to the work of our hands.
Cf. Ps 90 (89): 17

COLLECT

O God, by whose help we sow seeds in the earth
that will grow by the effect of your power,
grant that what we know to be lacking in our labors
may be supplied abundantly by you,
for you alone give increase.
Through our Lord Jesus Christ, your Son,
who lives and reigns with you
in the unity of the Holy Spirit,
one God, for ever and ever.

Other Prayers, p. 639.

PRAYER AFTER COMMUNION

O Lord, who renew us with your Sacraments,
assist, we pray, the work of our hands,
so that we, who live and move and have our being in you,
may, through your blessing of the seeds of the earth,
be fed by abundant crops.
Through Christ our Lord.

B
Other Prayers

COLLECT

Pour out your gracious blessing on your people, Lord God,
so that through your generosity
our land may yield its fruits
for us to enjoy with ever-grateful hearts,
to the honor of your holy name.
Through our Lord Jesus Christ, your Son,
who lives and reigns with you
in the unity of the Holy Spirit,
one God, for ever and ever.

PRAYER AFTER COMMUNION

Grant to your faithful, almighty God,
abundance of the earth's fruits,
that, nourished by these in the present age,
they may also grow in spiritual things
and so obtain the good things of eternity,
of which they have received a pledge in this Sacrament.
Through Christ our Lord.

28. After the Harvest

Entrance Antiphon

The earth has yielded its fruit;
may God, our God, bless us. Ps 67 (66): 7

COLLECT

O Lord, good Father, who in your providence
have entrusted the earth to the human race,
grant, we pray, that with the fruits harvested from it
we may be able to sustain life
and, with your help, always use them
to promote your praise and the well-being of all.
Through our Lord Jesus Christ, your Son,
who lives and reigns with you
in the unity of the Holy Spirit,
one God, for ever and ever.

Or:

We give you thanks, O Lord,
for the fruits that earth has given
to benefit the human family
and we pray
that, as the working of your supreme providence
has produced them,
so you may cause the seed of justice
and the fruits of charity
to spring up in our hearts.
Through our Lord Jesus Christ, your Son,
who lives and reigns with you
in the unity of the Holy Spirit,
one God, for ever and ever.

PRAYER AFTER COMMUNION

Grant, we pray, O Lord,
that, as we give you thanks in this saving mystery
for the crops harvested from the earth,
we may, through the same mystery working within us,
be worthy to receive still greater blessings.
Through Christ our Lord.

29. For the Progress of Peoples

Entrance Antiphon

When a person who has worldly means
sees a brother in need and refuses him compassion,
how can the love of God remain in him? 1 Jn 3: 17

COLLECT

O God, who gave one origin to all peoples
and willed to gather from them one family for yourself,
fill all hearts, we pray, with the fire of your love
and kindle in them a desire
for the just advancement of their neighbor,
that, through the good things
which you richly bestow upon all,
each human person may be brought to perfection,
every division may be removed,
and equity and justice may be established
in human society.
Through our Lord Jesus Christ, your Son,
who lives and reigns with you
in the unity of the Holy Spirit,
one God, for ever and ever.

PRAYER AFTER COMMUNION

Having been fed with the one Bread
by which you constantly renew the human family,
we pray, O Lord,
that from participation in this Sacrament of unity
we may draw a love strong and pure
to help peoples in their development
and, prompted by charity, to fulfill what justice requires.
Through Christ our Lord.

30. For the Preservation of Peace and Justice

This Mass may not be used on the Solemnity of Mary, the Holy Mother of God, on January 1.

A

Entrance Antiphon

Give peace, O Lord, to those who wait for you;
hear the prayers of your servants
and guide us in the way of justice. Cf. Sir 36: 18, 19

COLLECT

O God, who have revealed
that peacemakers are to be called your children,
grant, we pray,
that we may work without ceasing to establish that justice
which alone ensures true and lasting peace.
Through our Lord Jesus Christ, your Son,
who lives and reigns with you
in the unity of the Holy Spirit,
one God, for ever and ever.

Or:

O God, who show a father's care for all,
grant, in your mercy,
that the members of the human race,
to whom you have given a single origin,
may form in peace a single family
and always be united by a fraternal spirit.
Through our Lord Jesus Christ, your Son,
who lives and reigns with you
in the unity of the Holy Spirit,
one God, for ever and ever.

Other Prayers, p. 643.

PRAYER AFTER COMMUNION

Bestow on us, we pray, O Lord, the spirit of charity,
so that, sustained by the Body and Blood
of your Only Begotten Son,
we may be effective in nurturing among all
the peace that he has left us.
Who lives and reigns for ever and ever.

B

Other Prayers for Peace

COLLECT

**O God, Creator of the world,
under whose governance
the design for all the ages unfolds,
be attentive, we pray, to our petitions
and grant to our times tranquility and peace,
that we may exult with unceasing joy
in praise of your great mercy.
Through our Lord Jesus Christ, your Son,
who lives and reigns with you
in the unity of the Holy Spirit,
one God, for ever and ever.**

Or:

**O God of peace, who are peace itself
and whom a spirit of discord cannot grasp,
nor a violent mind receive,
grant that those who are one in heart
may persevere in what is good
and that those in conflict
may forget evil and so be healed.
Through our Lord Jesus Christ, your Son,
who lives and reigns with you
in the unity of the Holy Spirit,
one God, for ever and ever.**

The Mass for Promoting Harmony, p. 625, may also be used.

31. In Time of War or Civil Disturbance

Entrance Antiphon

The Lord said: I think thoughts of peace and not of affliction.
You will call upon me, and I will answer you,
and I will lead back your captives from every place.
Jer 29: 11-12, 14

Or:

The waves of death rose about me;
the pains of the netherworld surrounded me.
In my anguish I called to the Lord,
and from his holy temple he heard my voice. Cf. Ps 18 (17): 5-7

COLLECT

O God, merciful and strong,
who crush wars and cast down the proud,
be pleased to banish violence swiftly from our midst
and to wipe away all tears,
so that we may all truly deserve to be called your children.
Through our Lord Jesus Christ, your Son,
who lives and reigns with you
in the unity of the Holy Spirit,
one God, for ever and ever.

Or:

O God, author and lover of peace,
to know you is to live, to serve you is to reign;
defend against every attack those who cry to you,
so that we, who trust in your protection,
may not fear the weapons of any foe.
Through our Lord Jesus Christ, your Son,
who lives and reigns with you
in the unity of the Holy Spirit,
one God, for ever and ever.

PRAYER AFTER COMMUNION

Grant to us, O Lord,
that, nourished with the delights of the one Bread
that fortifies the human heart,
we may successfully overcome the fury of war
and resolutely keep your law of love and justice.
Through Christ our Lord.

32. For Refugees and Exiles

Entrance Antiphon

For you has God commanded his angels
to keep you in all your ways. Ps 91 (90): 11

Or:

The Lord said: I think thoughts of peace and not of affliction.
You will call upon me, and I will answer you,
and I will lead back your captives from every place.
Jer 29: 11-12, 14

COLLECT

O Lord, to whom no one is a stranger
and from whose help no one is ever distant,
look with compassion on refugees and exiles,
on segregated persons and on lost children;
restore them, we pray, to a homeland,
and give us a kind heart for the needy and for strangers.
Through our Lord Jesus Christ, your Son,
who lives and reigns with you
in the unity of the Holy Spirit,
one God, for ever and ever.

PRAYER AFTER COMMUNION

O Lord, who have renewed us
with the one Bread and the one Chalice,
grant that in sincerity of heart
we may show true compassion
toward strangers and the abandoned
and that all of us may deserve
to be gathered together at last
in the land of the living.
Through Christ our Lord.

33. In Time of Famine or for Those Suffering Hunger

A

Entrance Antiphon

Look to your covenant, O Lord,
and forget not the life of your poor ones for ever.
Ps 74 (73): 20, 19

COLLECT

O God, who, being both good and almighty,
provide for all creatures,
give us, we pray, an effective love
for our brothers and sisters who suffer hunger,
so that famine may be banished
and that they may have strength to serve you
with free and untroubled hearts.
Through our Lord Jesus Christ, your Son,
who lives and reigns with you
in the unity of the Holy Spirit,
one God, for ever and ever.

Other Prayers, to Be Said by Those Suffering Hunger, p. 647.

PRAYER AFTER COMMUNION

O God, almighty Father,
we humbly ask you that the living Bread,
which has come down from heaven,
may give us strength
to relieve our brothers and sisters in their need.
Through Christ our Lord.

B

Other Prayers, to Be Said by Those Suffering Hunger

COLLECT

O God, who did not create death
and who provide food for all living things,
drive out, in your compassion,
the hunger of your servants,
that our hearts may serve you
with greater readiness and joy.
Through our Lord Jesus Christ, your Son,
who lives and reigns with you
in the unity of the Holy Spirit,
one God, for ever and ever.

PRAYER AFTER COMMUNION

Having received the Bread of heaven
from your abundance, O Lord,
we pray that it may give us
such hope and strength for our labor,
that we may provide effectively for our own needs
and for those of our brothers and sisters.
Through Christ our Lord.

34. In Time of Earthquake

COLLECT

O God, who set the earth on its firm foundation,
spare those who are fearful
and show favor to those who implore you,
so that, with all dangers of earthquake entirely gone,
we may continue to experience your mercy
and serve you in thankfulness,
safe under your protection.
Through our Lord Jesus Christ, your Son,
who lives and reigns with you
in the unity of the Holy Spirit,
one God, for ever and ever.

35. For Rain

COLLECT

O God, in whom we live and move and have our being,
grant us sufficient rain,
so that, being supplied with what sustains us
in this present life,
we may seek more confidently
what sustains us for eternity.
Through our Lord Jesus Christ, your Son,
who lives and reigns with you
in the unity of the Holy Spirit,
one God, for ever and ever.

36. For Fine Weather

COLLECT

Almighty ever-living God,
who heal us through correction
and save us by your forgiveness,
grant to those who seek your favor
that we may rejoice at the good weather
for which we hope
and always use what in your goodness you bestow
for the glory of your name and for our well-being.
Through our Lord Jesus Christ, your Son,
who lives and reigns with you
in the unity of the Holy Spirit,
one God, for ever and ever.

37. For an End to Storms

COLLECT

O God, to whose commands
all the elements give obedience,
we humbly entreat you,
that the stilling of fearsome storms
may turn a powerful menace
into an occasion for us to praise you.
Through our Lord Jesus Christ, your Son,
who lives and reigns with you
in the unity of the Holy Spirit,
one God, for ever and ever.

III. FOR VARIOUS OCCASIONS

38. For the Forgiveness of Sins

A

Entrance Antiphon

You have mercy on all, O Lord,
and despise nothing that you have made.
You overlook people's sins,
to bring them to repentance,
and you spare them, for you are the Lord our God.
Cf. Wis 11: 23, 24, 26

COLLECT

Graciously hear the prayers of those who call upon you,
we ask, O Lord,
and forgive the sins of those who confess to you,
granting us in your kindness both pardon and peace.
Through our Lord Jesus Christ, your Son,
who lives and reigns with you
  in the unity of the Holy Spirit,
one God, for ever and ever.

Or:

Be merciful to your people, O Lord,
and absolve them from all sins,
so that what we deserve by our offenses
may be avoided by your pardon.
Through our Lord Jesus Christ, your Son,
who lives and reigns with you
  in the unity of the Holy Spirit,
one God, for ever and ever.

Other Prayers, p. 650.

PRAYER AFTER COMMUNION

Grant us, merciful God,
that, receiving in this gift the forgiveness of sins,
we may be able by your grace
to avoid sinning from now on
and to serve you in sincerity of heart.
Through Christ our Lord.

B

Other Prayers

COLLECT

Almighty and most gentle God,
who brought forth from the rock
a fountain of living water for your thirsty people,
bring forth, we pray,
from the hardness of our heart, tears of sorrow,
that we may lament our sins
and merit forgiveness from your mercy.
Through our Lord Jesus Christ, your Son,
who lives and reigns with you
in the unity of the Holy Spirit,
one God, for ever and ever.

PRAYER AFTER COMMUNION

May the reverent reception of your Sacrament, O Lord,
lead us to wash away the stains of our sins
with sighs and tears,
and in your generosity
grant that the pardon we seek may have its effect on us.
Through Christ our Lord.

39. For Chastity

COLLECT

Purify our hearts, O Lord,
by the heavenly fire of the Holy Spirit,
that we may serve you with a chaste body
and please you with a pure heart.
Through our Lord Jesus Christ, your Son,
who lives and reigns with you
in the unity of the Holy Spirit,
one God, for ever and ever.

PRAYER AFTER COMMUNION

Through the Sacraments we have received, O Lord,
may our heart and our body flourish anew
by a keen sense of modesty and renewed chastity,
so that what has passed our lips as food
we may possess in purity of heart.
Through Christ our Lord.

40. For Charity

Entrance Antiphon

Thus says the Lord:
I will take from your bodies your stony hearts
and give you natural hearts.
I will put my spirit within you.
You will be my people, and I will be your God. Ez 36: 26-28

COLLECT

Set our hearts aflame, O Lord,
with the Spirit of your charity, we pray,
that we may always think thoughts
worthy and pleasing to your majesty
and love you sincerely in our brothers and sisters.
Through our Lord Jesus Christ, your Son,
who lives and reigns with you
in the unity of the Holy Spirit,
one God, for ever and ever.

PRAYER AFTER COMMUNION

Pour out the grace of the Holy Spirit, O Lord,
on those you have replenished
with the one Bread of heaven
and refresh us, we pray,
with the delights of perfect charity.
Through Christ our Lord.

41. For Relatives and Friends

Entrance Antiphon

For the peace of Jerusalem pray,
and may they prosper, those who love you.
For the sake of my family and friends,
I will say: Peace be upon you. Cf. Ps 122 (121): 6, 8

COLLECT

O God, who by the grace of the Holy Spirit
have filled the hearts of your faithful with gifts of charity,
grant health of mind and body to your servants,
for whom we beseech your mercy,
that they may love you with all their strength
and, with all their love, do what is pleasing to you.
Through our Lord Jesus Christ, your Son,
who lives and reigns with you
in the unity of the Holy Spirit,
one God, for ever and ever.

PRAYER AFTER COMMUNION

We ask you, Lord, as we receive the divine mysteries:
grant your servants,
to whom you have given a love for us,
pardon for sins,
consolation in this life
and unfailing guidance,
that all of us, united in your service,
may rejoice together before your face.
Through Christ our Lord.

42. For Our Oppressors

Entrance Antiphon

Love your enemies, says the Lord.
Do good to those who hate you,
bless those who curse you,
pray for those who mistreat you. Lk 6: 27-28

COLLECT

O God, who have laid down by your precept of charity
that we should sincerely love those who afflict us,
grant that we may follow the commands of the New Law,
striving to return good for evil
and bearing one another's burdens.
Through our Lord Jesus Christ, your Son,
who lives and reigns with you
in the unity of the Holy Spirit,
one God, for ever and ever.

PRAYER AFTER COMMUNION

Through these mysteries of our peace,
grant, O God, that we may live in harmony with all
and bring those who are against us
to find favor with you and be reconciled to us.
Through Christ our Lord.

43. For Those Held in Captivity

Entrance Antiphon

O Lord and God of my salvation,
I have cried before you day and night.
Let my prayer come into your presence.
Incline your ear to my cry. Ps 88 (87): 2-3

COLLECT

O God, whose Son humbled himself
and took the form of a slave
to redeem the human race from being captive to sin,
grant to your servants held in confinement
that they may obtain the freedom you destine to all,
for we are your sons and daughters.
Through our Lord Jesus Christ, your Son,
who lives and reigns with you
in the unity of the Holy Spirit,
one God, for ever and ever.

PRAYER AFTER COMMUNION

Mindful of the price paid for our deliverance,
we implore your mercy, O Lord,
upon our brothers and sisters,
that they may be released from captivity
and become servants of your justice.
Through Christ our Lord.

44. For Those in Prison

COLLECT

Almighty and merciful God,
to whom alone the secrets of the heart lie open,
who recognize the just and make righteous the guilty,
hear our prayers for your servants held in prison,
and grant that through patience and hope
they may find relief in their affliction
and soon return unhindered to their own.
Through our Lord Jesus Christ, your Son,
who lives and reigns with you
in the unity of the Holy Spirit,
one God, for ever and ever.

For those imprisoned for the sake of the Gospel, the prayers For Persecuted Christians may be used, p. 632.

45. For the Sick

Entrance Antiphon

Have mercy on me, Lord, for I languish;
Lord, heal me; my bones are trembling,
and my soul is greatly shaken. Ps 6: 3-4

Or:

Truly the Lord has borne our infirmities,
and he has carried our sorrows. Cf. Is 53: 4

COLLECT

O God, who willed that our infirmities
be borne by your Only Begotten Son
to show the value of human suffering,
listen in kindness to our prayers
for our brothers and sisters who are sick;
grant that all who are oppressed
by pain, distress or other afflictions
may know that they are chosen
among those proclaimed blessed
and are united to Christ
in his suffering for the salvation of the world.
Through our Lord Jesus Christ, your Son,
who lives and reigns with you
in the unity of the Holy Spirit,
one God, for ever and ever.

Or:

Almighty ever-living God, eternal health of believers,
hear our prayers for your servants who are sick:
grant them, we implore you, your merciful help,
so that, with their health restored,
they may give you thanks in the midst of your Church.
Through our Lord Jesus Christ, your Son,
who lives and reigns with you
in the unity of the Holy Spirit,
one God, for ever and ever.

PRAYER AFTER COMMUNION

O God, only support of our human weakness,
show the power of your protection
over your servants who are sick,
that, sustained by your merciful help,
they may be restored to your holy Church in good health.
Through Christ our Lord.

46. For the Dying

Entrance Antiphon

No one lives for himself, and no one dies for himself.
For if we live, we live for the Lord,
and if we die, we die for the Lord;
so then, whether we live or die, we are the Lord's. Rom 14: 7-8

Or:

Truly the Lord has borne our infirmities,
and he has carried our sorrows. Cf. Is 53: 4

COLLECT

Almighty and merciful God,
who through the fact of death itself
have mercifully unlocked for the human race
the gate to eternal life,
look kindly on your servant in his (her) final struggle,
so that, united to your Son's Passion
and sealed with his Blood,
he (she) may come without blemish into your presence.
Through our Lord Jesus Christ, your Son,
who lives and reigns with you
in the unity of the Holy Spirit,
one God, for ever and ever.

Or, for those who will die today:

Almighty and merciful God,
who show your love to all creatures everywhere,
hear graciously the prayers we make
for those who will die today,
that, redeemed by your Son's Precious Blood,
they may leave this world without stain of sin
and find eternal rest in the embrace of your mercy.
Through our Lord Jesus Christ, your Son,
who lives and reigns with you
in the unity of the Holy Spirit,
one God, for ever and ever.

PRAYER AFTER COMMUNION

By the power of this Sacrament, O Lord,
be pleased to sustain your servant
with your merciful grace,
that at the hour of death
he (she) may not see the enemy prevail against him (her)
but may be worthy to pass over to life eternal
in the company of your Angels.
Through Christ our Lord.

47. For the Grace of a Happy Death

Entrance Antiphon

Though I should walk in the valley of the shadow of death,
no evil will I fear, for you are with me, Lord, my God.
Your crook and your staff have given me comfort. Ps 23 (22): 4

COLLECT

O God, who have created us in your image
and willed that your Son
should undergo death for our sake,
grant that those who call upon you
may be watchful in prayer at all times,
so that we may leave this world without stain of sin
and may merit to rest with joy in your merciful embrace.
Through our Lord Jesus Christ, your Son,
who lives and reigns with you
in the unity of the Holy Spirit,
one God, for ever and ever.

PRAYER AFTER COMMUNION

Having received the pledge of immortality
through these mysteries, O Lord,
we humbly entreat your fatherly help
for the moment when we depart in death,
so that, overcoming the snares of the enemy,
we may be restored to life
in the embrace of your eternal glory.
Through Christ our Lord.

48. In Any Need

A

Entrance Antiphon

I am the salvation of the people, says the Lord.
Should they cry to me in any distress,
I will hear them, and I will be their Lord for ever.

COLLECT

O God, our refuge in trials,
our strength in sickness, our comfort in sorrow,
spare your people, we pray,
that, though rightly chastised now by affliction,
they may find relief at last through your loving mercy.
Through our Lord Jesus Christ, your Son,
who lives and reigns with you
in the unity of the Holy Spirit,
one God, for ever and ever.

PRAYER AFTER COMMUNION

We pray, O Lord, that in receiving your Sacrament
we may experience help in mind and body,
so that, kept safe in both,
we may glory in the fullness of heavenly healing.
Through Christ our Lord.

B

Entrance Antiphon

Arise, O Lord, come to our help;
redeem us with your merciful love. Cf. Ps 44 (43): 26

COLLECT

Almighty and merciful God,
look with compassion on our affliction,
and so lighten your children's burden
and confirm their faith,
that they may always trust without hesitation
in your fatherly providence.
Through our Lord Jesus Christ, your Son,
who lives and reigns with you
in the unity of the Holy Spirit,
one God, for ever and ever.

PRAYER AFTER COMMUNION

We humbly entreat you, Lord,
that, nourished and fortified by this divine banquet,
we may have strength to face future trials with fortitude
and to lend more generous help
to our brothers and sisters in time of trouble.
Through Christ our Lord.

C

Other Prayers

COLLECT

O God, who know that because of human frailty
we cannot stand firm amid such great dangers,
grant us health of mind and body,
that what we suffer for our sins
we may overcome with your help.
Through our Lord Jesus Christ, your Son,
who lives and reigns with you
  in the unity of the Holy Spirit,
one God, for ever and ever.

Or:

Grant, we pray, O Lord,
that your people may avoid the contagion of the devil
and follow you, the only God, in purity of heart.
Through our Lord Jesus Christ, your Son,
who lives and reigns with you
  in the unity of the Holy Spirit,
one God, for ever and ever.

PRAYER AFTER COMMUNION

Look with pity on our tribulation, O Lord, we pray,
and, though our sins deserve your anger,
mercifully turn it away from us
through the Passion of your Son.
Who lives and reigns for ever and ever.

[In the Dioceses of the United States]

48/1. For Giving Thanks to God for the Gift of Human Life

A

Entrance Antiphon

For the sake of your name, O Lord, give me life.

Cf. Ps 143 (142): 11

COLLECT

God our Creator,
we give thanks to you,
who alone have the power to impart the breath of life
as you form each of us in our mother's womb;
grant, we pray,
that we, whom you have made stewards of creation,
may remain faithful to this sacred trust
and constant in safeguarding the dignity
of every human life.
Through our Lord Jesus Christ, your Son,
who lives and reigns with you
in the unity of the Holy Spirit,
one God, for ever and ever.

PRAYER AFTER COMMUNION

Increase your love within us, Lord God,
by the saving mysteries we have celebrated,
and bring people everywhere
to respect your gift of human life.
Through Christ our Lord.

B

Entrance Antiphon

I trust in you, O Lord; I say, you are my God.
My life is in your hands. Cf. Ps 31 (30): 15-16

COLLECT

O God, who adorn creation with splendor and beauty
and fashion human lives in your image and likeness,
awaken in every heart
reverence for the work of your hands,
and renew among your people
a readiness to nurture and sustain
your precious gift of human life.
Through our Lord Jesus Christ, your Son,
who lives and reigns with you
in the unity of the Holy Spirit,
one God, for ever and ever.

PRAYER AFTER COMMUNION

Confirm our resolve, O God,
by the life-giving Body and Blood of your Son,
that we may live always for others
and cherish your sacred gift of human life.
Through Christ our Lord.

49. For Giving Thanks to God

A

Entrance Antiphon

**Sing and make music to the Lord in your hearts,
always thanking God the Father for all things
in the name of our Lord Jesus Christ.** Eph 5: 19-20

COLLECT

**O God, who always listen mercifully
to your servants in distress,
we humbly beseech you,
as we give thanks for your kindness,
that, free from all evil,
we may constantly serve you in gladness.
Through our Lord Jesus Christ, your Son,
who lives and reigns with you
in the unity of the Holy Spirit,
one God, for ever and ever.**

Other Prayers, p. 663.

PRAYER AFTER COMMUNION

**Almighty God, who through this Bread of Life
are pleased to free your servants from the bond of sin
and in your compassion to restore their strength,
grant us to advance without hindrance
towards the hope of glory.
Through Christ our Lord.**

B

Other Prayers

COLLECT

O God, the Father of every gift,
we confess that all we have and are
comes down from you;
teach us to recognize the effects of your boundless care
and to love you with a sincere heart
and with all our strength.
Through our Lord Jesus Christ, your Son,
who lives and reigns with you
in the unity of the Holy Spirit,
one God, for ever and ever.

PRAYER AFTER COMMUNION

O God, who have given to us as spiritual food
the saving Sacrament of your Son,
which we have offered you in thanksgiving,
grant that, being strengthened by gifts of courage and joy,
we may serve you more devotedly
and be worthy of still further blessings.
Through Christ our Lord.

VOTIVE MASSES

If some serious pastoral benefit is to be gained, an appropriately corresponding Votive Mass may be used, at the direction of the Ordinary, or with his permission, except on Solemnities, on the Sundays of Advent, Lent, and Easter, on days within the Octave of Easter, on the Commemoration of All the Faithful Departed (All Souls' Day), on Ash Wednesday, and on the weekdays of Holy Week.

Votive Masses are in principle forbidden on days on which there occurs an Obligatory Memorial, on a weekday of Advent up to and including December 16, on a weekday of Christmas Time from January 2, or on a weekday of Easter Time after the Octave of Easter. However, for pastoral reasons, as determined by the rector of the church or the Priest Celebrant himself, an appropriately corresponding Votive Mass may be used in celebration of Mass with the people.

On weekdays in Ordinary Time, even if an Optional Memorial occurs, a Votive Mass may be chosen by the Priest Celebrant for the sake of the devotion of the faithful.

1. THE MOST HOLY TRINITY

In this Mass, the color white is used.

Entrance Antiphon

Blest be God the Father, and the Only Begotten Son of God,
and also the Holy Spirit, for he has shown us his merciful love.

COLLECT

God our Father, who, by sending into the world
the Word of truth and the Spirit of sanctification,
made known to the human race your wondrous mystery,
grant us, we pray, that in professing the true faith
we may acknowledge the Trinity of eternal glory
and adore your Unity, powerful in majesty.
Through our Lord Jesus Christ, your Son,
who lives and reigns with you
in the unity of the Holy Spirit,
one God, for ever and ever.

PRAYER AFTER COMMUNION

May receiving this Sacrament, O Lord our God,
bring us health of body and soul,
as we confess your eternal holy Trinity
and undivided Unity.
Through Christ our Lord.

2. THE MERCY OF GOD

In this Mass, the color white is used. This Mass may not be said on the Second Sunday of Easter.

Entrance Antiphon

God has loved us with an everlasting love;
he sent his Only Begotten Son as an expiation for our sins
and not for our sins alone, but for those of all the world.
Cf. Jer 31: 3; 1 Jn 2: 2

Or:

I will sing for ever of your mercies, O Lord;
through all ages my mouth will proclaim your fidelity.
Ps 89 (88): 2

COLLECT

O God, whose mercies are without number
and whose treasure of goodness is infinite,
graciously increase the faith
of the people consecrated to you,
that all may grasp and rightly understand
by whose love they have been created,
through whose Blood they have been redeemed,
and by whose Spirit they have been reborn.
Through our Lord Jesus Christ, your Son,
who lives and reigns with you
in the unity of the Holy Spirit,
one God, for ever and ever.

PRAYER AFTER COMMUNION

Grant to us, O merciful God,
that, nourished by the Body and Blood of your Son,
we may draw confidently from the wellsprings of mercy
and show ourselves ever more compassionate
towards our brothers and sisters.
Through Christ our Lord.

3. OUR LORD JESUS CHRIST, THE ETERNAL HIGH PRIEST

In this Mass, the color white is used.

Entrance Antiphon

The Lord has sworn an oath he will not change:
You are a priest for ever,
according to the order of Melchizedek. Ps 110 (109): 4

COLLECT

O God, who for your glory
and the salvation of the human race
willed to establish Christ as the eternal High Priest,
grant that the people he has gained for you by his Blood
may, through their participation in his memorial,
experience the power of his Cross and Resurrection.
Who lives and reigns with you
in the unity of the Holy Spirit,
one God, for ever and ever.

PRAYER AFTER COMMUNION

We pray, O Lord,
that through our partaking in this sacrifice,
which your Son commanded to be offered in his memory,
you may make us together with him
an everlasting oblation to you.
Through Christ our Lord.

4. THE MYSTERY OF THE HOLY CROSS

In this Mass, the color red is used.

Entrance Antiphon

We should glory in the Cross of our Lord Jesus Christ,
in whom is our salvation, life and resurrection,
through whom we are saved and delivered. Cf. Gal 6: 14

COLLECT

O God, who willed that your Only Begotten Son
should undergo the Cross to save the human race,
grant, we pray,
that we, who have known his mystery on earth,
may merit the grace of his redemption in heaven.
Through our Lord Jesus Christ, your Son,
who lives and reigns with you
in the unity of the Holy Spirit,
one God, for ever and ever.

PRAYER AFTER COMMUNION

Having been nourished by your holy banquet,
we beseech you, Lord Jesus Christ,
to bring those you have redeemed
by the wood of your life-giving Cross
to the glory of the resurrection.
Who live and reign for ever and ever.

5. THE MOST HOLY EUCHARIST

In this Mass, the color white is used.

Entrance Antiphon

The Lord opened the gates of heaven,
and rained down manna upon them to eat,
and gave them bread from heaven:
man ate the bread of angels. Ps 78 (77): 23-25

COLLECT

O God, who have accomplished the work
of human redemption
through the Paschal Mystery of your Only Begotten Son,
graciously grant that we, who confidently proclaim,
under sacramental signs,
the Death and Resurrection of Christ,
may experience continued increase of your saving grace.
Through our Lord Jesus Christ, your Son,
who lives and reigns with you
in the unity of the Holy Spirit,
one God, for ever and ever.

PRAYER AFTER COMMUNION

May sharing at the heavenly table
sanctify us, Lord, we pray,
so that through the Body and Blood of Christ
the whole family of believers may be bound together.
Through Christ our Lord.

As a Votive Mass of the Most Holy Eucharist, the Votive Mass of our Lord Jesus Christ, the Eternal High Priest may also be used, pp. 668-669; or the Mass of the Solemnity of the Most Holy Body and Blood of Christ, p. 286.

6. THE MOST HOLY NAME OF JESUS

In this Mass, the color white is used.

Entrance Antiphon

At the name of Jesus every knee should bend,
of those in heaven and on earth and under the earth,
and every tongue confess
that Jesus Christ is Lord, to the glory of God the Father.
Phil 2: 10-11

COLLECT

As we venerate the most holy Name of Jesus,
mercifully grant us, Lord,
that, savoring its sweetness in this life,
we may be filled with everlasting joy
in our heavenly homeland.
Through our Lord Jesus Christ, your Son,
who lives and reigns with you
in the unity of the Holy Spirit,
one God, for ever and ever.

PRAYER AFTER COMMUNION

Grant us in your mercy, O Lord, we pray,
that in these sacred mysteries
we may do worthy homage to the Lord Jesus,
for it is your will that at his Name
every knee should bend
and in him all people find salvation.
Who lives and reigns for ever and ever.

7. THE MOST PRECIOUS BLOOD OF OUR LORD JESUS CHRIST

In this Mass, the color red is used.

Entrance Antiphon

You have redeemed us, Lord, by your Blood,
from every tribe and tongue and people and nation,
and have made us into a kingdom for our God. Cf. Rev 5: 9-10

COLLECT

O God, who by the Precious Blood
of your Only Begotten Son
have redeemed the whole world,
preserve in us the work of your mercy,
so that, ever honoring the mystery of our salvation,
we may merit to obtain its fruits.
Through our Lord Jesus Christ, your Son,
who lives and reigns with you
in the unity of the Holy Spirit,
one God, for ever and ever.

PRAYER AFTER COMMUNION

Refreshed, O Lord, by this saving food and drink,
we pray that we may always be bathed
in the Blood of our Savior,
so that it may become for us
a spring of water welling up to eternal life.
Through Christ our Lord.

Or:

Restored with heavenly food and drink,
we beseech you, almighty God,
to protect from fear of their enemies
those you have redeemed
by the Precious Blood of your Son.
Who lives and reigns for ever and ever.

8. THE MOST SACRED HEART OF JESUS

In this Mass, the color white is used.

Entrance Antiphon

The designs of his Heart are from age to age,
to rescue their souls from death
and to keep them alive in famine. Ps 33 (32): 11, 19

COLLECT

Clothe us, Lord God,
with the virtues of the Heart of your Son
and set us aflame with his love,
that, conformed to his image,
we may merit a share in eternal redemption.
Through our Lord Jesus Christ, your Son,
who lives and reigns with you
in the unity of the Holy Spirit,
one God, for ever and ever.

PRAYER AFTER COMMUNION

Made partakers in your Sacrament of charity,
we humbly implore your mercy, Lord,
that we may be conformed to Christ on earth
and merit to be coheirs of his glory in heaven.
Who lives and reigns for ever and ever.

As a Votive Mass, the Mass of the Solemnity of the Most Sacred Heart of Jesus may also be used, p. 287.

9. THE HOLY SPIRIT

In this Mass, the color red is used.

A

Entrance Antiphon

The love of God has been poured into our hearts
through the Spirit of God dwelling within us. Rom 5: 5; cf. 8: 11

COLLECT

O God, who have taught the hearts of the faithful
by the light of the Holy Spirit,
grant that in the same Spirit we may be truly wise
and ever rejoice in his consolation.
Through our Lord Jesus Christ, your Son,
who lives and reigns with you
in the unity of the Holy Spirit,
one God, for ever and ever.

PRAYER AFTER COMMUNION

May the outpouring of the Holy Spirit
cleanse our hearts, O Lord,
and make them fruitful by the inner sprinkling of his dew.
Through Christ our Lord.

B

Entrance Antiphon

When the Spirit of truth comes,
he will teach you all truth, says the Lord. Cf. Jn 14: 26; 15: 26

COLLECT

May the Paraclete who proceeds from you,
we pray, O Lord,
enlighten our minds and lead us into all truth,
just as your Son has promised.
Who lives and reigns with you
in the unity of the Holy Spirit,
one God, for ever and ever.

Or:

O God, to whom every heart lies open,
every desire speaks plainly
and from whom no secret is hidden,
cleanse, we pray, the thoughts of our heart
by the outpouring of the Holy Spirit,
that we may merit to love you perfectly
and offer you worthy praise.
Through our Lord Jesus Christ, your Son,
who lives and reigns with you
in the unity of the Holy Spirit,
one God, for ever and ever.

PRAYER AFTER COMMUNION

Lord our God, who have been pleased
to nourish us with heavenly food,
pour, we pray, the delights of your Spirit
into the recesses of our heart,
that what we have devoutly received in time
we may possess as a gift for eternity.
Through Christ our Lord.

C

Entrance Antiphon

The Spirit of the Lord is upon me,
he has sent me to preach the good news to the poor,
says the Lord. Cf. Lk 4: 18

COLLECT

O God, who sanctify your universal Church
in every people and nation,
pour out, we pray, the gifts of your Spirit
across the face of the earth,
so that your divine grace, which was at work
when the Gospel was first proclaimed,
may now spread through the hearts
of those who believe in you.
Through our Lord Jesus Christ, your Son,
who lives and reigns with you
in the unity of the Holy Spirit,
one God, for ever and ever.

Or:

O God, by whose Spirit we are governed
and by whose protection we are kept safe,
extend over us your mercy
and give ear to our supplications,
that the faith of those who believe in you
may always be sustained by your gifts.
Through our Lord Jesus Christ, your Son,
who lives and reigns with you
in the unity of the Holy Spirit,
one God, for ever and ever.

PRAYER AFTER COMMUNION

May these gifts we have consumed
benefit us, O Lord,
that we may always be aflame with the same Spirit
whom you wondrously poured out on your Apostles.
Through Christ our Lord.

10. THE BLESSED VIRGIN MARY

In these Masses, the color white is used.

A

Any Mass from the Common of the Blessed Virgin Mary (p. 518) is used, in accordance with the various times of the year.

B

Our Lady, Mother of the Church

Entrance Antiphon The disciples devoted themselves with one accord to prayer with Mary, the Mother of Jesus. Cf. Acts 1: 14

COLLECT

O God, Father of mercies,
whose Only Begotten Son, as he hung upon the Cross,
chose the Blessed Virgin Mary, his Mother,
to be our Mother also,
grant, we pray, that with her loving help
your Church may be more fruitful day by day
and, exulting in the holiness of her children,
may draw to her embrace all the families of the peoples.
Through our Lord Jesus Christ, your Son,
who lives and reigns with you
in the unity of the Holy Spirit,
one God, for ever and ever.

PRAYER AFTER COMMUNION

Having received the pledge of redemption and of life,
we humbly pray, O Lord,
that, with the Blessed Virgin's motherly help,
your Church may teach all nations
by proclaiming the Gospel
and, through the grace of the outpouring of the Spirit,
fill the whole earth.
Through Christ our Lord.

C

The Most Holy Name of Mary

Entrance Antiphon

Blessed are you, O Virgin Mary, by the Lord God Most High,
above all women on the earth;
for he has so exalted your Name
that your praise shall be undying on our lips. Cf. Jdt 13: 18-19

COLLECT

O God, who chose the Blessed Virgin Mary,
full of your grace, from among women
to become the Mother of your Son, our Redeemer,
mercifully grant that, venerating her holy name,
we may escape the dangers of this present age
and obtain with her life eternal.
Through our Lord Jesus Christ, your Son,
who lives and reigns with you
in the unity of the Holy Spirit,
one God, for ever and ever.

Or:

O God, whose Son, dying on the altar of the Cross,
willed that the most Blessed Virgin Mary,
whom he had chosen as his Mother,
should be our Mother also,
graciously grant, we pray,
that we, who fly to her protection,
may find comfort by invoking our Mother's name.
Through our Lord Jesus Christ, your Son,
who lives and reigns with you
in the unity of the Holy Spirit,
one God, for ever and ever.

PRAYER AFTER COMMUNION

Grant us, we pray, O Lord,
whom you have strengthened
at the table of word and Sacrament,
that, with Blessed Mary as our patron and guide,
we may reject whatever is contrary
to the name of Christian
and follow whatever accords with it.
Through Christ our Lord.

D

Our Lady, Queen of Apostles

Entrance Antiphon The disciples devoted themselves with one accord to prayer with Mary, the Mother of Jesus. Cf. Acts 1: 14

COLLECT

O God, who gave the Holy Spirit to your Apostles
as they prayed with Mary the Mother of Jesus,
grant that through her intercession
we may faithfully serve your majesty
and extend, by word and example, the glory of your name.
Through our Lord Jesus Christ, your Son,
who lives and reigns with you
in the unity of the Holy Spirit,
one God, for ever and ever.

PRAYER AFTER COMMUNION

Having partaken, O Lord, of these helps to our salvation
in our commemoration of the Blessed Virgin Mary,
Queen of Apostles,
we humbly beseech you,
that, persevering in your will
and in service of the human family,
your people may draw ever closer to salvation.
Through Christ our Lord.

11. THE HOLY ANGELS

In this Mass, the color white is used.

Entrance Antiphon

Bless the Lord, all you his angels, mighty in power,
fulfilling his word and heeding his voice. Cf. Ps 103 (102): 20

COLLECT

O God, who dispose in marvelous order
ministries both angelic and human,
graciously grant
that our life on earth may be defended
by those who watch over us
as they minister perpetually to you in heaven.
Through our Lord Jesus Christ, your Son,
who lives and reigns with you
in the unity of the Holy Spirit,
one God, for ever and ever.

PRAYER AFTER COMMUNION

Having been nourished upon heavenly bread
we beseech you humbly, O Lord,
that, drawing from it new strength,
under the faithful protection of your Angels,
we may advance boldly along the way of salvation.
Through Christ our Lord.

As a Votive Mass, the Mass of the Holy Guardian Angels may also be used, as on October 2 (p. 465).

12. SAINT JOHN THE BAPTIST

In this Mass, the color white is used.

Entrance Antiphon

He will be great in the sight of the Lord
and will be filled with the Holy Spirit,
even from his mother's womb;
and many will rejoice at his birth. Lk 1: 15, 14

COLLECT

Grant, we pray, almighty God,
that your family may walk in the way of salvation,
and, attentive to what Saint John the Precursor urged,
may come safely to the One he foretold,
our Lord Jesus Christ.
Who lives and reigns with you
in the unity of the Holy Spirit,
one God, for ever and ever.

PPRAYER AFTER COMMUNION

May the marvelous prayer of Saint John the Baptist
accompany us who have eaten our fill
at this sacrificial feast, O Lord,
and, since Saint John proclaimed your Son
to be the Lamb who would take away our sins,
may he now implore for us your favor.
Through Christ our Lord.

13. SAINT JOSEPH

In this Mass, the color white is used.

Entrance Antiphon

Behold a faithful and prudent steward,
whom the Lord set over his household. Cf. Lk 12: 42

COLLECT

O God, who in your inexpressible providence
were pleased to choose Saint Joseph
as spouse of the most holy Mother of your Son,
grant, we pray,
that we, who revere him as our protector on earth,
may be worthy of his heavenly intercession.
Through our Lord Jesus Christ, your Son,
who lives and reigns with you
in the unity of the Holy Spirit,
one God, for ever and ever.

PRAYER AFTER COMMUNION

**Restored by these life-giving Sacraments, Lord,
may we live for you always in justice and holiness,
helped by the example and intercession of Saint Joseph,
who in carrying out your great mysteries
served you as a man just and obedient.
Through Christ our Lord.**

If appropriate, the Mass of the Solemnity, as on March 19 (p. 364), or of Saint Joseph the Worker, as on May 1 (p. 377), may also be said.

14. ALL THE HOLY APOSTLES

In this Mass, the color red is used.

Entrance Antiphon

**It was not you who chose me, says the Lord,
but I who chose you and appointed you to go and bear fruit,
fruit that will last (E.T. alleluia).** Jn 15: 16

COLLECT

**May your Church always exult, O Lord,
in the honor given through the ages
to the blessed Apostles,
that she may be guided by these protectors,
in whose teaching and merits she finds joy.
Through our Lord Jesus Christ, your Son,
who lives and reigns with you
in the unity of the Holy Spirit,
one God, for ever and ever.**

PRAYER AFTER COMMUNION

**Grant that we may persevere, O God,
with rejoicing and simplicity of heart
in the teaching of the Apostles,
in the breaking of the bread,
and in the prayers.
Through Christ our Lord.**

15. SAINTS PETER AND PAUL, APOSTLES

In this Mass, the color red is used.

Entrance Antiphon

Peter the Apostle, and Paul the teacher of the Gentiles:
these have taught us your law, O Lord.

COLLECT

Grant, we pray, O Lord our God,
that we may be sustained by the intercession
of the blessed Apostles Peter and Paul,
that, as through them you gave your Church
the foundations of her heavenly office,
so through them you may help her to eternal salvation.
Through our Lord Jesus Christ, your Son,
who lives and reigns with you
in the unity of the Holy Spirit,
one God, for ever and ever.

PRAYER AFTER COMMUNION

By this heavenly Sacrament, O Lord, we pray,
strengthen your faithful,
whom you have enlightened
with the teaching of the Apostles.
Through Christ our Lord.

16. SAINT PETER, APOSTLE

In this Mass, the color red is used.

Entrance Antiphon

The Lord says to Simon Peter:
I have prayed for you that your faith may not fail,
and once you have turned back, strengthen your brothers.
Lk 22: 32

COLLECT

O God, who gave the keys of the Kingdom of Heaven
to your blessed Apostle Peter
and handed over to him
the pontifical office of binding and loosing,
grant, we pray, that through the help of his intercession
we may be set free from the bonds of our sins.
Through our Lord Jesus Christ, your Son,
who lives and reigns with you
in the unity of the Holy Spirit,
one God, for ever and ever.

PRAYER AFTER COMMUNION

Having been admitted, O Lord, to the banquet of salvation
as we venerate the memory of the blessed Apostle Peter,
we ask with gladness
that we may always hold fast to your Son,
who alone has the words of life,
so that, as faithful sheep of your flock,
we may be happily led to eternal pastures.
Through Christ our Lord.

17. SAINT PAUL, APOSTLE

In this Mass, the color red is used.

Entrance Antiphon

I know the one in whom I have believed
and I am sure that he, the just judge, the mighty,
will keep safe what is my due until that day. 2 Tm 1: 12; 4: 8

COLLECT

Lord God, who in a wondrous way
chose the blessed Apostle Paul to preach the Gospel,
grant, we pray, that the whole world
may be imbued with that faith
which he brought before rulers and nations,
for the unceasing growth of your Church.
Through our Lord Jesus Christ, your Son,
who lives and reigns with you
in the unity of the Holy Spirit,
one God, for ever and ever.

PRAYER AFTER COMMUNION

Grant Lord, to those refreshed
by communion in the Body and Blood of your Son,
that Christ himself may be life to us,
that nothing may separate us from his love,
and that, attentive to the teaching
of the blessed Apostle Paul,
we may walk in charity with our neighbor.
Through Christ our Lord.

18. ONE HOLY APOSTLE

In this Mass, the color red is used. The Mass of his Feast is said. But if he is honored together with another Apostle and the texts of the Mass are not appropriate for that Apostle, the following Mass is said with the color red.

Entrance Antiphon

Proclaim the salvation of God day by day;
tell among the nations his glory. Ps 96 (95): 2-3

COLLECT

Strengthen in us, O Lord, the faith,
by which the blessed Apostle N.
clung wholeheartedly to your Son,
and grant that through the help of his prayers
your Church may become for all the nations
the sacrament of salvation.
Through our Lord Jesus Christ, your Son,
who lives and reigns with you
in the unity of the Holy Spirit,
one God, for ever and ever.

PRAYER AFTER COMMUNION

As we celebrate the memory of the blessed Apostle N.,
we have received the pledge of eternal salvation, O Lord,
and we pray that it may be of help to us,
both now and for the life to come.
Through Christ our Lord.

19. ALL SAINTS

In this Mass, the color white is used.

Entrance Antiphon

The souls of the Saints are rejoicing in heaven,
the Saints who followed the footsteps of Christ,
and so now exult with Christ for ever.

COLLECT

O God, fount of all holiness,
make us each walk worthily in our vocation,
through the intercession of your Saints,
on whom you bestowed
a great variety of graces on earth
and a single glorious reward in heaven.
Through our Lord Jesus Christ, your Son,
who lives and reigns with you
in the unity of the Holy Spirit,
one God, for ever and ever.

PRAYER AFTER COMMUNION

O God, who refresh us with the one Bread
and sustain us with one hope,
strengthen us likewise, we pray, by your grace,
that, as we are one with your Saints,
one body and one spirit in Christ,
we may rise with him to glory.
Who lives and reigns for ever and ever.

MASSES FOR THE DEAD

1. Although for the sake of convenience, complete Masses with their own antiphons and prayers are given here, all the texts may be exchanged one for another, especially the prayers. In these latter, however, changes should be made, according to circumstances, in gender and number.

   Similarly, if the prayers given here for funerals and anniversaries are used in other circumstances, the phrasing that appears less suited should be omitted.

2. In Easter Time, the Alleluia at the end of the antiphons may, if appropriate, be omitted.

I. FOR THE FUNERAL

The Funeral Mass may be celebrated on any day, except on Solemnities that are Holydays of Obligation, on Thursday of Holy Week, during the Paschal Triduum, and on the Sundays of Advent, Lent and Easter Time.

A

Outside Easter Time

Entrance Antiphon

Eternal rest grant unto them, O Lord,
and let perpetual light shine upon them. Cf. 4 Esdr 2: 34-35

Or:

Eternal rest grant unto him (her), O Lord,
and let perpetual light shine upon him (her).

COLLECT

O God, almighty Father,
our faith professes that your Son died and rose again;
mercifully grant, that through this mystery
your servant N., who has fallen asleep in Christ,
may rejoice to rise again through him.
Who lives and reigns with you
in the unity of the Holy Spirit,
one God, for ever and ever.

Or:

O God, whose nature
is always to forgive and to show mercy,
we humbly implore you for your servant N.,
whom you have called (this day) to journey to you,
and, since he (she) hoped and believed in you,
grant that he (she) may be led to our true homeland
to delight in its everlasting joys.
Through our Lord Jesus Christ, your Son,
who lives and reigns with you
in the unity of the Holy Spirit,
one God, for ever and ever.

PRAYER AFTER COMMUNION

Lord God, whose Son left us,
in the Sacrament of his Body,
food for the journey,
mercifully grant that, strengthened by it,
our brother (sister) N. may come
to the eternal table of Christ.
Who lives and reigns for ever and ever.

B

Outside Easter Time

Entrance Antiphon

May the Lord open to him (her) the gates of Paradise,
that he (she) may return to that homeland
where there is no death, where eternal joy endures.

COLLECT

O God, who are mercy for sinners
and the happiness of your Saints,
give, we pray, to your servant N.,
for whom (today) we perform
the fraternal offices of burial,
a share with your chosen ones in the blessedness you give,
so that on the day of resurrection,
freed from the bonds of mortality,
he (she) may come before your face.
Through our Lord Jesus Christ, your Son,
who lives and reigns with you
in the unity of the Holy Spirit,
one God, for ever and ever.

Or:

O God, who have set a limit to this present life,
so as to open up an entry into eternity,
we humbly beseech you,
that by the grace of your mercy
you may command the name of your servant N.
to be inscribed in the book of life.
Through our Lord Jesus Christ, your Son,
who lives and reigns with you
in the unity of the Holy Spirit,
one God, for ever and ever.

PRAYER AFTER COMMUNION

Grant, we pray, almighty God,
that your servant N.,
who (today) has journeyed from this world,
may by this sacrifice be cleansed and freed from sin
and so receive the everlasting joys of the resurrection.
Through Christ our Lord.

C

During Easter Time

Entrance Antiphon

Just as Jesus died and rose again,
so, through Jesus, God will bring with him
those who have fallen asleep;
and as in Adam all die,
so also in Christ will all be brought to life, alleluia.
1 Thes 4: 14; 1 Cor 15: 22

COLLECT

Listen kindly to our prayers, O Lord:
as our faith in your Son,
raised from the dead, is deepened,
may our hope of resurrection for your departed servant N.,
also find new strength.
Through our Lord Jesus Christ, your Son,
who lives and reigns with you
in the unity of the Holy Spirit,
one God, for ever and ever.

Or:

O God, who through the ending of present things
open up the beginning of things to come,
grant, we pray, that the soul of your servant N.
may be led by you
to attain the inheritance of eternal redemption.
Through our Lord Jesus Christ, your Son,
who lives and reigns with you
in the unity of the Holy Spirit,
one God, for ever and ever.

PRAYER AFTER COMMUNION

Grant, we pray, O Lord, that your servant N.,
for whom we have celebrated this paschal Sacrament,
may pass over to a dwelling place of light and peace.
Through Christ our Lord.

D

Other Prayers for the Funeral Mass

COLLECT

O God, who alone are able to give life after death,
free your servant N. from all sins,
that he (she),
who believed in the Resurrection of your Christ,
may, when the day of resurrection comes,
be united with you in glory.
Through our Lord Jesus Christ, your Son,
who lives and reigns with you
in the unity of the Holy Spirit,
one God, for ever and ever.

PRAYER AFTER COMMUNION

Having received the Sacrament
of your Only Begotten Son,
who was sacrificed for us and rose in glory,
we humbly implore you, O Lord,
for your departed servant N.,
that, cleansed by the paschal mysteries,
he (she) may glory in the gift of the resurrection to come.
Through Christ our Lord.

E

For the Funeral of a Baptized Child

1

Entrance Antiphon

Come, you blessed of my Father, says the Lord;
receive the kingdom prepared for you
from the foundation of the world (E.T. alleluia). Mt 25: 34

COLLECT

Most compassionate God,
who in the counsels of your wisdom
have called this little child to yourself
on the very threshold of life,
listen kindly to our prayers
and grant that one day
we may inherit eternal life with him (her),
whom, by the grace of Baptism,
you have adopted as your own child
and who we believe is dwelling even now
in your Kingdom.
Through our Lord Jesus Christ, your Son,
who lives and reigns with you
in the unity of the Holy Spirit,
one God, for ever and ever.

PRAYER AFTER COMMUNION

Having received the Communion
of your Son's Body and Blood, O Lord,
we ask you faithfully
to comfort amid the sorrows of this life
those whom you have graciously nourished
by these sacred mysteries,
so as to strengthen their hope of life eternal.
Through Christ our Lord.

2
Other Prayers

COLLECT

O God, who know that our hearts
are weighed down by grief
at the death of this young child,
grant that, while we weep for him (her),
who at your bidding has departed this life so soon,
we may have faith that he (she) has gained
an eternal home in heaven.
Through our Lord Jesus Christ, your Son,
who lives and reigns with you
in the unity of the Holy Spirit,
one God, for ever and ever.

PRAYER AFTER COMMUNION

**Nourished by your divine gifts,
we pray, O Lord,
that, just as you have given this little child
a place at the table in your heavenly Kingdom,
we, too, may find a place there.
Through Christ our Lord.**

F

For the Funeral of a Child Who Died before Baptism

Should a child whom the parents wished to be baptized, die before Baptism, the Diocesan Bishop, taking into consideration pastoral circumstances, may permit the funeral to be celebrated in the home of the deceased child, or even according to the form of funeral rites otherwise customarily used in the region.

In funerals of this kind there should ordinarily be a Liturgy of the Word, as described in the Roman Ritual. Nevertheless, if at times the celebration of Mass is judged opportune, the following texts should be used.

In catechesis, however, proper care is to be taken that the doctrine of the necessity of Baptism is not obscured in the minds of the faithful.

Entrance Antiphon

**God will wipe every tear from their eyes,
and there shall be no more death
or mourning, crying or pain,
for former things have passed away.** Rev 21: 4

COLLECT

**Receive the prayers of your faithful, Lord,
and grant that those you allow to be weighed down
by their longing for the child taken from them
may be raised up by faith to hope in your compassion.
Through our Lord Jesus Christ, your Son,
who lives and reigns with you
in the unity of the Holy Spirit,
one God, for ever and ever.**

Or:

O God, searcher of hearts and most loving consoler,
who know the faith of these parents,
grant that, as they mourn their child,
now departed from this life,
they may be assured
that he (she) has been entrusted
to your divine compassion.
Through our Lord Jesus Christ, your Son,
who lives and reigns with you
in the unity of the Holy Spirit,
one God, for ever and ever.

PRAYER AFTER COMMUNION

Having received the Communion
of your Son's Body and Blood, O Lord,
we ask you faithfully
to comfort amid the sorrows of this life
those whom you have graciously nourished
by these sacred mysteries,
so as to strengthen their hope of life eternal.
Through Christ our Lord.

II. ON THE ANNIVERSARY

This Mass may be celebrated on the first anniversary even on days within the Octave of the Nativity of the Lord, and on days when an Obligatory Memorial occurs and on weekdays, with the exception of Ash Wednesday and weekdays during Holy Week.

On other anniversaries, this Mass may be celebrated on weekdays in Ordinary Time even when an Optional Memorial occurs.

A

Outside Easter Time

Entrance Antiphon

God will wipe every tear from their eyes,
and there shall be no more death
or mourning, crying or pain,
for former things have passed away. Rev 21: 4

COLLECT

O God, glory of the faithful and life of the just,
by the Death and Resurrection of whose Son
we have been redeemed,
look mercifully on your departed servant N.,
that, just as he (she) professed
the mystery of our resurrection,
so he (she) may merit to receive
the joys of eternal happiness.
Through our Lord Jesus Christ, your Son,
who lives and reigns with you
in the unity of the Holy Spirit,
one God, for ever and ever.

PRAYER AFTER COMMUNION

Restored by these sacred mysteries,
we humbly beseech you, O Lord,
that your servant N. may be cleansed from all offenses
and merit for all eternity
the precious gift of the resurrection.
Through Christ our Lord.

B

Outside Easter Time

Entrance Antiphon

Lord Jesus, grant eternal rest to those,
for whom you poured out your precious Blood.

COLLECT

Send down, we pray, O Lord,
the lasting dew of your mercy on your servant N.,
whose anniversary we commemorate,
and be pleased to grant him (her)
the company of your Saints.
Through our Lord Jesus Christ, your Son,
who lives and reigns with you
in the unity of the Holy Spirit,
one God, for ever and ever.

PRAYER AFTER COMMUNION

Just as you have lovingly accepted, O Lord,
our prayers and sacrificial offerings
for the soul of your servant N.,
so, we humbly entreat you:
if any stain of sin has clung to him (her),
may it be wiped away by your merciful forgiveness.
Through Christ our Lord.

C

During Easter Time

Entrance Antiphon

God, who raised Jesus from the dead,
will give life also to your mortal bodies,
through his Spirit that dwells in you, alleluia. Cf. Rom 8: 11

COLLECT

Almighty and merciful God,
whose Son, for our sake,
willingly underwent death in the flesh,
grant mercifully, we pray,
that your servant N. may have part
in the wondrous victory of Christ's Resurrection.
Who lives and reigns with you
in the unity of the Holy Spirit,
one God, for ever and ever.

PRAYER AFTER COMMUNION

Having received the Sacrament
of your Only Begotten Son,
who was sacrificed for us and rose in glory,
we humbly implore you, O Lord,
for your departed servant N.,
that, cleansed by the paschal mysteries,
he (she) may glory in the gift of the resurrection to come.
Through Christ our Lord.

D

Other Prayers on the Anniversary

COLLECT

Grant, we pray, O Lord,
through the blessed Passion of your Son,
that your servant N. may receive
the forgiveness for his (her) sins he (she) always desired,
so that, knowing you in truth,
he (she) may be worthy to rejoice
at being called to behold you for ever.
Through our Lord Jesus Christ, your Son,
who lives and reigns with you
in the unity of the Holy Spirit,
one God, for ever and ever.

PRAYER AFTER COMMUNION

Replenished by the food that renews and gives life,
we pray, O Lord,
that our brother (sister) N.,
strengthened by it and cleansed from all sins,
may pass over to the company of heaven.
Through Christ our Lord.

E

Other Prayers on the Anniversary

COLLECT

O God of all forgiveness,
grant to the soul of your servant N.,
whose anniversary we celebrate,
a place of refreshment, of blessed rest
and resplendent light.
Through our Lord Jesus Christ, your Son,
who lives and reigns with you
in the unity of the Holy Spirit,
one God, for ever and ever.

PRAYER AFTER COMMUNION

Grant, we pray, almighty God,
that the soul of your servant N.,
for whom we have offered
this sacrifice to your majesty,
may by the power of this Sacrament
be cleansed of all sins
and receive from your mercy
the happiness of perpetual light.
Through Christ our Lord.

III. VARIOUS COMMEMORATIONS

This Mass may be celebrated when the news of a death is first received or on the day of final burial, even on days within the Octave of the Nativity of the Lord, on days when an Obligatory Memorial occurs, and on weekdays, with the exception of Ash Wednesday and weekdays during Holy Week.

"Daily" Masses for the Dead may be celebrated on weekdays in Ordinary Time, even if an Optional Memorial occurs, provided such Masses are actually applied for the dead.

A. For One Deceased Person

1

Entrance Antiphon

May the Lord open to him (her) the gates of Paradise,
that he (she) may return to that homeland,
where there is no death, where eternal joy endures.

COLLECT

O God, almighty Father,
who have strengthened us by the mystery of the Cross
and promise us a share
in the mystery of your Son's Resurrection,
mercifully grant, we pray,
that your departed servant N. may be gathered
into the company of your chosen ones.
Through our Lord Jesus Christ, your Son,
who lives and reigns with you
in the unity of the Holy Spirit,
one God, for ever and ever.

Or:

Incline your ear, O Lord, to our prayers,
by which we humbly entreat your mercy,
that, as you graciously numbered your servant N.
among your people in this world,
you may now set him (her) in a place of peace and light
and grant him (her) a share
in the company of your Saints.
Through our Lord Jesus Christ, your Son,
who lives and reigns with you
in the unity of the Holy Spirit,
one God, for ever and ever.

PRAYER AFTER COMMUNION

Renewed by this life-giving Sacrament,
we pray, O Lord,
that the soul of our brother (sister) N.,
to whom you gave a part in your covenant,
may be purified by the power of this mystery
and rejoice without end in the peace of Christ.
Who lives and reigns for ever and ever.

2

Entrance Antiphon

I know that my Redeemer lives,
and that he will at last stand forth upon the dust;
and from my flesh I shall see God. Jb 19: 25, 26

COLLECT

Free your servant N., we pray, O Lord,
from every bond of sin,
that he (she), who in this world
was found worthy to be conformed to Christ,
may be raised to the glory of the resurrection
and draw the breath of new life among your Saints.
Through our Lord Jesus Christ, your Son,
who lives and reigns with you
in the unity of the Holy Spirit,
one God, for ever and ever.

PRAYER AFTER COMMUNION

May the sacrifice of your Church, we pray, O Lord,
benefit the soul of your servant N.,
so that he (she), who received
the Sacrament of Christ's mercy,
may enter his company, together with your Saints.
Through Christ our Lord.

3
Other Prayers

COLLECT

O God, in whose presence the dead are alive
and in whom your Saints rejoice full of happiness,
grant our supplication, that your servant N.,
for whom the fleeting light of this world shines no more,
may enjoy the comfort of your light for all eternity.
Through our Lord Jesus Christ, your Son,
who lives and reigns with you
in the unity of the Holy Spirit,
one God, for ever and ever.

PRAYER AFTER COMMUNION

As we receive these heavenly gifts,
we give you thanks, O Lord,
and humbly pray that the soul of your servant N.,
freed through your Son's Passion from the bonds of sin,
may come happily into your presence.
Through Christ our Lord.

4
Other Prayers

COLLECT

May our prayers rise up to you, O Lord,
and may the soul of N. your servant
be welcomed into eternal joy;
for as you were pleased
to create him (her) in your own image
and adopt him (her) as your own,
so command, we pray,
that he (she) may have a share in your inheritance.
Through our Lord Jesus Christ, your Son,
who lives and reigns with you
in the unity of the Holy Spirit,
one God, for ever and ever.

PRAYER AFTER COMMUNION

Renewed by the nourishment of this sacred gift,
we pray, O Lord,
that our brother (sister) N., freed from the bonds of death,
may rejoice to have a share
in the Resurrection of your Son.
Who lives and reigns for ever and ever.

5
Other Prayers

COLLECT

Incline your merciful ear to our prayers, O Lord,
and grant to the soul of your servant N.
the remission of all his (her) sins,
that he (she) may have life on the day of resurrection
and may rest in the splendor of eternal light.
Through our Lord Jesus Christ, your Son,
who lives and reigns with you
in the unity of the Holy Spirit,
one God, for ever and ever.

PRAYER AFTER COMMUNION

As we receive the pledge of eternal life,
we humbly implore you, O Lord,
for the soul of your servant N.,
that, freed from the bonds of mortality,
he (she) may join the company of the redeemed.
Through Christ our Lord.

B. For Several Deceased Persons or for All the Dead

1

Entrance Antiphon

Eternal rest grant unto them, O Lord,
and fill their souls with splendor.

COLLECT

O God, who willed that your Only Begotten Son,
having conquered death,
should pass over into the realm of heaven,
grant, we pray, to your departed servants (N. and N.)
that, with the mortality of this life overcome,
they may gaze eternally on you,
their Creator and Redeemer.
Through our Lord Jesus Christ, your Son,
who lives and reigns with you
in the unity of the Holy Spirit,
one God, for ever and ever.

PRAYER AFTER COMMUNION

Through these sacrificial gifts
which we have received, O Lord,
bestow on your departed servants your great mercy,
and, to those you have endowed with the grace of Baptism,
grant also the fullness of eternal joy.
Through Christ our Lord.

2

Entrance Antiphon

God so loved the world that he gave his Only Begotten Son,
so that all who believe in him may not perish,
but may have eternal life. Jn 3: 16

COLLECT

Almighty ever-living God,
life of all that is mortal and joy of the Saints,
we humbly pray to you for your servants (N. and N.)
that, freed from the bonds of mortality,
they may possess your Kingdom in everlasting glory.
Through our Lord Jesus Christ, your Son,
who lives and reigns with you
in the unity of the Holy Spirit,
one God, for ever and ever.

PRAYER AFTER COMMUNION

As we participate in the divine mysteries
we pray, almighty God,
that they may advance our salvation
and bring pardon to the souls of your servants,
for whom we implore your mercy.
Through Christ our Lord.

3

Entrance Antiphon

Blessed are the dead who die in the Lord.
Let them rest from their labors,
for their works accompany them. Cf. Rev 14: 13

COLLECT

O God, by whose mercy the souls of the faithful find rest,
graciously grant pardon for their sins
to your servants (N. and N.)
and to all who sleep in Christ,
so that, freed from all guilt,
they may have a share in the Resurrection of your Christ.
Who lives and reigns with you
in the unity of the Holy Spirit,
one God, for ever and ever.

PRAYER AFTER COMMUNION

We have received, O Lord, the Sacrament of redemption
and entreat your mercy, that in your compassion
you may give protection to us, the living,
and, to our departed brothers and sisters,
everlasting pardon.
Through Christ our Lord.

4

Entrance Antiphon

In you, O Lord, I put my trust, let me never be put to shame;
in your justice, deliver me. Cf. Ps 31 (30): 2

COLLECT

O God, Creator and Redeemer of all the faithful,
grant to your departed servants
the remission of all their sins,
so that through our devout supplications
they may obtain that pardon
which they have always desired.
Through our Lord Jesus Christ, your Son,
who lives and reigns with you
in the unity of the Holy Spirit,
one God, for ever and ever.

PRAYER AFTER COMMUNION

May the prayer of those who plead before you
benefit the souls of your servants, we pray, O Lord,
so that through this sacrifice,
you may free them from all their sins
and make them sharers in eternal salvation.
Through Christ our Lord.

5

Entrance Antiphon

Let the hearts that seek the Lord rejoice;
turn to the Lord and his strength;
constantly seek his face. Cf. Ps 105 (104): 3-4

COLLECT

Almighty ever-living God,
who rule both the living and the dead
and are merciful to all,
we humbly beseech you,
that those for whom we pour out our prayers
may obtain pardon for their sins
through your tender mercy,
rejoicing together, blessed in your sight,
and praising you without end.
Through our Lord Jesus Christ, your Son,
who lives and reigns with you
in the unity of the Holy Spirit,
one God, for ever and ever.

PRAYER AFTER COMMUNION

Hear, O God, your children,
nourished now by the Sacrament of salvation,
and, as through the Holy Spirit,
you raised Christ, your Only Begotten Son, from the dead,
so grant to your faithful servants (N. and N.)
the joy of life and immortality.
Through Christ our Lord.

6

Entrance Antiphon

Look, O God, on the face of your anointed one;
one day within your courts is better than a thousand elsewhere.
Ps 84 (83): 10-11

COLLECT

Grant perpetual mercy to your departed servants,
we pray, O Lord,
that the hope and faith they had in you
may benefit them for all eternity.
Through our Lord Jesus Christ, your Son,
who lives and reigns with you
in the unity of the Holy Spirit,
one God, for ever and ever.

PRAYER AFTER COMMUNION

May your departed servants,
and all who sleep in Christ
inherit eternal light, we pray, O Lord,
for while still in this life
they received this, your holy Sacrament.
Through Christ our Lord.

7
Other Prayers

COLLECT

Be favorable, Lord, to your servants (N. and N.),
whom you washed clean in the font of rebirth,
and bring them to the happiness of heavenly life.
Through our Lord Jesus Christ, your Son,
who lives and reigns with you
in the unity of the Holy Spirit,
one God, for ever and ever.

PRAYER AFTER COMMUNION

Having received your heavenly Sacrament, O Lord,
we humbly ask your mercy,
that your departed servants,
obtaining, through this gift, pardon for sins,
may be counted worthy to enter your Kingdom,
there to praise you for eternity.
Through Christ our Lord.

8
Other Prayers

COLLECT

To you, O Lord, we commend your servants (N. and N.)
that, having died to this world, they may live for you,
and we beseech you,
that whatever sins they committed
through the frailty of the flesh during their earthly lives
you may in your most tender mercy
pardon and wipe away.
Through our Lord Jesus Christ, your Son,
who lives and reigns with you
in the unity of the Holy Spirit,
one God, for ever and ever.

PRAYER AFTER COMMUNION

Grant, we pray, almighty God,
that through the power of this Sacrament
your departed servants be made partakers
of eternal happiness
in the gathering of the just.
Through Christ our Lord.

9
Other Prayers

COLLECT

Almighty ever-living God,
to whom we never pray without hope of your mercy,
be gracious to your servants (N. and N.),
who departed this life confessing your name,
and admit them to the company of your Saints.
Through our Lord Jesus Christ, your Son,
who lives and reigns with you
in the unity of the Holy Spirit,
one God, for ever and ever.

PRAYER AFTER COMMUNION

May the Sacrament we have received
purify us, almighty and merciful God,
and grant, we pray,
that this sacrifice may be for us
a plea for pardon,
strength for the weak,
a stronghold in all danger;
and may it be for the living and the dead
remission of all their sins
and the pledge of eternal redemption.
Through Christ our Lord.

IV. VARIOUS PRAYERS FOR THE DEAD

1. For a Pope

A

COLLECT

O God, faithful rewarder of souls,
grant that your departed servant Pope N.,
whom you made successor of Peter
and shepherd of your Church,
may happily enjoy for ever in your presence in heaven
the mysteries of your grace and compassion,
which he faithfully ministered on earth.
Through our Lord Jesus Christ, your Son,
who lives and reigns with you
in the unity of the Holy Spirit,
one God, for ever and ever.

PRAYER AFTER COMMUNION

Renewed by the Sacrament
of our communion with you, our God,
we pray, O Lord,
that your servant Pope N.,
who served by your will on earth
as the visible foundation of your Church's unity,
may be happily admitted to your blessed flock.
Through Christ our Lord.

B

COLLECT

O God, who in your wondrous providence
chose your servant Pope N. to preside over your Church,
grant, we pray,
that, having served as the Vicar of your Son on earth,
he may be welcomed by him into eternal glory.
Who lives and reigns with you
in the unity of the Holy Spirit,
one God, for ever and ever.

PRAYER AFTER COMMUNION

As we receive sacred sustenance
from your charity, O Lord,
we pray that your servant Pope N.,
who was a faithful steward of your mysteries on earth,
may praise your mercy for ever in the glory of the Saints.
Through Christ our Lord.

C

COLLECT

O God, immortal shepherd of souls,
look on your people's prayers
and grant that your servant Pope N.,
who presided over your Church in charity,
may, with the flock entrusted to his care,
receive from your mercy
the reward of a faithful steward.
Through our Lord Jesus Christ, your Son,
who lives and reigns with you
in the unity of the Holy Spirit,
one God, for ever and ever.

PRAYER AFTER COMMUNION

As we come to the table of your eternal banquet,
we humbly beg your mercy, Lord,
for the soul of your departed servant Pope N.,
that he may rejoice at last in possession of the truth
in which he faithfully confirmed your people.
Through Christ our Lord.

2. For a Bishop

A

For a Diocesan Bishop

COLLECT

Grant, we pray, almighty God,
that the soul of your departed servant Bishop N.,
to whom you committed the care of your family,
may, with the manifold fruit of his labors,
enter into the eternal gladness of his Lord.
Who lives and reigns with you
in the unity of the Holy Spirit,
one God, for ever and ever.

PRAYER AFTER COMMUNION

May your merciful kindness,
which we have implored, O Lord,
benefit the soul of your departed servant Bishop N.,
that, by these sacrificial gifts,
he may know the eternal company of Christ,
in whom he hoped and whom he preached.
Who lives and reigns for ever and ever.

B

For Another Bishop

COLLECT

O God, who chose your servant Bishop (Cardinal) N.
from among your Priests
and endowed him with pontifical dignity
in the apostolic priesthood,
grant, we pray,
that he may also be admitted to their company for ever.
Through our Lord Jesus Christ, your Son,
who lives and reigns with you
in the unity of the Holy Spirit,
one God, for ever and ever.

PRAYER AFTER COMMUNION

We pray, almighty and merciful God,
that, as you made your servant Bishop (Cardinal) N.
an ambassador for Christ on earth,
so you may raise him, purified by this sacrifice,
to be seated with Christ in heaven.
Who lives and reigns for ever and ever.

3. For a Priest

A

COLLECT

Grant, we pray, O Lord,
that the soul of N., your servant and Priest,
whom you honored with sacred office
while he lived in this world,
may exult for ever in the glorious home of heaven.
Through our Lord Jesus Christ, your Son,
who lives and reigns with you
in the unity of the Holy Spirit,
one God, for ever and ever.

PRAYER AFTER COMMUNION

Having received the Sacrament of salvation,
we implore your kindness, O God,
for N., your servant and Priest,
that, as you made him a steward of your mysteries
on earth,
so you may bring him to be nourished
by their truth and reality as unveiled in heaven.
Through Christ our Lord.

B

COLLECT

Hear with favor our prayers,
which we humbly offer, O Lord,
for the salvation of the soul of N.,
your servant and Priest,
that he, who devoted a faithful ministry to your name,
may rejoice in the perpetual company of your Saints.
Through our Lord Jesus Christ, your Son,
who lives and reigns with you
in the unity of the Holy Spirit,
one God, for ever and ever.

PRAYER AFTER COMMUNION

Renewed by food from your heavenly table,
we humbly beseech you, O Lord,
that by the power of this sacrifice
the soul of N., your servant and Priest,
who faithfully ministered in your Church,
may exult for ever in your sight.
Through Christ our Lord.

4. For a Deacon

COLLECT

Grant, we pray, O merciful God,
a share in eternal happiness
to the soul of N., your servant and Deacon,
on whom you bestowed the gift
of ministering in your Church.
Through our Lord Jesus Christ, your Son,
who lives and reigns with you
in the unity of the Holy Spirit,
one God, for ever and ever.

PRAYER AFTER COMMUNION

Replenished with these sacred gifts,
we humbly entreat you, O Lord,
graciously to grant through this sacrifice
that N., your servant and Deacon,
whom you called to be among those
who serve your Church,
once freed from the bonds of death,
may receive a share with those who have ministered well,
and enter into your joy.
Through Christ our Lord.

5. For a Religious

COLLECT

Grant, we pray, almighty God,
that the soul of your servant N.,
who for love of Christ walked the way of perfect charity,
may rejoice in the coming of your glory
and together with his brothers (her sisters)
may delight in the everlasting happiness
of your Kingdom.
Through our Lord Jesus Christ, your Son,
who lives and reigns with you
in the unity of the Holy Spirit,
one God, for ever and ever.

6. For One Who Worked in the Service of the Gospel

COLLECT

We humbly beseech your mercy, O Lord,
for your servant N.,
that, having worked tirelessly for the spread of the Gospel,
he (she) may merit to enter into the rewards
of the Kingdom.
Through our Lord Jesus Christ, your Son,
who lives and reigns with you
in the unity of the Holy Spirit,
one God, for ever and ever.

7. For a Young Person

COLLECT

O God, who direct our life in all its moments,
we humbly entrust to you this your servant N.,
whom we mourn as one whose life
was completed in so short a time;
grant that he (she) may flourish, for ever young,
in the happiness of your house.
Through our Lord Jesus Christ, your Son,
who lives and reigns with you
in the unity of the Holy Spirit,
one God, for ever and ever.

8. For One Who Suffered a Long Illness

COLLECT

O God, who called your servant N.
to serve you in affliction and sickness,
grant, we pray,
that he (she),
who followed your Son's example of suffering,
may also receive the reward of his glory.
Who lives and reigns with you
in the unity of the Holy Spirit,
one God, for ever and ever.

9. For One Who Died Suddenly

COLLECT

Show us, Lord, the immense power of your goodness,
that, as we weep for our brother (sister) N.,
taken from us by a sudden death,
we may be confident that he (she) has passed over
into your eternal company.
Through our Lord Jesus Christ, your Son,
who lives and reigns with you
in the unity of the Holy Spirit,
one God, for ever and ever.

10. For a Married Couple

COLLECT

**Grant merciful forgiveness, we pray, O Lord,
to your servants N. and N.,
that, just as faithful married love
bound them together in this life,
so the fullness of your charity
may unite them for all eternity.
Through our Lord Jesus Christ, your Son,
who lives and reigns with you
in the unity of the Holy Spirit,
one God, for ever and ever.**

Or, for one deceased spouse:

**Grant merciful forgiveness, we pray, O Lord,
to your departed servant N.
and keep in your constant care
your servant N. (living spouse),
that, just as faithful married love
bound them together in this life,
so the fullness of your charity
may unite them for all eternity.
Through our Lord Jesus Christ, your Son,
who lives and reigns with you
in the unity of the Holy Spirit,
one God, for ever and ever.**

11. For the Priest's Parents

COLLECT

O God, who commanded us to honor father and mother,
have mercy in your compassion
on my father and mother (our parents),
forgive them their sins,
and bring me (us) to see them one day
in the gladness of eternal glory.
Through our Lord Jesus Christ, your Son,
who lives and reigns with you
in the unity of the Holy Spirit,
one God, for ever and ever.

PRAYER AFTER COMMUNION

May participation in this heavenly Sacrament
obtain perpetual light and rest
for my father and mother (our parents),
we pray, O Lord,
and bring me (us), along with them,
to the fullness of your everlasting glory.
Through Christ our Lord.

12. For Relatives, Friends, and Benefactors

COLLECT

O God, giver of pardon and loving author of our salvation,
grant, we pray you, in your mercy,
that, through the intercession
of Blessed Mary, ever-Virgin, and all your Saints,
the members, friends, and benefactors of our community,
who have passed from this world,
may attain a share in eternal happiness.
Through our Lord Jesus Christ, your Son,
who lives and reigns with you
in the unity of the Holy Spirit,
one God, for ever and ever.

PRAYER AFTER COMMUNION

Grant, we pray, almighty and merciful God,
that the souls of our relatives, friends, and benefactors,
for whom we have offered
this sacrifice of praise to your majesty,
may, through the power of this Sacrament,
be cleansed of all their sins,
and receive from your mercy
the happiness of perpetual light.
Through Christ our Lord.

S. GREGORIVS

APPENDICES

APPENDIX I

The Creed

Credo III

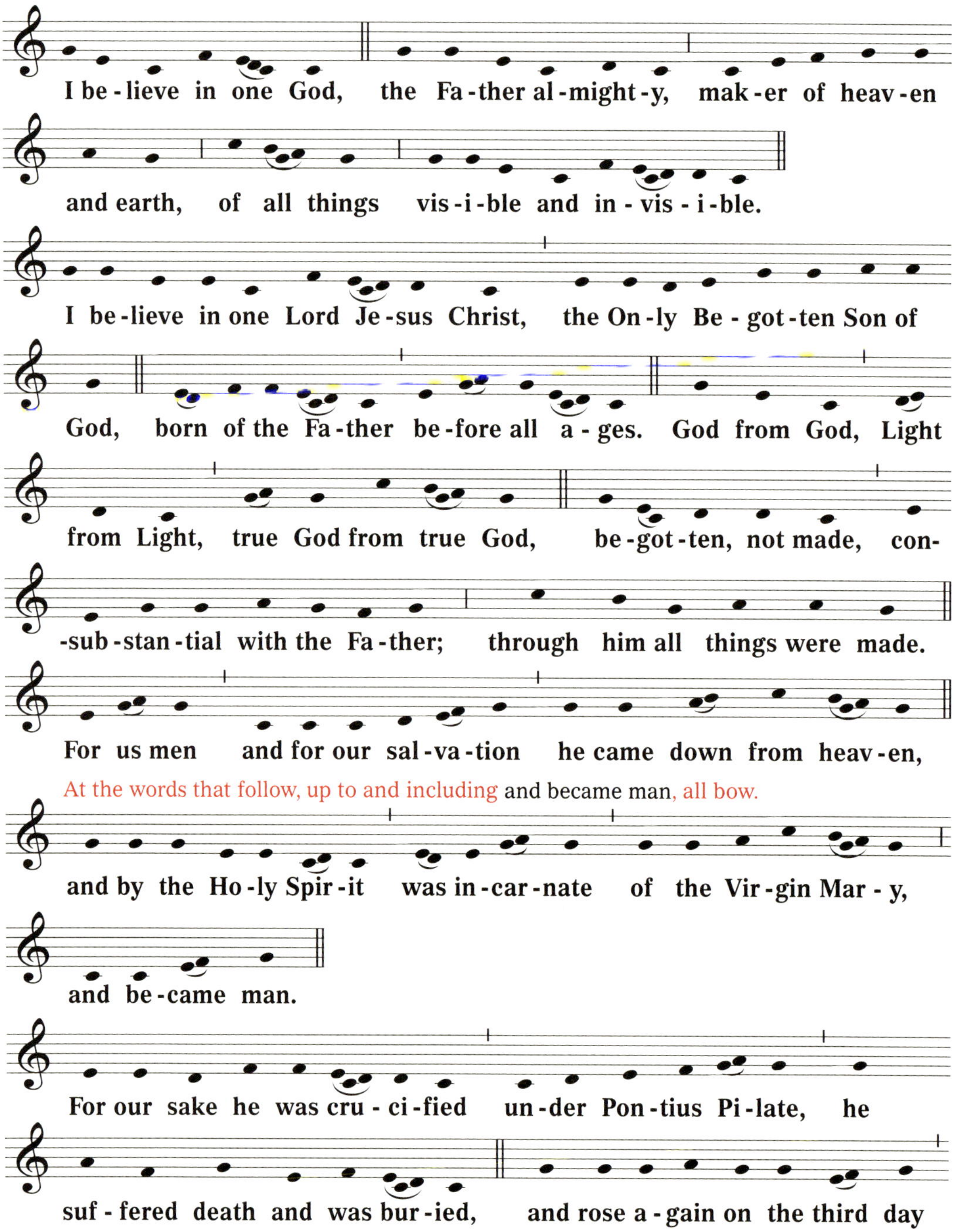

in ac-cord-ance with the Scrip-tures. He as-cend-ed in-to heav-en
and is seat-ed at the right hand of the Fa-ther. He will come a-gain
in glo-ry to judge the liv-ing and the dead and his king-dom
will have no end.
I be-lieve in the Ho-ly Spir-it, the Lord, the giv-er of life, who pro-
-ceeds from the Fa-ther and the Son, who with the Fa-ther and the
Son is a-dored and glo-ri-fied, who has spo-ken through the
proph-ets. I be-lieve in one, ho-ly, ca-tho-lic and a-pos-tol-ic
Church. I con-fess one Bap-tism for the for-give-ness of sins
and I look for-ward to the res-ur-rec-tion of the dead and the life
of the world to come. A - - men.

The Announcement of Easter and the Moveable Feasts

On the Epiphany of the Lord, after the singing of the Gospel, a Deacon or cantor, in keeping with an ancient practice of Holy Church, announces from the ambo the moveable feasts of the current year according to this formula:

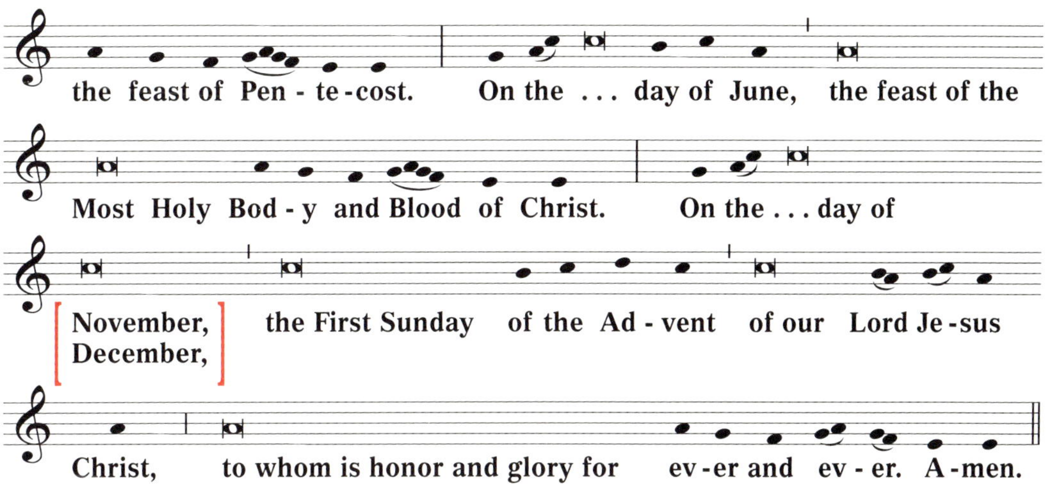
the feast of Pen - te - cost. On the . . . day of June, the feast of the
Most Holy Bod - y and Blood of Christ. On the . . . day of
[November, December,] the First Sunday of the Ad - vent of our Lord Je - sus
Christ, to whom is honor and glory for ev - er and ev - er. A - men.

APPENDIX II

RITE FOR THE BLESSING AND SPRINKLING OF WATER

1. On Sundays, especially in Easter Time, the blessing and sprinkling of water as a memorial of Baptism may take place from time to time in all churches and chapels, even in Masses anticipated on Saturday evenings.

If this rite is celebrated during Mass, it takes the place of the usual Penitential Act at the beginning of Mass.

2. After the greeting, the Priest stands at his chair and faces the people. With a vessel containing the water to be blessed before him, he calls upon the people to pray in these or similar words:

Dear brethren (brothers and sisters),
let us humbly beseech the Lord our God
to bless this water he has created,
which will be sprinkled on us
as a memorial of our Baptism.
May he help us by his grace
to remain faithful to the Spirit we have received.

And after a brief pause for silence, he continues with hands joined:

Almighty ever-living God,
who willed that through water,
the fountain of life and the source of purification,
even souls should be cleansed
and receive the gift of eternal life;
be pleased, we pray, to ✠ bless this water,
by which we seek protection on this your day, O Lord.
Renew the living spring of your grace within us
and grant that by this water we may be defended
from all ills of spirit and body,
and so approach you with hearts made clean
and worthily receive your salvation.
Through Christ our Lord.

℟. Amen.

Or:

Almighty Lord and God,
who are the source and origin of all life,
whether of body or soul,
we ask you to ✠ bless this water,
which we use in confidence
to implore forgiveness for our sins
and to obtain the protection of your grace
against all illness and every snare of the enemy.
Grant, O Lord, in your mercy,
that living waters may always spring up for our salvation,
and so may we approach you with a pure heart
and avoid all danger to body and soul.
Through Christ our Lord.

℟. Amen.

Or, during Easter Time:

Lord our God,
in your mercy be present to your people's prayers,
and, for us who recall the wondrous work of our creation
and the still greater work of our redemption,
graciously ✠ bless this water.
For you created water to make the fields fruitful
and to refresh and cleanse our bodies.
You also made water the instrument of your mercy:
for through water you freed your people from slavery
and quenched their thirst in the desert;
through water the Prophets proclaimed the new covenant
you were to enter upon with the human race;
and last of all,
through water, which Christ made holy in the Jordan,
you have renewed our corrupted nature
in the bath of regeneration.
Therefore, may this water be for us
a memorial of the Baptism we have received,
and grant that we may share
in the gladness of our brothers and sisters
who at Easter have received their Baptism.
Through Christ our Lord.

℟. Amen.

3. Where the circumstances of the place or the custom of the people suggest that the mixing of salt be preserved in the blessing of water, the Priest may bless salt, saying:

We humbly ask you, almighty God:
be pleased in your faithful love to bless ✠ this salt
you have created,
for it was you who commanded the prophet Elisha
to cast salt into water,
that impure water might be purified.
Grant, O Lord, we pray,
that, wherever this mixture of salt and water is sprinkled,
every attack of the enemy may be repulsed
and your Holy Spirit may be present
to keep us safe at all times.
Through Christ our Lord.

℟. Amen.

Then he pours the salt into the water, without saying anything.

4. Afterward, taking the aspergillum, the Priest sprinkles himself and the ministers, then the clergy and people, moving through the church, if appropriate.

Meanwhile, one of the following chants, or another appropriate chant is sung.

Outside Easter Time

Antiphon 1

Sprinkle me with hyssop, O Lord, and I shall be cleansed;
wash me and I shall be whiter than snow. Ps 51 (50): 9

Antiphon 2

I will pour clean water upon you,
and you will be made clean of all your impurities,
and I shall give you a new spirit, says the Lord. Ez 36: 25-26

Hymn

Blessed be the God and Father of our Lord Jesus Christ,
who in his great mercy has given us new birth into a living hope
through the Resurrection of Jesus Christ from the dead,
into an inheritance that will not perish,
preserved for us in heaven
for the salvation to be revealed in the last time! Cf. 1 Pt 1: 3-5

During Easter Time

Antiphon 1

I saw water flowing from the Temple,
from its right-hand side, alleluia:
and all to whom this water came
were saved and shall say: Alleluia, alleluia. Cf. Ez 47: 1-2, 9

Antiphon 2

On the day of my resurrection, says the Lord, alleluia,
I will gather the nations and assemble the kingdoms
and I will pour clean water upon you, alleluia.
Cf. Zeph 3: 8; Ez 36: 25

Antiphon 3

You springs and all that moves in the waters,
sing a hymn to God, alleluia. Cf. Dn 3: 77, 79

Antiphon 4

O chosen race, royal priesthood, holy nation,
proclaim the mighty works of him
who called you out of darkness into his wonderful light, alleluia.
1 Pt 2: 9

Antiphon 5

From your side, O Christ,
bursts forth a spring of water,
by which the squalor of the world is washed away
and life is made new again, alleluia.

5. When he returns to his chair and the singing is over, the Priest stands facing the people and, with hands joined, says:

May almighty God cleanse us of our sins,
and through the celebration of this Eucharist
make us worthy to share at the table of his Kingdom.

℟. Amen.

6. Then, when it is prescribed, the hymn Gloria in excelsis (Glory to God in the highest) is sung or said.

APPENDIX V

EXAMPLES OF FORMULARIES FOR THE UNIVERSAL PRAYER

1. GENERAL FORMULA I

PRIEST'S INTRODUCTION

To God the Father almighty,
dear brothers and sisters,
may every prayer of our heart be directed,
for his will it is that all humanity should be saved
and come to the knowledge of the truth.

INTENTIONS

1. **For the holy Church of God,**
that the Lord may graciously watch over her
and care for her,
let us pray to the Lord.
℟. Grant this, almighty God.

2. **For the peoples of all the world,**
that the Lord may graciously preserve harmony
among them,
let us pray to the Lord.
℟. Grant this, almighty God.

3. **For all who are oppressed by any kind of need,**
that the Lord may graciously grant them relief,
let us pray to the Lord.
℟. Grant this, almighty God.

4. **For ourselves and our own community,**
that the Lord may graciously receive us
as a sacrifice acceptable to himself,
let us pray to the Lord.
℟. Grant this, almighty God.

PRIEST'S PRAYER

O God, our refuge and our strength,
hear the prayers of your Church,
for you yourself are the source of all devotion,
and grant, we pray, that what we ask in faith
we may truly obtain.
Through Christ our Lord.
℟. Amen.

2. GENERAL FORMULA II

PRIEST'S INTRODUCTION

Brothers and sisters,
as we now make our prayer
for our community and for the world,
let us all pray to Christ the Lord,
not only for ourselves and our own needs,
but for the entire people.

INTENTIONS

1a. **For the whole Christian people,**
let us beseech the abundance of divine goodness.
℟. Christ, hear us. or Christ, graciously hear us.

1b. **For all who do not yet believe,**
let us implore the giver of all spiritual gifts.
℟. Christ, hear us.

2a. **For those who hold public office,**
let us call upon the power of the Lord.
℟. Christ, hear us.

2b. **For favorable weather and abundant fruits from the earth,**
let us entreat the Lord, the ruler of the world.
℟. Christ, hear us.

3a. **For our brothers and sisters**
who cannot be present at this sacred assembly,
let us beseech him who observes all things.
℟. Christ, hear us.

3b. **For the repose of the souls of the faithful departed,**
let us call upon the judge of all humanity.
℟. Christ, hear us.

4a. **For all of us who pray in faith**
and ask the mercy of the Lord,
let us entreat the compassion of our Savior.
℟. Christ, hear us.

4b. **For ourselves and those close to us**
who await the Lord's goodness,
let us call upon the mercy of Christ the Lord.
℟. Christ, hear us.

PRIEST'S PRAYER

**Incline your merciful ear to our prayers,
we ask, O Lord,
and listen in kindness to the supplications
of those who call on you.
Through Christ our Lord.**
℟. Amen.

3. ADVENT

PRIEST'S INTRODUCTION

**As we await with longing
the coming of our Lord Jesus Christ,
dear brothers and sisters,
let us with renewed devotion beseech his mercy,
that, as he came into the world
to bring the good news to the poor
and heal the contrite of heart,
so in our own time, also,
he may bring salvation to all in need.**

INTENTIONS

1a. **That Christ may visit his holy Church
and keep watch over her always,
let us pray to the Lord.**
℟. Lord, have mercy. or Kyrie, eleison.

1b. **That Christ may fill the Pope,
our Bishop, and the whole Order of Bishops
with spiritual gifts and graces,
let us pray to the Lord.**
℟. Lord, have mercy. or Kyrie, eleison.

2a. **That under the protection of Christ
our times may be peaceful,
let us pray to the Lord.**
℟. Lord, have mercy. or Kyrie, eleison.

2b. **That Christ may guide the minds of those who govern us
to promote the common good according to his will,
let us pray to the Lord.**
℟. Lord, have mercy. or Kyrie, eleison.

3a. **That Christ may banish disease,**
drive out hunger, and ward off every affliction,
let us pray to the Lord.
℟. Lord, have mercy. or Kyrie, eleison.

3b. **That Christ in his mercy may free**
all who suffer persecution,
let us pray to the Lord.
℟. Lord, have mercy. or Kyrie, eleison.

4a. **That as witnesses to Christ's love before all**
we may abide in the truth,
let us pray to the Lord.
℟. Lord, have mercy. or Kyrie, eleison.

4b. **That Christ may find us watching when he comes,**
let us pray to the Lord.
℟. Lord, have mercy. or Kyrie, eleison.

PRIEST'S PRAYER **Almighty ever-living God,**
who bring salvation to all
and desire that no one should perish,
hear the prayers of your people
and grant that the course of our world
may be directed by your peaceful rule
and your Church rejoice in tranquility and devotion.
Through Christ our Lord.
℟. Amen.

4. CHRISTMAS TIME

PRIEST'S INTRODUCTION

On this day (on this night, in this time)
when the goodness and kindness of God our Savior
have appeared,
let us, dear brothers and sisters,
humbly pour forth to him our prayers,
trusting not in our own good works, but in his mercy.

INTENTIONS

1. **For the Church of God,**
that in integrity of faith she may await
and may welcome with joy
him whom the immaculate Virgin conceived by a word
and wondrously brought to birth,
let us pray to the Lord.
℟. Lord, have mercy.

2. **For the progress and peace of the whole world,**
that what is given in time may become a reward in eternity,
let us pray to the Lord.
℟. Lord, have mercy.

3. **For those oppressed by hunger, sickness or loneliness,**
that through the mystery of the Nativity (Epiphany)
of Christ
they may find relief in both mind and body,
let us pray to the Lord.
℟. Lord, have mercy.

4. **For the families of our congregation,**
that, receiving Christ,
they may learn also to welcome him in the poor,
let us pray to the Lord.
℟. Lord, have mercy.

PRIEST'S PRAYER

We pray, O Lord our God,
that the Virgin Mary,
who merited to bear God and man in her chaste womb,
may commend the prayers of your faithful in your sight.
Through Christ our Lord.
℟. Amen.

5. LENT I

PRIEST'S INTRODUCTION

We should pour forth prayers at all times,
dear brothers and sisters,
but, above all, in these days of Lent
we ought to watch more intently with Christ
and direct our petitions more fervently to God.

INTENTIONS

1. For the whole Christian people,
that in this sacred time
they may be more abundantly nourished
by every word that comes from the mouth of God,
let us pray to the Lord.

2. For the whole world,
that in lasting tranquility and peace
our days may truly become
the acceptable time of grace and salvation,
let us pray to the Lord.

3. For sinners and the neglectful,
that in this time of reconciliation
they may return to Christ,
let us pray to the Lord.

4. For ourselves,
that God may at last stir up in our hearts
aversion for our sins,
let us pray to the Lord.

PRIEST'S PRAYER

Grant, we pray, O Lord,
that your people may turn to you with all their heart,
so that whatever they dare to ask in fitting prayer
they may receive by your mercy.
Through Christ our Lord.
℟. Amen.

6. LENT II

PRIEST'S INTRODUCTION

As the Solemnity of Easter approaches, dear friends,
let our prayer to the Lord be all the more insistent,
that all of us, and the whole multitude of the baptized,
together with the entire world,
may come to share more abundantly
in this sacred mystery.

INTENTIONS

1. That God may be pleased
to increase faith and understanding
in the catechumens who are to be initiated
by Holy Baptism
in the coming Paschal Solemnity,
let us pray to the Lord.

2. That peoples in need may find help
and that peace and security
may be firmly established everywhere,
let us pray to the Lord.

3. That all who are afflicted or suffering temptation
may be strengthened by his grace,
let us pray to the Lord.

4. That all of us may learn
to distribute the fruits of self-denial
for the good of those in need,
let us pray to the Lord.

PRIEST'S PRAYER

Have mercy, O Lord, on the prayers of your Church
and turn with compassion to the hearts
that bow before you,
that those you make sharers in the divine mystery
may never be left without your assistance.
Through Christ our Lord.
℟. Amen.

7. WEEKDAYS OF HOLY WEEK

PRIEST'S INTRODUCTION

In this time of the Lord's Passion,
when Christ offered prayers and supplications
to his Father
with loud cries and tears,
let us humbly beseech God,
that in answer to his Son's reverent submission
he may in mercy hear our prayers also.

INTENTIONS

1. That the Church, the Bride of Christ,
may be more fully cleansed by his Blood
in this time of his Passion,
let us pray to the Lord.

2. That through the Blood of Christ's Cross
all things in the world
may be brought to peace for the sake of salvation,
let us pray to the Lord.

3. That God may grant fortitude and patience
to all who through sickness or hardship
have a share in Christ's Passion,
let us pray to the Lord.

4. That we may all be led
through the Lord's Passion and Cross
to the glory of his Resurrection,
let us pray to the Lord.

PRIEST'S PRAYER

Be present, O Lord, to your people at prayer,
so that what they do not have the confidence
or presumption to ask
they may obtain by the merits of your Son's Passion.
Who lives and reigns for ever and ever.
℟. Amen.

8. EASTER TIME

PRIEST'S INTRODUCTION

Dear brothers and sisters,
filled with paschal joy,
let us pray more earnestly to God
that he, who graciously listened
to the prayers and supplications of his beloved Son,
may now be pleased to look upon us in our lowliness.

INTENTIONS

1. For the shepherds of our souls,
that they may have the strength to govern wisely
the flock entrusted to them by the Good Shepherd,
let us pray to the Lord.

2. For the whole world,
that it may truly know the peace given by Christ,
let us pray to the Lord.

3. For our brothers and sisters who suffer,
that their sorrow may be turned to gladness
which no one can take from them,
let us pray to the Lord.

4. For our own community,
that it may bear witness with great confidence
to the Resurrection of Christ,
let us pray to the Lord.

PRIEST'S PRAYER

O God, who know that our life in this present age
is subject to suffering and need,
hear the desires of those who cry to you
and receive the prayers of those who believe in you.
Through Christ our Lord.
℟. Amen.

9. ORDINARY TIME I

PRIEST'S INTRODUCTION

Dear brothers and sisters,
gathered as one to celebrate the good things
we have received from our God,
let us ask him to prompt in us
prayers that are worthy of his hearing.

INTENTIONS

1. For N. our Pope and N. our Bishop
and all the clergy,
with the people entrusted to their charge,
let us pray to the Lord.

2. For those who hold public office
and those who assist them
in promoting the common good,
let us pray to the Lord.

3. For those who travel by sea, land or air,
for captives and all held in prison,
let us pray to the Lord.

4. For all of us gathered in this sacred place
by faith and devotion
and by love and reverence for God,
let us pray to the Lord.

PRIEST'S PRAYER

May the petitions of your Church
be pleasing in your sight, O Lord,
so that we may receive from your mercy
what we cannot ask out of confidence in our own merits.
Through Christ our Lord.
℟. Amen.

10. ORDINARY TIME II

PRIEST'S INTRODUCTION

We have all gathered here,
dear brothers and sisters,
to celebrate the mysteries of our redemption;
let us therefore ask almighty God
that the whole world may be watered
from these springs of all blessing and life.

INTENTIONS

1. For all who have vowed themselves to God,
that with his help they may faithfully keep to their resolve,
let us pray to the Lord.

2. For peace among nations,
that, delivered from all turmoil,
the peoples may serve God in freedom of heart,
let us pray to the Lord.

3. For the elderly who suffer from isolation or sickness,
that they may be strengthened
by our love of them as brothers and sisters,
let us pray to the Lord.

4. For ourselves gathered here,
that, as God does not cease to sustain us
with the things of this life,
we may know how to use them in such a way
that we may hold even now
to the things that endure for ever,
let us pray to the Lord.

PRIEST'S PRAYER

May your mercy, we beseech you, O Lord,
be with your people who cry to you,
so that what they seek at your prompting
they may obtain by your ready generosity.
Through Christ our Lord.
℟. Amen.

The General Formulas printed above, nos. 1-2, may also be used in Ordinary Time.

11. IN MASSES FOR THE DEAD

PRIEST'S INTRODUCTION

Let us in faith call upon God the almighty Father,
who raised Christ his Son from the dead,
as we pray for the salvation of the living and the dead.

INTENTIONS

1. That God may establish the Christian people
in faith and unity,
let us pray to the Lord.

2. That he may rescue the entire world
from all the evils of war,
let us pray to the Lord.

3. That he may be pleased to show himself a father
to our brothers and sisters
who lack work, food or housing,
let us pray to the Lord.

4a. That he may be pleased
to admit for ever to the company of the Saints
his deceased servant N.,
who once through Baptism
received the seed of eternal life,
let us pray to the Lord.

4b. That on the last day he may raise up N.,
who fed on the Body of Christ,
the Bread of eternal life,
let us pray to the Lord.

(Or for a Priest):

That he may grant N. a share in the heavenly liturgy,
for he exercised the priestly office in the Church,
let us pray to the Lord.

4c. That he may grant to the souls
of our brothers and sisters, friends, and benefactors
the reward of their labors,
let us pray to the Lord.

4d. **That he may welcome into the light of his face**
all who have fallen asleep in the hope of the resurrection,
let us pray to the Lord.

4e. **That he may graciously help and comfort**
our brothers and sisters who are suffering affliction,
let us pray to the Lord.

4f. **That he may be pleased to gather**
into his glorious Kingdom
all who have gathered here in faith and devotion,
let us pray to the Lord.

PRIEST'S PRAYER **May the prayer of those who cry to you**
benefit the souls of your servants, O Lord:
free them, we pray, from all their sins
and make them sharers in your redemption.
Through Christ our Lord.
℟. Amen.

APPENDIX VI

[In the Dioceses of the United States]

SAMPLE INVOCATIONS FOR THE PENITENTIAL ACT

Brethren (brothers and sisters),
let us acknowledge our sins,
and so prepare ourselves to celebrate the sacred mysteries.

A brief pause for silence follows.

The Priest, or a Deacon or another minister, then may use one of the following invocations with Kyrie, eleison (Lord, have mercy):

I

The Priest: **Lord Jesus, you came to gather the nations**
into the peace of God's Kingdom:
Lord, have mercy.

The people reply: Lord, have mercy.

The Priest: **Lord Jesus, you come in word and sacrament**
to strengthen us in holiness:
Christ, have mercy.

The people: Christ, have mercy.

The Priest: **Lord Jesus, you will come in glory**
with salvation for your people:
Lord, have mercy.

The people: Lord, have mercy.

The absolution by the Priest follows:

May almighty God have mercy on us,
forgive us our sins
and bring us to everlasting life.

The people reply: Amen.

II

The Priest: **Lord Jesus, you are mighty God and Prince of peace:**
Lord, have mercy.

The people reply: Lord, have mercy.

The Priest: **Lord Jesus, you are the Son of God and Son of Mary:**
Christ, have mercy.

The people: Christ, have mercy.

The Priest: **Lord Jesus, you are Word made flesh**
and splendor of the Father:
Lord, have mercy.

The people: Lord, have mercy.

The absolution by the Priest follows:

May almighty God have mercy on us,
forgive us our sins
and bring us to everlasting life.

The people reply: Amen.

III

The Priest: **Lord Jesus, you came to reconcile us to one another and to the Father:**
Lord, have mercy.

The people reply: Lord, have mercy.

The Priest: **Lord Jesus, you heal the wounds of sin and division:**
Christ, have mercy.

The people: Christ, have mercy.

The Priest: **Lord Jesus, you intercede for us with your Father:**
Lord, have mercy.

The people: Lord, have mercy.

The absolution by the Priest follows:

May almighty God have mercy on us,
forgive us our sins
and bring us to everlasting life.

The people reply: Amen.

IV

The Priest: **Lord Jesus, you raise the dead to life in the Spirit:**
Lord, have mercy.

The people reply: Lord, have mercy.

The Priest: **Lord Jesus, you bring pardon and peace to the sinner:**
Christ, have mercy.

The people: Christ, have mercy.

The Priest: **Lord Jesus, you bring light to those in darkness:**
Lord, have mercy.

The people: Lord, have mercy.

The absolution by the Priest follows:

May almighty God have mercy on us,
forgive us our sins
and bring us to everlasting life.

The people reply: Amen.

V

The Priest: **Lord Jesus, you raise us to new life:**
Lord, have mercy.

The people reply: Lord, have mercy.

The Priest: **Lord Jesus, you forgive us our sins:**
Christ, have mercy.

The people: Christ, have mercy.

The Priest: **Lord Jesus, you feed us with your Body and Blood:**
Lord, have mercy.

The people: Lord, have mercy.

The absolution by the Priest follows:

May almighty God have mercy on us,
forgive us our sins
and bring us to everlasting life.

The people reply: Amen.

VI

The Priest: **Lord Jesus, you have shown us the way to the Father:**
Lord, have mercy.

The people reply: Lord, have mercy.

The Priest: **Lord Jesus, you have given us the consolation**
of the truth:
Christ, have mercy.

The people: Christ, have mercy.

The Priest: **Lord Jesus, you are the Good Shepherd,**
leading us into everlasting life:
Lord, have mercy.

The people: Lord, have mercy.

The absolution by the Priest follows:

May almighty God have mercy on us,
forgive us our sins
and bring us to everlasting life.

The people reply: Amen.

VII

The Priest: **Lord Jesus, you healed the sick:**
Lord, have mercy.

The people reply: Lord, have mercy.

The Priest: **Lord Jesus, you forgave sinners:**
Christ, have mercy.

The people: Christ, have mercy.

The Priest: **Lord Jesus, you gave yourself to heal us**
and bring us strength:
Lord, have mercy.

The people: Lord, have mercy.

The absolution by the Priest follows:

May almighty God have mercy on us,
forgive us our sins
and bring us to everlasting life.

The people reply: Amen.

PREPARATION FOR MASS

Prayer of Saint Ambrose

I draw near, loving Lord Jesus Christ,
to the table of your most delightful banquet
in fear and trembling,
a sinner, presuming not upon my own merits,
but trusting rather in your goodness and mercy.
I have a heart and body defiled by my many offenses,
a mind and tongue
over which I have kept no good watch.
Therefore, O loving God, O awesome Majesty,
I turn in my misery, caught in snares,
to you the fountain of mercy,
hastening to you for healing,
flying to you for protection;
and while I do not look forward to having you as Judge,
I long to have you as Savior.
To you, O Lord, I display my wounds,
to you I uncover my shame.
I am aware of my many and great sins,
for which I fear,
but I hope in your mercies,
which are without number.
Look upon me, then, with eyes of mercy,
Lord Jesus Christ, eternal King,
God and Man, crucified for mankind.
Listen to me, as I place my hope in you,
have pity on me, full of miseries and sins,
you, who will never cease
to let the fountain of compassion flow.
Hail, O Saving Victim,
offered for me and for the whole human race
on the wood of the Cross.
Hail, O noble and precious Blood,
flowing from the wounds
of Jesus Christ, my crucified Lord,
and washing away the sins of all the world.

**Remember, Lord, your creature,
whom you redeemed by your Blood.
I am repentant of my sins,
I desire to put right what I have done.
Take from me, therefore, most merciful Father,
all my iniquities and sins,
so that, purified in mind and body,
I may worthily taste the Holy of Holies.
And grant that this sacred foretaste
of your Body and Blood
which I, though unworthy, intend to receive,
may be the remission of my sins,
the perfect cleansing of my faults,
the banishment of shameful thoughts,
and the rebirth of right sentiments;
and may it encourage
a wholesome and effective performance
of deeds pleasing to you
and be a most firm defense of body and soul
against the snares of my enemies.
Amen.**

Prayer of Saint Thomas Aquinas

Almighty eternal God,
behold, I come to the Sacrament
of your Only Begotten Son,
our Lord Jesus Christ,
as one sick to the physician of life,
as one unclean to the fountain of mercy,
as one blind to the light of eternal brightness,
as one poor and needy to the Lord of heaven and earth.
I ask, therefore, for the abundance of your immense generosity,
that you may graciously cure my sickness,
wash away my defilement,
give light to my blindness,
enrich my poverty,
clothe my nakedness,
so that I may receive the bread of Angels,
the King of kings and Lord of lords,
with such reverence and humility,
such contrition and devotion,
such purity and faith,
such purpose and intention
as are conducive to the salvation of my soul.
Grant, I pray, that I may receive
not only the Sacrament of the Lord's Body and Blood,
but also the reality and power of that Sacrament.
O most gentle God,
grant that I may so receive
the Body of your Only Begotten Son our Lord Jesus Christ,
which he took from the Virgin Mary,
that I may be made worthy to be incorporated into his Mystical Body
and to be counted among its members.
O most loving Father,
grant that I may at last gaze for ever
upon the unveiled face of your beloved Son,
whom I, a wayfarer,
propose to receive now veiled under these species:
Who lives and reigns with you for ever and ever.
Amen.

Prayer to the Blessed Virgin Mary

O most blessed Virgin Mary,
Mother of tenderness and mercy,
I, a miserable and unworthy sinner,
fly to you with all the affection of my heart
and I beseech your motherly love,
that, as you stood by your most dear Son,
while he hung on the Cross,
so, in your kindness,
you may be pleased to stand by me, a poor sinner,
and all Priests who today are offering the Sacrifice
here and throughout the entire holy Church,
so that with your gracious help
we may offer a worthy and acceptable oblation
in the sight of the most high and undivided Trinity.
Amen.

Formula of Intent

My intention is to celebrate Mass
and to consecrate the Body and Blood of our Lord Jesus Christ
according to the Rite of Holy Roman Church,
to the praise of almighty God
and all the Church triumphant,
for my good
and that of all the Church militant,
for all who have commended themselves to my prayers
in general and in particular,
and for the welfare of Holy Roman Church.
Amen.

May the almighty and merciful Lord
grant us joy with peace,
amendment of life,
room for true repentance,
the grace and consolation of the Holy Spirit
and perseverance in good works.
Amen.

THANKSGIVING AFTER MASS

Prayer of Saint Thomas Aquinas

I give you thanks,
Lord, holy Father, almighty and eternal God,
who have been pleased to nourish me,
a sinner and your unworthy servant,
with the precious Body and Blood
of your Son, our Lord Jesus Christ:
this through no merits of mine,
but due solely to the graciousness of your mercy.

And I pray that this Holy Communion
may not be for me an offense to be punished,
but a saving plea for forgiveness.
May it be for me the armor of faith,
and the shield of good will.
May it cancel my faults,
destroy concupiscence and carnal passion,
increase charity and patience, humility and obedience
and all the virtues,
may it be a firm defense against the snares of all my enemies,
both visible and invisible,
the complete calming of my impulses,
both of the flesh and of the spirit,
a firm adherence to you, the one true God,
and the joyful completion of my life's course.

And I beseech you to lead me, a sinner,
to that banquet beyond all telling,
where with your Son and the Holy Spirit
you are the true light of your Saints,
fullness of satisfied desire, eternal gladness,
consummate delight and perfect happiness.
Through Christ our Lord.
Amen.

Prayer to the Most Holy Redeemer

Soul of Christ, sanctify me.
Body of Christ, save me.
Blood of Christ, embolden me.
Water from the side of Christ, wash me.
Passion of Christ, strengthen me.
O good Jesus, hear me.
Within your wounds hide me.
Never permit me to be parted from you.
From the evil Enemy defend me.
At the hour of my death call me
and bid me come to you,
that with your Saints I may praise you
for age upon age.
Amen.

Prayer of Self-Offering

Receive, Lord, my entire freedom.
Accept the whole of my memory,
my intellect and my will.
Whatever I have or possess,
it was you who gave it to me;
I restore it to you in full,
and I surrender it completely
to the guidance of your will.
Give me only love of you
together with your grace,
and I am rich enough
and ask for nothing more.
Amen.

Prayer to Our Lord Jesus Christ Crucified

Behold, O good and loving Jesus,
that I cast myself on my knees before you
and, with the greatest fervor of spirit,
I pray and beseech you to instill into my heart
ardent sentiments of faith, hope and charity,
with true repentance for my sins
and a most firm purpose of amendment.

With deep affection and sorrow
I ponder intimately
and contemplate in my mind your five wounds,
having before my eyes what the prophet David
had already put in your mouth about yourself, O good Jesus:
They have pierced my hands and my feet;
they have numbered all my bones (Ps 21:17-18).

The Universal Prayer Attributed to Pope Clement XI

I believe, O Lord, but may I believe more firmly;
I hope, but may I hope more securely;
I love, but may I love more ardently;
I sorrow, but may I sorrow more deeply.

I adore you as my first beginning;
I long for you as my last end;
I praise you as my constant benefactor;
I invoke you as my gracious protector.

By your wisdom direct me,
by your righteousness restrain me,
by your indulgence console me,
by your power protect me.

I offer you, Lord, my thoughts to be directed to you,
my words, to be about you,
my deeds, to respect your will,
my trials, to be endured for you.

I will whatever you will,
I will it because you will it,
I will it in the way you will it,
I will it for as long as you will it.

Lord, enlighten my understanding, I pray:
arouse my will,
cleanse my heart,
sanctify my soul.

May I weep for past sins,
repel future temptations,
correct evil inclinations,
nurture appropriate virtues.

Give me, good God,
love for you, hatred for myself,
zeal for my neighbor,
contempt for the world.

May I strive to obey superiors,
to help those dependent on me,
to have care for my friends,
forgiveness for my enemies.

May I conquer sensuality by austerity,
avarice by generosity,
anger by gentleness,
lukewarmness by fervor.

Render me prudent in planning,
steadfast in dangers,
patient in adversity,
humble in prosperity.

Make me, O Lord, attentive at prayer,
moderate at meals,
diligent in work,
steadfast in intent.

May I be careful to maintain interior innocence,
outward modesty,
exemplary behavior,
a regular life.

May I be always watchful in subduing nature,
in nourishing grace,
in observing your law,
in winning salvation.

May I learn from you
how precarious are earthly things,
how great divine things,
how fleeting is time,
how lasting things eternal.

Grant that I may prepare for death,
fear judgment,
flee hell,
gain paradise.
Through Christ our Lord.
Amen.

Prayers to the Blessed Virgin Mary

**O Mary, Virgin and Mother most holy,
behold, I have received your most dear Son,
whom you conceived in your immaculate womb,
brought forth, nursed and embraced most tenderly.
Behold him at whose sight
you used to rejoice and be filled with all delight;
him whom, humbly and lovingly,
once again I present
and offer him to you
to be clasped in your arms,
to be loved by your heart,
and to be offered up to the Most Holy Trinity
as the supreme worship of adoration,
for your own honor and glory
and for my needs and for those of the whole world.
I ask you therefore, most loving Mother:
entreat for me the forgiveness of all my sins
and, in abundant measure, the grace
of serving him in the future more faithfully,
and at the last, final grace,
so that with you I may praise him
for all the ages of ages.
Amen.**

**Hail, Mary, full of grace, the Lord is with you;
blessed are you among women,
and blessed is the fruit of your womb, Jesus.
Holy Mary, Mother of God,
pray for us sinners
now and at the hour of our death.
Amen.**

INDEX

ALPHABETICAL INDEX OF CELEBRATIONS